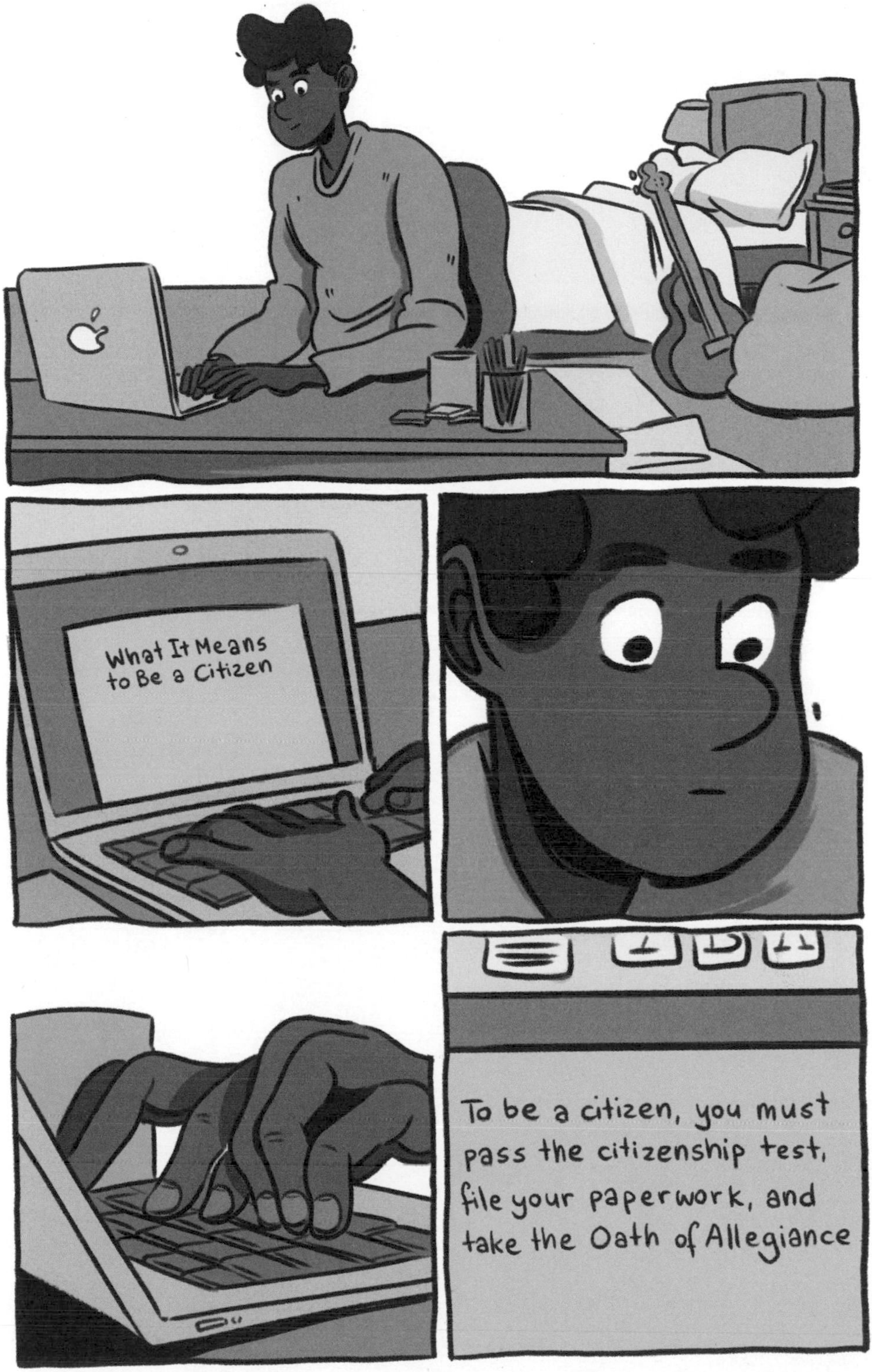
What It Means
to Be a Citizen
To be a citizen, you must pass the citizenship test, file your paperwork, and take the Oath of Allegiance

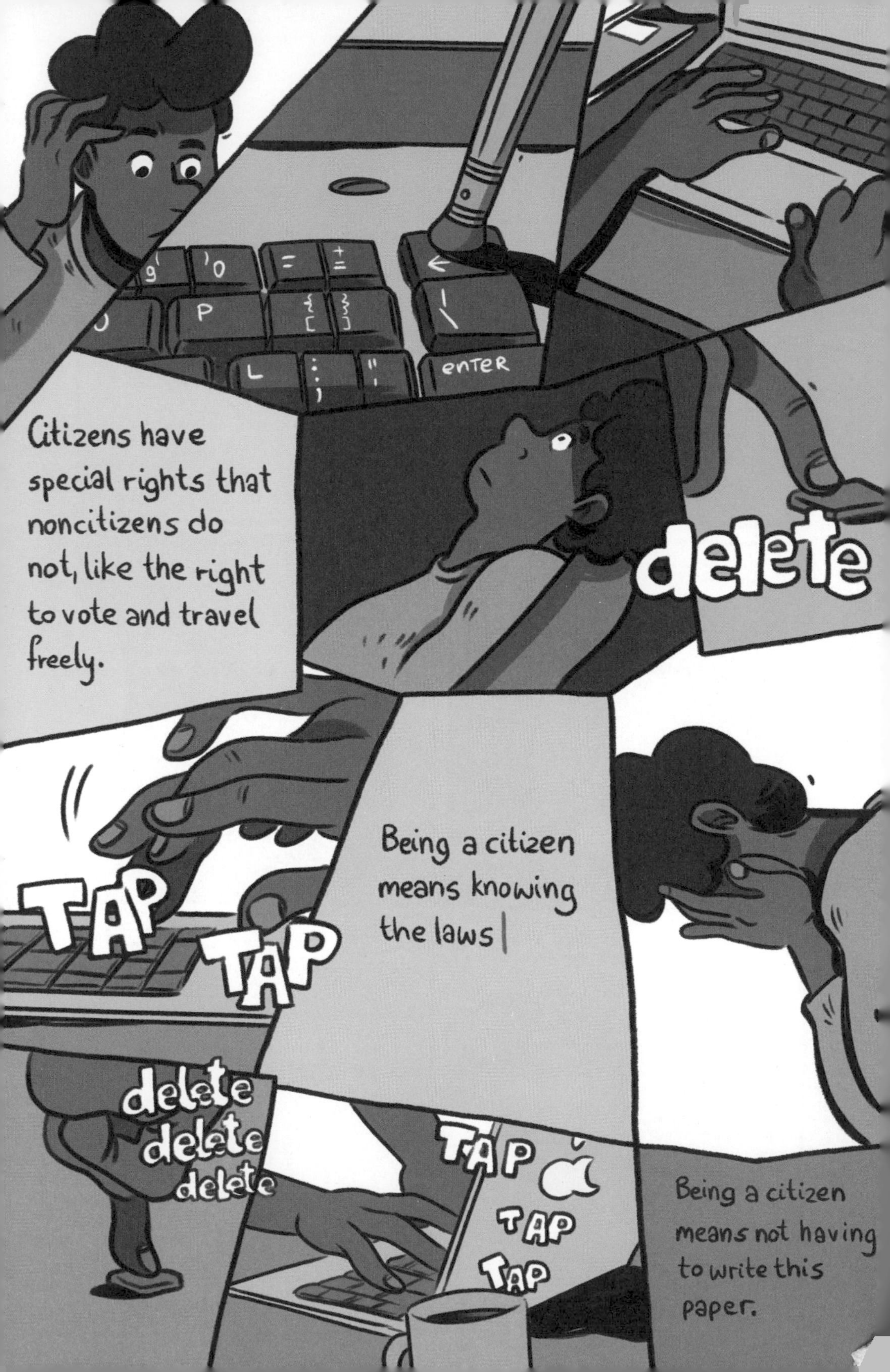
enter
Citizens have special rights that noncitizens do not, like the right to vote and travel freely.
delete
TAP
TAP
Being a citizen means knowing the laws
delete
delete
delete
TAP
TAP
TAP
Being a citizen means not having to write this paper.

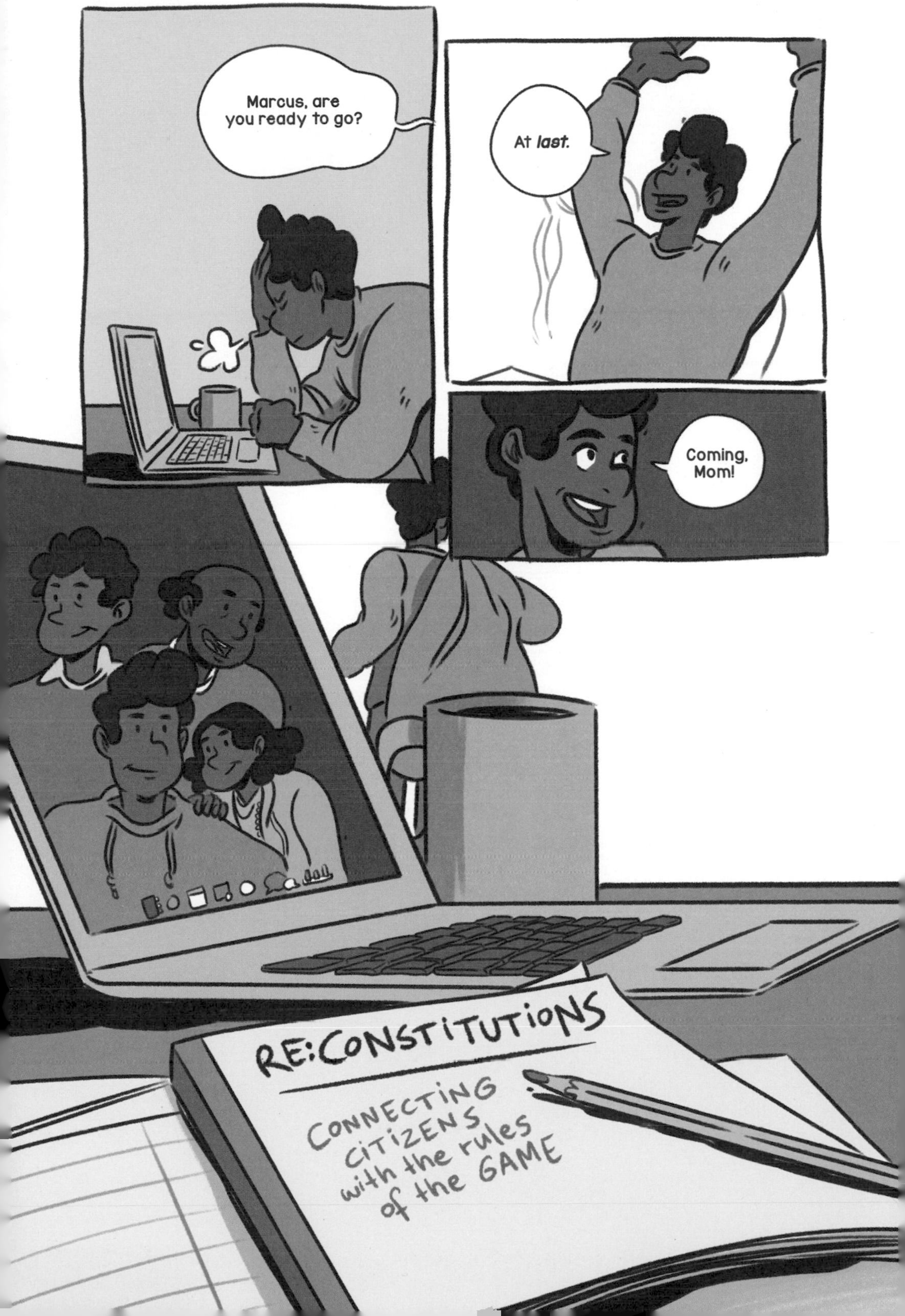
Marcus, are you ready to go?
At *last.*
Coming, Mom!
RE:CONSTITUTIONS
CONNECTING CITIZENS with the rules of the GAME

RE:constitutions

connecting citizens
with the rules of the game

BEKA FEATHERS
art by *KASIA BABIS*

First Second

NEW YORK

For my Grandpa Lou, who was the first to
teach me what it means to be a citizen

—Beka Feathers

Chapter 1

Community
Picnic

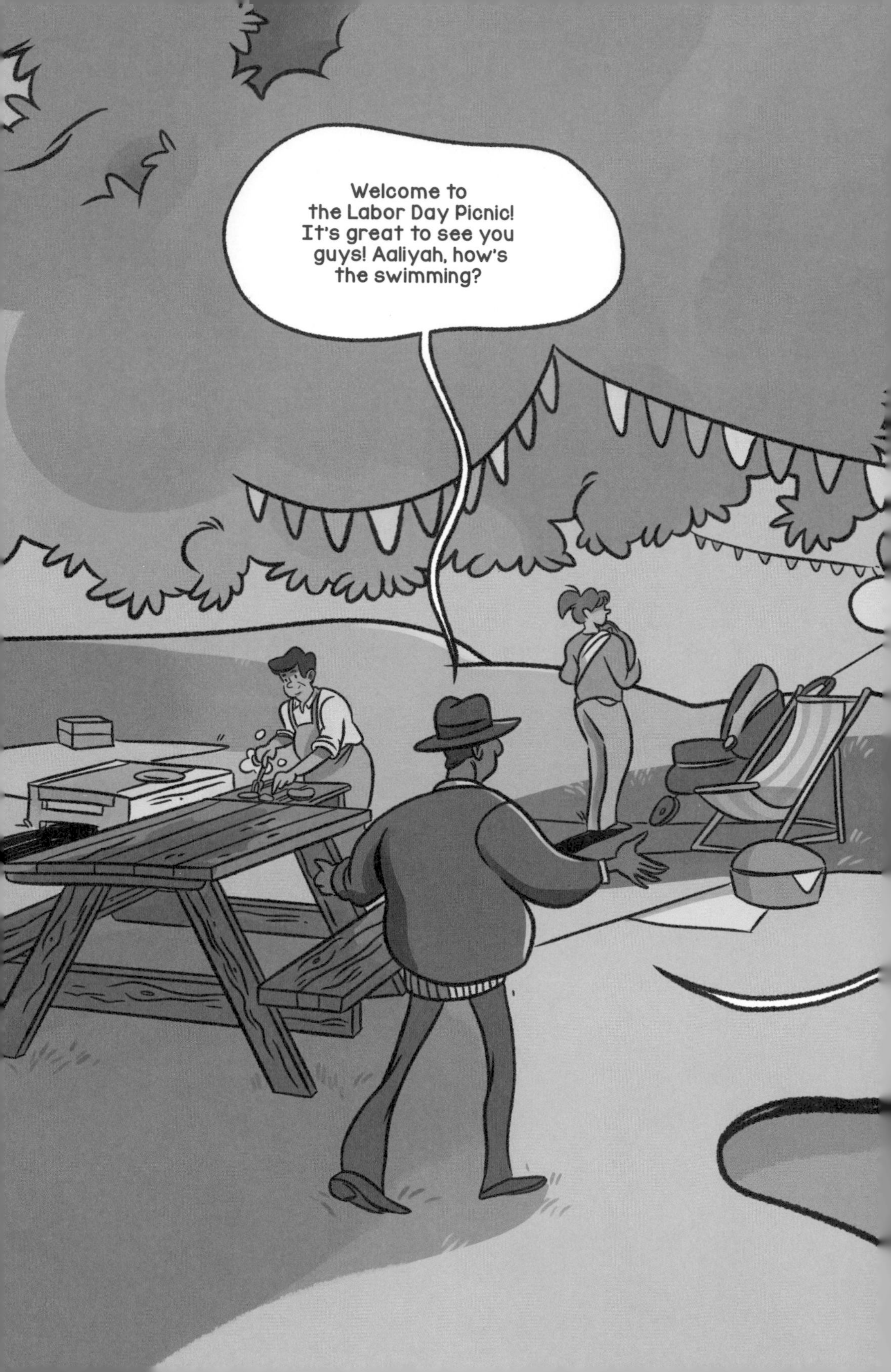
Welcome to the Labor Day Picnic! It's great to see you guys! Aaliyah, how's the swimming?

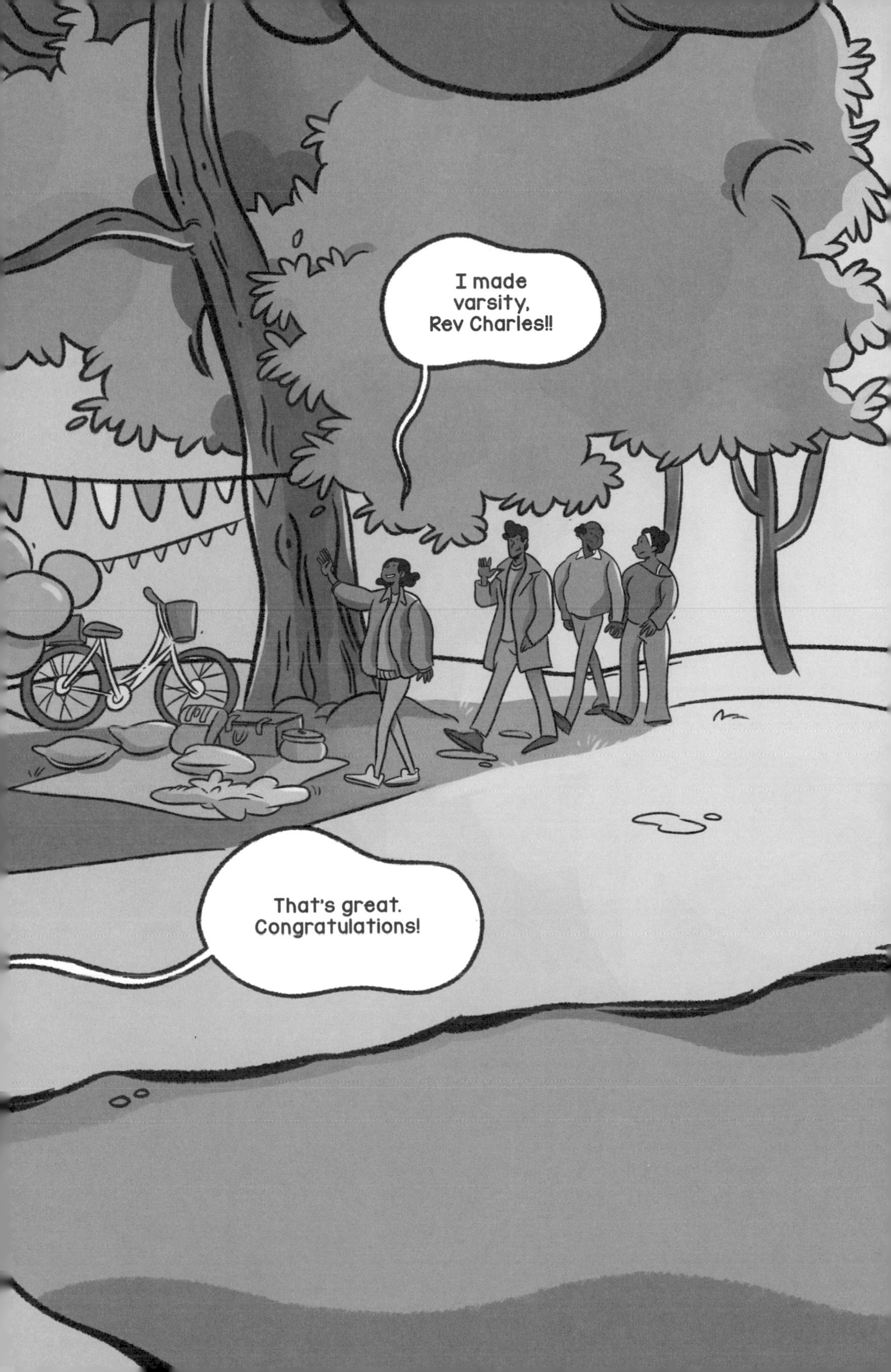
I made varsity, Rev Charles!!
That's great. Congratulations!

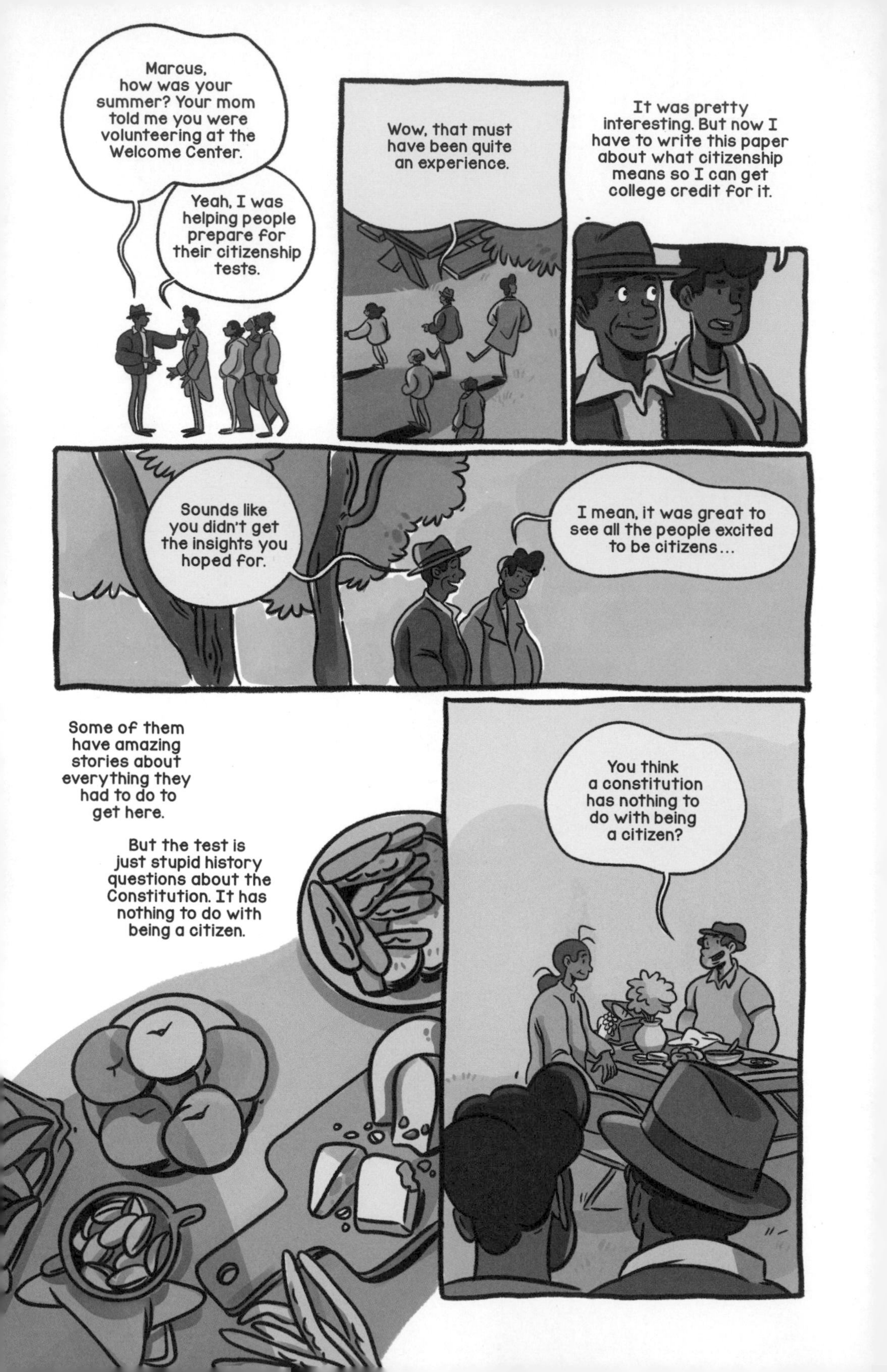
Marcus, how was your summer? Your mom told me you were volunteering at the Welcome Center.
Yeah, I was helping people prepare for their citizenship tests.
Wow, that must have been quite an experience.
It was pretty interesting. But now I have to write this paper about what citizenship means so I can get college credit for it.
Sounds like you didn't get the insights you hoped for.
I mean, it was great to see all the people excited to be citizens...
Some of them have amazing stories about everything they had to do to get here.
But the test is just stupid history questions about the Constitution. It has nothing to do with being a citizen.
You think a constitution has nothing to do with being a citizen?

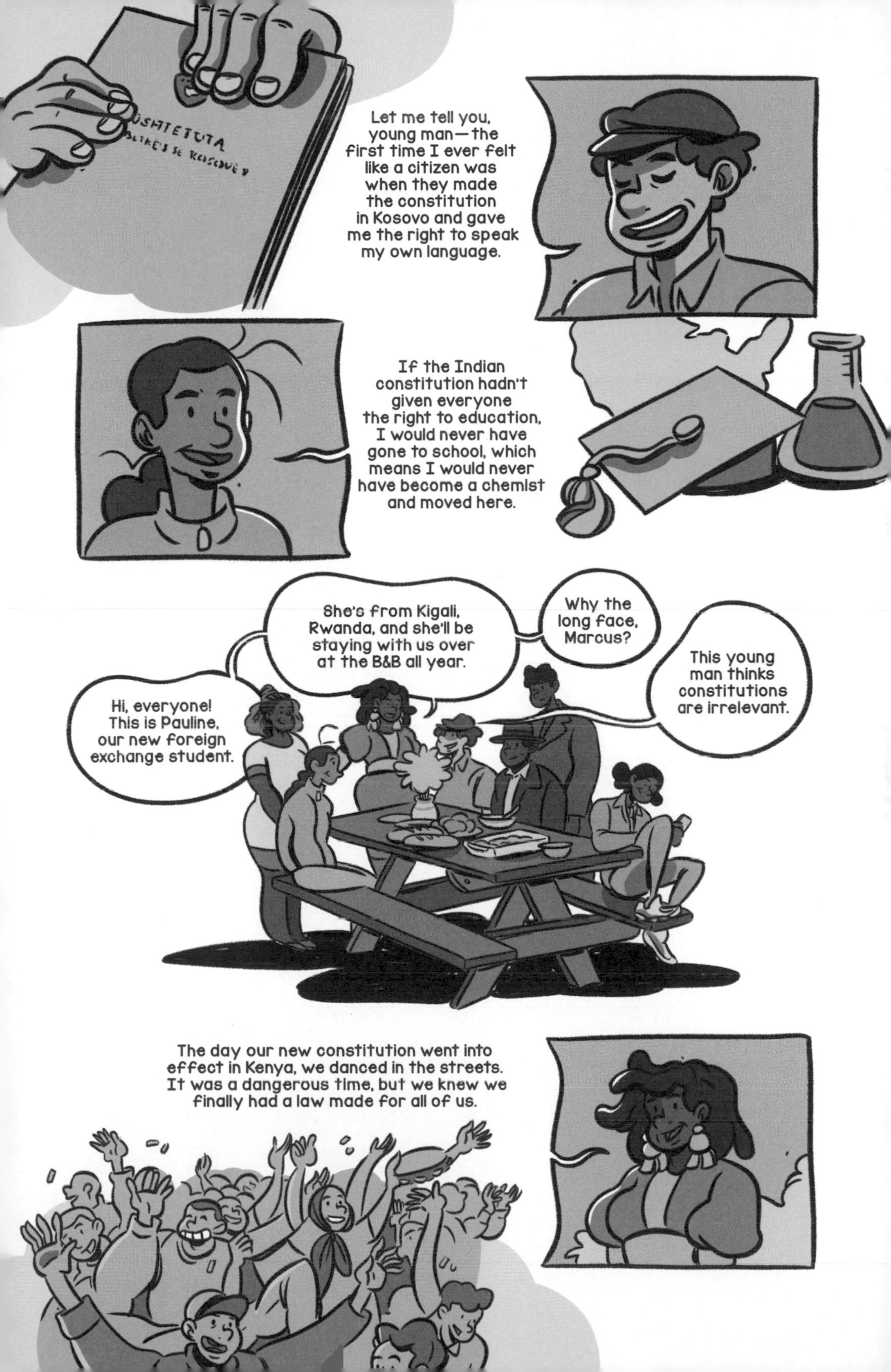
Let me tell you, young man—the first time I ever felt like a citizen was when they made the constitution in Kosovo and gave me the right to speak my own language.
If the Indian constitution hadn't given everyone the right to education, I would never have gone to school, which means I would never have become a chemist and moved here.
Hi, everyone! This is Pauline, our new foreign exchange student.
She's from Kigali, Rwanda, and she'll be staying with us over at the B&B all year.
Why the long face, Marcus?
This young man thinks constitutions are irrelevant.
The day our new constitution went into effect in Kenya, we danced in the streets. It was a dangerous time, but we knew we finally had a law made for all of us.

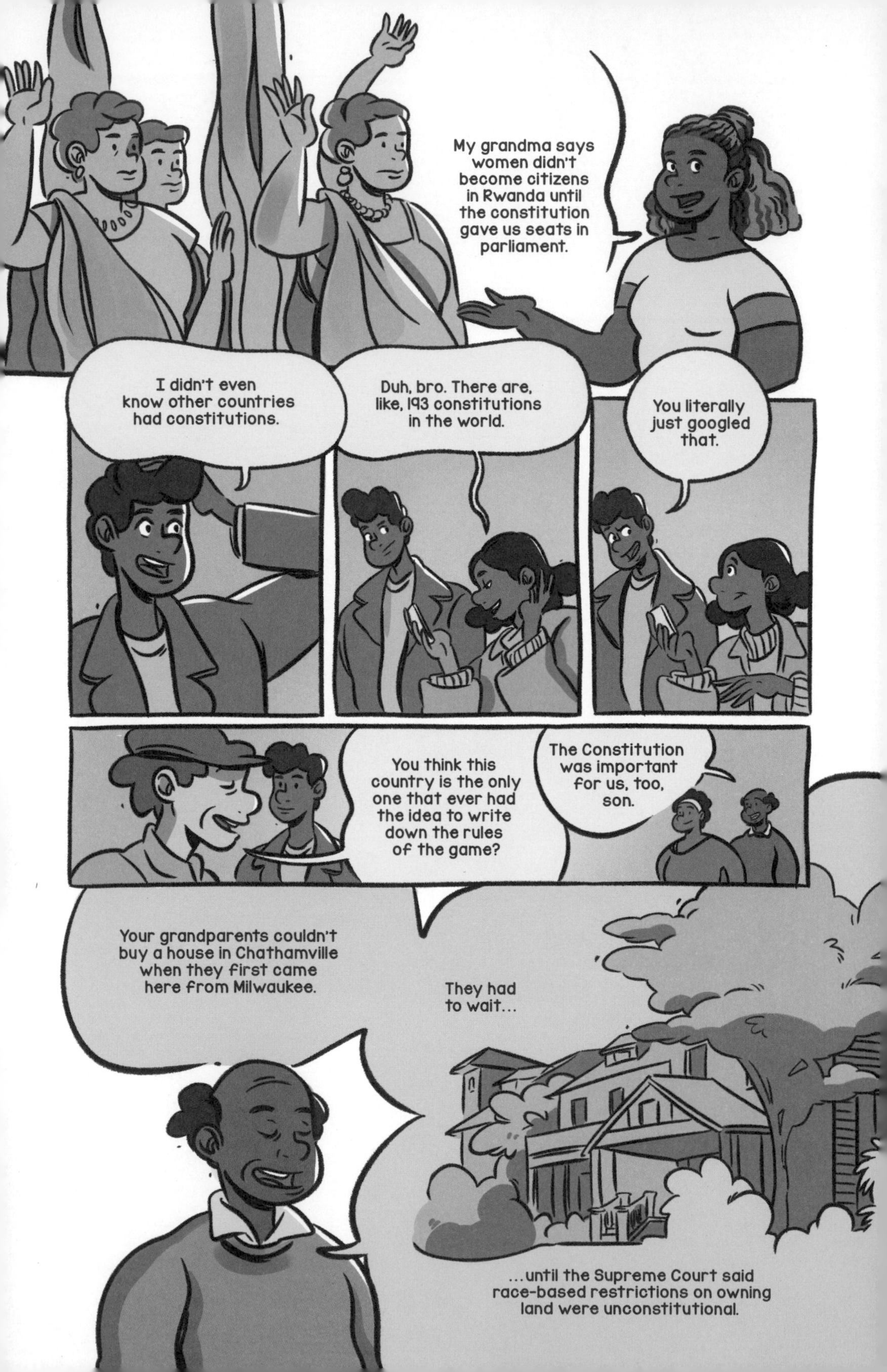
My grandma says women didn't become citizens in Rwanda until the constitution gave us seats in parliament.
I didn't even know other countries had constitutions.
Duh, bro. There are, like, 193 constitutions in the world.
You literally just googled that.
You think this country is the only one that ever had the idea to write down the rules of the game?
The Constitution was important for us, too, son.
Your grandparents couldn't buy a house in Chathamville when they first came here from Milwaukee.
They had to wait...
...until the Supreme Court said race-based restrictions on owning land were unconstitutional.

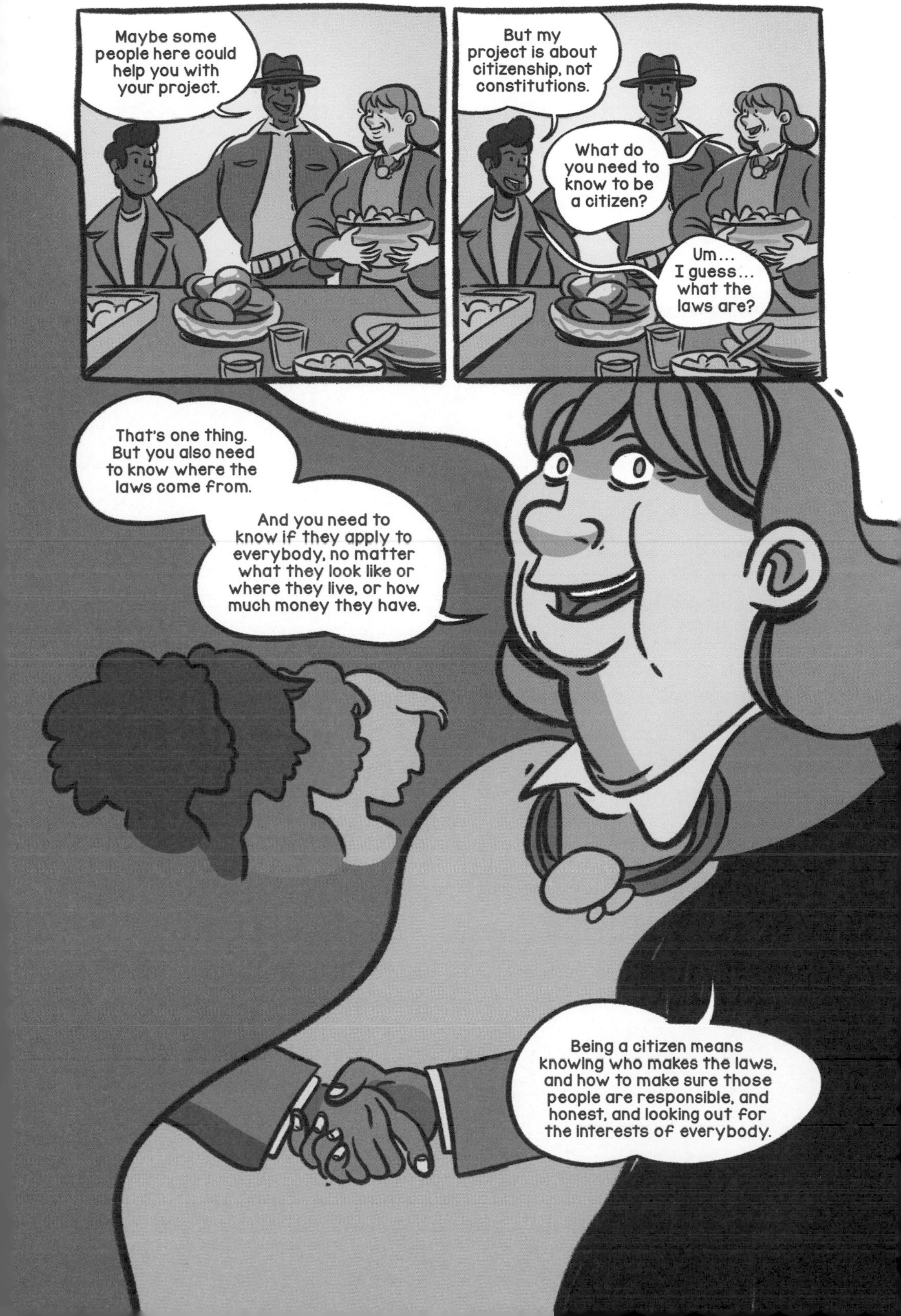
Maybe some people here could help you with your project.
But my project is about citizenship, not constitutions.
What do you need to know to be a citizen?
Um... I guess... what the laws are?
That's one thing. But you also need to know where the laws come from.
And you need to know if they apply to everybody, no matter what they look like or where they live, or how much money they have.
Being a citizen means knowing who makes the laws, and how to make sure those people are responsible, and honest, and looking out for the interests of everybody.

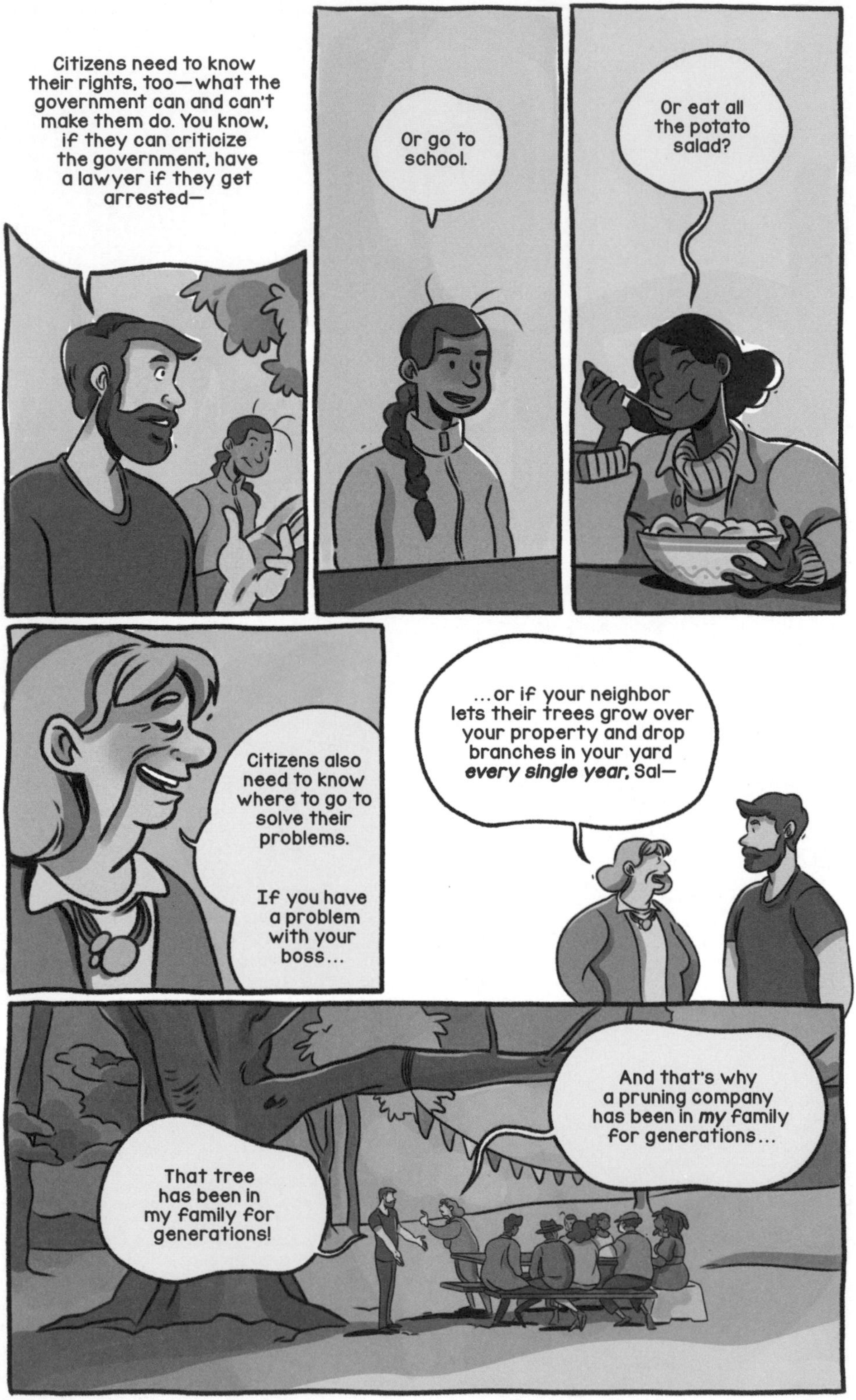
Citizens need to know their rights, too—what the government can and can't make them do. You know, if they can criticize the government, have a lawyer if they get arrested—
Or go to school.
Or eat all the potato salad?
Citizens also need to know where to go to solve their problems.
If you have a problem with your boss...
...or if your neighbor lets their trees grow over your property and drop branches in your yard *every single year,* Sal—
That tree has been in my family for generations!
And that's why a pruning company has been in *my* family for generations...

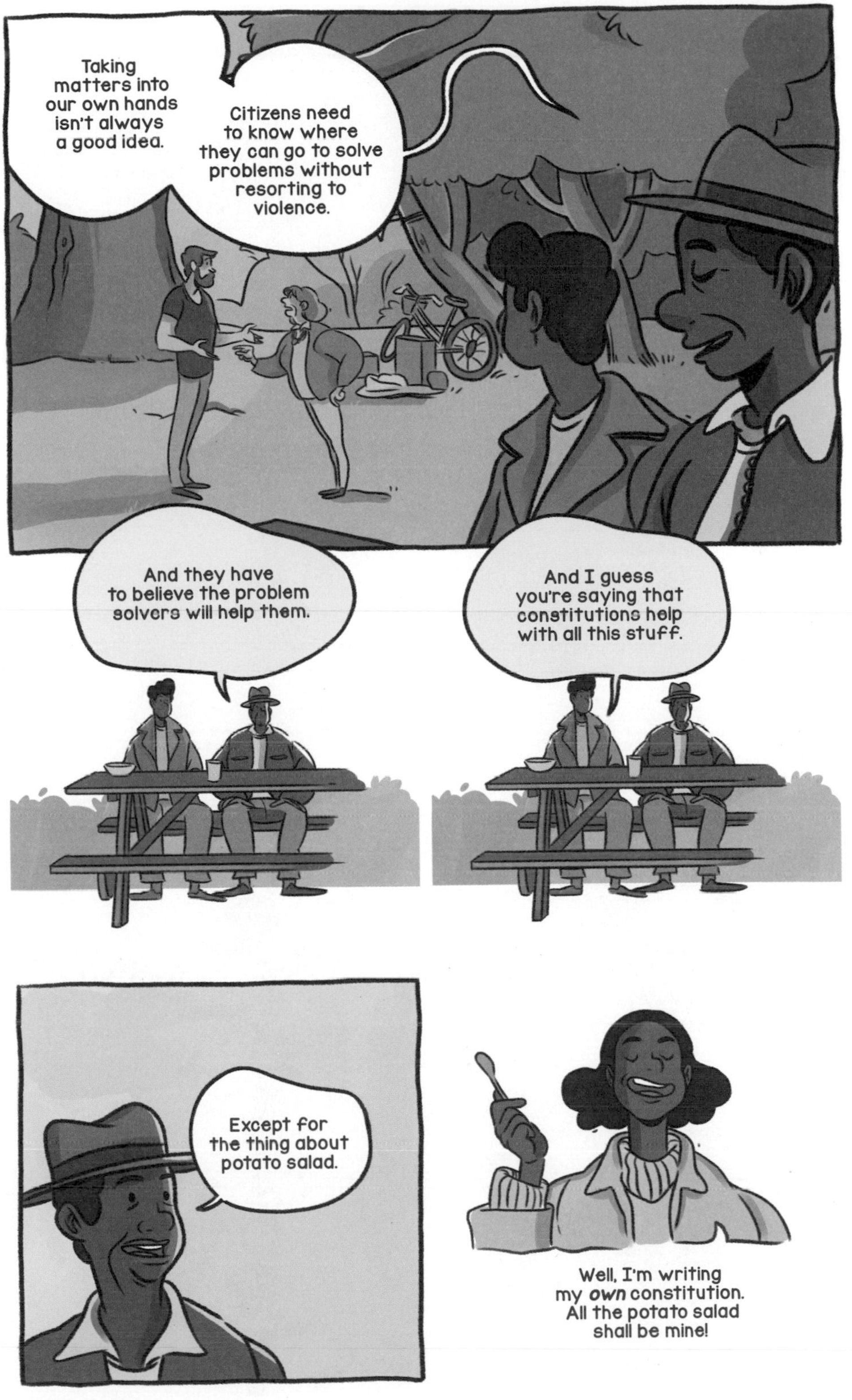
Taking matters into our own hands isn't always a good idea.
Citizens need to know where they can go to solve problems without resorting to violence.
And they have to believe the problem solvers will help them.
And I guess you're saying that constitutions help with all this stuff.
Except for the thing about potato salad.
Well, I'm writing my *own* constitution. All the potato salad shall be mine!

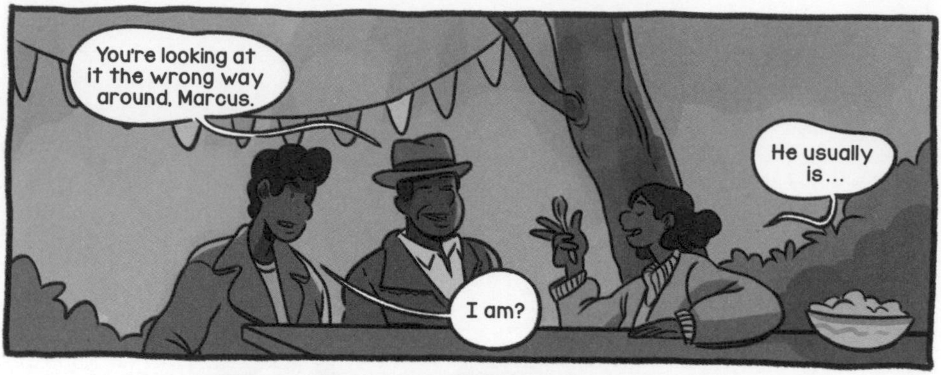
You're looking at it the wrong way around, Marcus.
I am?
He usually is…

Don't ask "What should citizens know about their constitution?"
Ask "What should a constitution do for its citizens?"

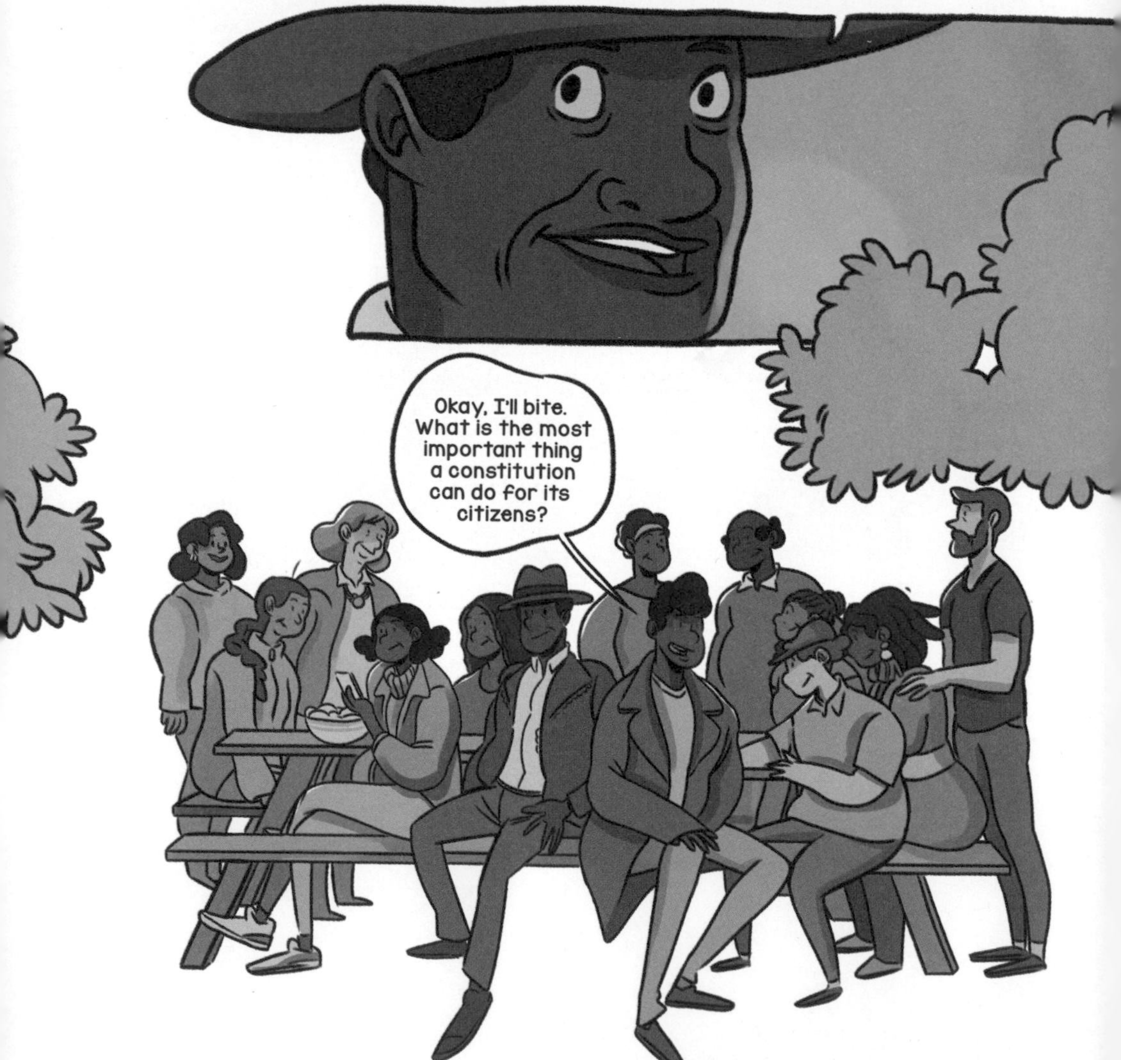
Okay, I'll bite. What is the most important thing a constitution can do for its citizens?

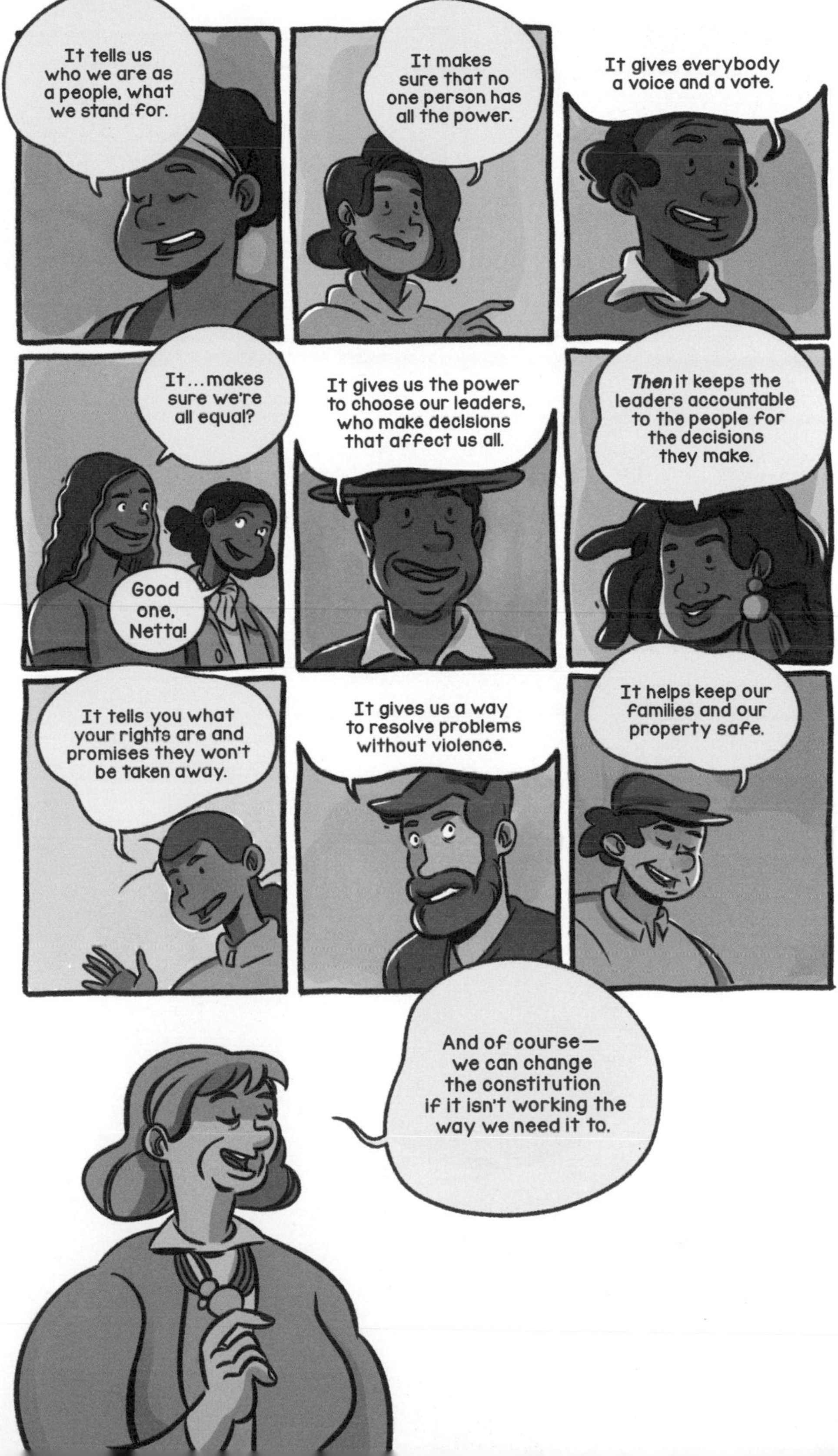

It tells us who we are as a people, what we stand for.
It makes sure that no one person has all the power.
It gives everybody a voice and a vote.
It...makes sure we're all equal?
Good one, Netta!
It gives us the power to choose our leaders, who make decisions that affect us all.
Then it keeps the leaders accountable to the people for the decisions they make.
It tells you what your rights are and promises they won't be taken away.
It gives us a way to resolve problems without violence.
It helps keep our families and our property safe.
And of course— we can change the constitution if it isn't working the way we need it to.

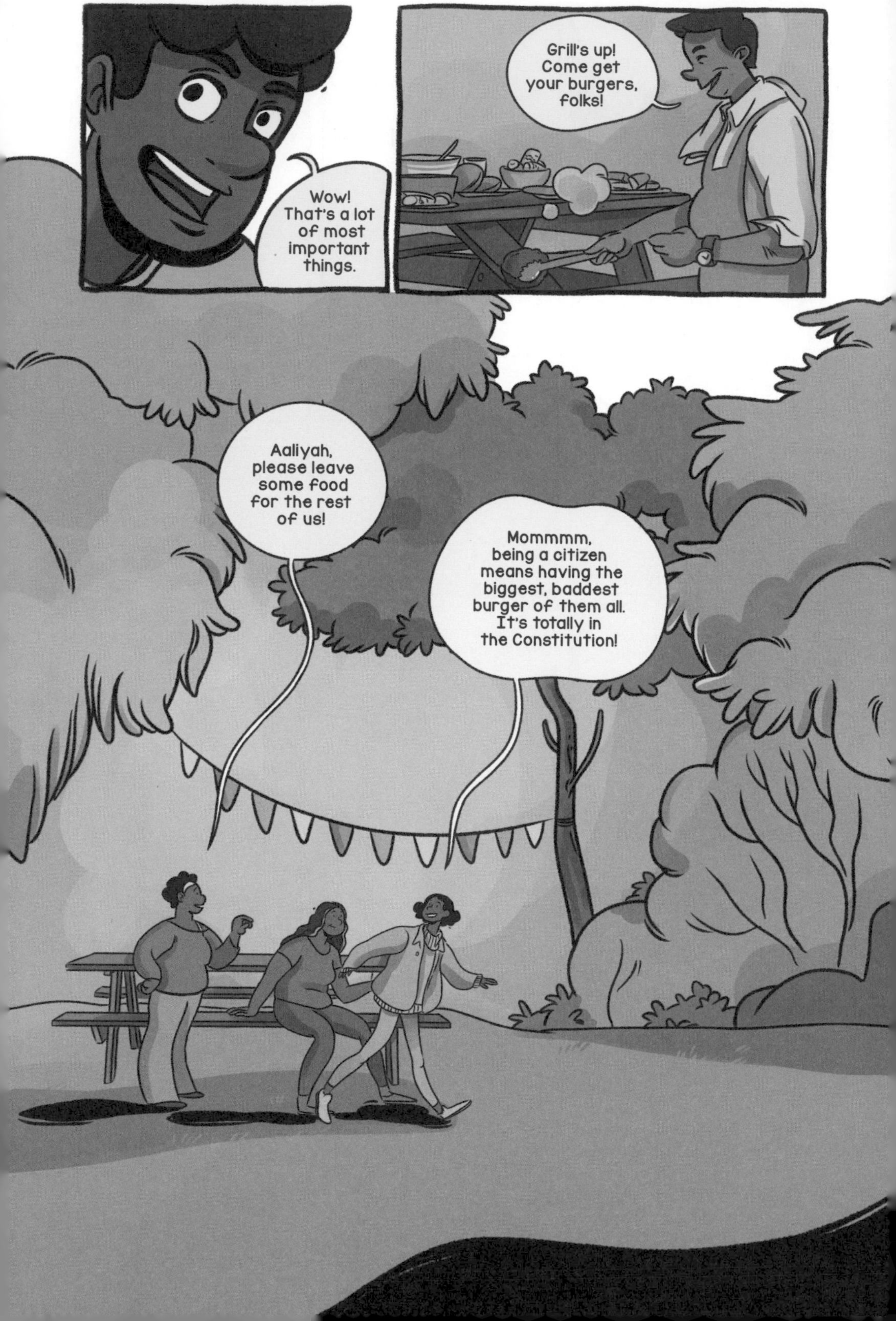
Wow! That's a lot of most important things.
Grill's up! Come get your burgers, folks!
Aaliyah, please leave some food for the rest of us!
Mommmm, being a citizen means having the biggest, baddest burger of them all. It's totally in the Constitution!

Chapter 11

What Does
a Constitution
Look Like?

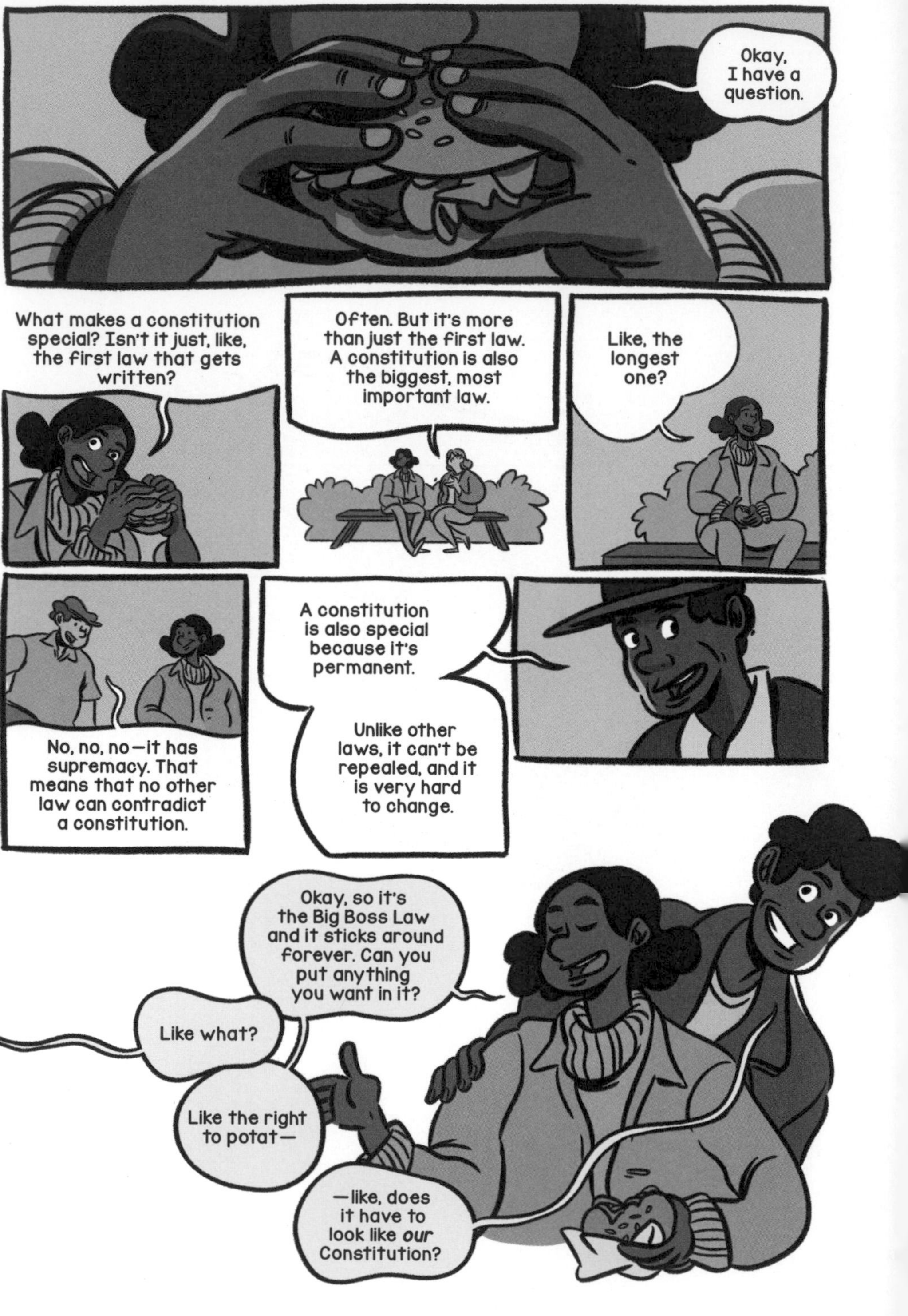
Okay, I have a question.
What makes a constitution special? Isn't it just, like, the first law that gets written?
Often. But it's more than just the first law. A constitution is also the biggest, most important law.
Like, the longest one?
No, no, no—it has supremacy. That means that no other law can contradict a constitution.
A constitution is also special because it's permanent.
Unlike other laws, it can't be repealed, and it is very hard to change.
Okay, so it's the Big Boss Law and it sticks around forever. Can you put anything you want in it?
Like what?
Like the right to potat—
—like, does it have to look like *our* Constitution?

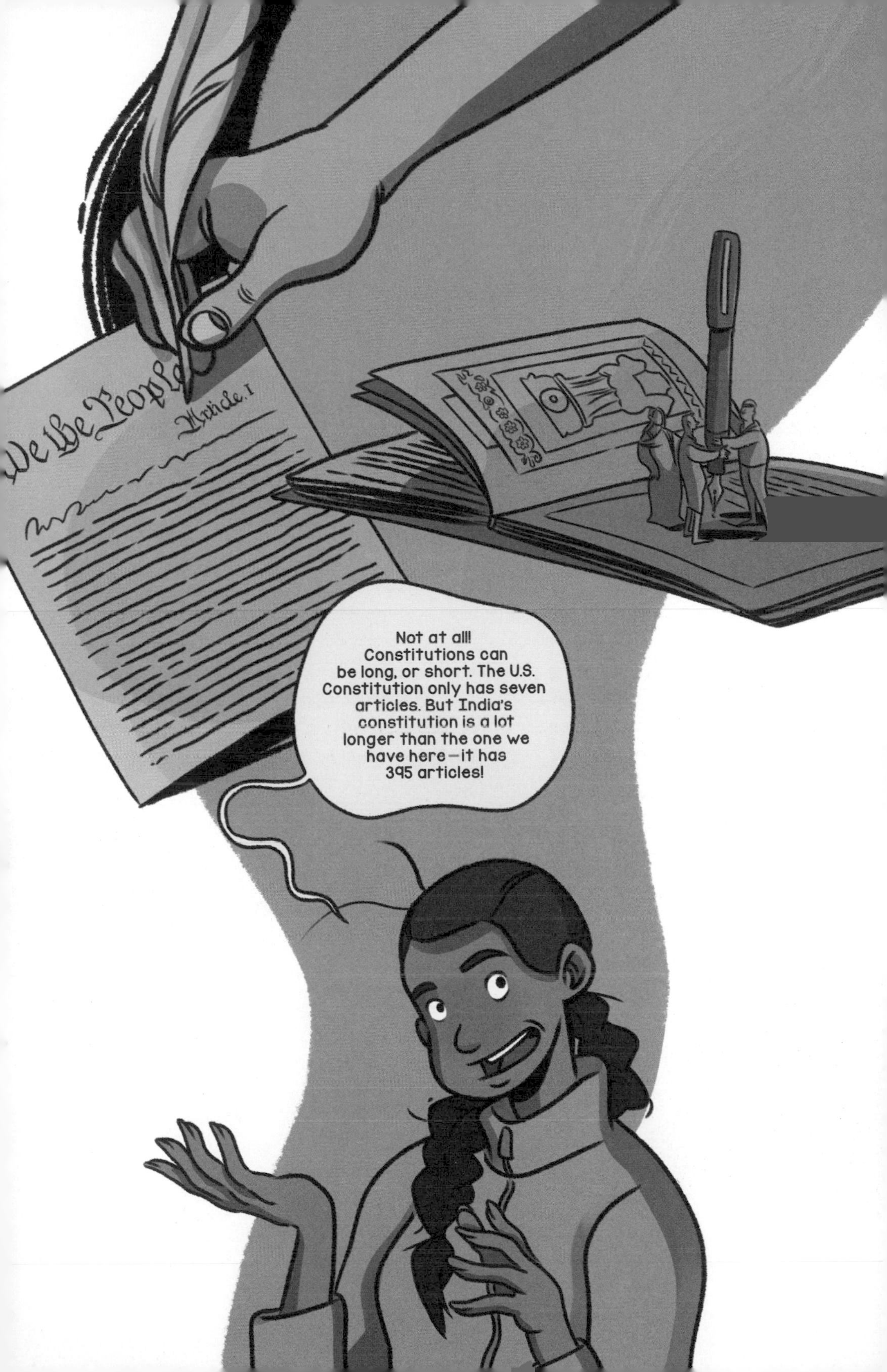
We the People
Article. I
Not at all! Constitutions can be long, or short. The U.S. Constitution only has seven articles. But India's constitution is a lot longer than the one we have here—it has 395 articles!

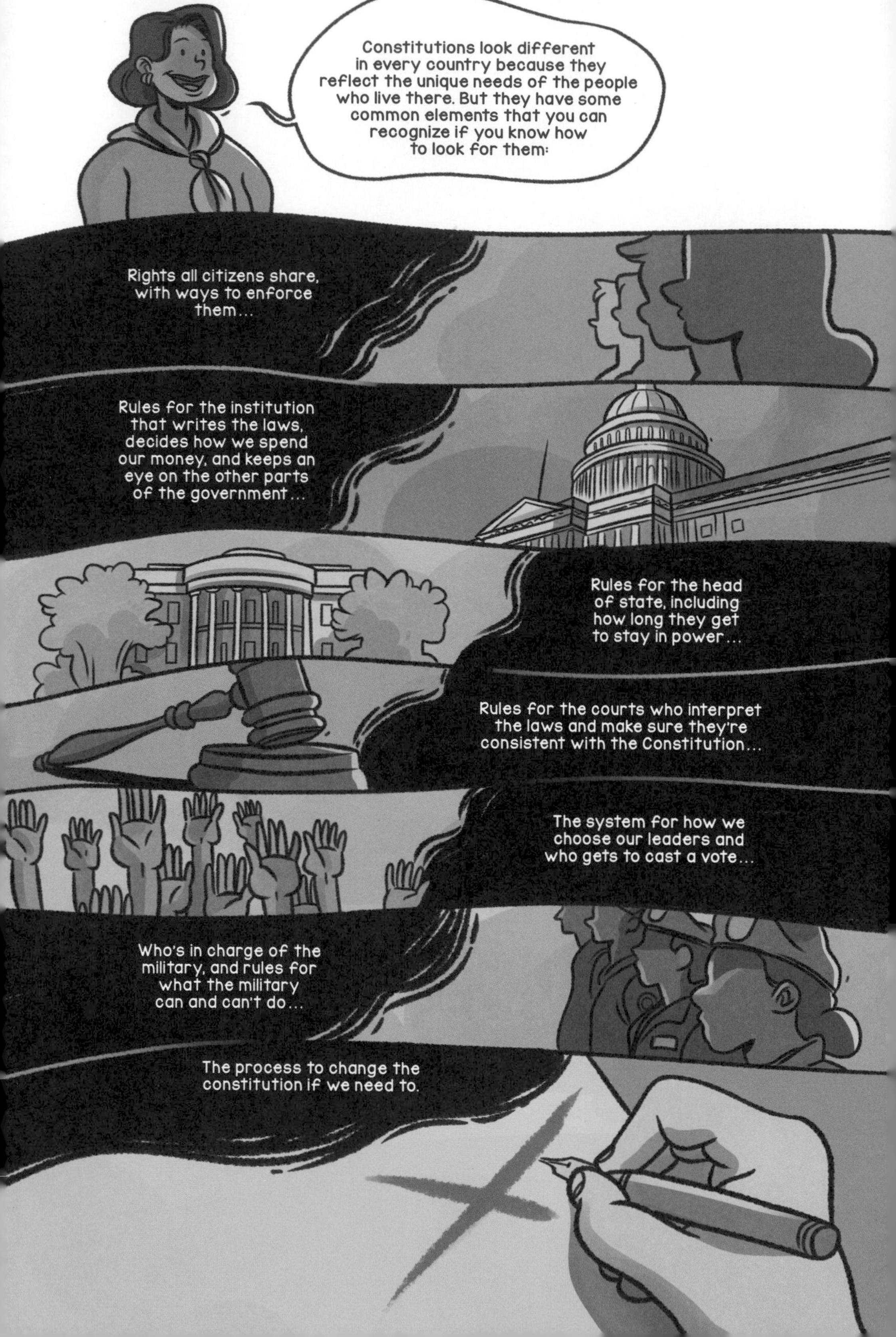

Constitutions look different in every country because they reflect the unique needs of the people who live there. But they have some common elements that you can recognize if you know how to look for them:
Rights all citizens share, with ways to enforce them...
Rules for the institution that writes the laws, decides how we spend our money, and keeps an eye on the other parts of the government...
Rules for the head of state, including how long they get to stay in power...
Rules for the courts who interpret the laws and make sure they're consistent with the Constitution...
The system for how we choose our leaders and who gets to cast a vote...
Who's in charge of the military, and rules for what the military can and can't do...
The process to change the constitution if we need to.

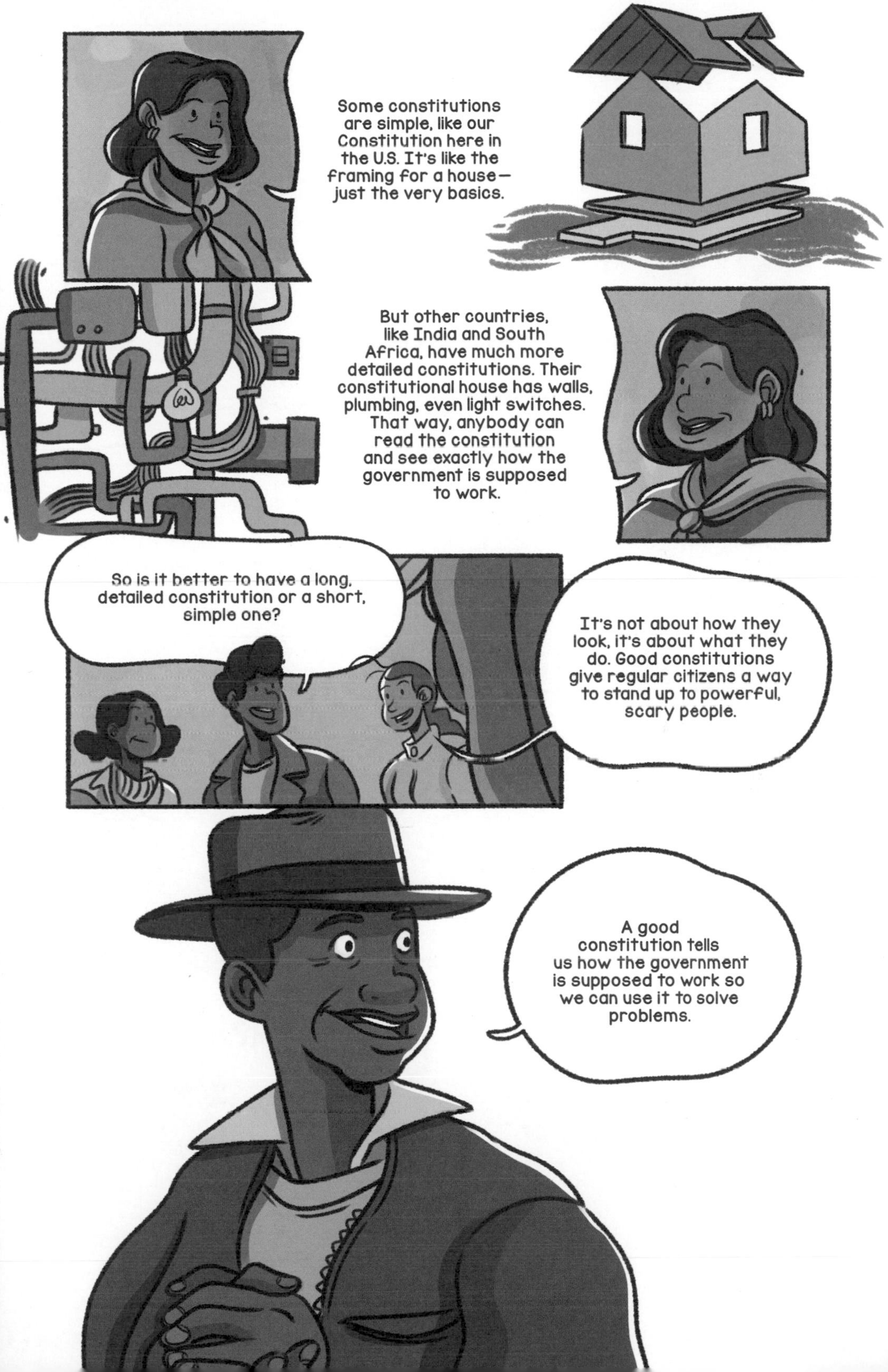
Some constitutions are simple, like our Constitution here in the U.S. It's like the framing for a house—just the very basics.
But other countries, like India and South Africa, have much more detailed constitutions. Their constitutional house has walls, plumbing, even light switches. That way, anybody can read the constitution and see exactly how the government is supposed to work.
So is it better to have a long, detailed constitution or a short, simple one?
It's not about how they look, it's about what they do. Good constitutions give regular citizens a way to stand up to powerful, scary people.
A good constitution tells us how the government is supposed to work so we can use it to solve problems.

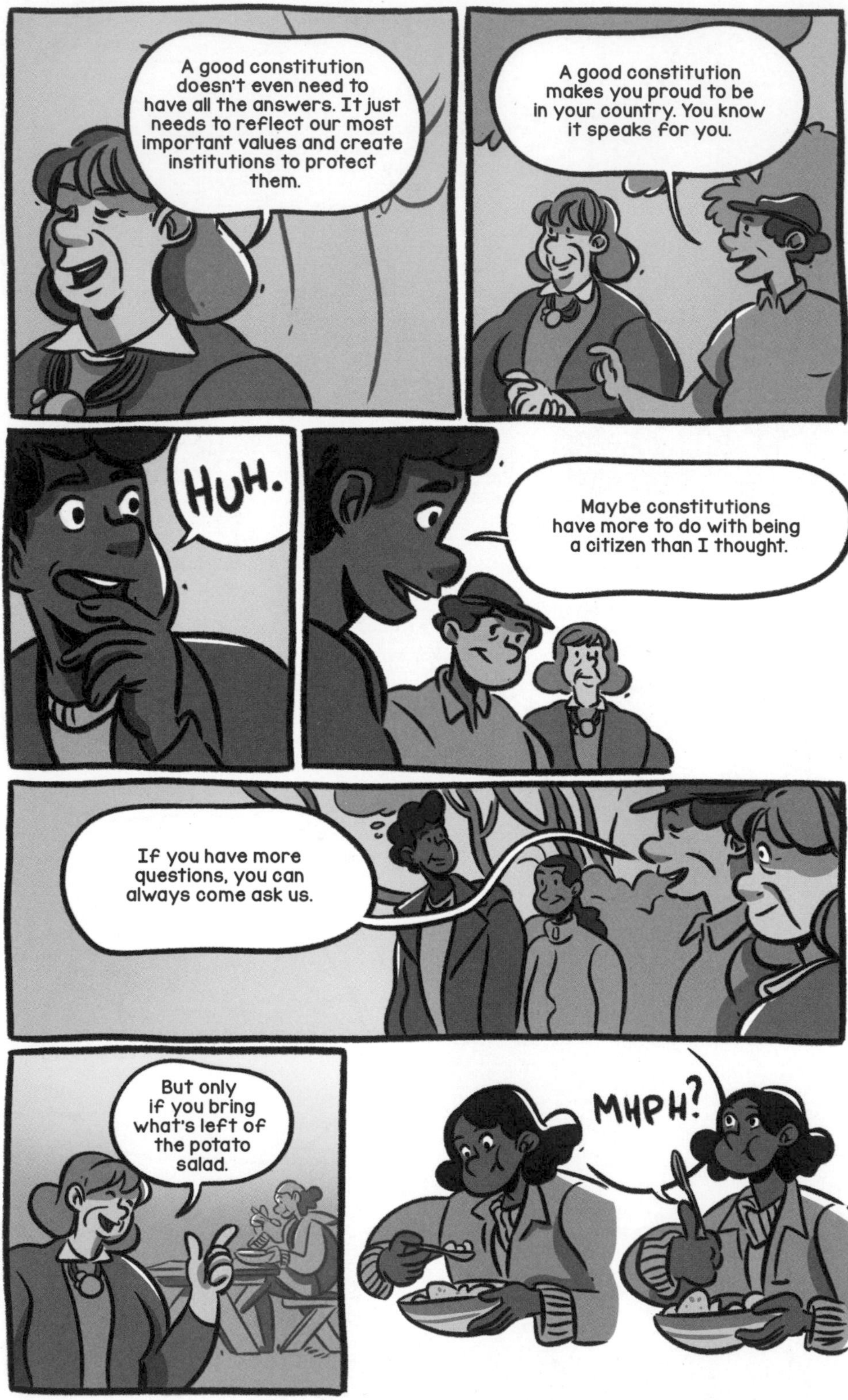
A good constitution doesn't even need to have all the answers. It just needs to reflect our most important values and create institutions to protect them.
A good constitution makes you proud to be in your country. You know it speaks for you.
HUH.
Maybe constitutions have more to do with being a citizen than I thought.
If you have more questions, you can always come ask us.
But only if you bring what's left of the potato salad.
MHPH?

Chapter III
We All
Belong Here

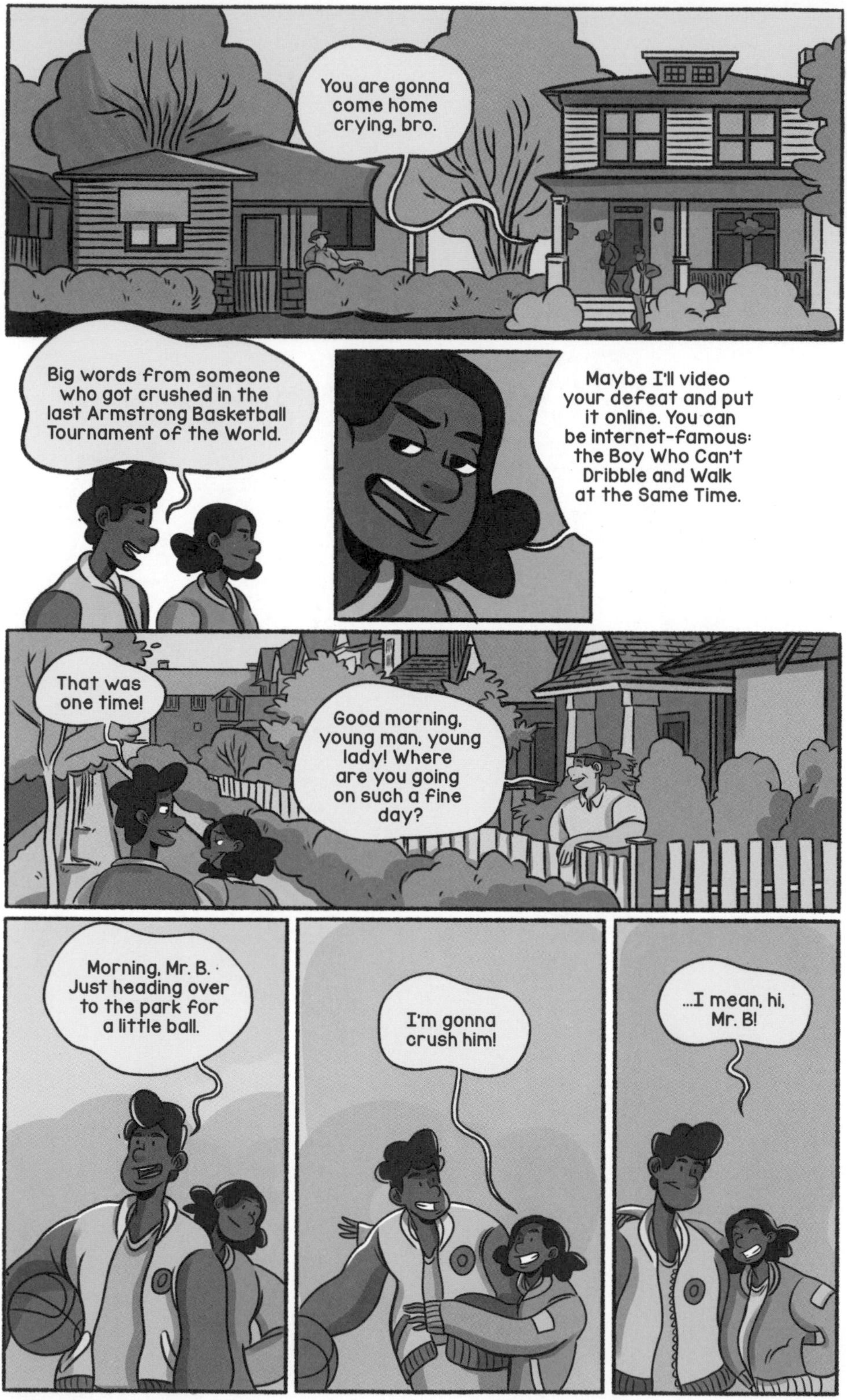
You are gonna come home crying, bro.
Big words from someone who got crushed in the last Armstrong Basketball Tournament of the World.
Maybe I'll video your defeat and put it online. You can be internet-famous: the Boy Who Can't Dribble and Walk at the Same Time.
That was one time!
Good morning, young man, young lady! Where are you going on such a fine day?
Morning, Mr. B. Just heading over to the park for a little ball.
I'm gonna crush him!
...I mean, hi, Mr. B!

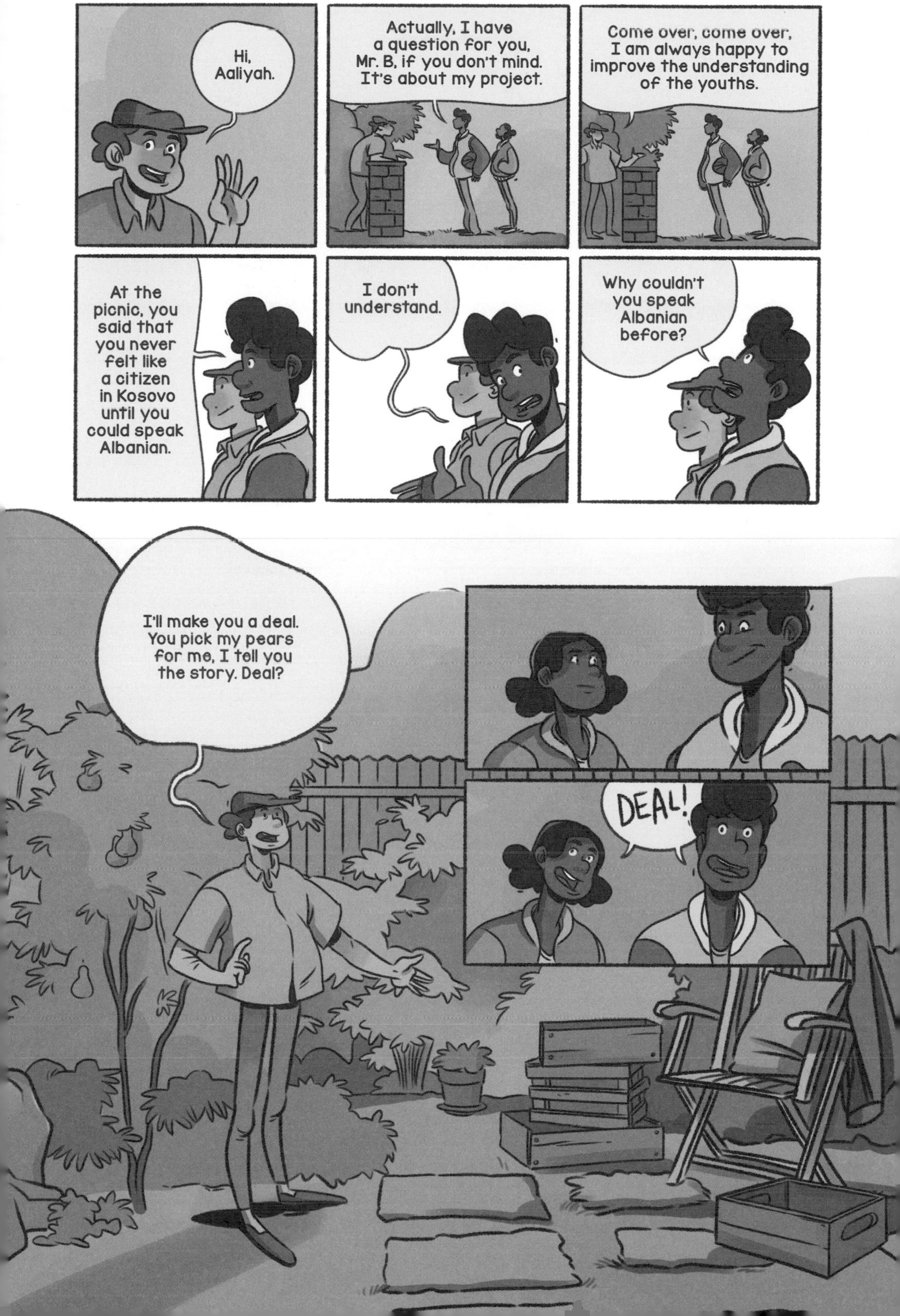
Hi, Aaliyah.
Actually, I have a question for you, Mr. B, if you don't mind. It's about my project.
Come over, come over, I am always happy to improve the understanding of the youths.
At the picnic, you said that you never felt like a citizen in Kosovo until you could speak Albanian.
I don't understand.
Why couldn't you speak Albanian before?
I'll make you a deal. You pick my pears for me, I tell you the story. Deal?
DEAL!

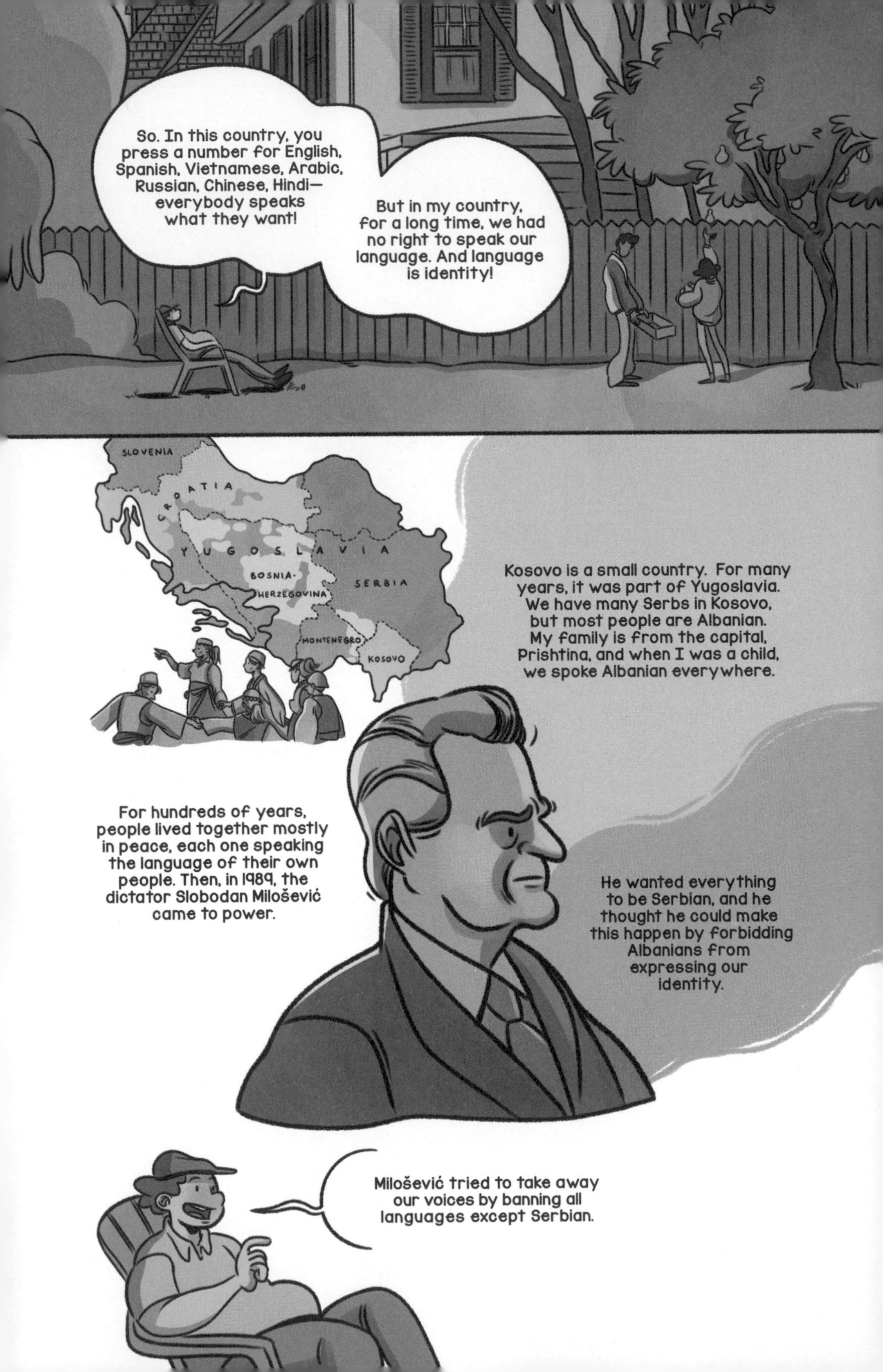
So. In this country, you press a number for English, Spanish, Vietnamese, Arabic, Russian, Chinese, Hindi—everybody speaks what they want!
But in my country, for a long time, we had no right to speak our language. And language is identity!
SLOVENIA
CROATIA
YUGOSLAVIA
BOSNIA-HERZEGOVINA
SERBIA
MONTENEGRO
KOSOVO
Kosovo is a small country. For many years, it was part of Yugoslavia. We have many Serbs in Kosovo, but most people are Albanian. My family is from the capital, Prishtina, and when I was a child, we spoke Albanian everywhere.
For hundreds of years, people lived together mostly in peace, each one speaking the language of their own people. Then, in 1989, the dictator Slobodan Milošević came to power.
He wanted everything to be Serbian, and he thought he could make this happen by forbidding Albanians from expressing our identity.
Milošević tried to take away our voices by banning all languages except Serbian.

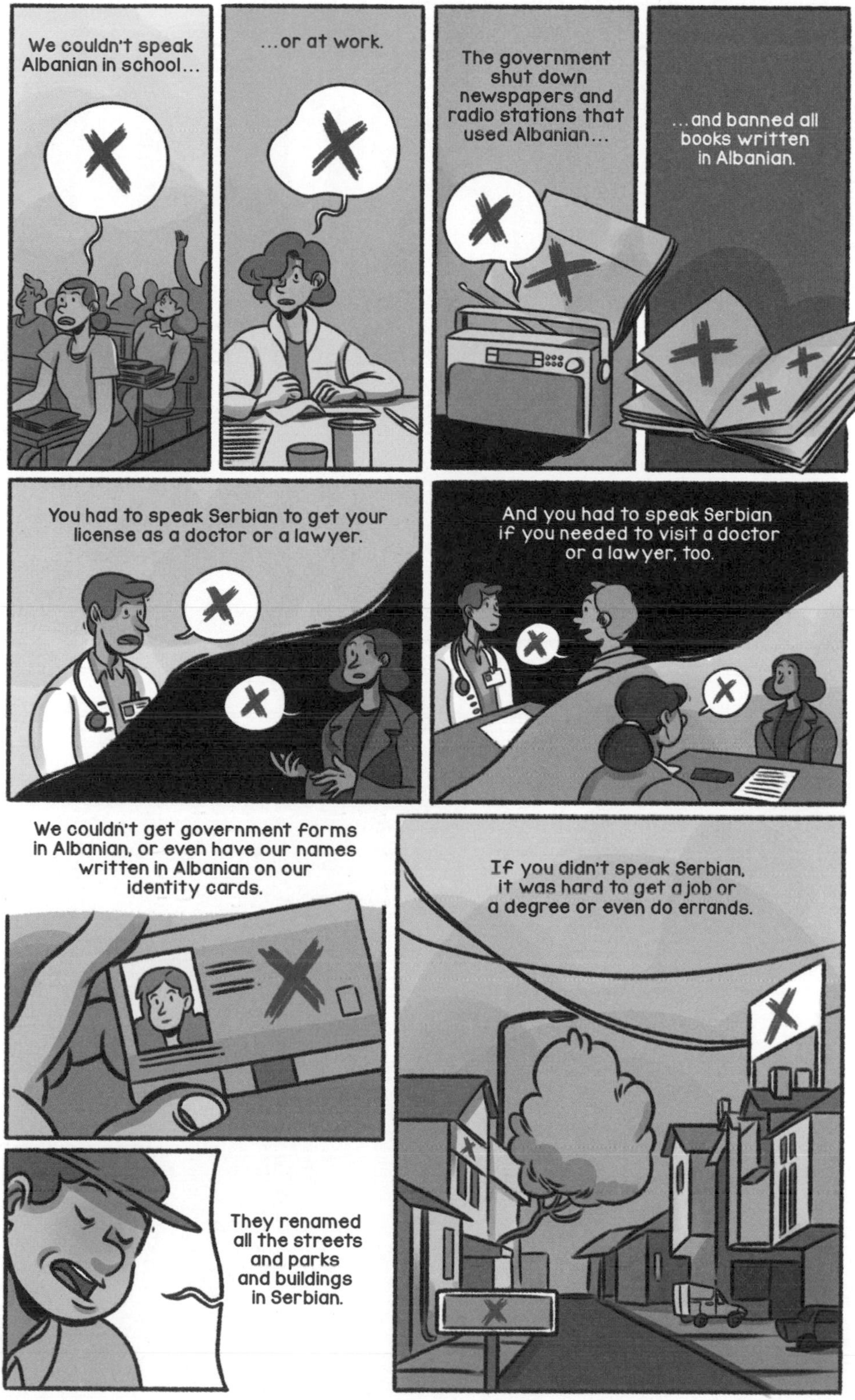
We couldn't speak Albanian in school...
...or at work.
The government shut down newspapers and radio stations that used Albanian...
...and banned all books written in Albanian.
You had to speak Serbian to get your license as a doctor or a lawyer.
And you had to speak Serbian if you needed to visit a doctor or a lawyer, too.
We couldn't get government forms in Albanian, or even have our names written in Albanian on our identity cards.
If you didn't speak Serbian, it was hard to get a job or a degree or even do errands.
They renamed all the streets and parks and buildings in Serbian.

If the police heard you speaking Albanian, they would follow you, harass you. Sometimes, groups of thugs would beat people they heard speaking Albanian, and the police— they would do nothing.

...

They took away our language, and it was like they were taking away our right to exist. We spoke Albanian to one another at home, we made secret Albanian schools and Albanian courts, but in public, we felt like nobody. How can your country want you if it doesn't even want to hear your language?

Mr. B, you're a lawyer! Couldn't you do something?

Here, you can sue everybody if you don't like something. But there was no law to make a lawsuit under. We didn't have any right to our own language.

Anyway, I couldn't practice the law back then— only Serbian speakers could get law licenses.

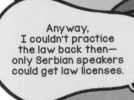

So what happened?

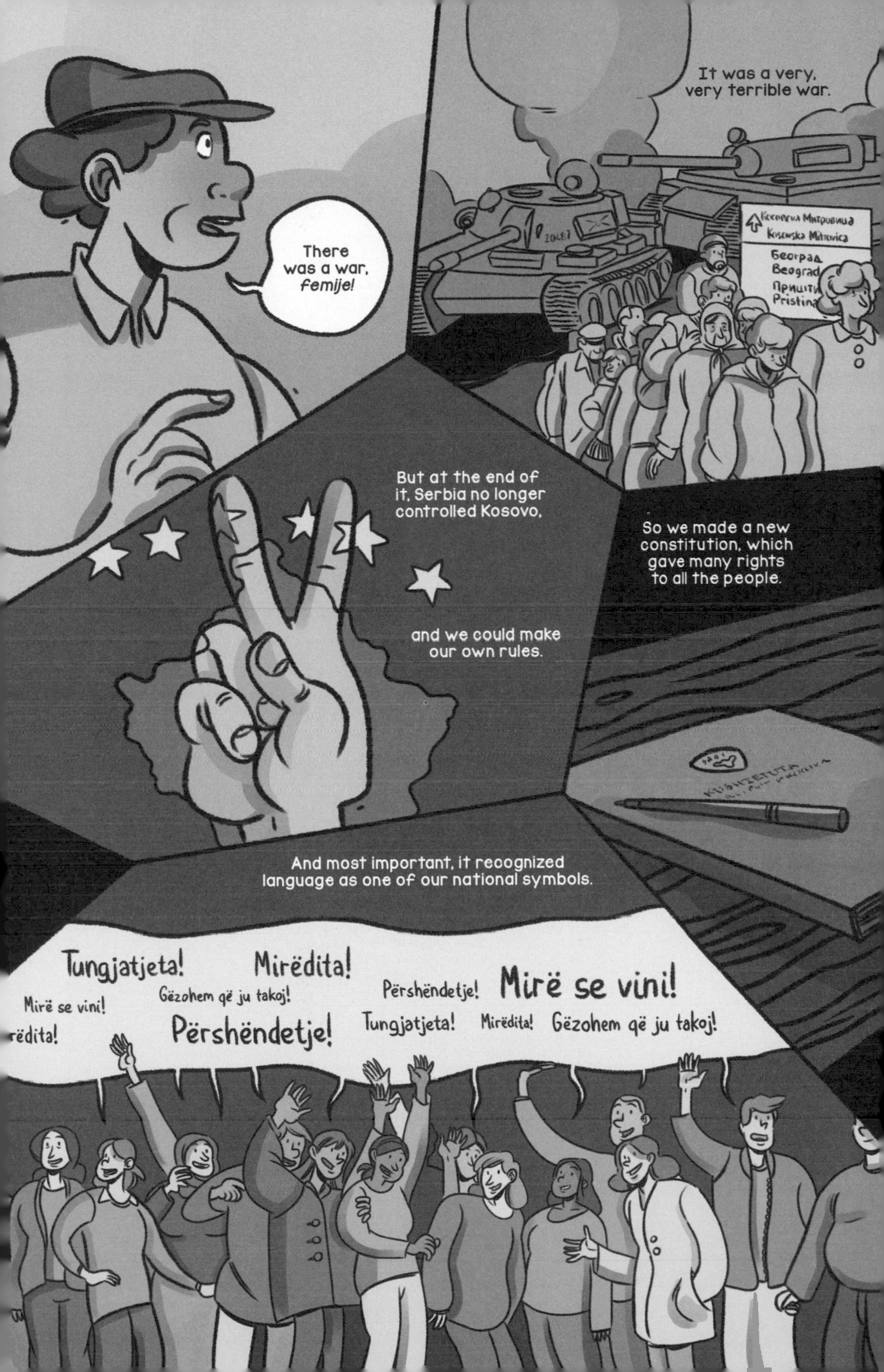
There was a war, *femije!*
It was a very, very terrible war.
Косовска Митровица
Kosovska Mitrovica
Београд
Beograd
Приштина
Pristina
But at the end of it, Serbia no longer controlled Kosovo,
and we could make our own rules.
So we made a new constitution, which gave many rights to all the people.
And most important, it recognized language as one of our national symbols.
Tungjatjeta!
Mirëdita!
Përshëndetje!
Mirë se vini!
Mirë se vini!
Gëzohem që ju takoj!
rëdita!
Përshëndetje!
Tungjatjeta!
Mirëdita!
Gëzohem që ju takoj!

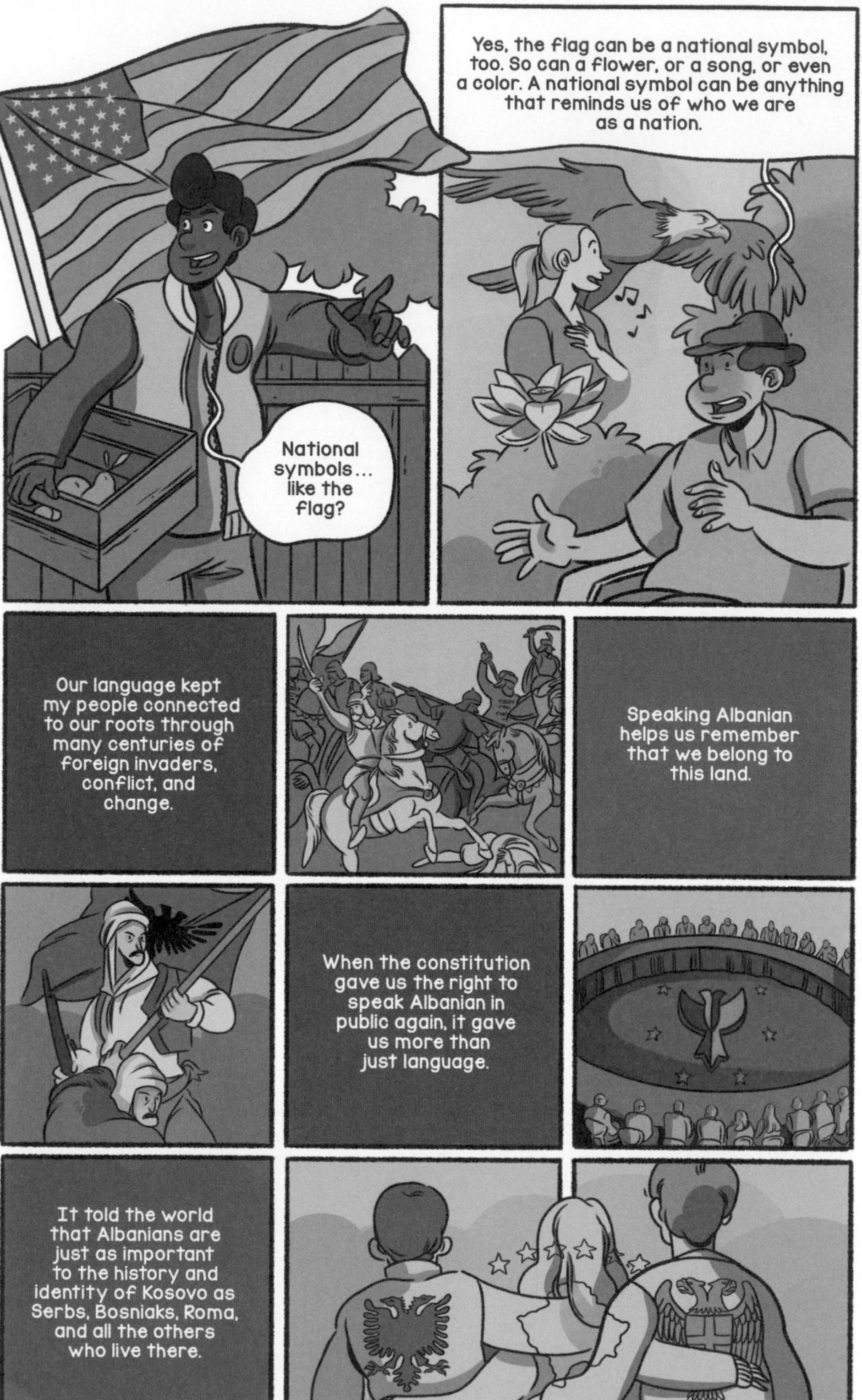

National symbols... like the flag?
Yes, the flag can be a national symbol, too. So can a flower, or a song, or even a color. A national symbol can be anything that reminds us of who we are as a nation.
Our language kept my people connected to our roots through many centuries of foreign invaders, conflict, and change.
Speaking Albanian helps us remember that we belong to this land.
When the constitution gave us the right to speak Albanian in public again, it gave us more than just language.
It told the world that Albanians are just as important to the history and identity of Kosovo as Serbs, Bosniaks, Roma, and all the others who live there.

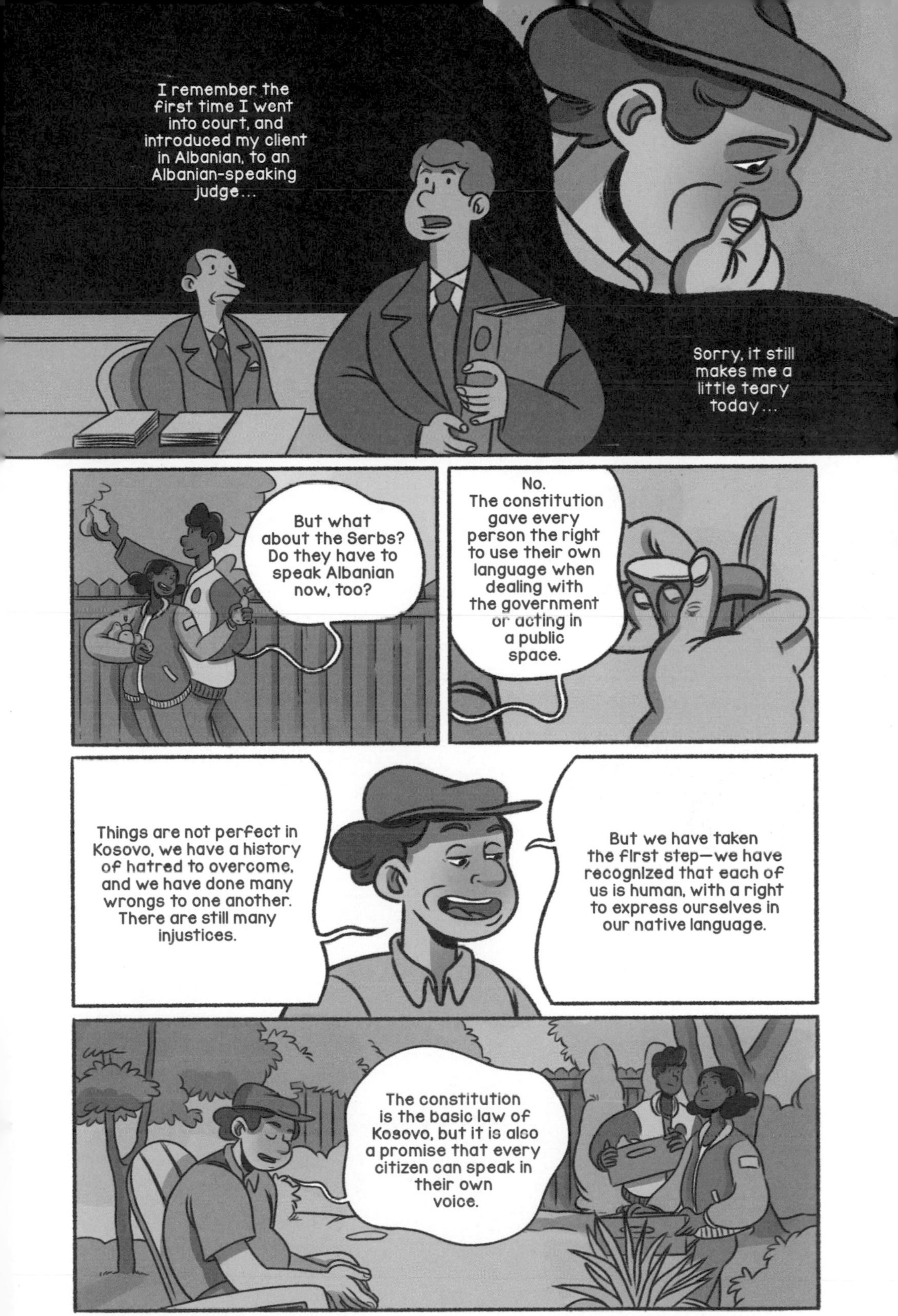
I remember the first time I went into court, and introduced my client in Albanian, to an Albanian-speaking judge...
Sorry, it still makes me a little teary today...
But what about the Serbs? Do they have to speak Albanian now, too?
No. The constitution gave every person the right to use their own language when dealing with the government or acting in a public space.
Things are not perfect in Kosovo, we have a history of hatred to overcome, and we have done many wrongs to one another. There are still many injustices.
But we have taken the first step—we have recognized that each of us is human, with a right to express ourselves in our native language.
The constitution is the basic law of Kosovo, but it is also a promise that every citizen can speak in their own voice.

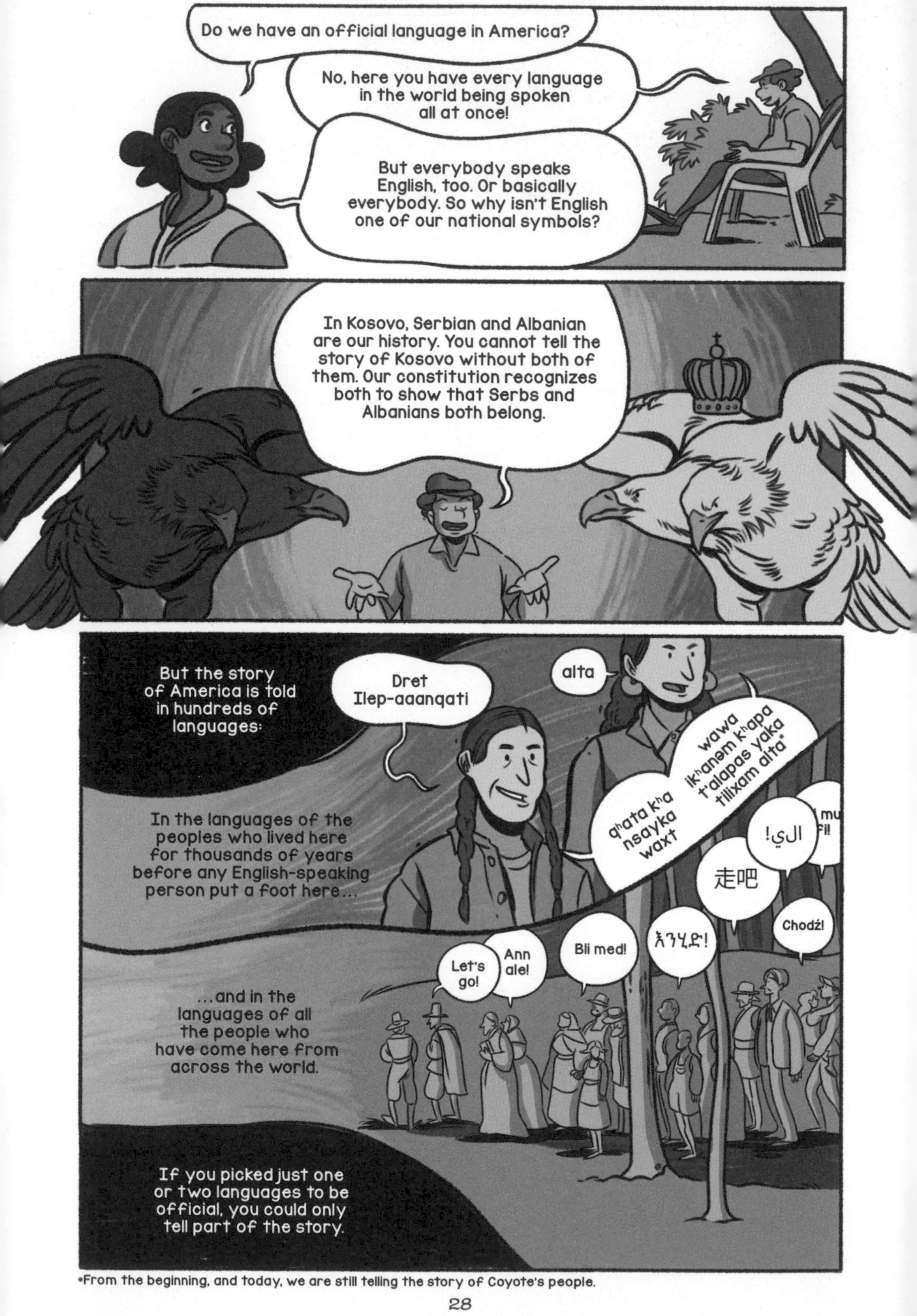
Do we have an official language in America?
No, here you have every language in the world being spoken all at once!
But everybody speaks English, too. Or basically everybody. So why isn't English one of our national symbols?
In Kosovo, Serbian and Albanian are our history. You cannot tell the story of Kosovo without both of them. Our constitution recognizes both to show that Serbs and Albanians both belong.
But the story of America is told in hundreds of languages:
Dret Ilep-aaanqati
alta
q^{h}ata k^{h}a nsayka waxt
wawa ik^{h}anəm k^{h}apa t'alapas yaka tilixam alta*
In the languages of the peoples who lived here for thousands of years before any English-speaking person put a foot here...
!الي
走吧
Chodź!
Let's go!
Ann ale!
Bli med!
እንሂድ!
...and in the languages of all the people who have come here from across the world.
If you picked just one or two languages to be official, you could only tell part of the story.

*From the beginning, and today, we are still telling the story of Coyote's people.

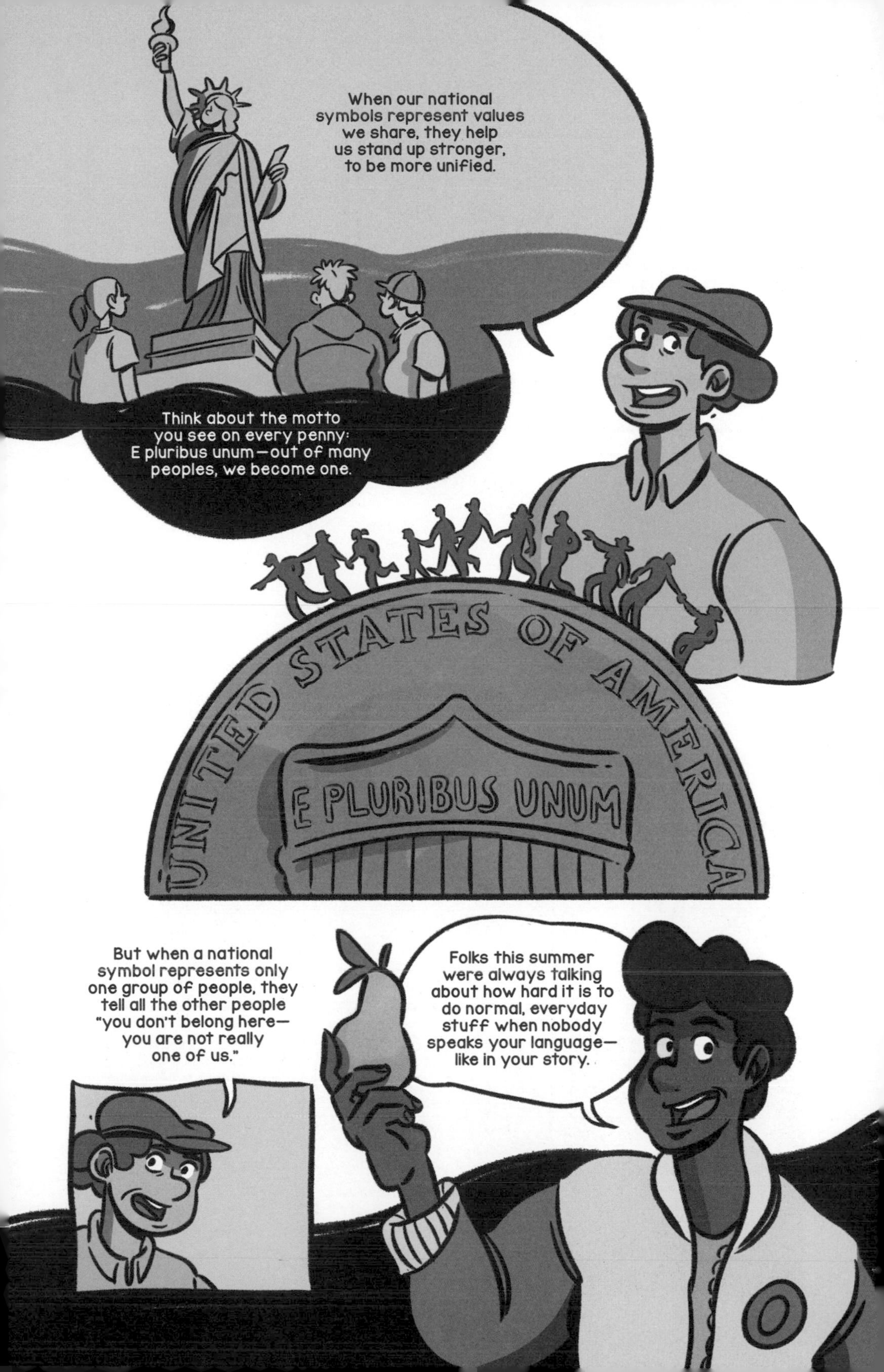
When our national symbols represent values we share, they help us stand up stronger, to be more unified.
Think about the motto you see on every penny: E pluribus unum—out of many peoples, we become one.
UNITED STATES OF AMERICA
E PLURIBUS UNUM
But when a national symbol represents only one group of people, they tell all the other people "you don't belong here—you are not really one of us."
Folks this summer were always talking about how hard it is to do normal, everyday stuff when nobody speaks your language—like in your story.

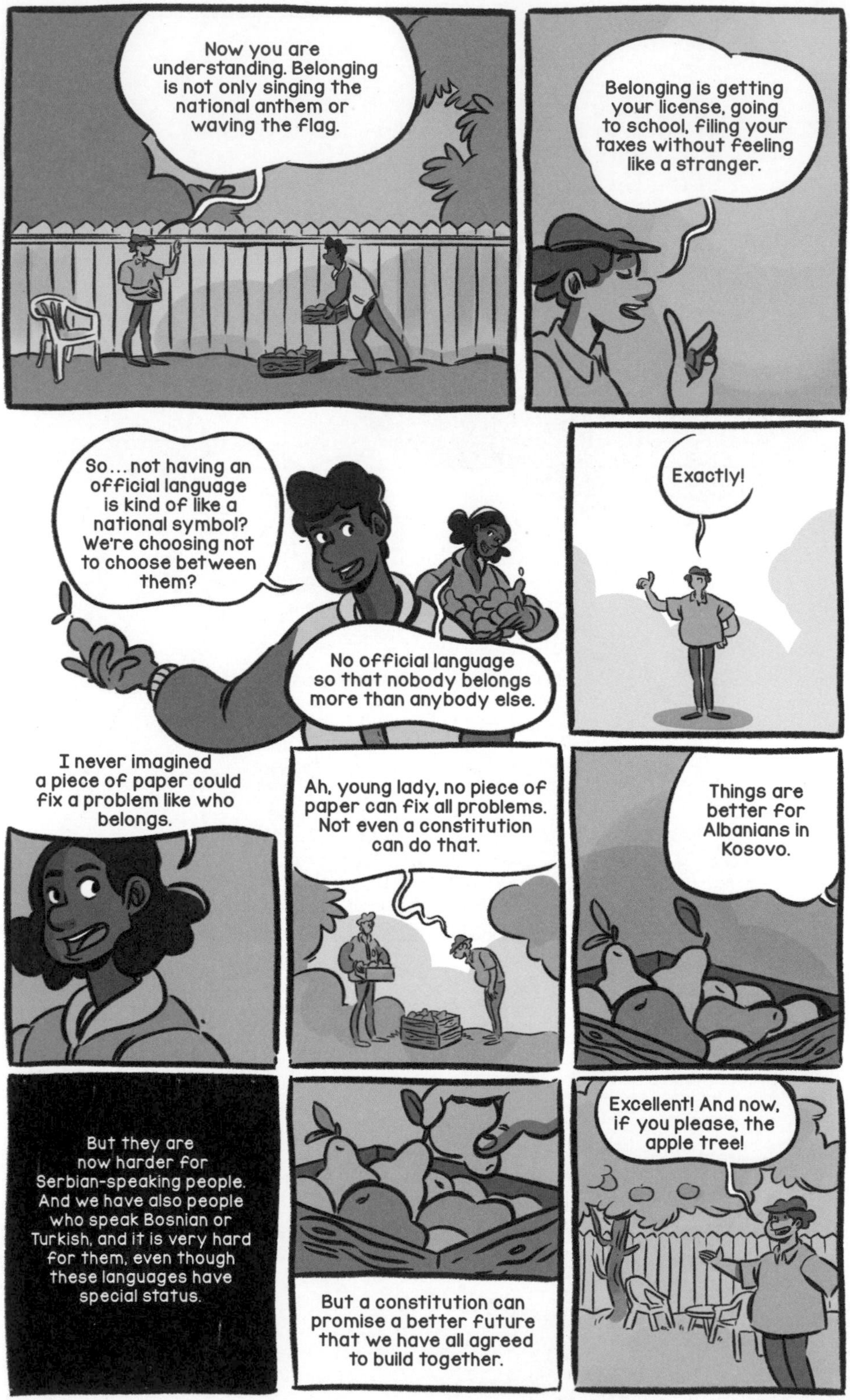
Now you are understanding. Belonging is not only singing the national anthem or waving the flag.
Belonging is getting your license, going to school, filing your taxes without feeling like a stranger.
So... not having an official language is kind of like a national symbol? We're choosing not to choose between them?
No official language so that nobody belongs more than anybody else.
Exactly!
I never imagined a piece of paper could fix a problem like who belongs.
Ah, young lady, no piece of paper can fix all problems. Not even a constitution can do that.
Things are better for Albanians in Kosovo.
But they are now harder for Serbian-speaking people. And we have also people who speak Bosnian or Turkish, and it is very hard for them, even though these languages have special status.
But a constitution can promise a better future that we have all agreed to build together.
Excellent! And now, if you please, the apple tree!

Chapter IV
No One Gets
All the Power

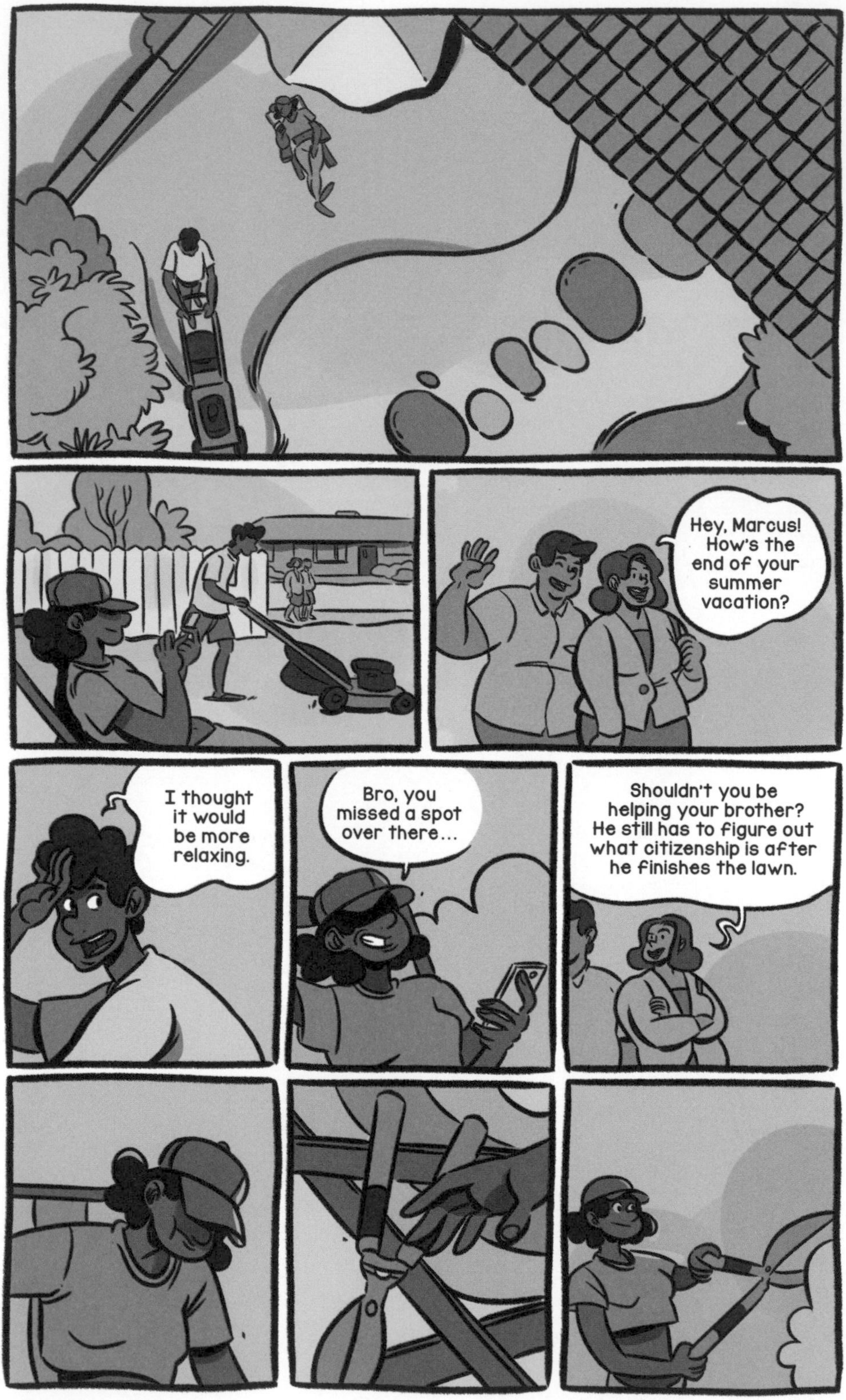
Hey, Marcus! How's the end of your summer vacation?
I thought it would be more relaxing.
Bro, you missed a spot over there...
Shouldn't you be helping your brother? He still has to figure out what citizenship is after he finishes the lawn.

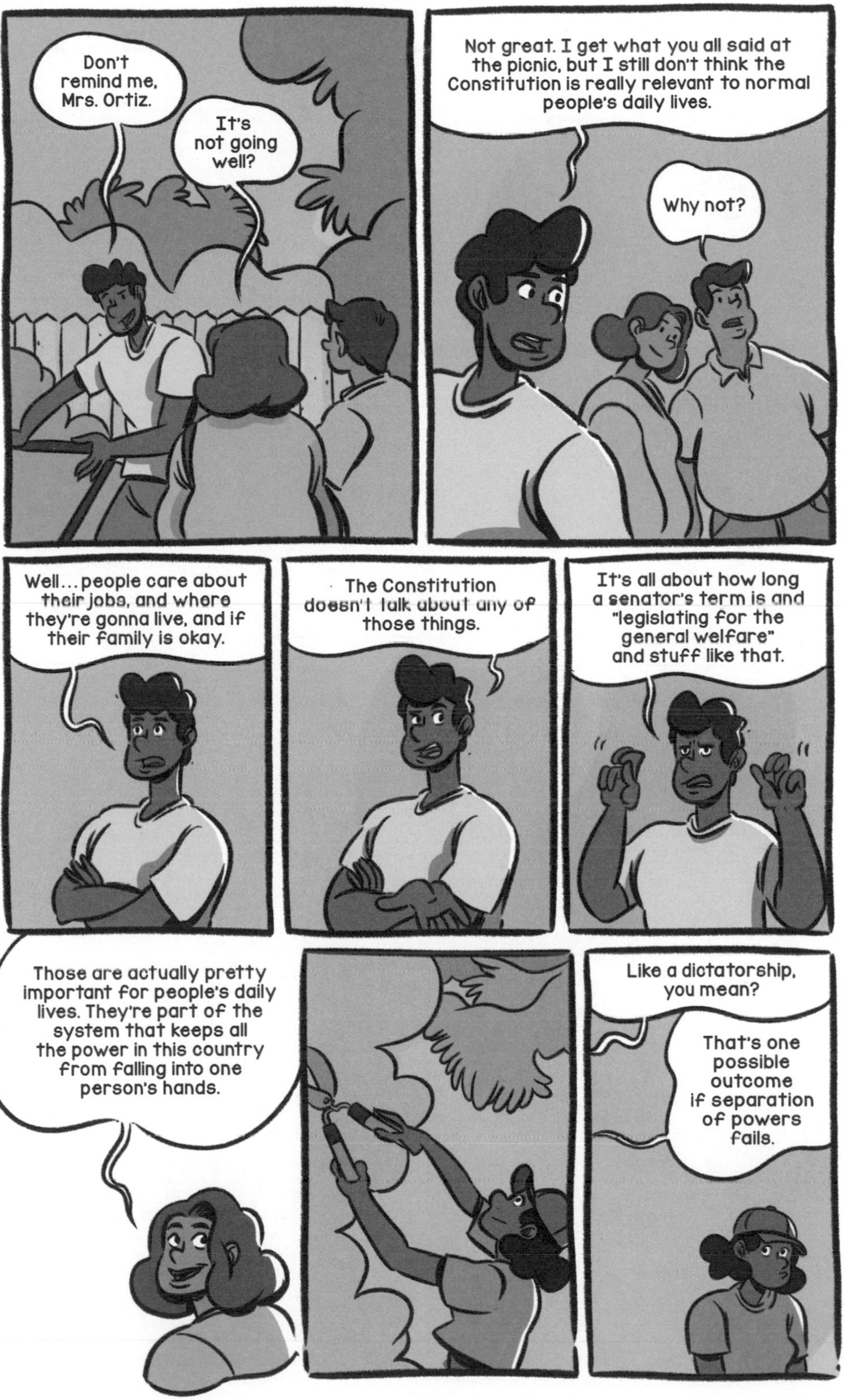
Don't remind me, Mrs. Ortiz.
It's not going well?
Not great. I get what you all said at the picnic, but I still don't think the Constitution is really relevant to normal people's daily lives.
Why not?
Well... people care about their jobs, and where they're gonna live, and if their family is okay.
The Constitution doesn't talk about any of those things.
It's all about how long a senator's term is and "legislating for the general welfare" and stuff like that.
Those are actually pretty important for people's daily lives. They're part of the system that keeps all the power in this country from falling into one person's hands.
Like a dictatorship, you mean?
That's one possible outcome if separation of powers fails.

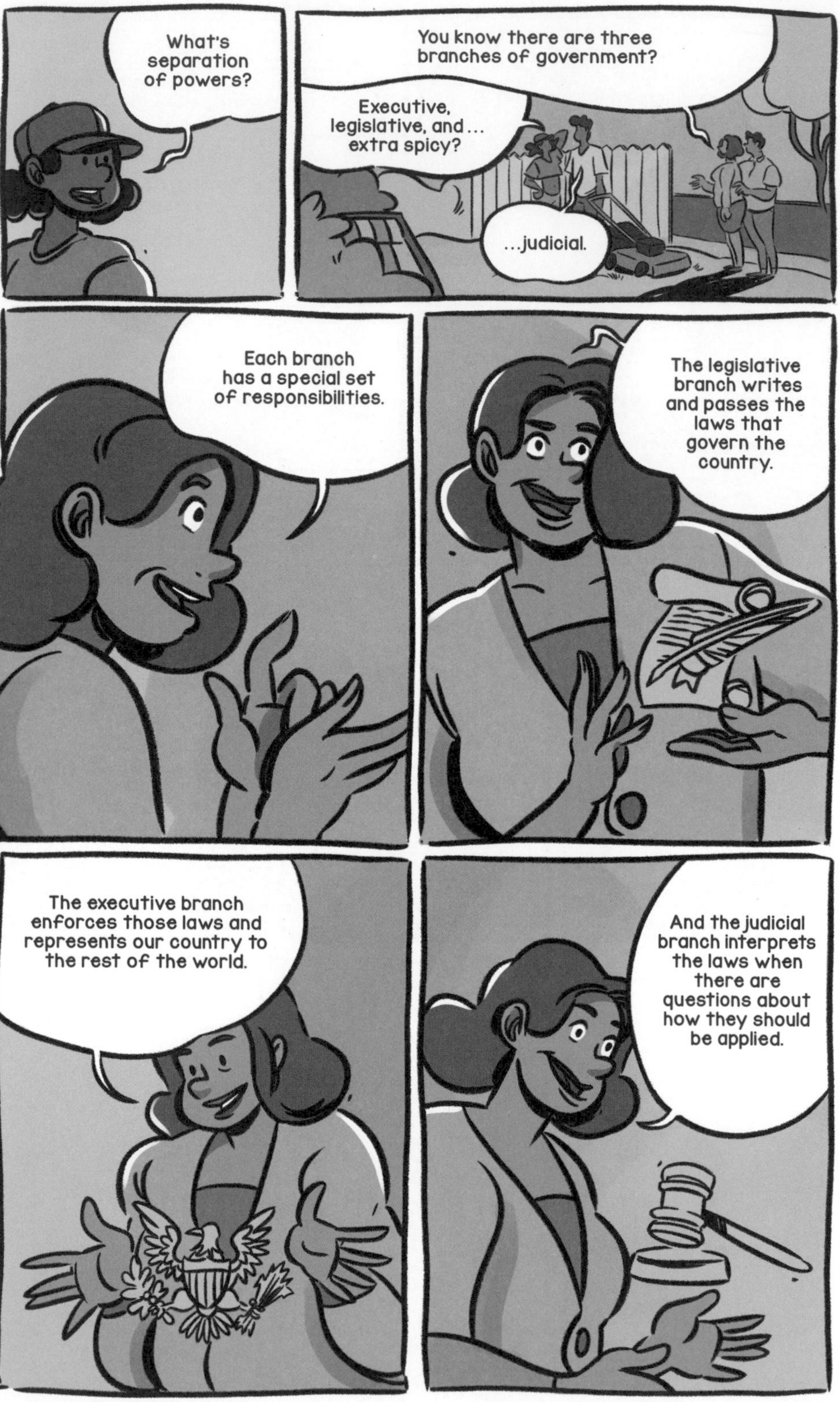
What's separation of powers?
You know there are three branches of government?
Executive, legislative, and... extra spicy?
...judicial.
Each branch has a special set of responsibilities.
The legislative branch writes and passes the laws that govern the country.
The executive branch enforces those laws and represents our country to the rest of the world.
And the judicial branch interprets the laws when there are questions about how they should be applied.

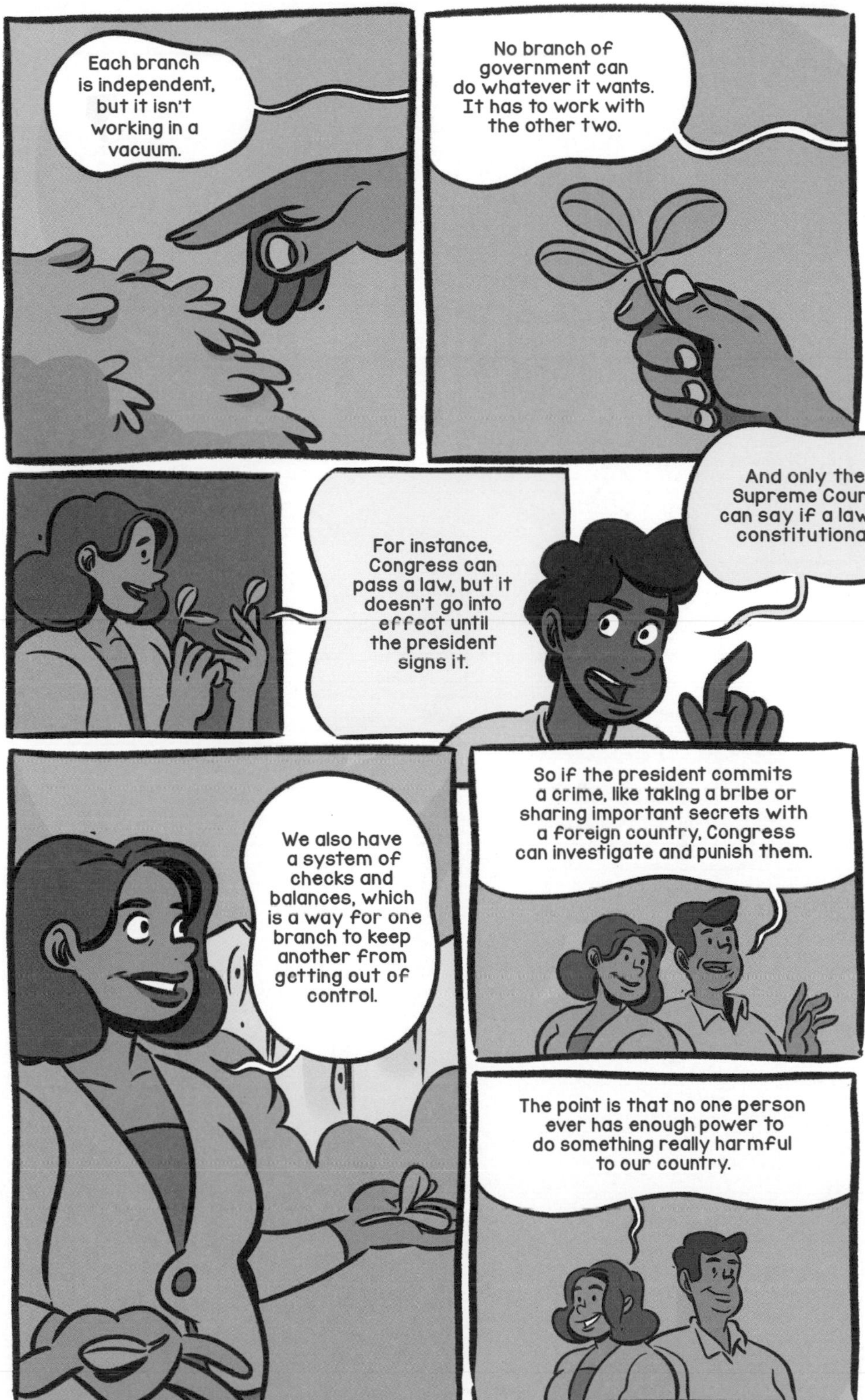
Each branch is independent, but it isn't working in a vacuum.
No branch of government can do whatever it wants. It has to work with the other two.
For instance, Congress can pass a law, but it doesn't go into effect until the president signs it.
And only the Supreme Court can say if a law is constitutional.
We also have a system of checks and balances, which is a way for one branch to keep another from getting out of control.
So if the president commits a crime, like taking a bribe or sharing important secrets with a foreign country, Congress can investigate and punish them.
The point is that no one person ever has enough power to do something really harmful to our country.

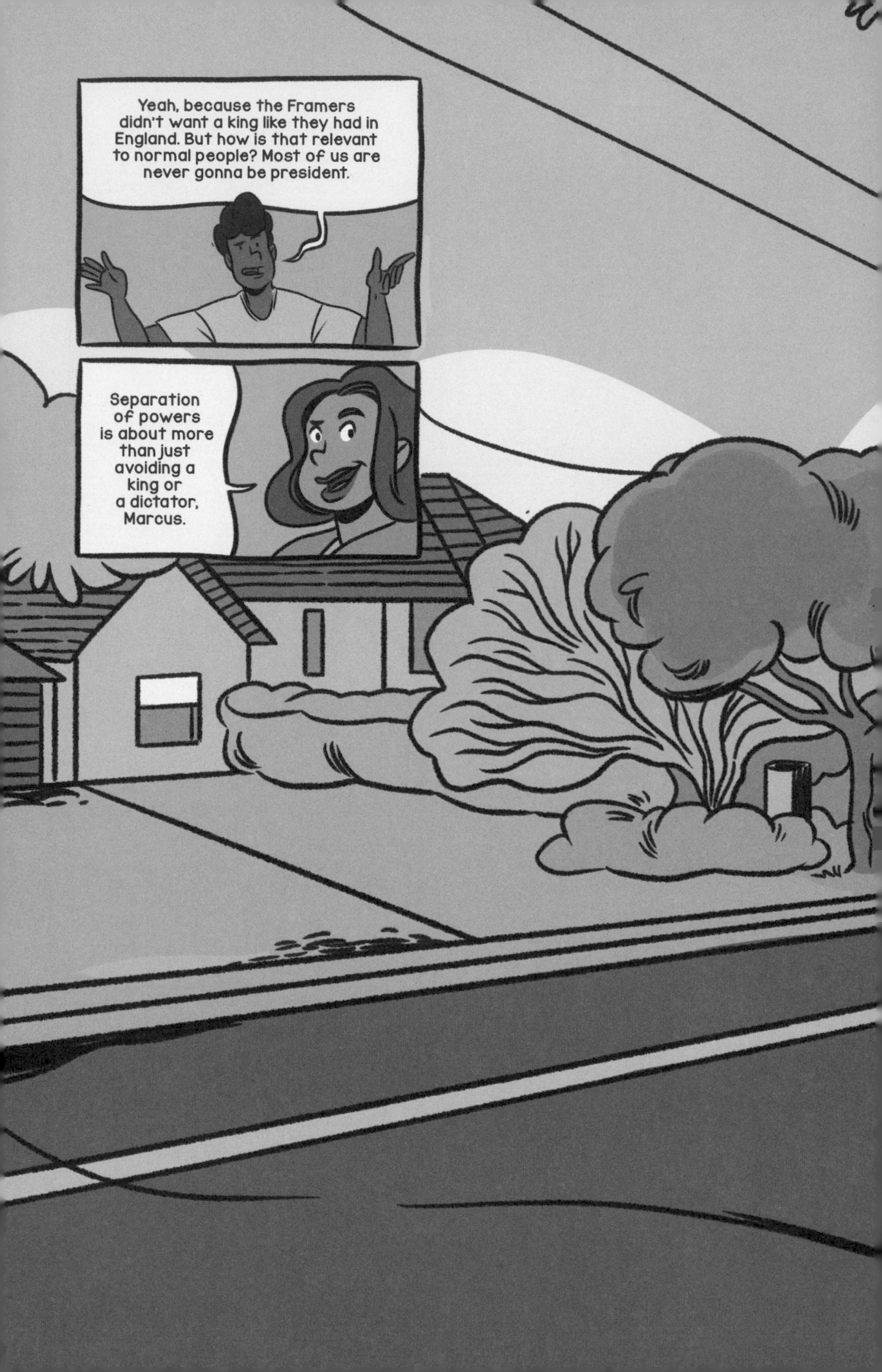
Yeah, because the Framers didn't want a king like they had in England. But how is that relevant to normal people? Most of us are never gonna be president.
Separation of powers is about more than just avoiding a king or a dictator, Marcus.

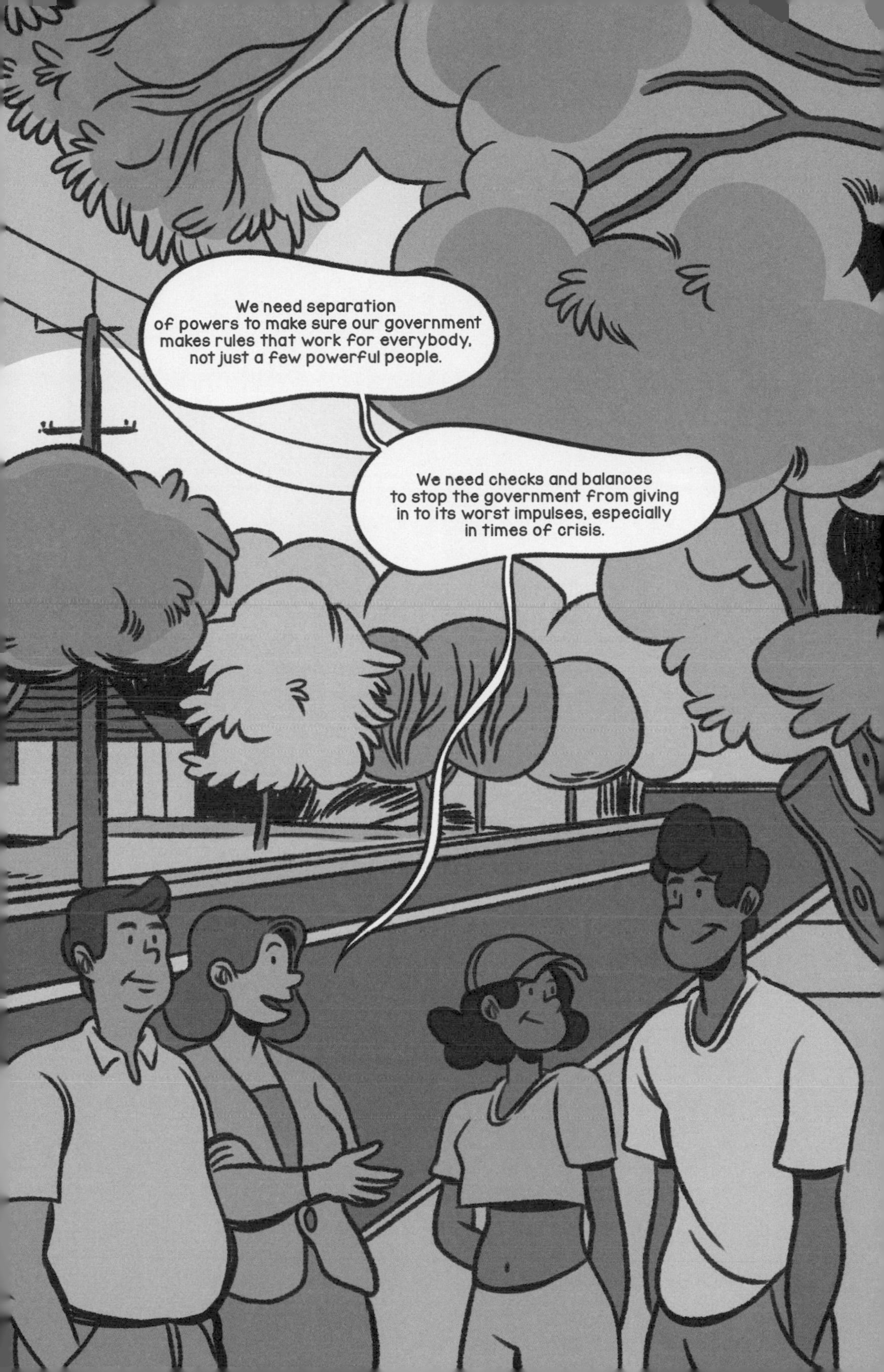
We need separation of powers to make sure our government makes rules that work for everybody, not just a few powerful people.
We need checks and balances to stop the government from giving in to its worst impulses, especially in times of crisis.

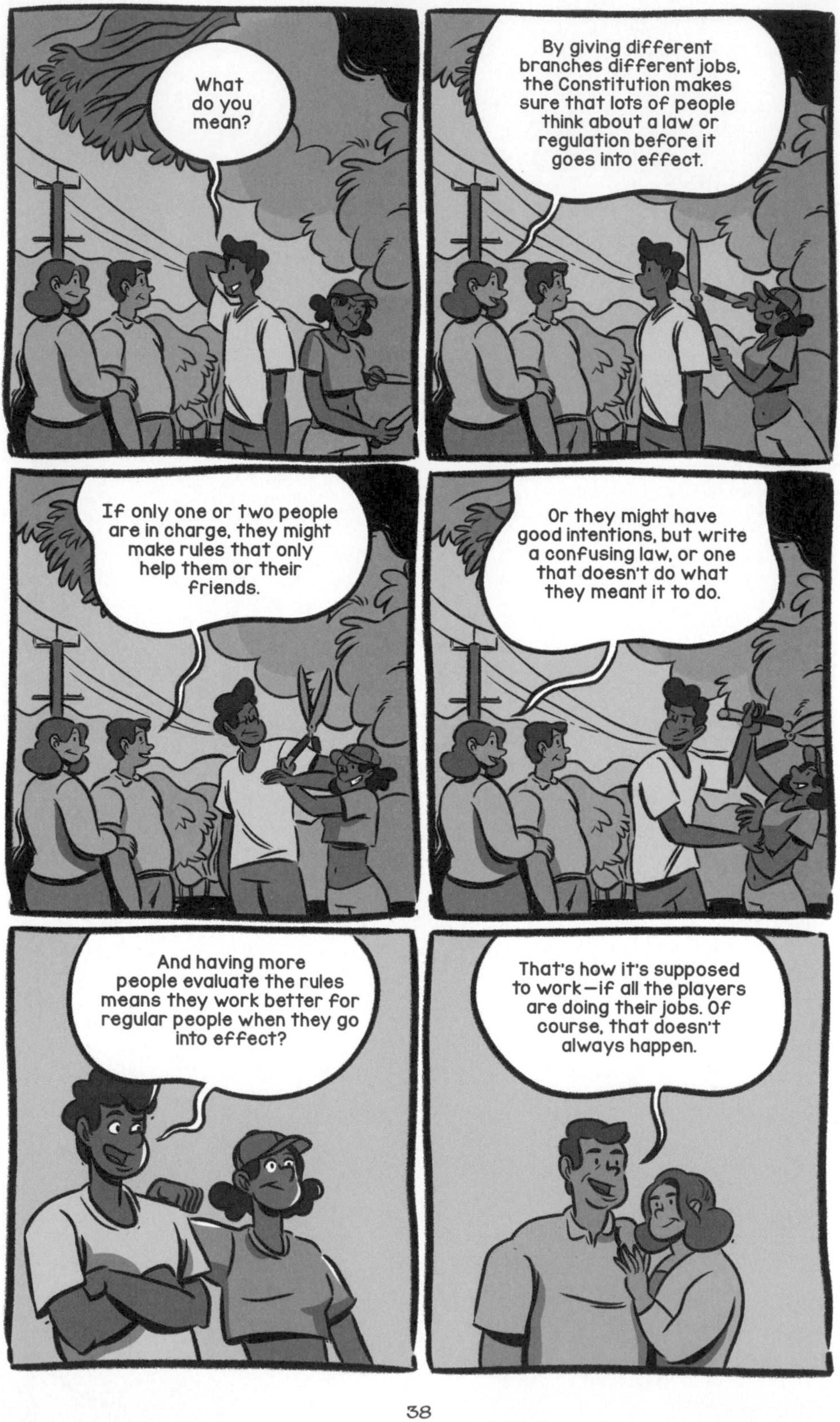
What do you mean?
By giving different branches different jobs, the Constitution makes sure that lots of people think about a law or regulation before it goes into effect.
If only one or two people are in charge, they might make rules that only help them or their friends.
Or they might have good intentions, but write a confusing law, or one that doesn't do what they meant it to do.
And having more people evaluate the rules means they work better for regular people when they go into effect?
That's how it's supposed to work—if all the players are doing their jobs. Of course, that doesn't always happen.

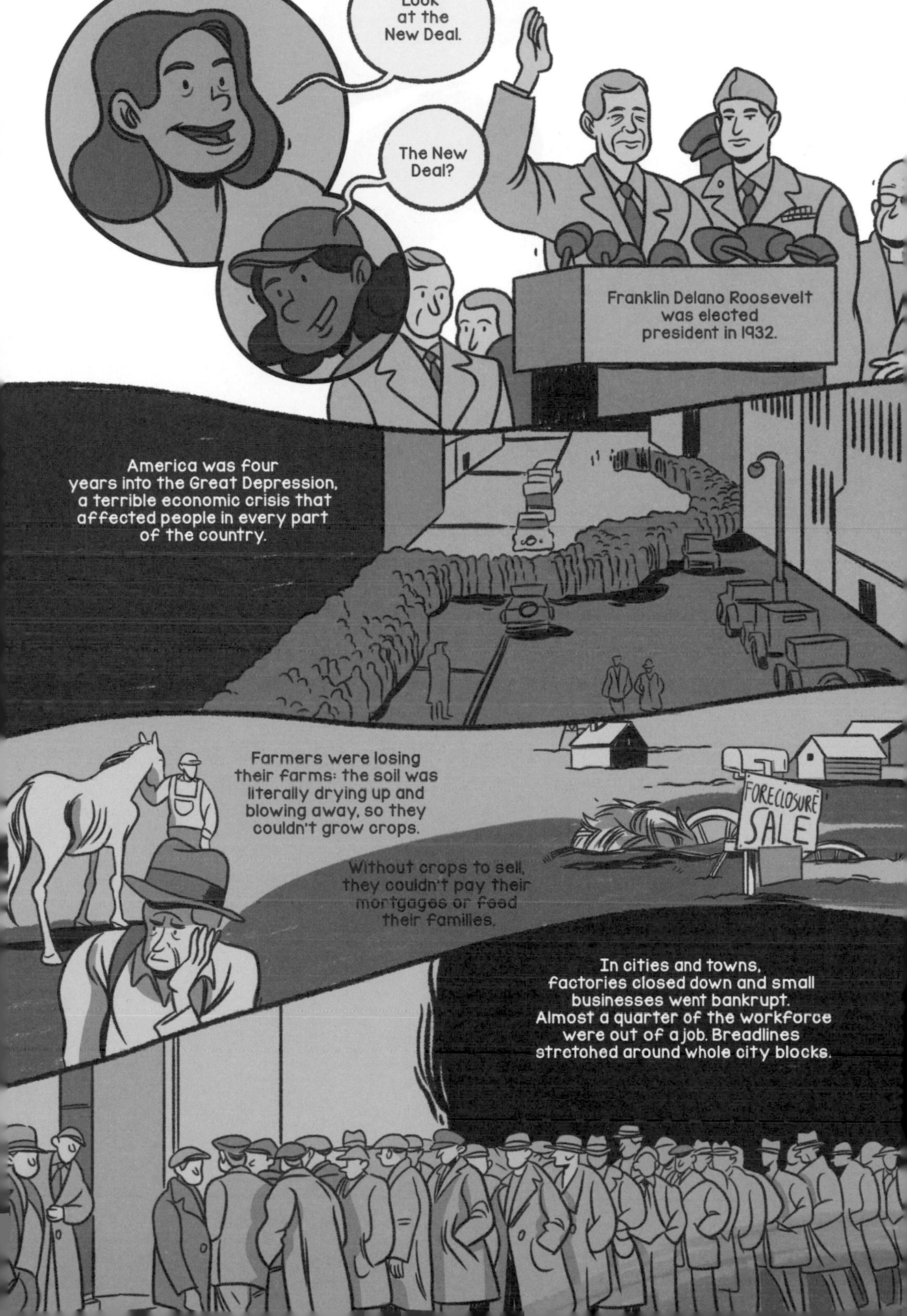
Look at the New Deal.
The New Deal?
Franklin Delano Roosevelt was elected president in 1932.
America was four years into the Great Depression, a terrible economic crisis that affected people in every part of the country.
Farmers were losing their farms: the soil was literally drying up and blowing away, so they couldn't grow crops.
FORECLOSURE SALE
Without crops to sell, they couldn't pay their mortgages or feed their families.
In cities and towns, factories closed down and small businesses went bankrupt. Almost a quarter of the workforce were out of a job. Breadlines stretched around whole city blocks.

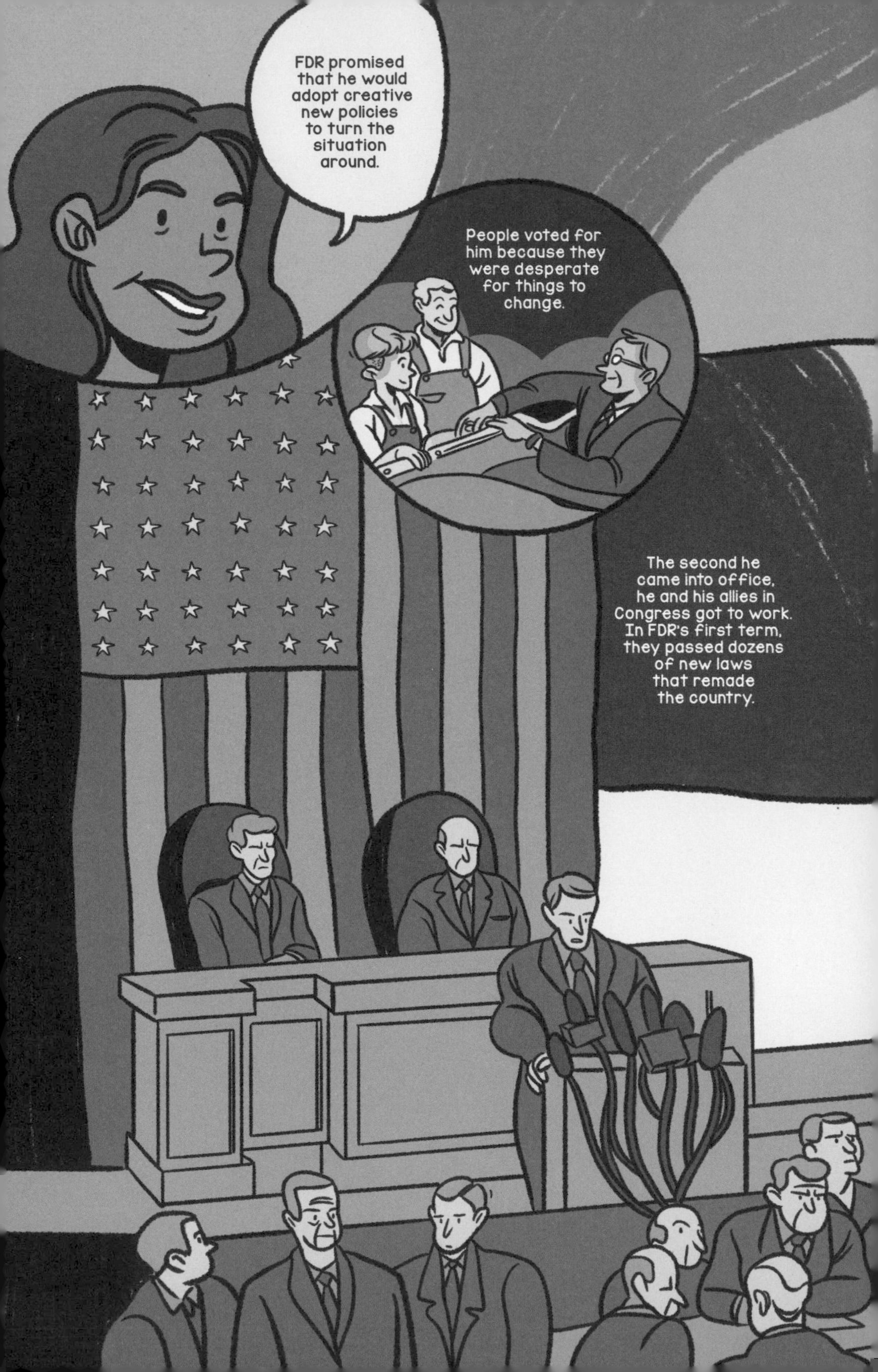
FDR promised that he would adopt creative new policies to turn the situation around.
People voted for him because they were desperate for things to change.
The second he came into office, he and his allies in Congress got to work. In FDR's first term, they passed dozens of new laws that remade the country.

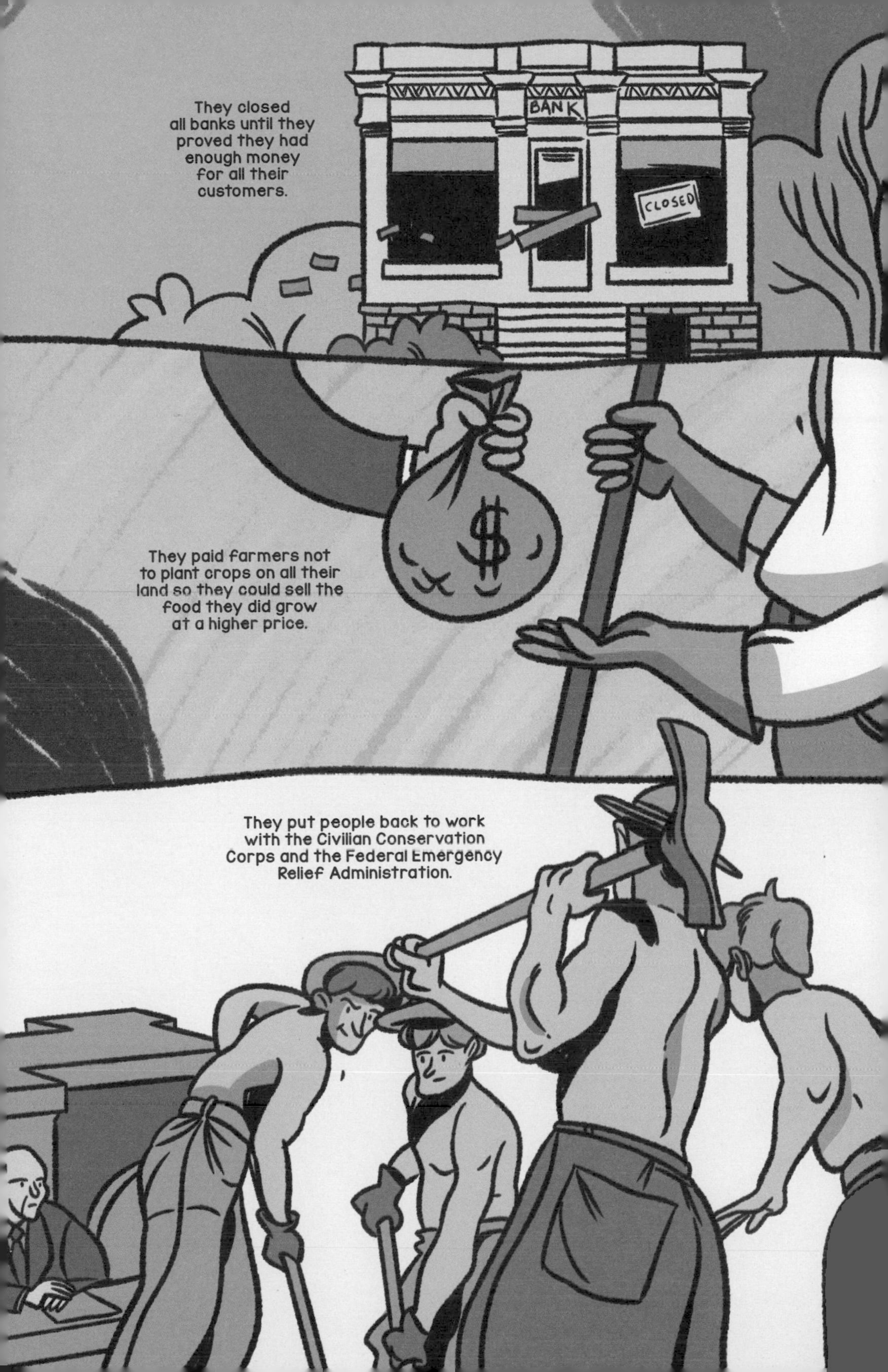
They closed all banks until they proved they had enough money for all their customers.
BANK
CLOSED
They paid farmers not to plant crops on all their land so they could sell the food they did grow at a higher price.
They put people back to work with the Civilian Conservation Corps and the Federal Emergency Relief Administration.

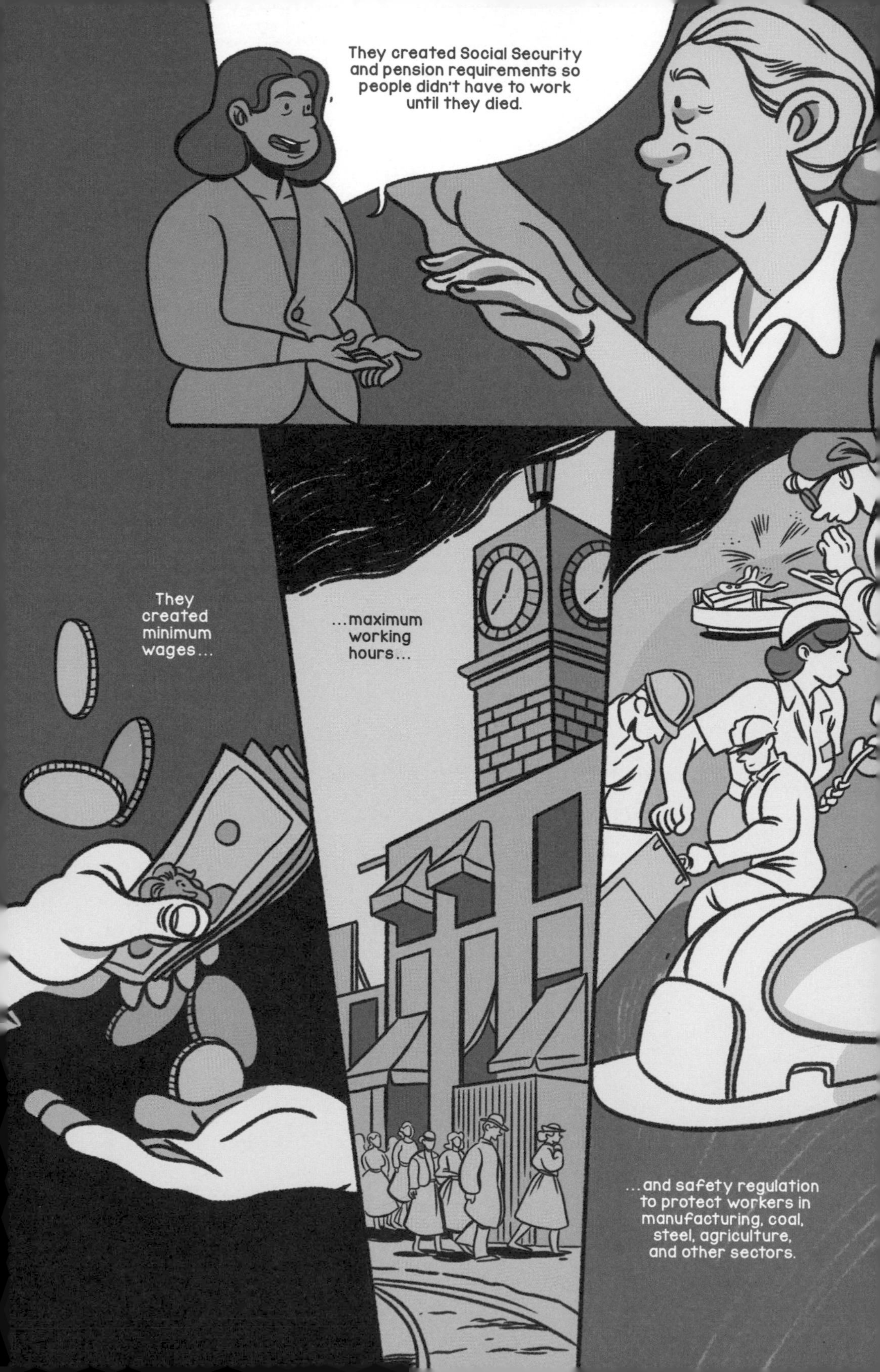
They created Social Security and pension requirements so people didn't have to work until they died.
They created minimum wages...
...maximum working hours...
...and safety regulation to protect workers in manufacturing, coal, steel, agriculture, and other sectors.

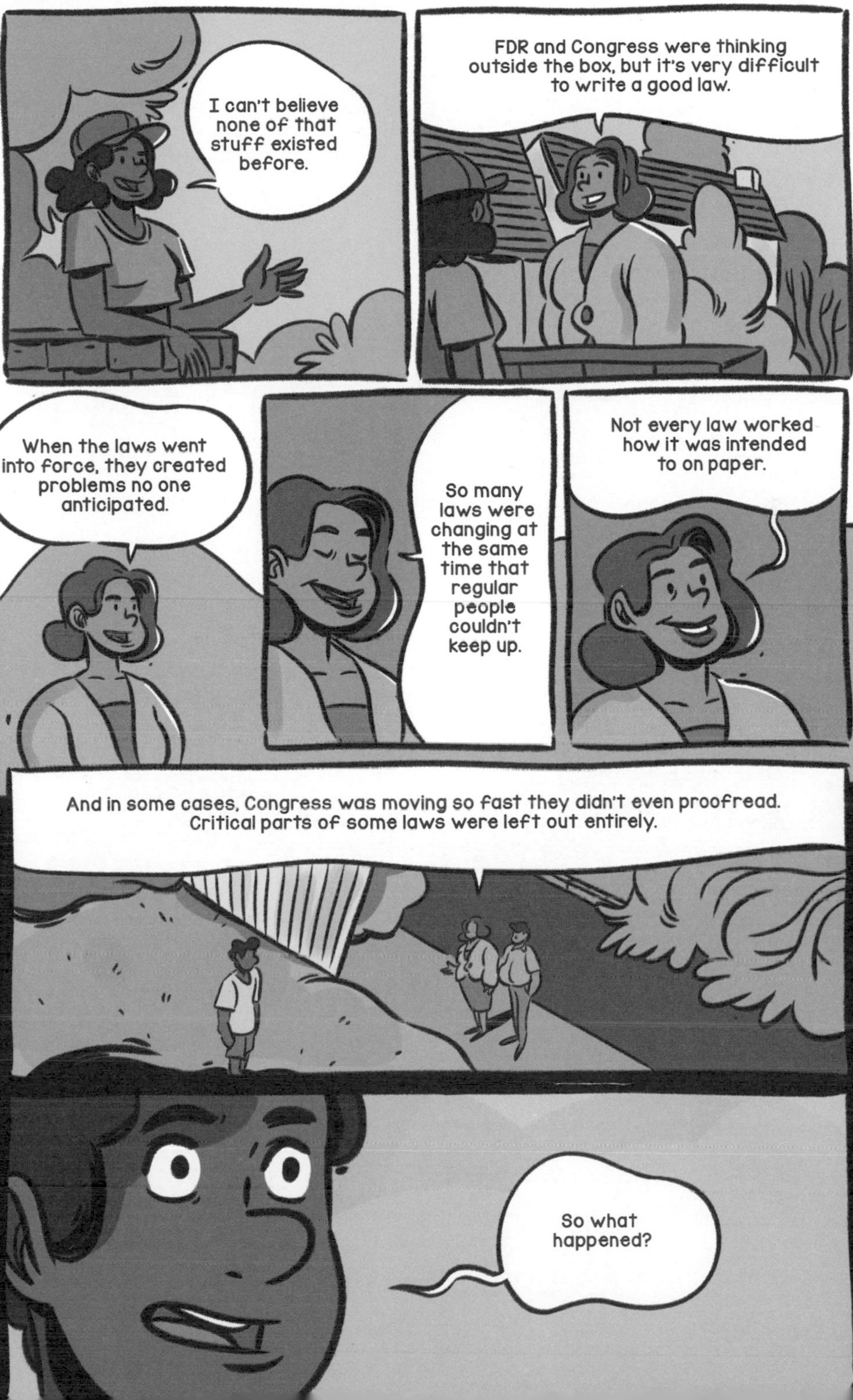

I can't believe none of that stuff existed before.
FDR and Congress were thinking outside the box, but it's very difficult to write a good law.
When the laws went into force, they created problems no one anticipated.
So many laws were changing at the same time that regular people couldn't keep up.
Not every law worked how it was intended to on paper.
And in some cases, Congress was moving so fast they didn't even proofread. Critical parts of some laws were left out entirely.
So what happened?

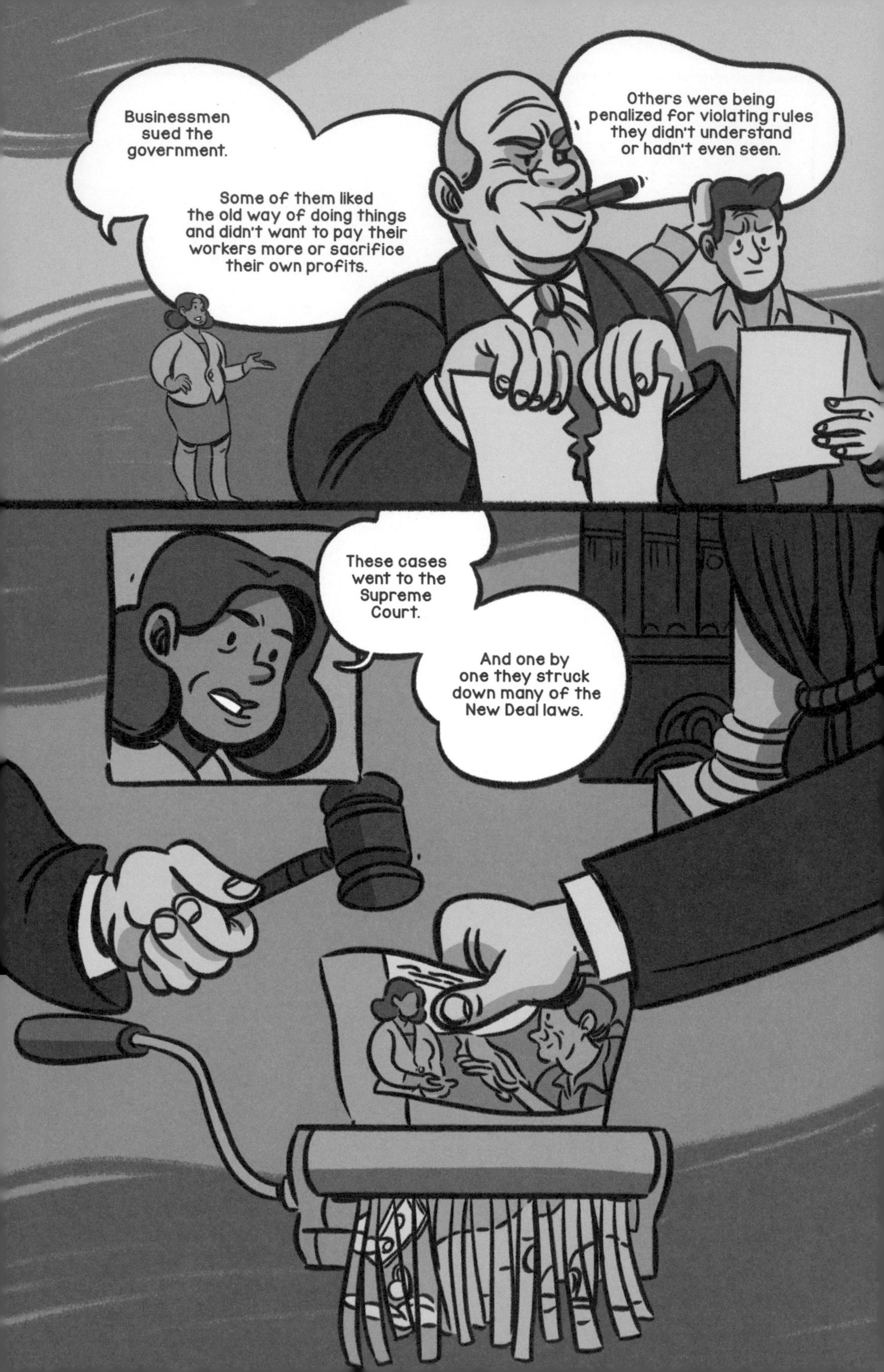
Businessmen sued the government.
Some of them liked the old way of doing things and didn't want to pay their workers more or sacrifice their own profits.
Others were being penalized for violating rules they didn't understand or hadn't even seen.
These cases went to the Supreme Court.
And one by one they struck down many of the New Deal laws.

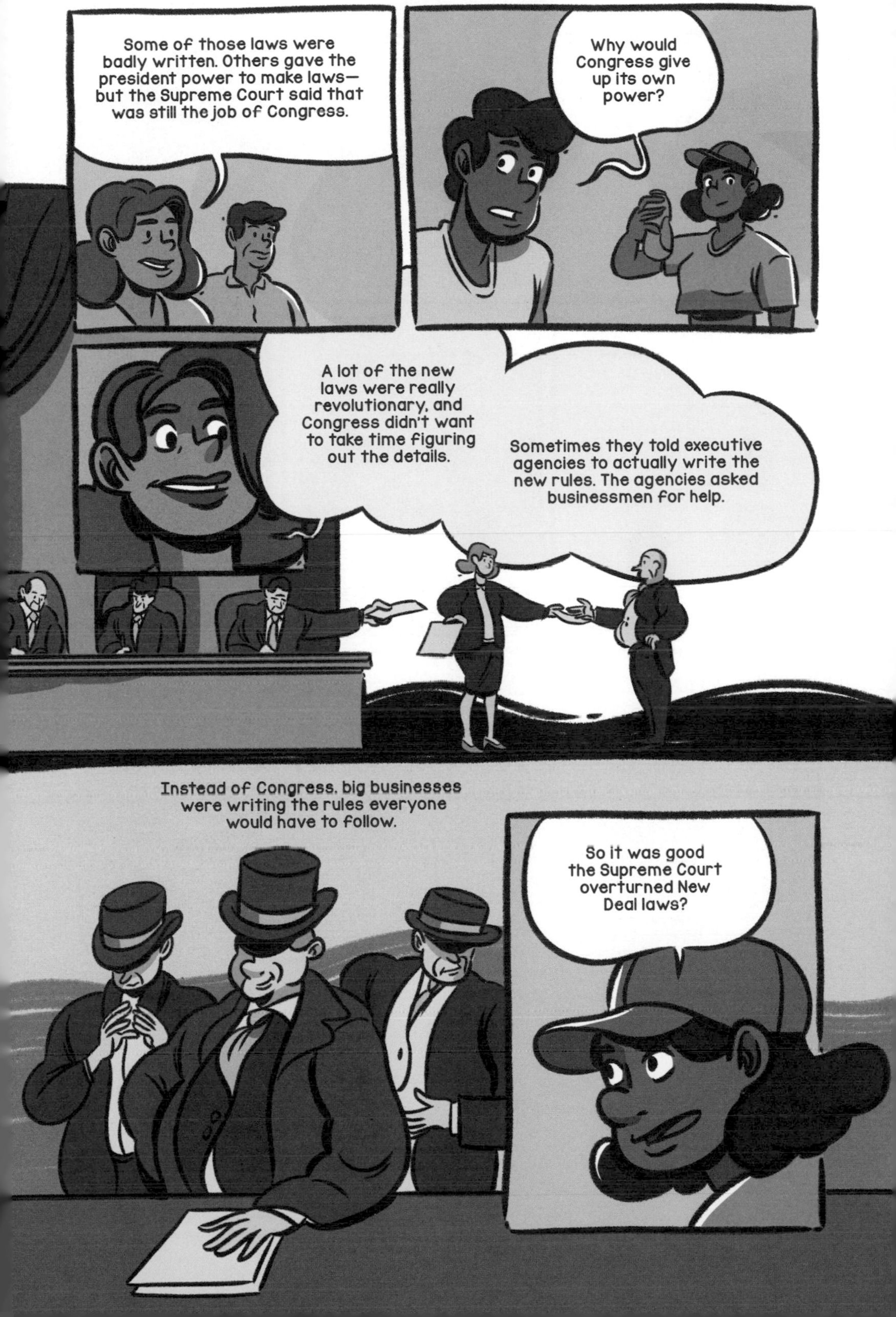
Some of those laws were badly written. Others gave the president power to make laws—but the Supreme Court said that was still the job of Congress.
Why would Congress give up its own power?
A lot of the new laws were really revolutionary, and Congress didn't want to take time figuring out the details.
Sometimes they told executive agencies to actually write the new rules. The agencies asked businessmen for help.
Instead of Congress, big businesses were writing the rules everyone would have to follow.
So it was good the Supreme Court overturned New Deal laws?

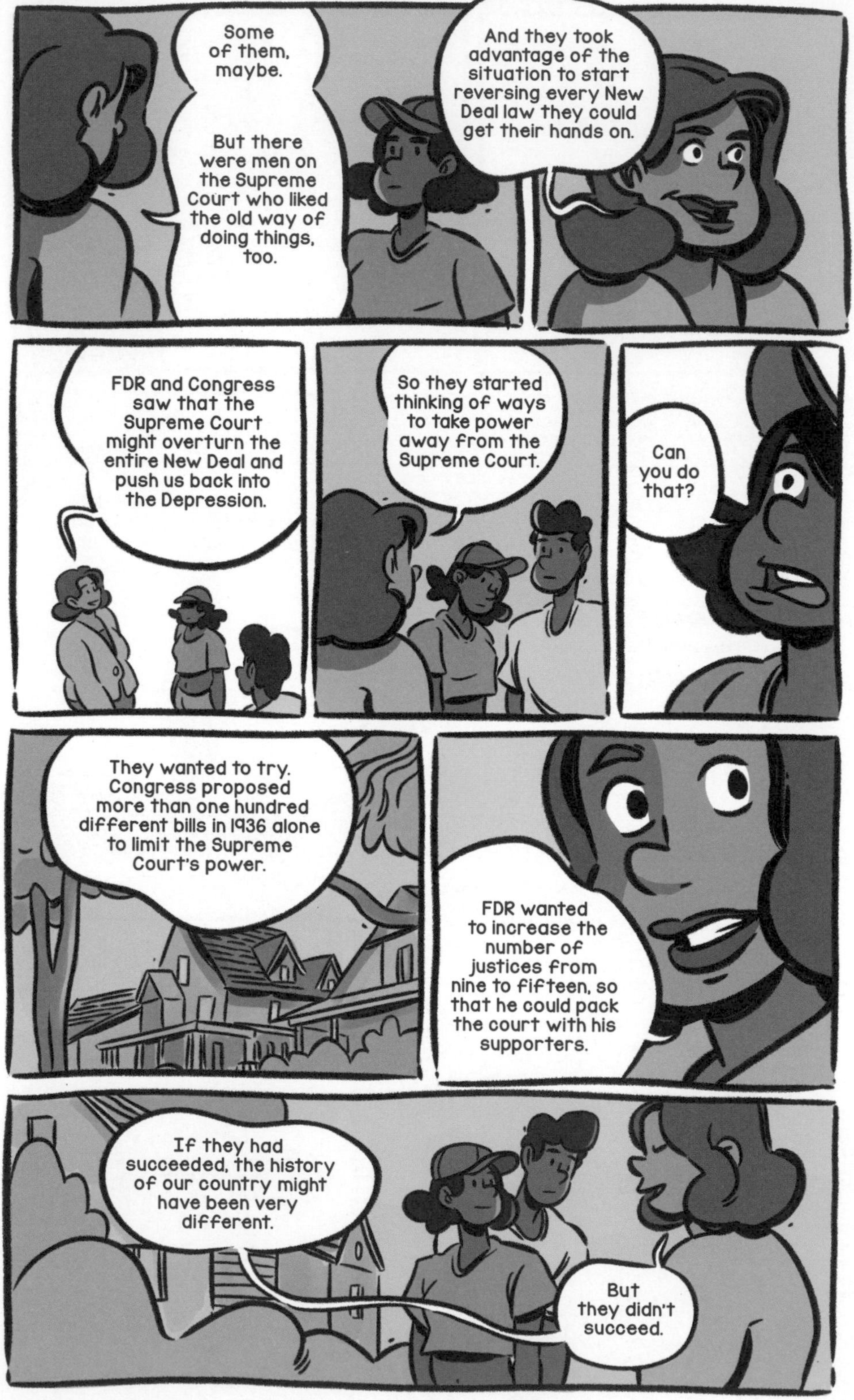
Some of them, maybe.
But there were men on the Supreme Court who liked the old way of doing things, too.
And they took advantage of the situation to start reversing every New Deal law they could get their hands on.
FDR and Congress saw that the Supreme Court might overturn the entire New Deal and push us back into the Depression.
So they started thinking of ways to take power away from the Supreme Court.
Can you do that?
They wanted to try. Congress proposed more than one hundred different bills in 1936 alone to limit the Supreme Court's power.
FDR wanted to increase the number of justices from nine to fifteen, so that he could pack the court with his supporters.
If they had succeeded, the history of our country might have been very different.
But they didn't succeed.

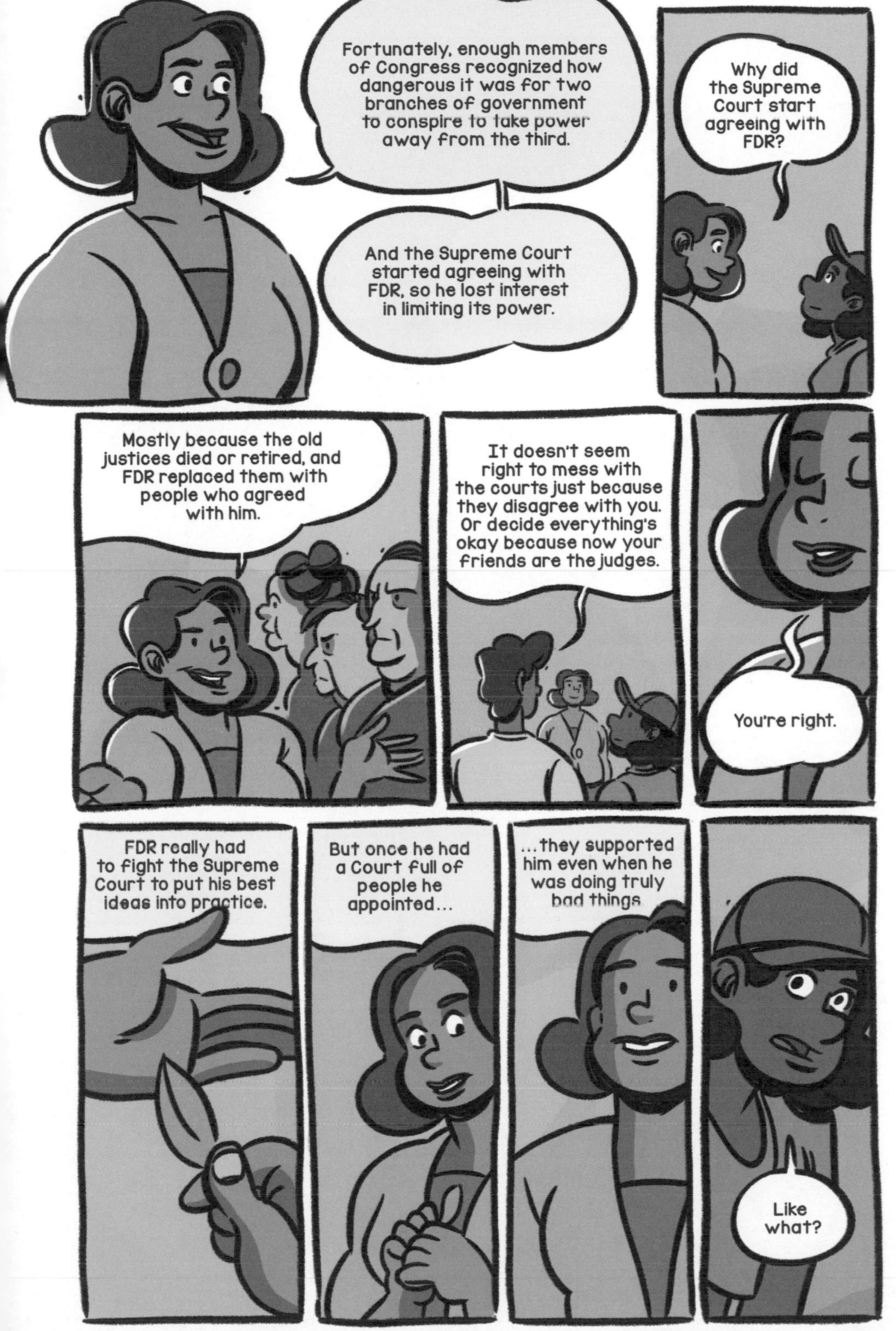
Fortunately, enough members of Congress recognized how dangerous it was for two branches of government to conspire to take power away from the third.
And the Supreme Court started agreeing with FDR, so he lost interest in limiting its power.
Why did the Supreme Court start agreeing with FDR?
Mostly because the old justices died or retired, and FDR replaced them with people who agreed with him.
It doesn't seem right to mess with the courts just because they disagree with you. Or decide everything's okay because now your friends are the judges.
You're right.
FDR really had to fight the Supreme Court to put his best ideas into practice.
But once he had a Court full of people he appointed...
...they supported him even when he was doing truly bad things.
Like what?

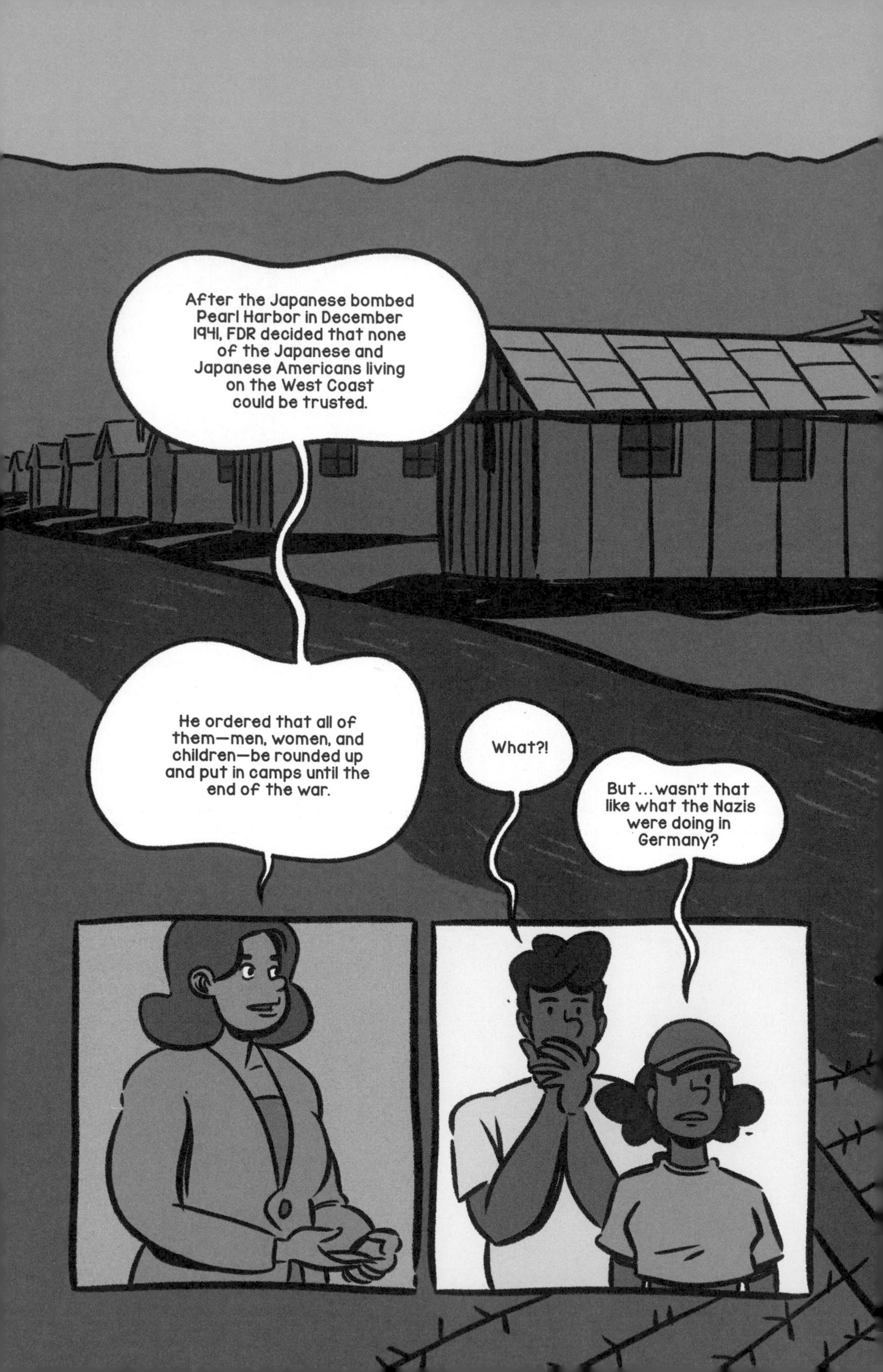
After the Japanese bombed Pearl Harbor in December 1941, FDR decided that none of the Japanese and Japanese Americans living on the West Coast could be trusted.
He ordered that all of them—men, women, and children—be rounded up and put in camps until the end of the war.
What?!
But...wasn't that like what the Nazis were doing in Germany?

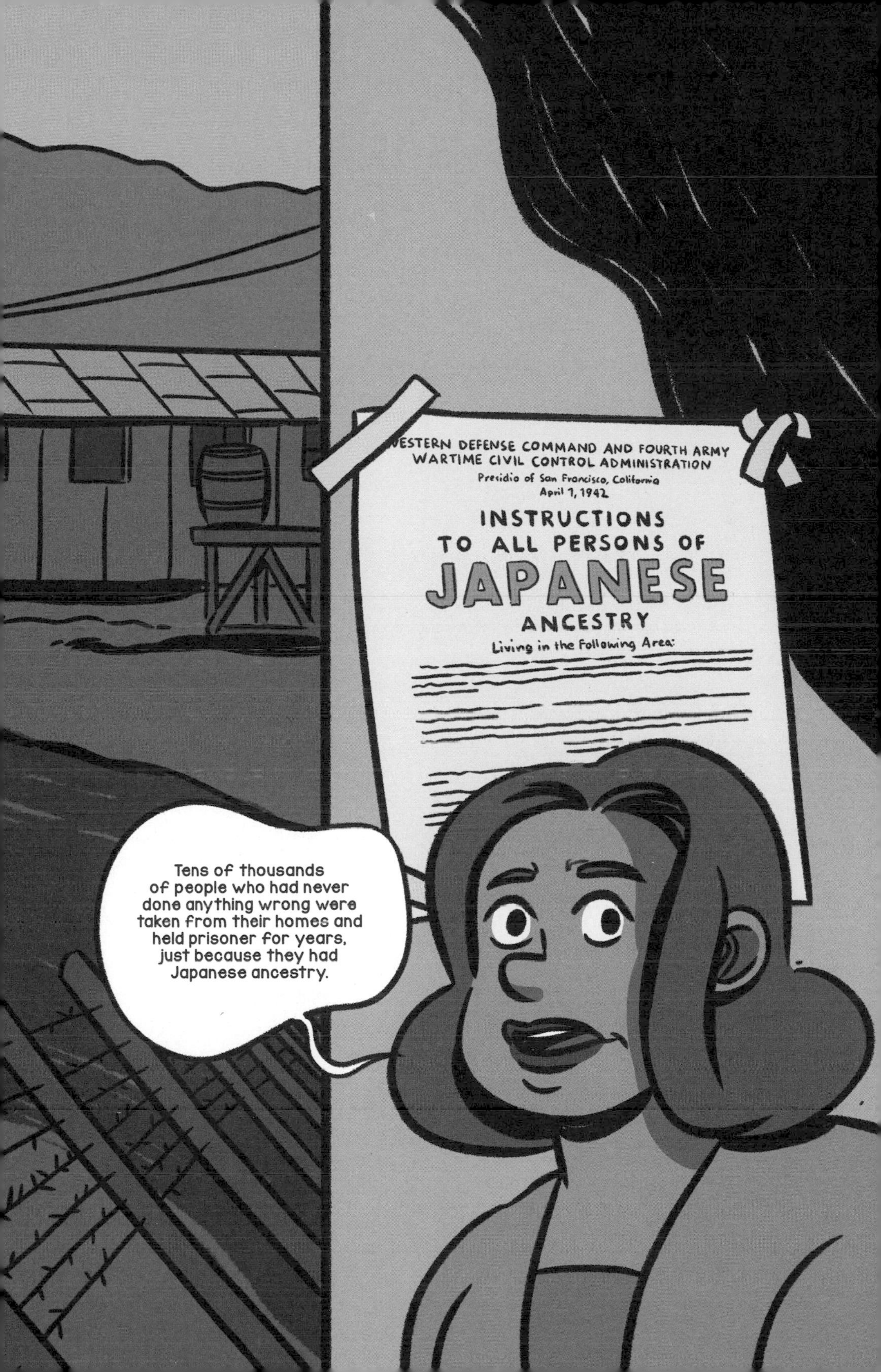
WESTERN DEFENSE COMMAND AND FOURTH ARMY
WARTIME CIVIL CONTROL ADMINISTRATION
Presidio of San Francisco, California
April 1, 1942
INSTRUCTIONS
TO ALL PERSONS OF
JAPANESE
ANCESTRY
Living in the Following Area:
Tens of thousands of people who had never done anything wrong were taken from their homes and held prisoner for years, just because they had Japanese ancestry.

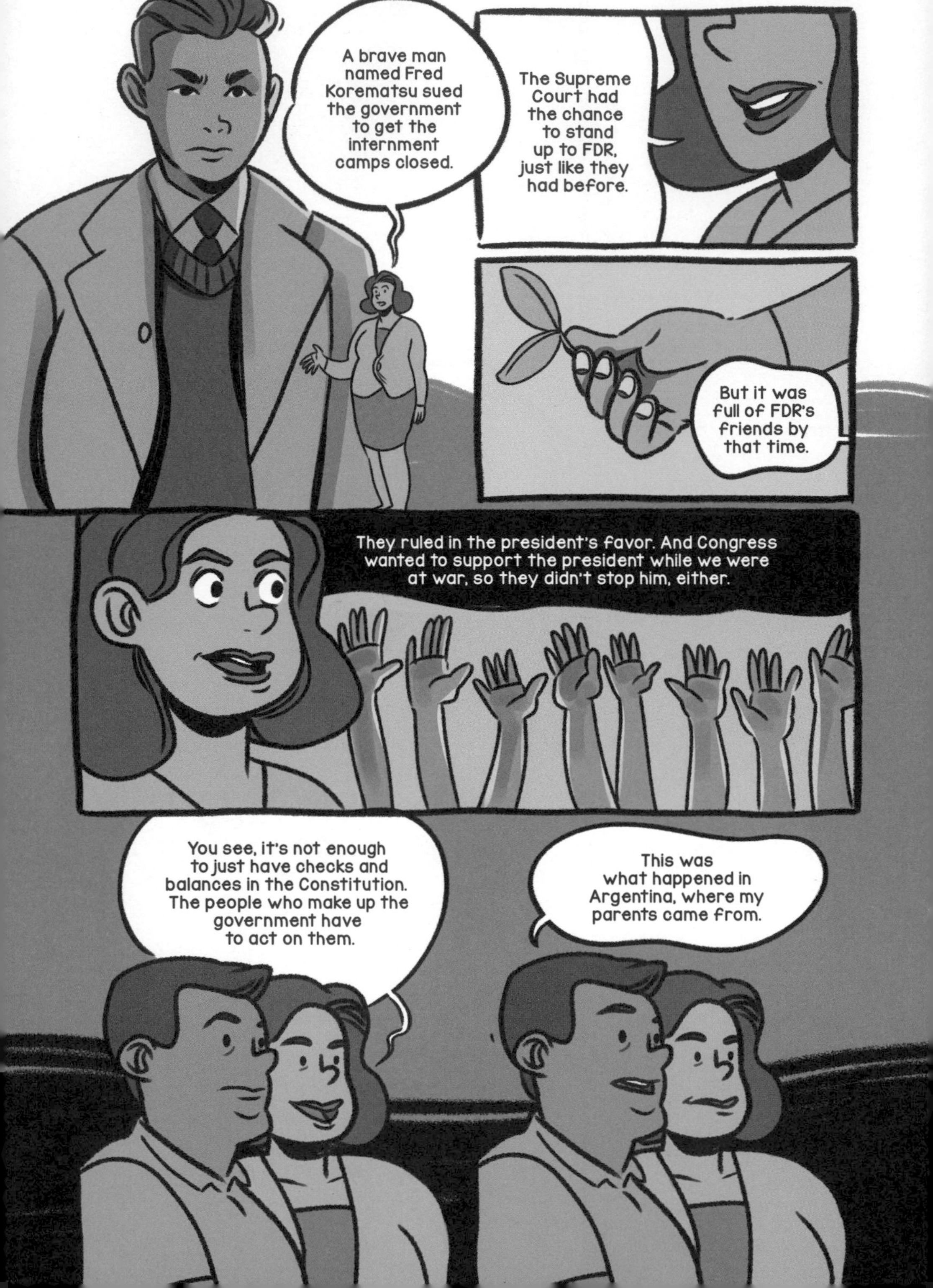
A brave man named Fred Korematsu sued the government to get the internment camps closed.
The Supreme Court had the chance to stand up to FDR, just like they had before.
But it was full of FDR's friends by that time.
They ruled in the president's favor. And Congress wanted to support the president while we were at war, so they didn't stop him, either.
You see, it's not enough to just have checks and balances in the Constitution. The people who make up the government have to act on them.
This was what happened in Argentina, where my parents came from.

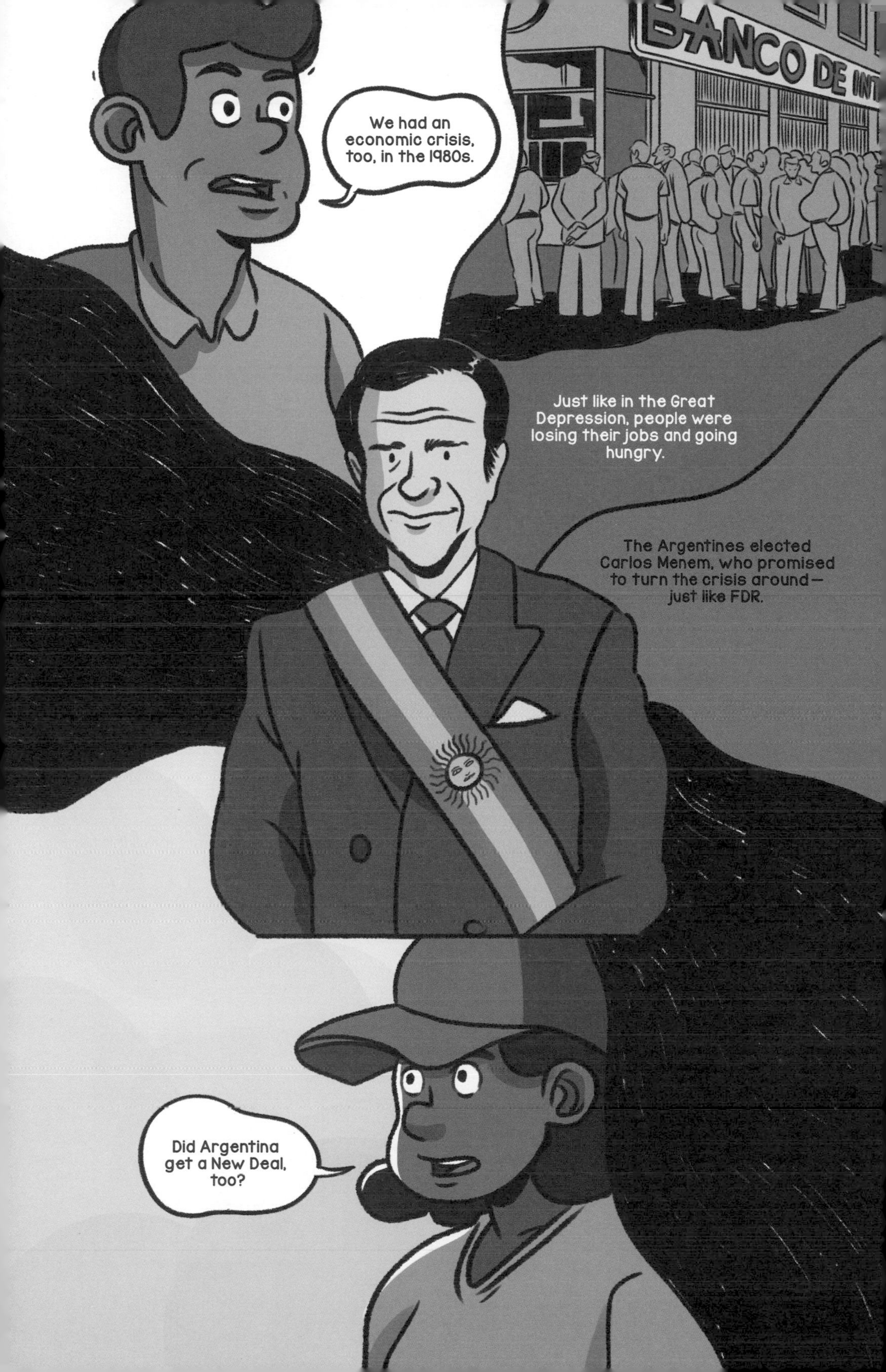

BANCO DE INT
We had an economic crisis, too, in the 1980s.
Just like in the Great Depression, people were losing their jobs and going hungry.
The Argentines elected Carlos Menem, who promised to turn the crisis around—just like FDR.
Did Argentina get a New Deal, too?

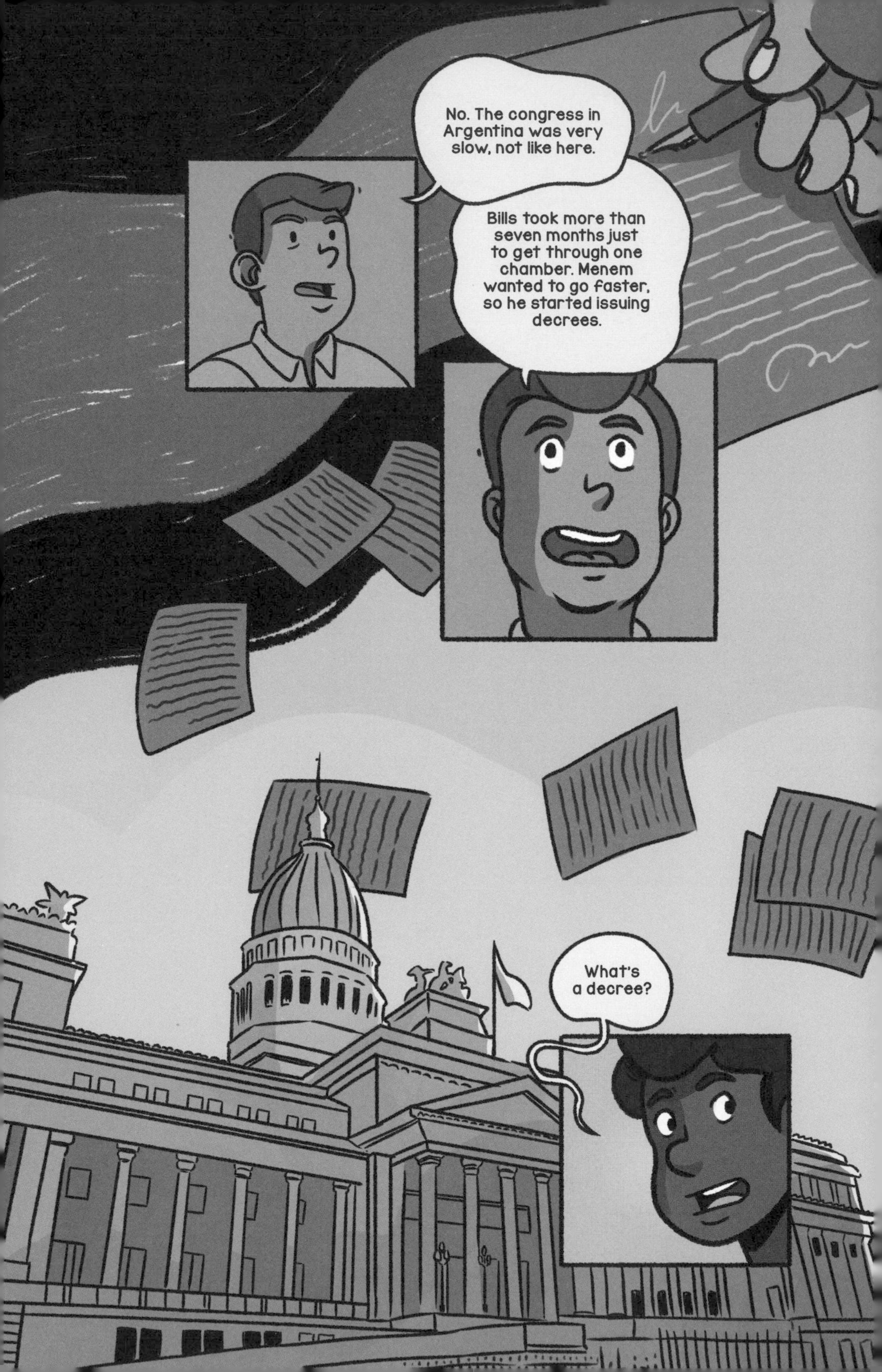
No. The congress in Argentina was very slow, not like here.
Bills took more than seven months just to get through one chamber. Menem wanted to go faster, so he started issuing decrees.
What's a decree?

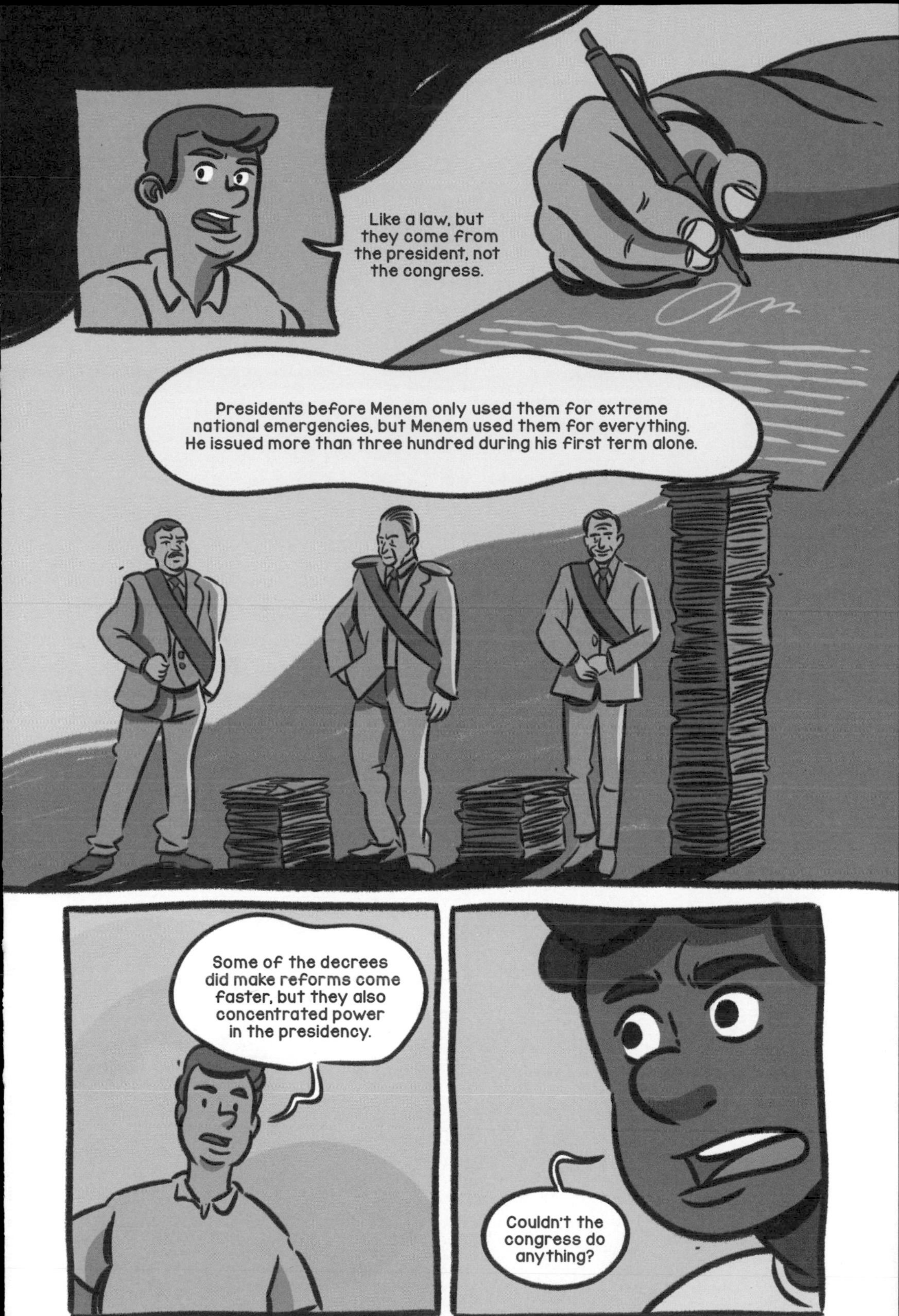
Like a law, but they come from the president, not the congress.
Presidents before Menem only used them for extreme national emergencies, but Menem used them for everything. He issued more than three hundred during his first term alone.
Some of the decrees did make reforms come faster, but they also concentrated power in the presidency.
Couldn't the congress do anything?

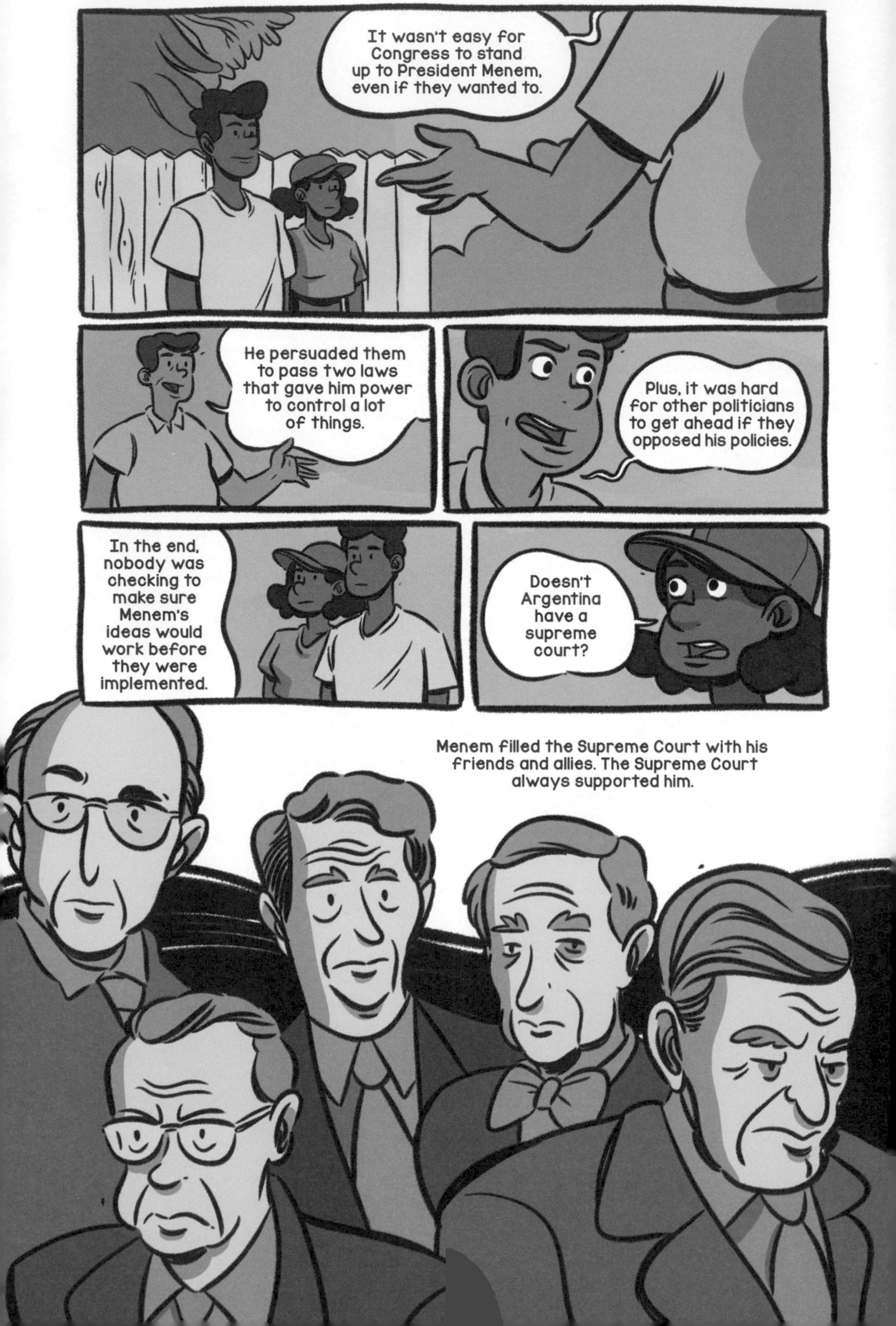
It wasn't easy for Congress to stand up to President Menem, even if they wanted to.
He persuaded them to pass two laws that gave him power to control a lot of things.
Plus, it was hard for other politicians to get ahead if they opposed his policies.
In the end, nobody was checking to make sure Menem's ideas would work before they were implemented.
Doesn't Argentina have a supreme court?
Menem filled the Supreme Court with his friends and allies. The Supreme Court always supported him.

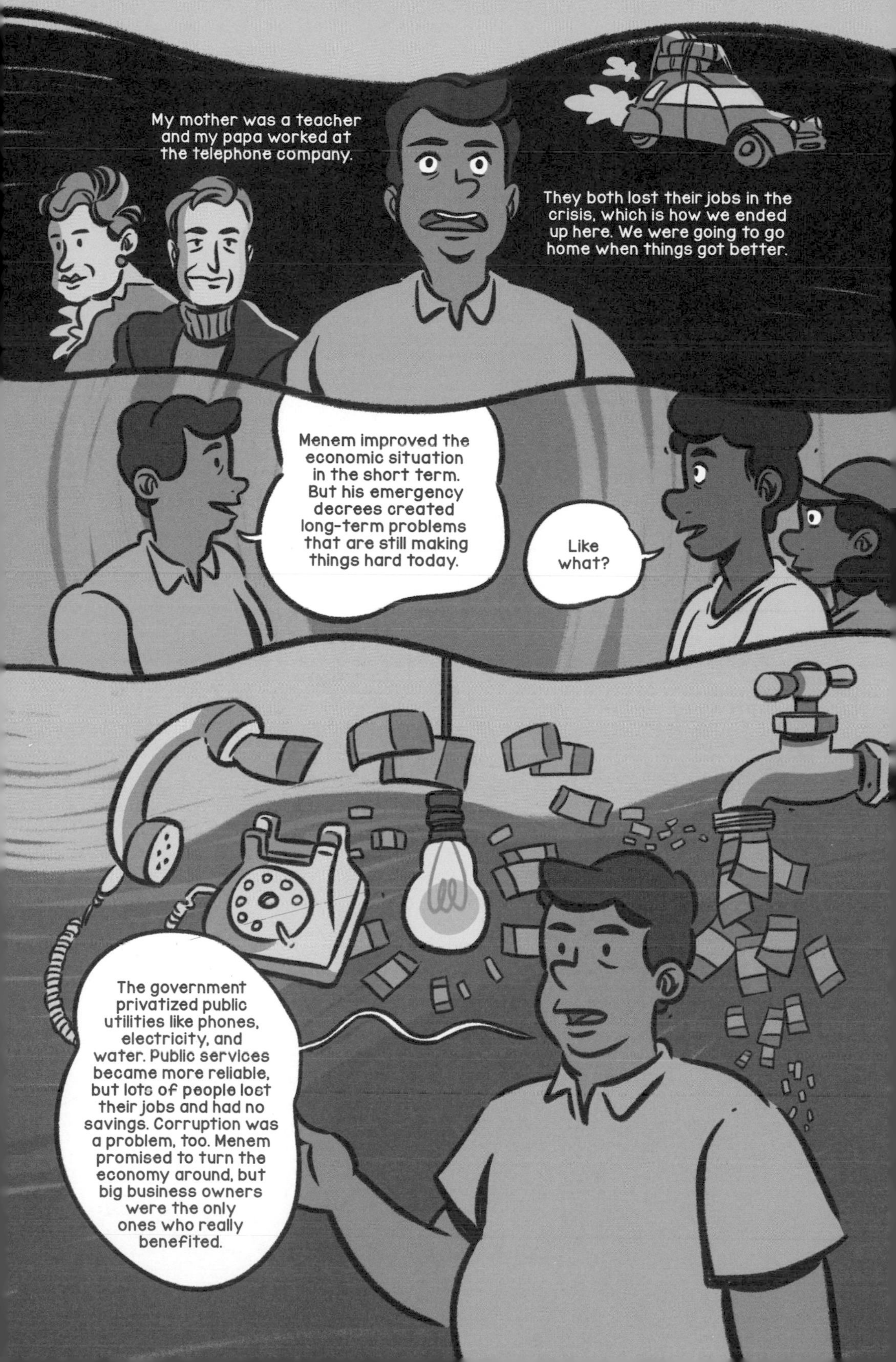
My mother was a teacher and my papa worked at the telephone company.
They both lost their jobs in the crisis, which is how we ended up here. We were going to go home when things got better.
Menem improved the economic situation in the short term. But his emergency decrees created long-term problems that are still making things hard today.
Like what?
The government privatized public utilities like phones, electricity, and water. Public services became more reliable, but lots of people lost their jobs and had no savings. Corruption was a problem, too. Menem promised to turn the economy around, but big business owners were the only ones who really benefited.

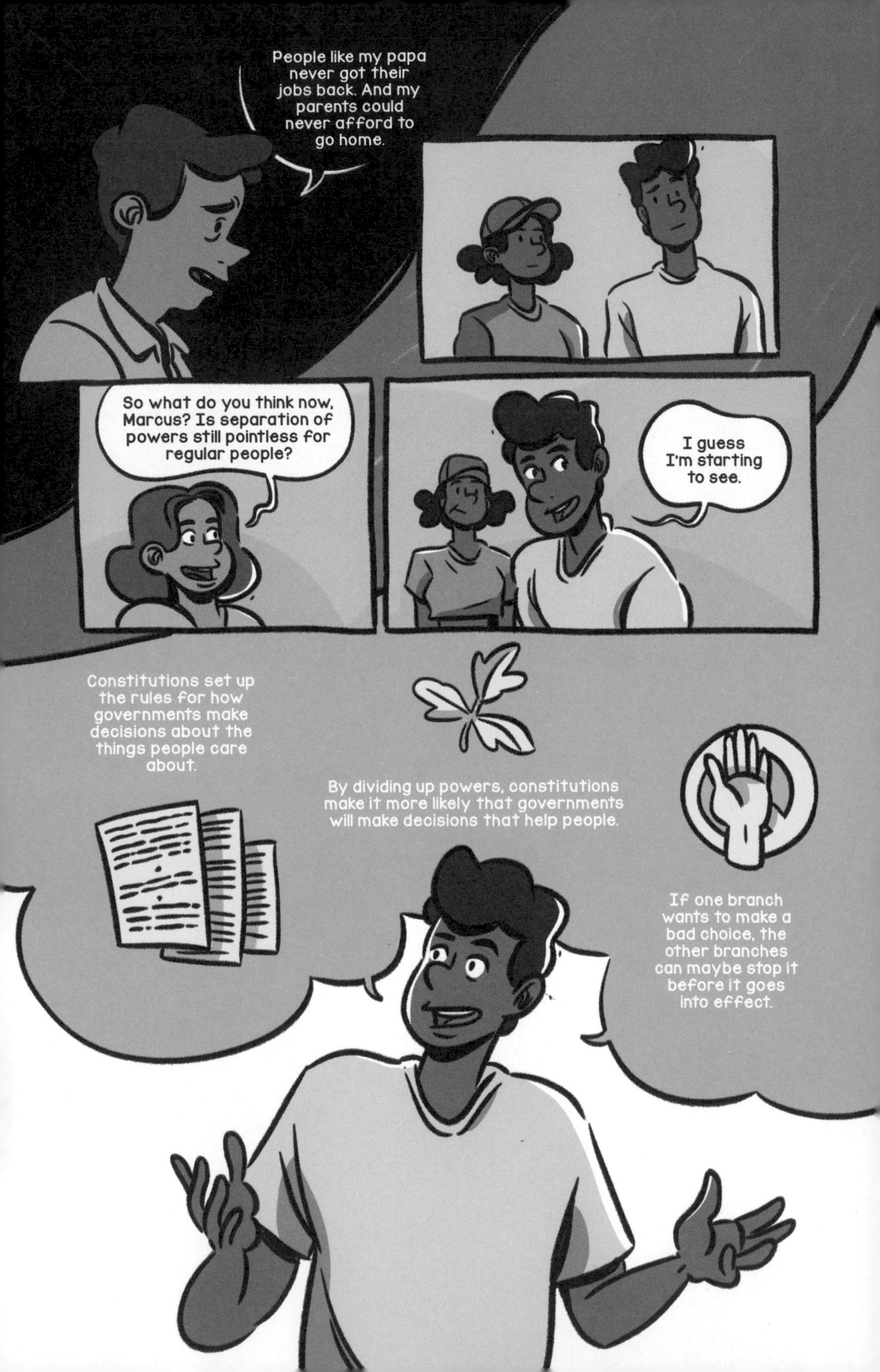
People like my papa never got their jobs back. And my parents could never afford to go home.
So what do you think now, Marcus? Is separation of powers still pointless for regular people?
I guess I'm starting to see.
Constitutions set up the rules for how governments make decisions about the things people care about.
By dividing up powers, constitutions make it more likely that governments will make decisions that help people.
If one branch wants to make a bad choice, the other branches can maybe stop it before it goes into effect.

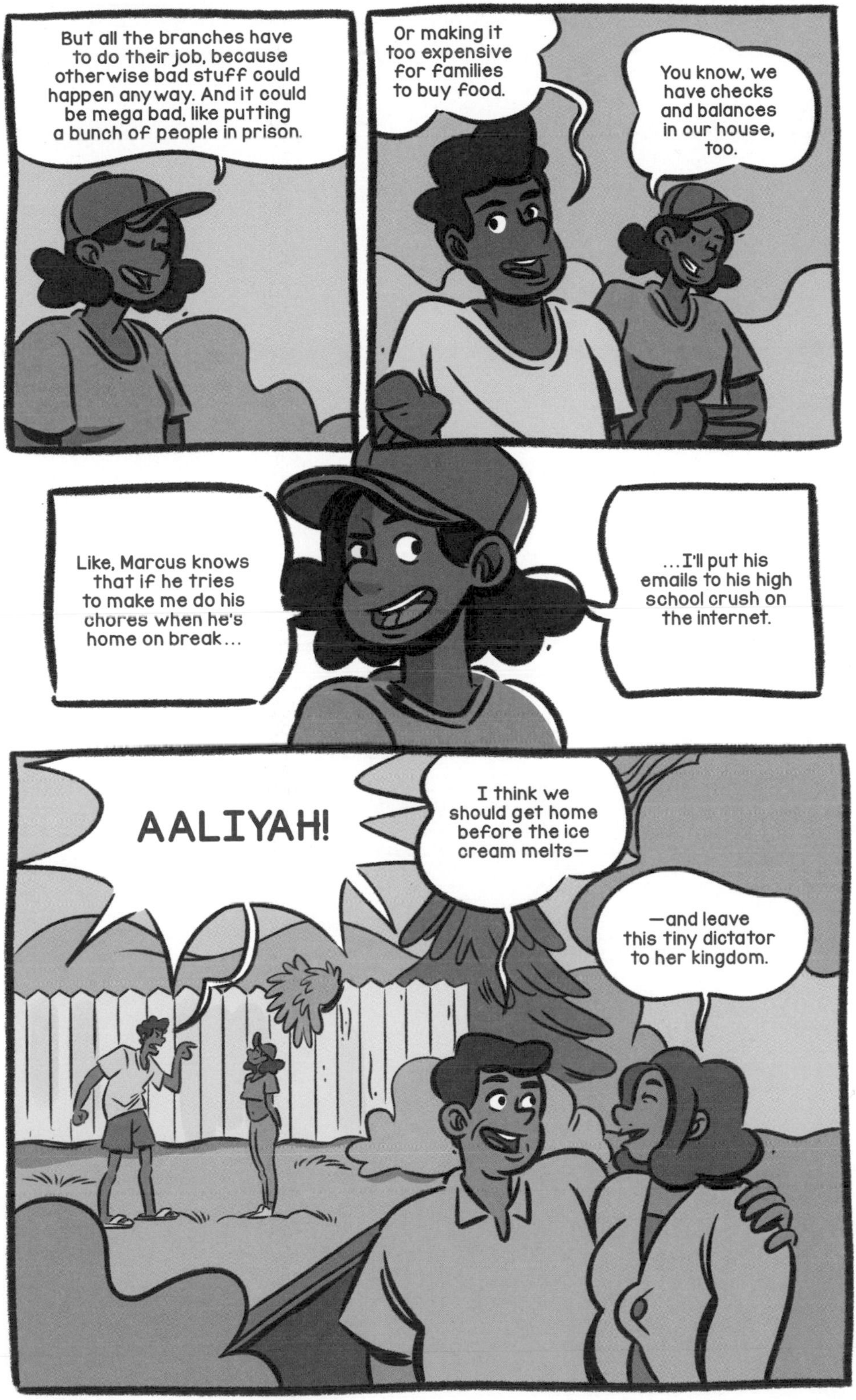

But all the branches have to do their job, because otherwise bad stuff could happen anyway. And it could be mega bad, like putting a bunch of people in prison.
Or making it too expensive for families to buy food.
You know, we have checks and balances in our house, too.
Like, Marcus knows that if he tries to make me do his chores when he's home on break...
...I'll put his emails to his high school crush on the internet.
AALIYAH!
I think we should get home before the ice cream melts—
—and leave this tiny dictator to her kingdom.

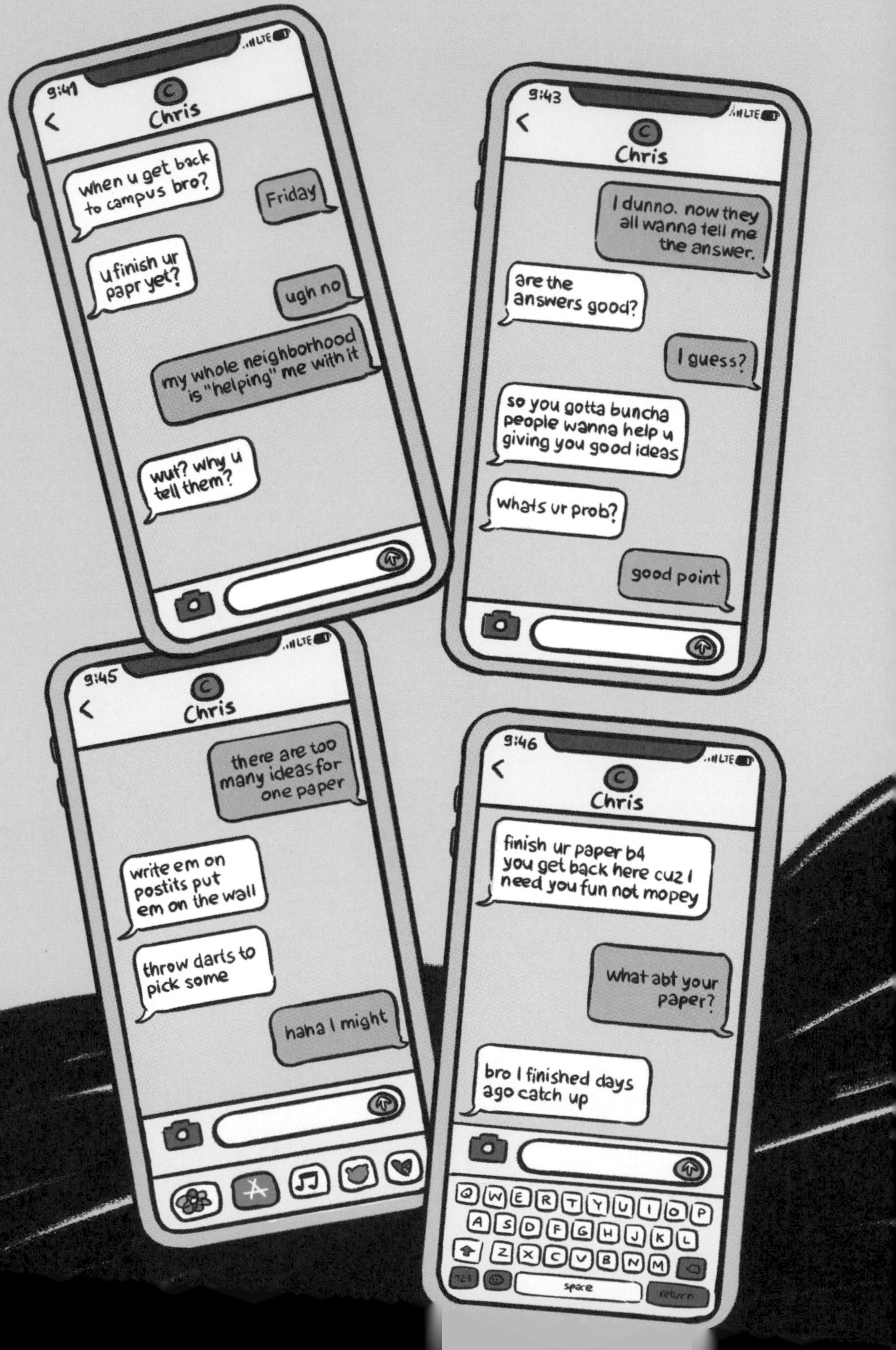
9:41
Chris
when u get back to campus bro?
Friday
u finish ur papr yet?
ugh no
my whole neighborhood is "helping" me with it
wut? why u tell them?
9:43
Chris
I dunno. now they all wanna tell me the answer.
are the answers good?
I guess?
so you gotta buncha people wanna help u giving you good ideas
whats ur prob?
good point
9:45
Chris
there are too many ideas for one paper
write em on postits put em on the wall
throw darts to pick some
haha I might
9:46
Chris
finish ur paper b4 you get back here cuz I need you fun not mopey
what abt your paper?
bro I finished days ago catch up

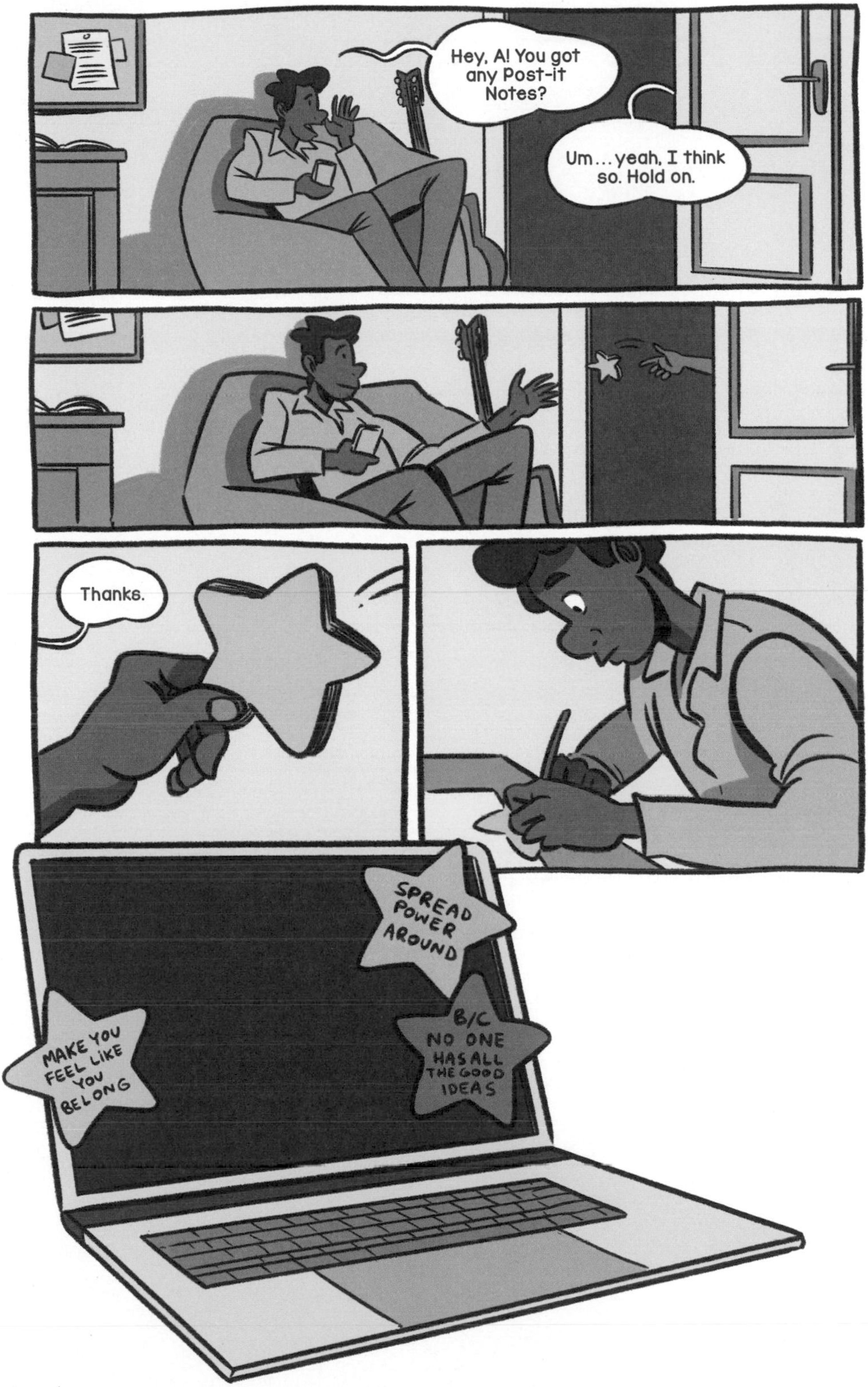
Hey, A! You got any Post-it Notes?
Um... yeah, I think so. Hold on.
Thanks.
SPREAD POWER AROUND
B/C NO ONE HAS ALL THE GOOD IDEAS
MAKE YOU FEEL LIKE YOU BELONG

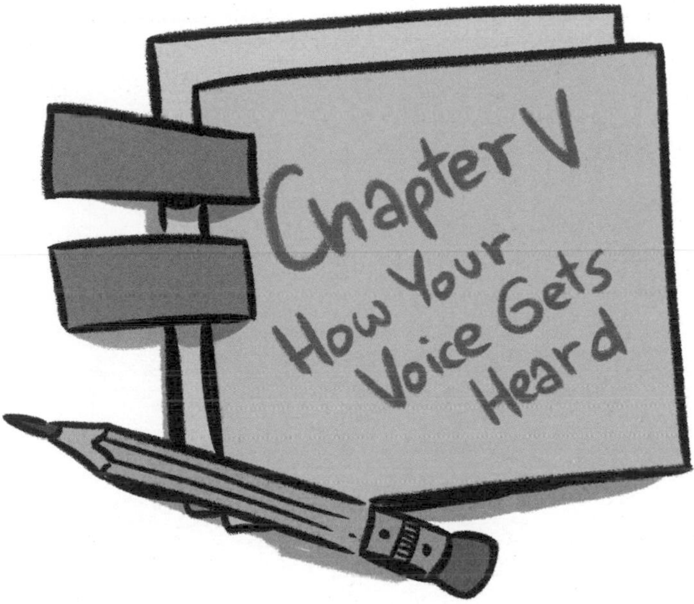
Chapter V
How Your Voice Gets Heard

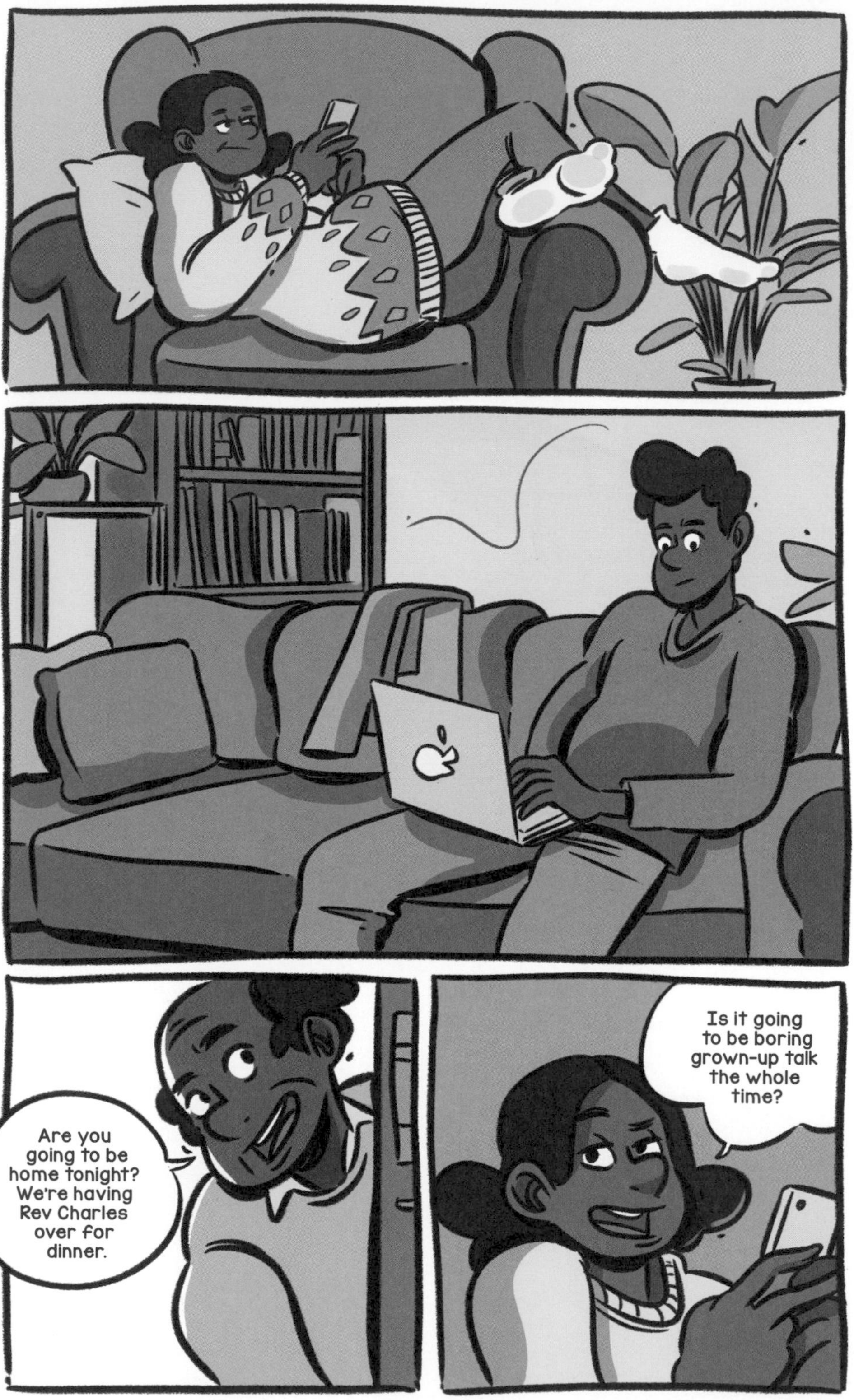
Are you going to be home tonight? We're having Rev Charles over for dinner.
Is it going to be boring grown-up talk the whole time?

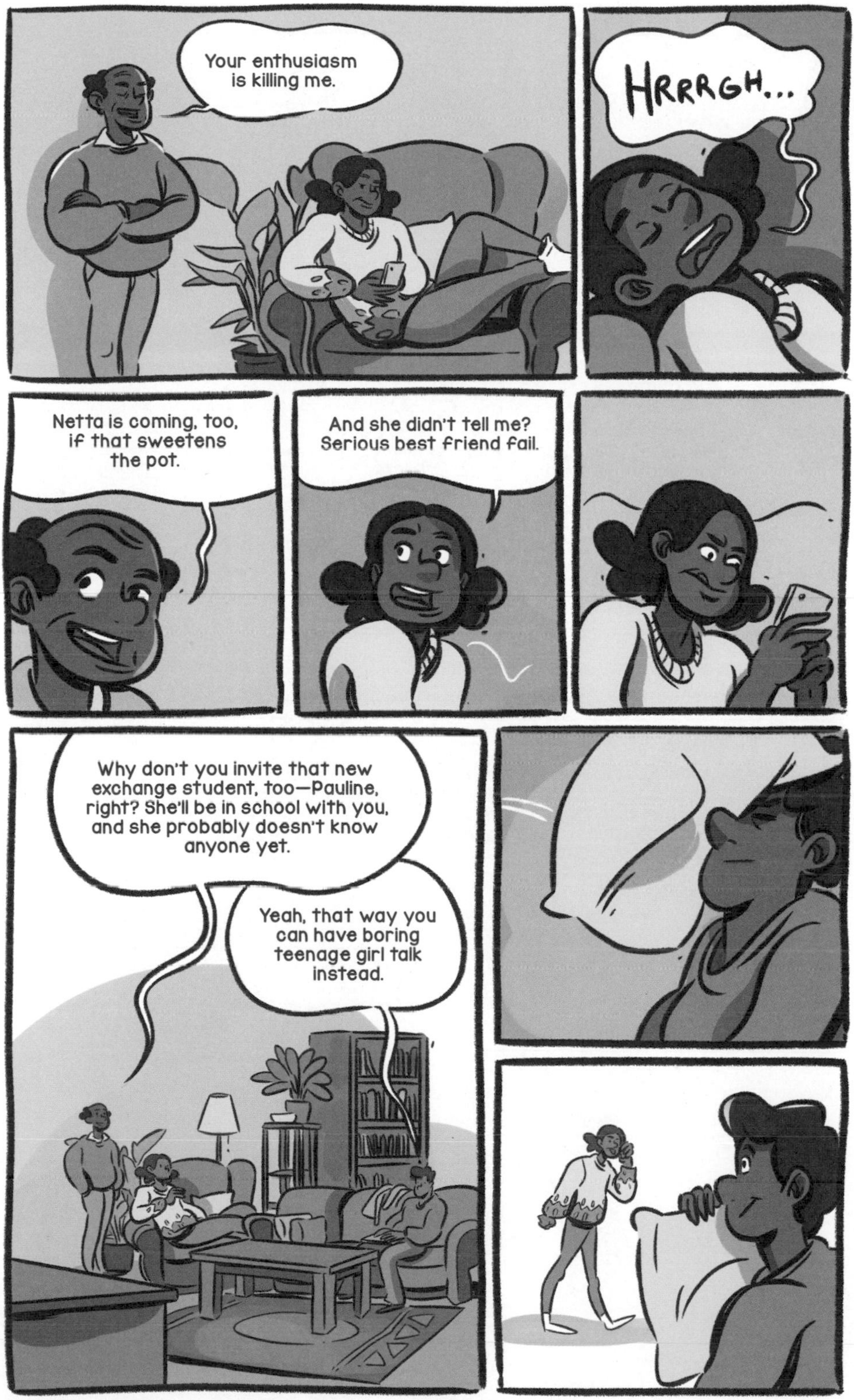
Your enthusiasm is killing me.
HRRRGH...
Netta is coming, too, if that sweetens the pot.
And she didn't tell me? Serious best friend fail.
Why don't you invite that new exchange student, too—Pauline, right? She'll be in school with you, and she probably doesn't know anyone yet.
Yeah, that way you can have boring teenage girl talk instead.

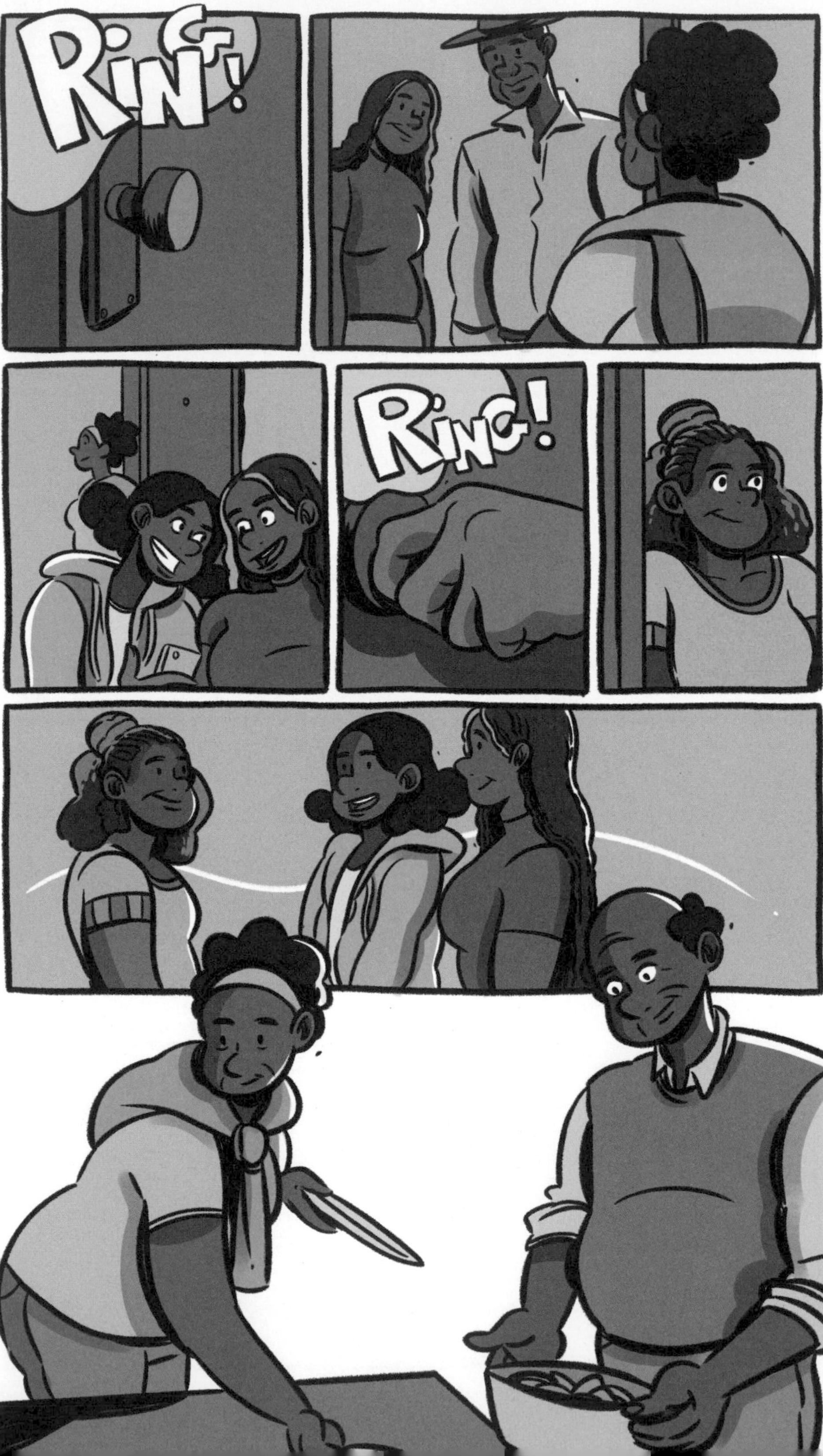
RING!
RING!

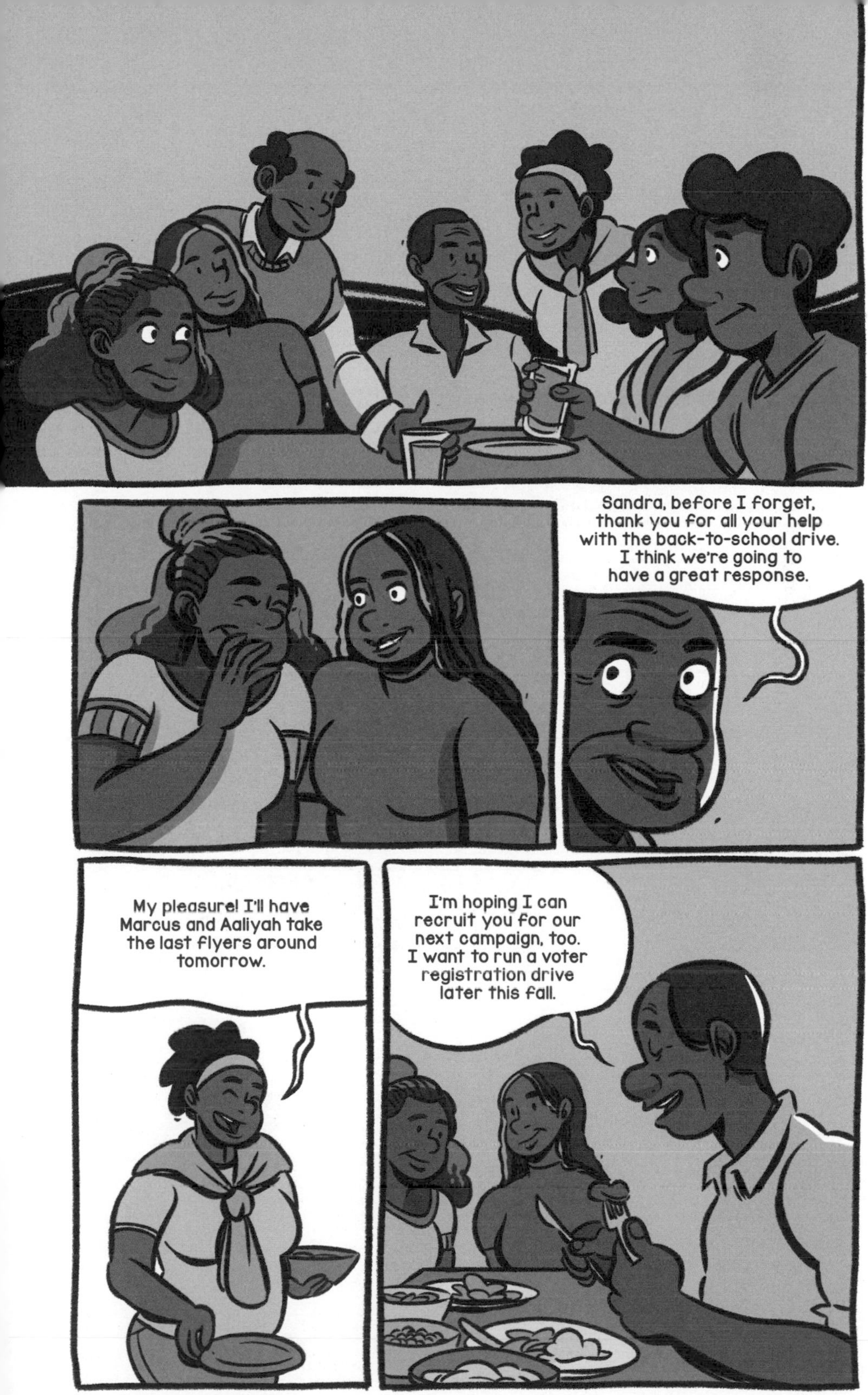
Sandra, before I forget, thank you for all your help with the back-to-school drive. I think we're going to have a great response.
My pleasure! I'll have Marcus and Aaliyah take the last flyers around tomorrow.
I'm hoping I can recruit you for our next campaign, too. I want to run a voter registration drive later this fall.

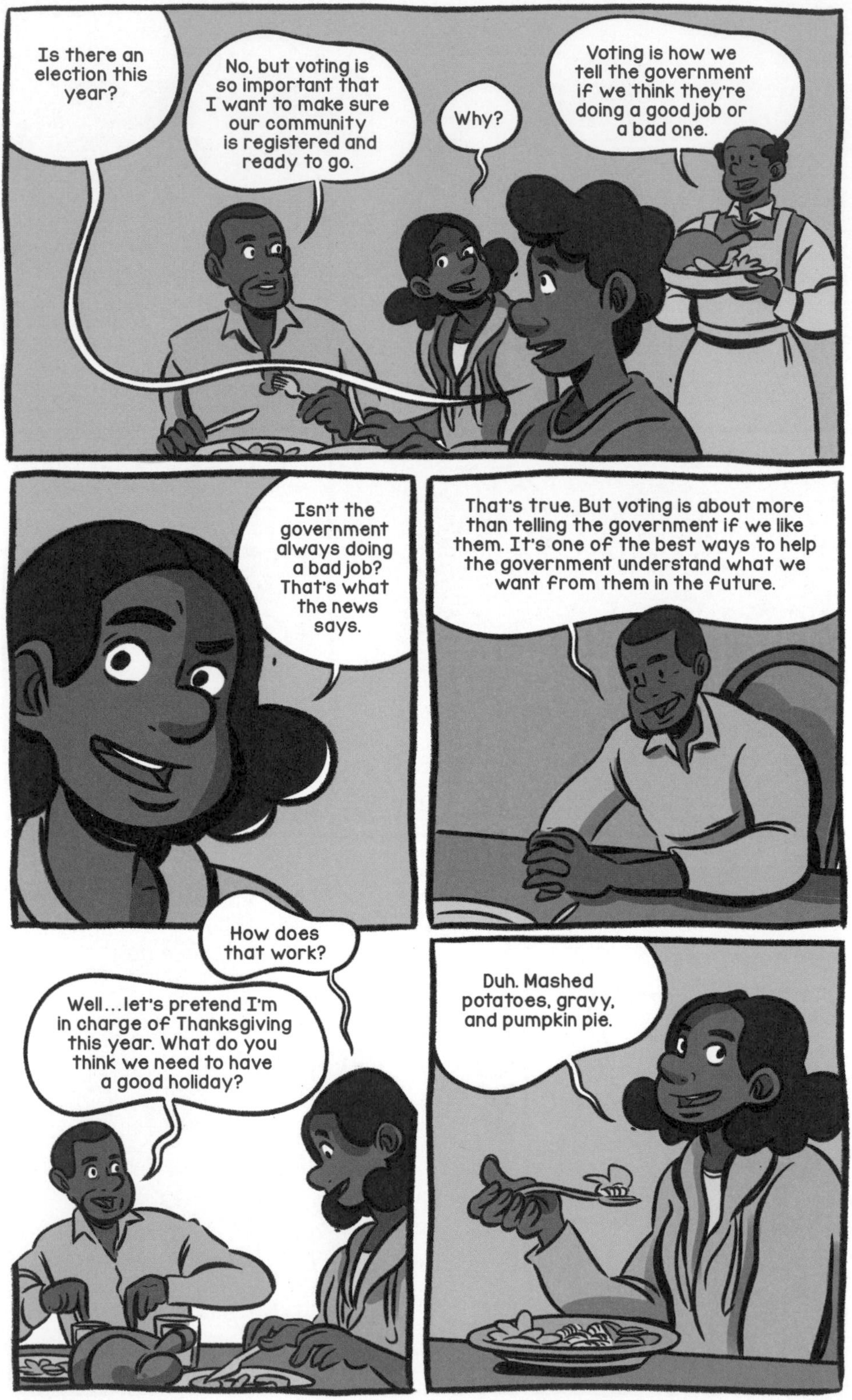
Is there an election this year?
No, but voting is so important that I want to make sure our community is registered and ready to go.
Why?
Voting is how we tell the government if we think they're doing a good job or a bad one.
Isn't the government always doing a bad job? That's what the news says.
That's true. But voting is about more than telling the government if we like them. It's one of the best ways to help the government understand what we want from them in the future.
How does that work?
Well... let's pretend I'm in charge of Thanksgiving this year. What do you think we need to have a good holiday?
Duh. Mashed potatoes, gravy, and pumpkin pie.

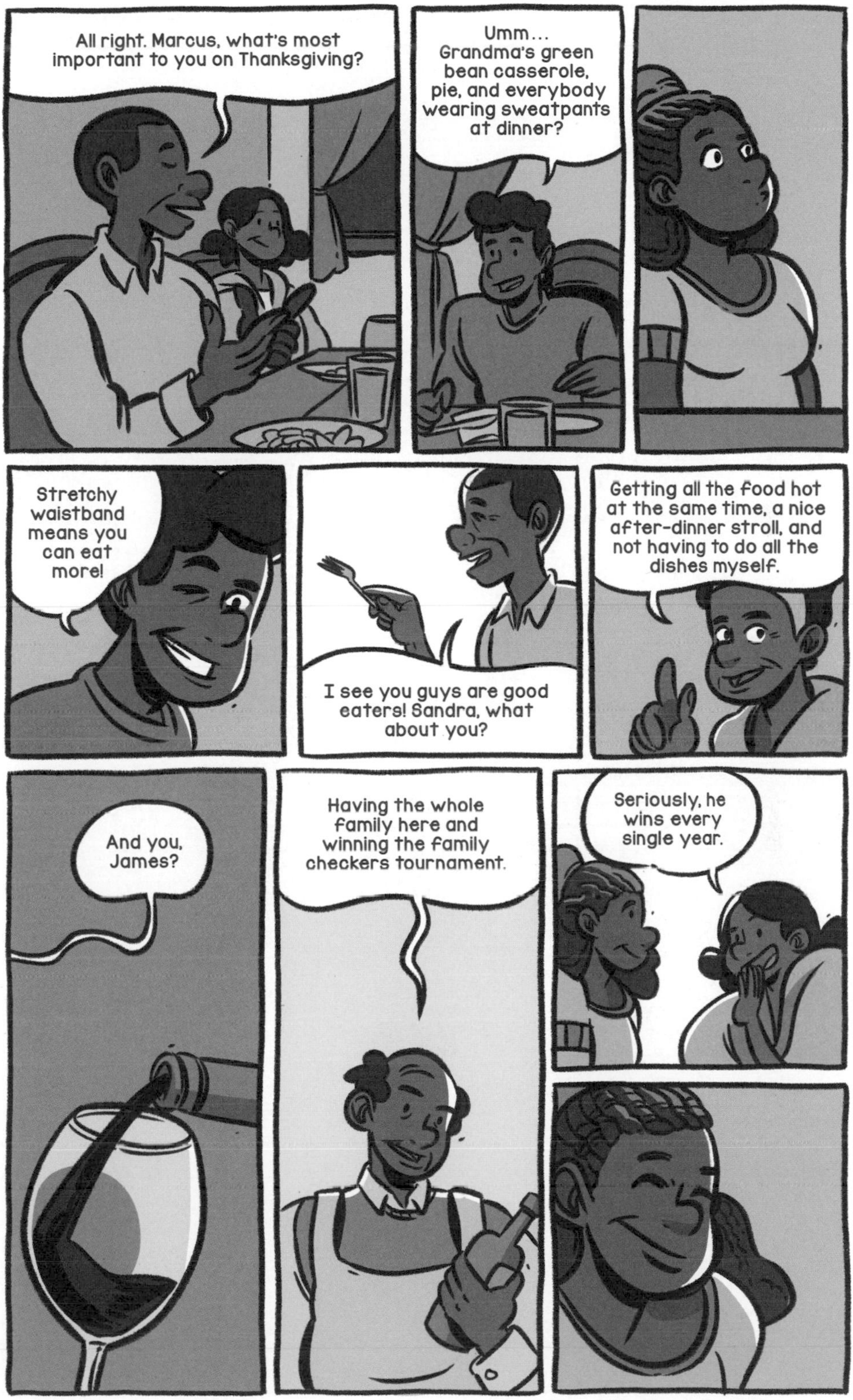
All right. Marcus, what's most important to you on Thanksgiving?
Umm... Grandma's green bean casserole, pie, and everybody wearing sweatpants at dinner?
Stretchy waistband means you can eat more!
I see you guys are good eaters! Sandra, what about you?
Getting all the food hot at the same time, a nice after-dinner stroll, and not having to do all the dishes myself.
And you, James?
Having the whole family here and winning the family checkers tournament.
Seriously, he wins every single year.

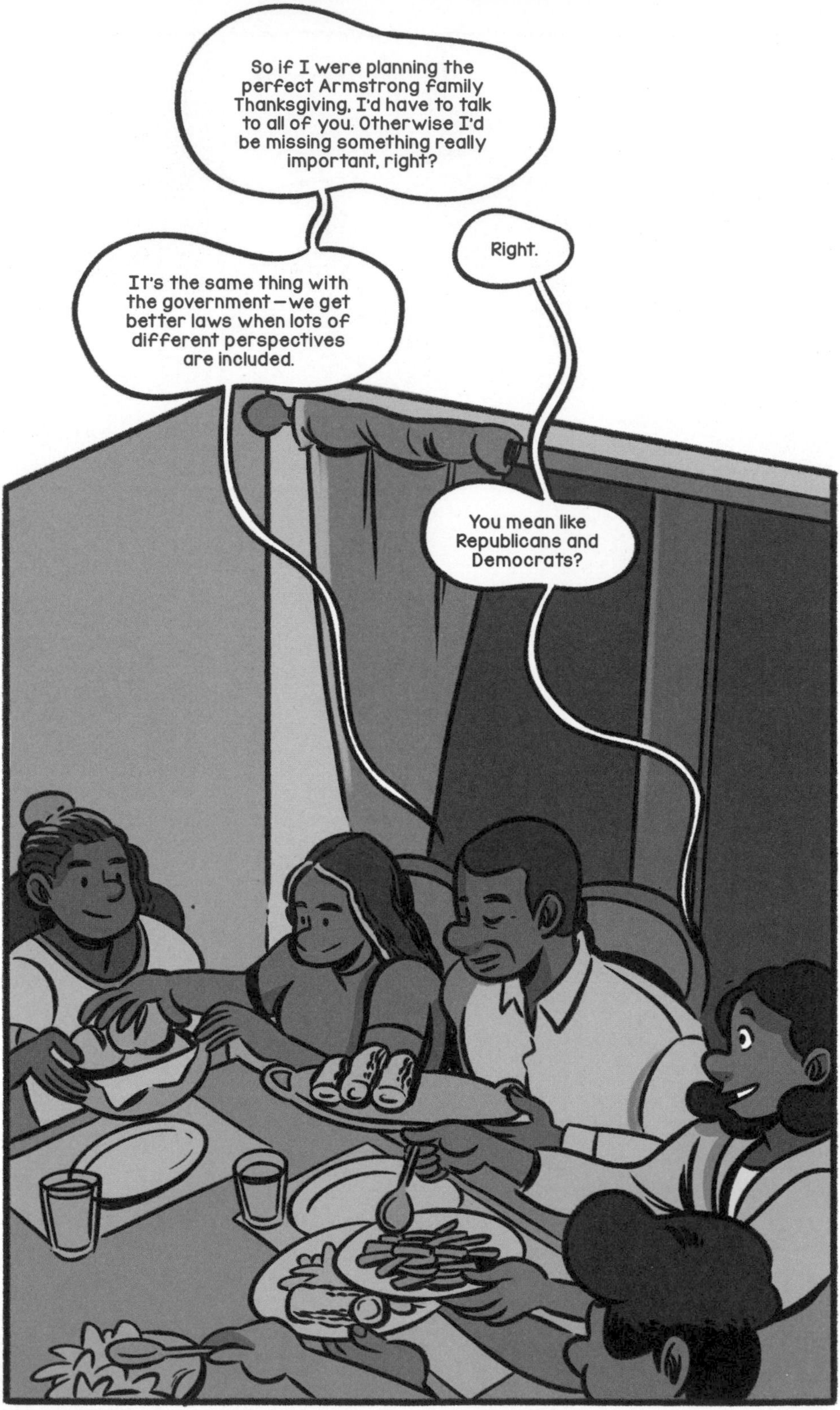
So if I were planning the perfect Armstrong family Thanksgiving, I'd have to talk to all of you. Otherwise I'd be missing something really important, right?
It's the same thing with the government—we get better laws when lots of different perspectives are included.
Right.
You mean like Republicans and Democrats?

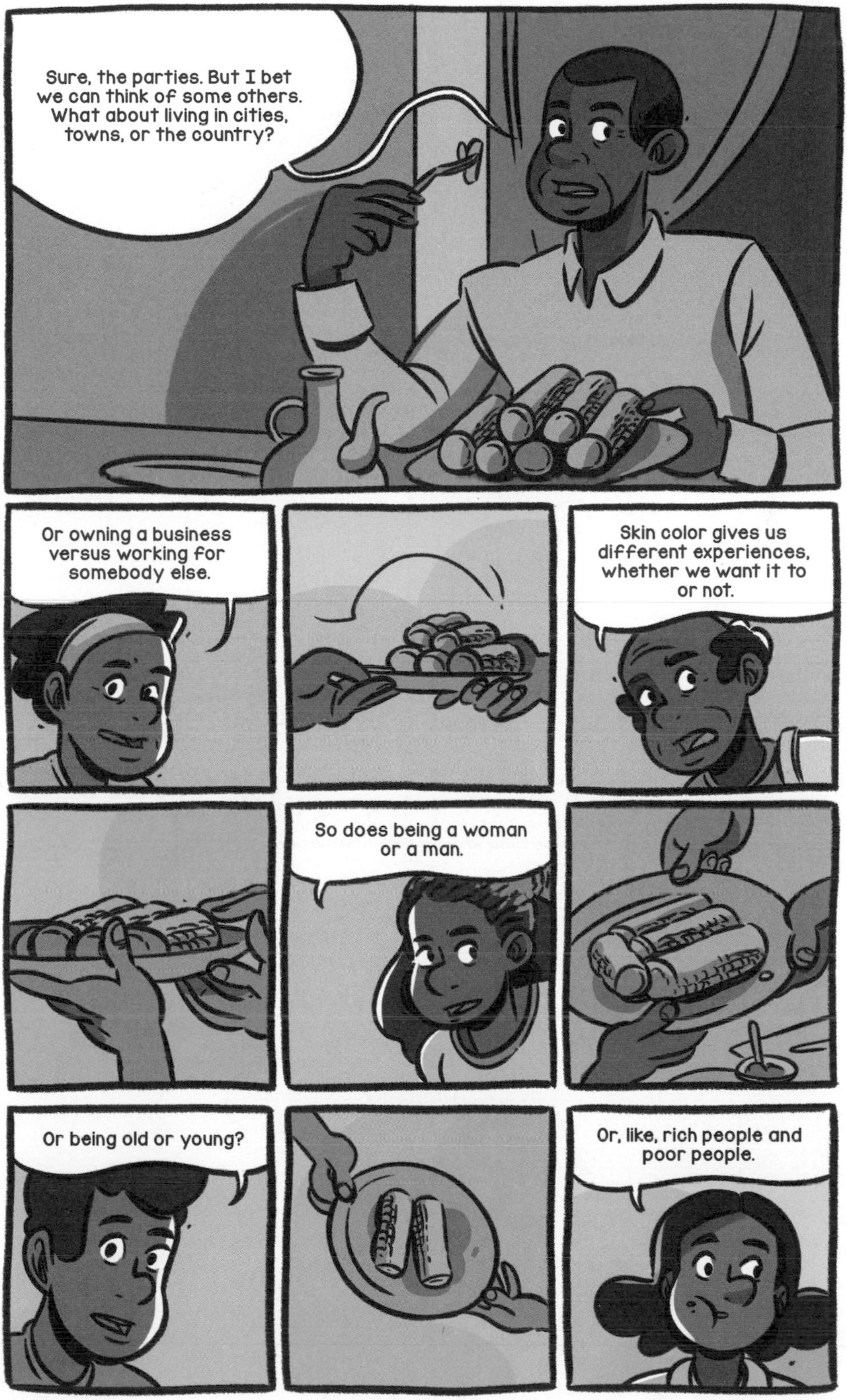
Sure, the parties. But I bet we can think of some others. What about living in cities, towns, or the country?
Or owning a business versus working for somebody else.
Skin color gives us different experiences, whether we want it to or not.
So does being a woman or a man.
Or being old or young?
Or, like, rich people and poor people.

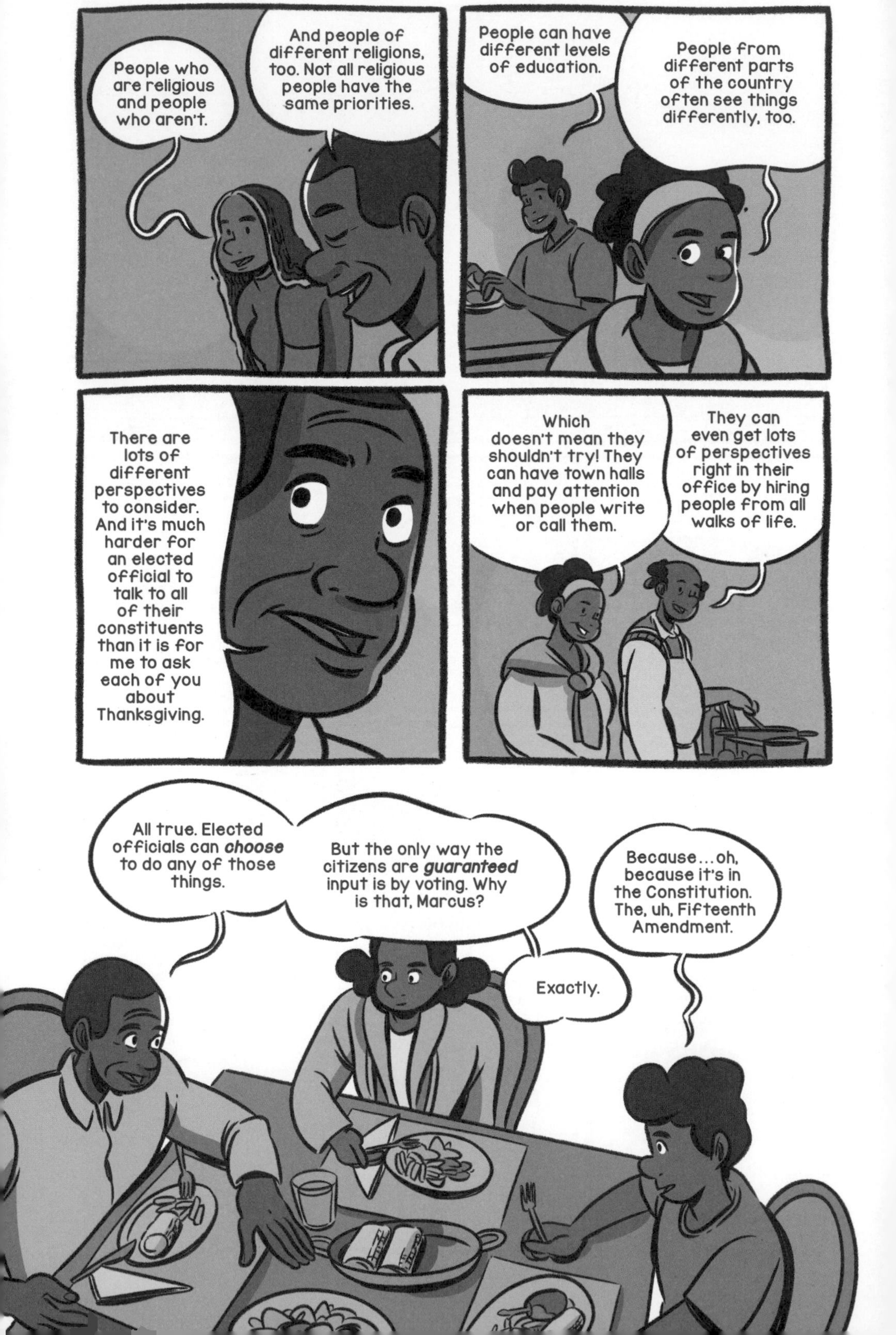
People who are religious and people who aren't.
And people of different religions, too. Not all religious people have the same priorities.
People can have different levels of education.
People from different parts of the country often see things differently, too.
There are lots of different perspectives to consider. And it's much harder for an elected official to talk to all of their constituents than it is for me to ask each of you about Thanksgiving.
Which doesn't mean they shouldn't try! They can have town halls and pay attention when people write or call them.
They can even get lots of perspectives right in their office by hiring people from all walks of life.
All true. Elected officials can *choose* to do any of those things.
But the only way the citizens are *guaranteed* input is by voting. Why is that, Marcus?
Because... oh, because it's in the Constitution. The, uh, Fifteenth Amendment.
Exactly.

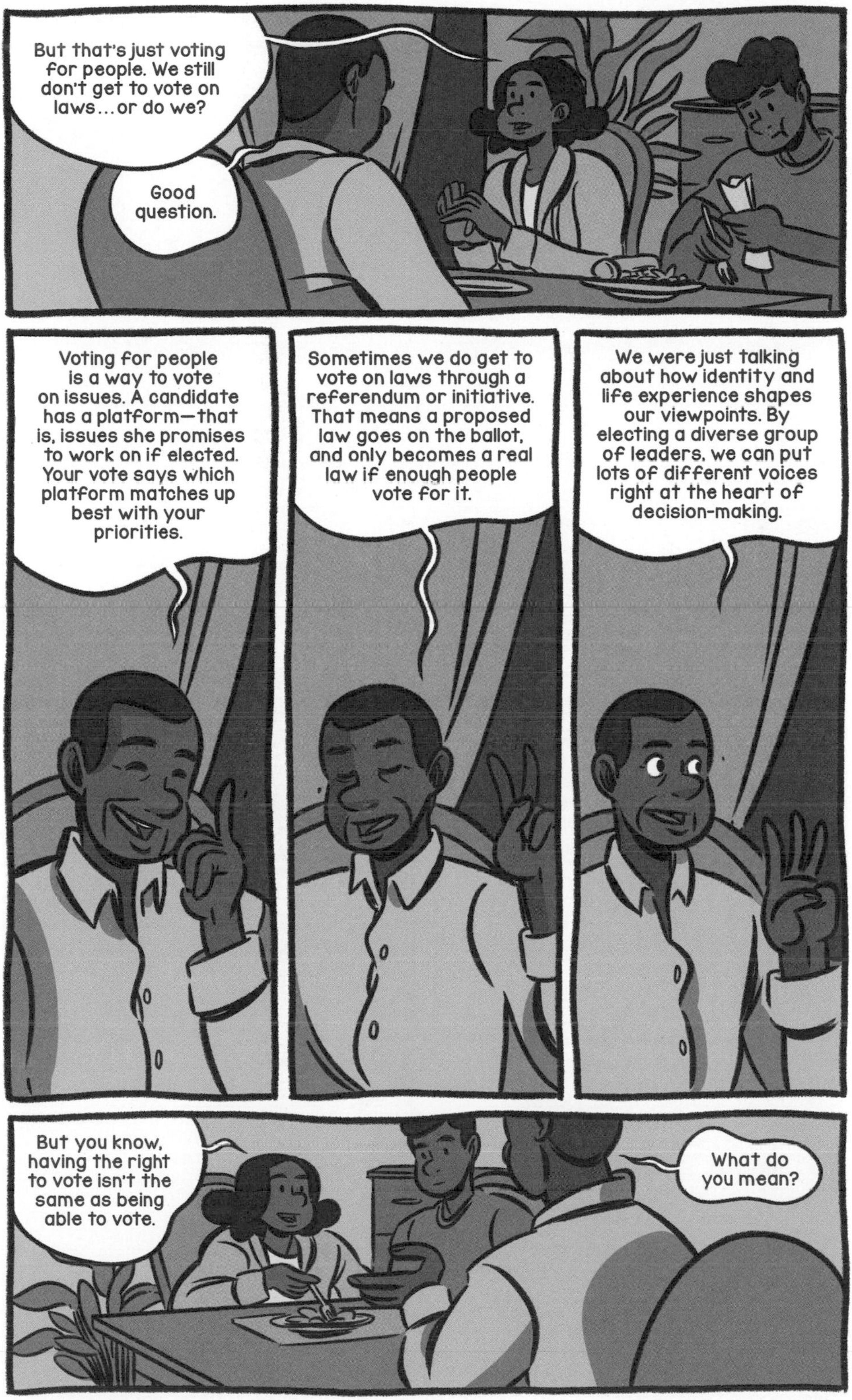

But that's just voting for people. We still don't get to vote on laws... or do we?
Good question.
Voting for people is a way to vote on issues. A candidate has a platform—that is, issues she promises to work on if elected. Your vote says which platform matches up best with your priorities.
Sometimes we do get to vote on laws through a referendum or initiative. That means a proposed law goes on the ballot, and only becomes a real law if enough people vote for it.
We were just talking about how identity and life experience shapes our viewpoints. By electing a diverse group of leaders, we can put lots of different voices right at the heart of decision-making.
But you know, having the right to vote isn't the same as being able to vote.
What do you mean?

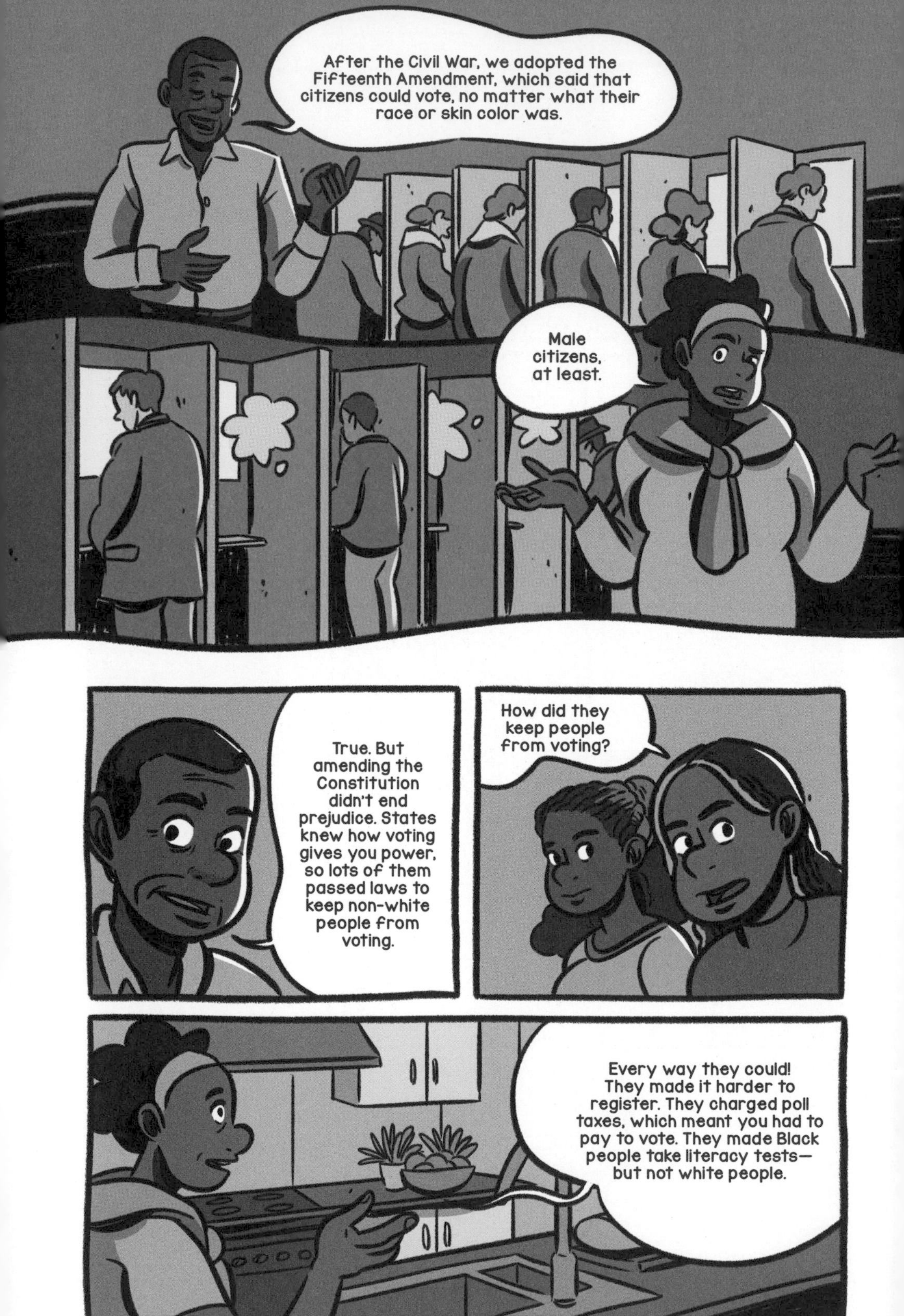
After the Civil War, we adopted the Fifteenth Amendment, which said that citizens could vote, no matter what their race or skin color was.
Male citizens, at least.
True. But amending the Constitution didn't end prejudice. States knew how voting gives you power, so lots of them passed laws to keep non-white people from voting.
How did they keep people from voting?
Every way they could! They made it harder to register. They charged poll taxes, which meant you had to pay to vote. They made Black people take literacy tests—but not white people.

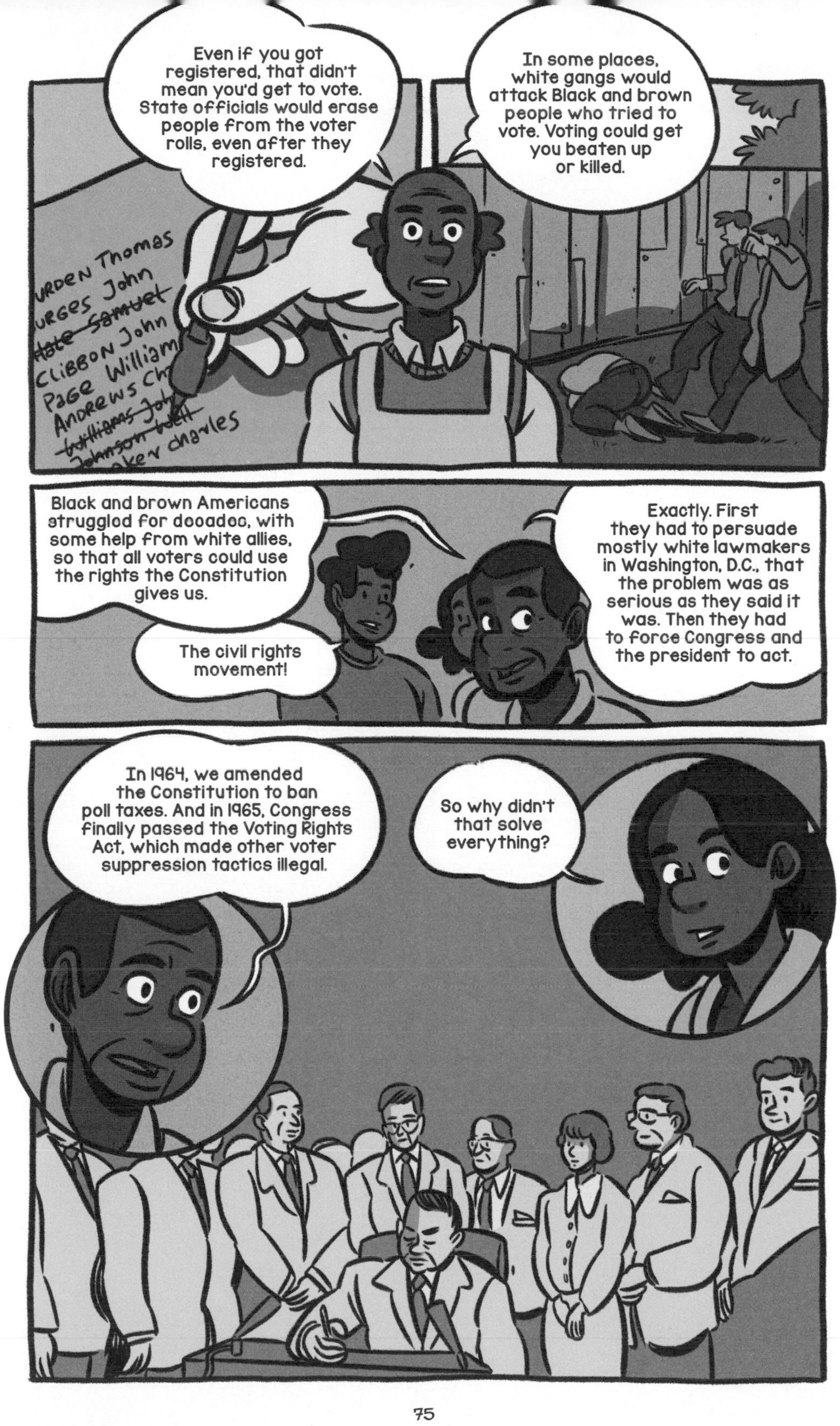
Even if you got registered, that didn't mean you'd get to vote. State officials would erase people from the voter rolls, even after they registered.
URDEN Thomas
URGES John
Hale Samuel
CLIBBON John
Page William
Andrews Ch
Williams John
Johnson Well
aker charles
In some places, white gangs would attack Black and brown people who tried to vote. Voting could get you beaten up or killed.
Black and brown Americans struggled for decades, with some help from white allies, so that all voters could use the rights the Constitution gives us.
The civil rights movement!
Exactly. First they had to persuade mostly white lawmakers in Washington, D.C., that the problem was as serious as they said it was. Then they had to force Congress and the president to act.
In 1964, we amended the Constitution to ban poll taxes. And in 1965, Congress finally passed the Voting Rights Act, which made other voter suppression tactics illegal.
So why didn't that solve everything?

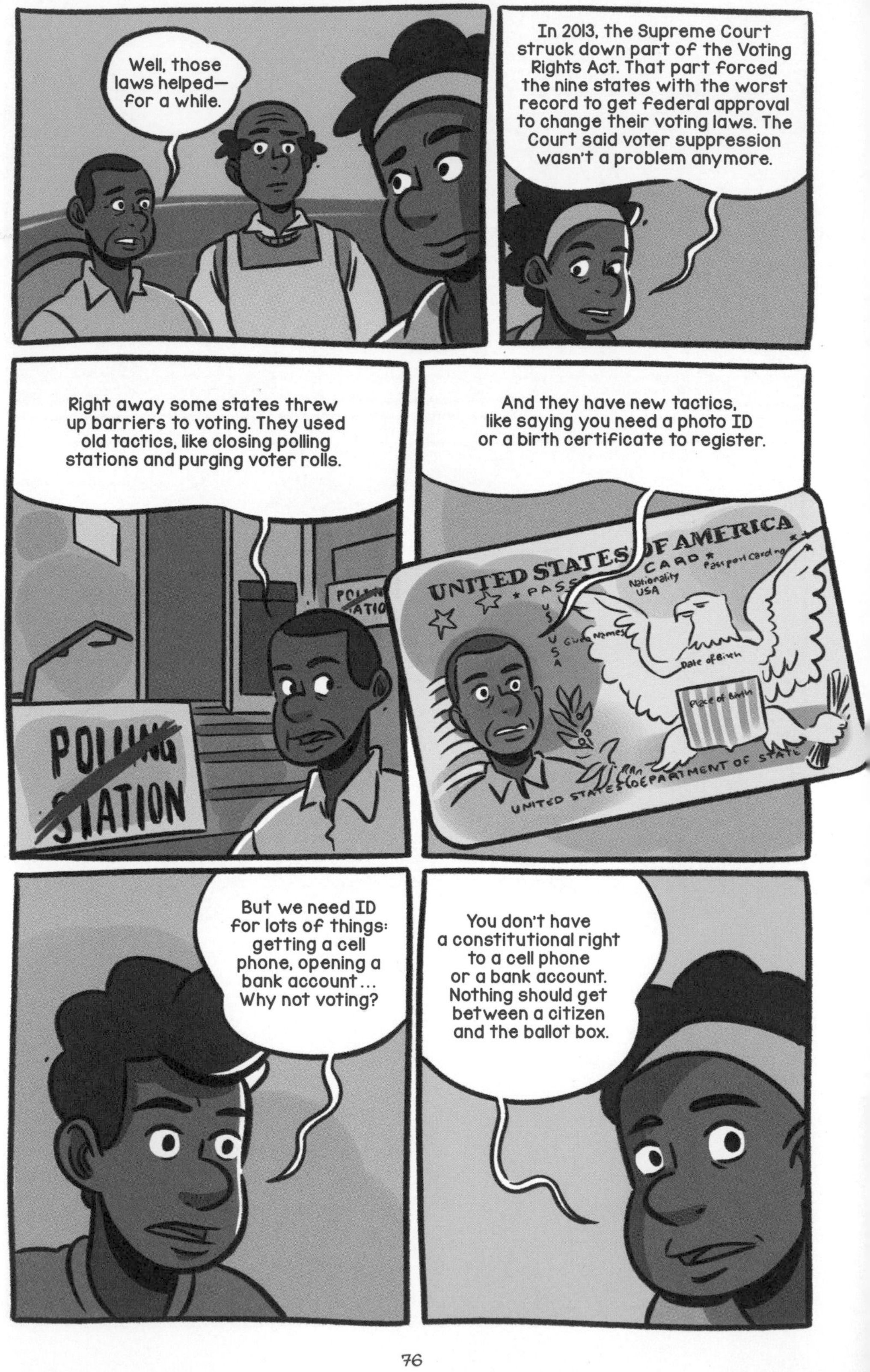
Well, those laws helped— for a while.
In 2013, the Supreme Court struck down part of the Voting Rights Act. That part forced the nine states with the worst record to get federal approval to change their voting laws. The Court said voter suppression wasn't a problem anymore.
Right away some states threw up barriers to voting. They used old tactics, like closing polling stations and purging voter rolls.
POLLING STATION
And they have new tactics, like saying you need a photo ID or a birth certificate to register.
UNITED STATES OF AMERICA
CARD
Nationality USA
Date of Birth
Place of Birth
UNITED STATES DEPARTMENT OF STATE
But we need ID for lots of things: getting a cell phone, opening a bank account... Why not voting?
You don't have a constitutional right to a cell phone or a bank account. Nothing should get between a citizen and the ballot box.

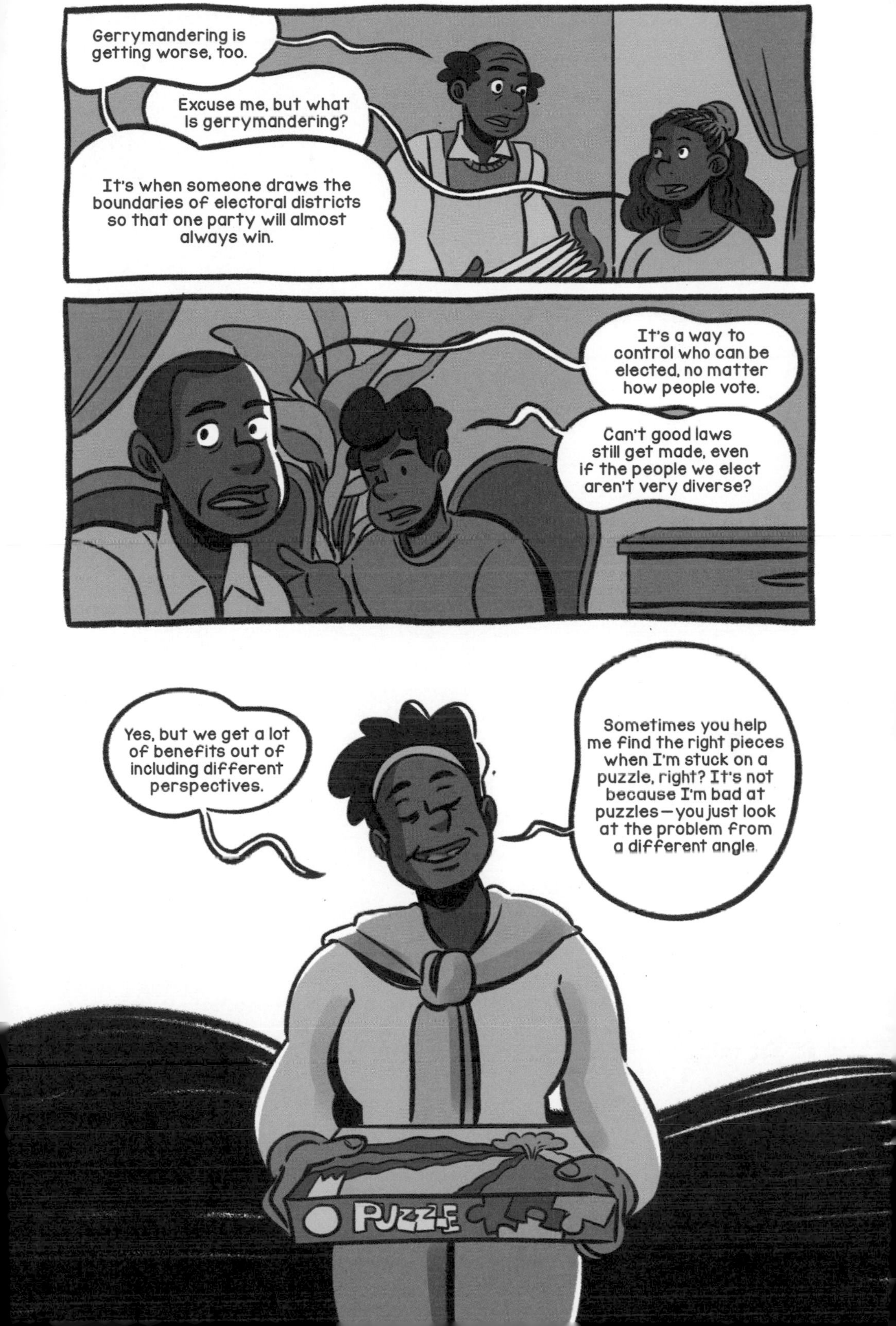

Gerrymandering is getting worse, too.
Excuse me, but what is gerrymandering?
It's when someone draws the boundaries of electoral districts so that one party will almost always win.
It's a way to control who can be elected, no matter how people vote.
Can't good laws still get made, even if the people we elect aren't very diverse?
Yes, but we get a lot of benefits out of including different perspectives.
Sometimes you help me find the right pieces when I'm stuck on a puzzle, right? It's not because I'm bad at puzzles—you just look at the problem from a different angle.
PUZZLE

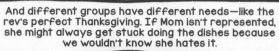
And different groups have different needs—like the rev's perfect Thanksgiving. If Mom isn't represented, she might always get stuck doing the dishes because we wouldn't know she hates it.

Oh, I think you *know* how I feel about doing dishes...

Rev?

I want to help out with the voter registration drive.

Me, too, Dad.

I can't think of two more persuasive—

—or persistent—

—helpers in all of Chathamville.

Sounds like we should have some dessert to celebrate!

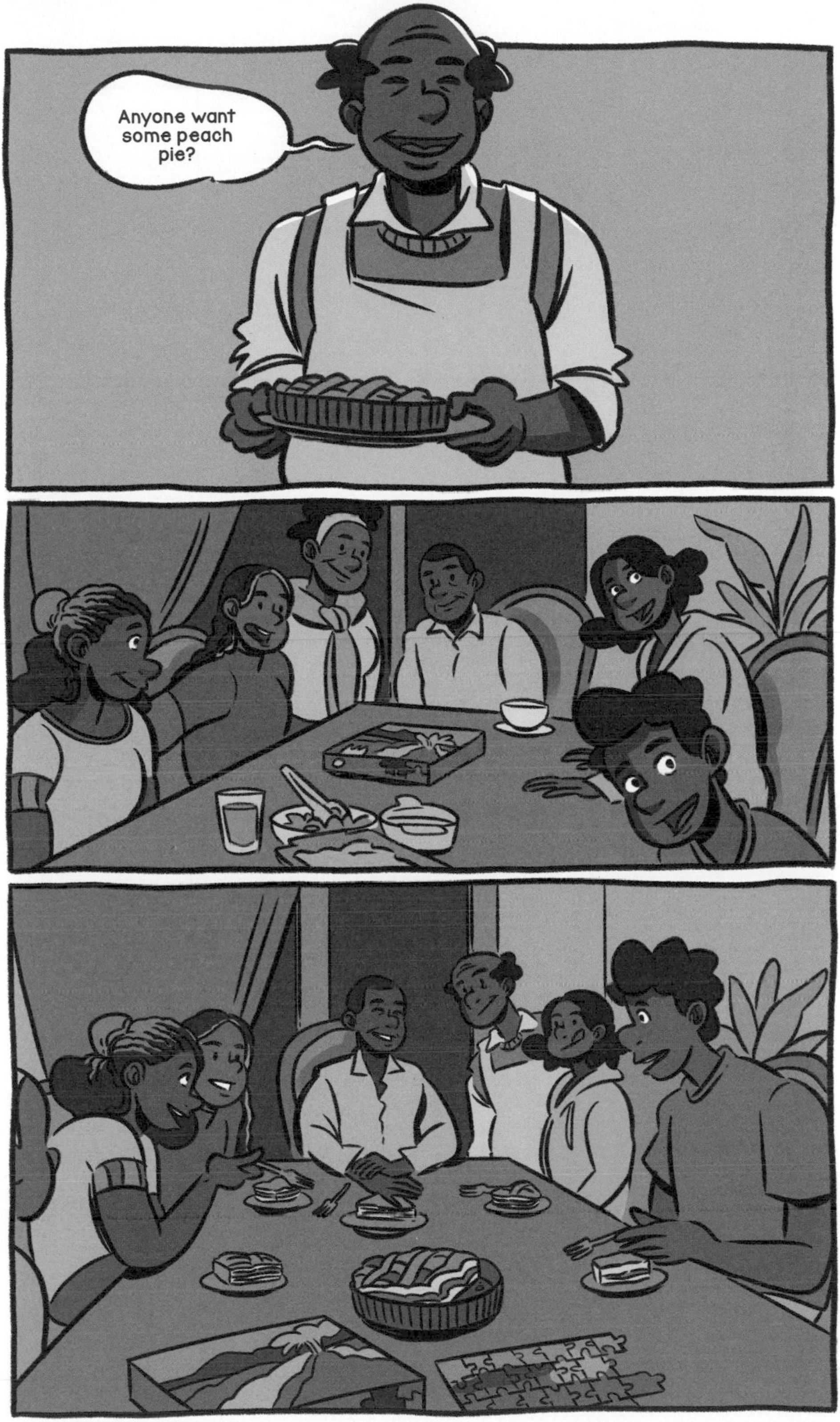
Anyone want some peach pie?

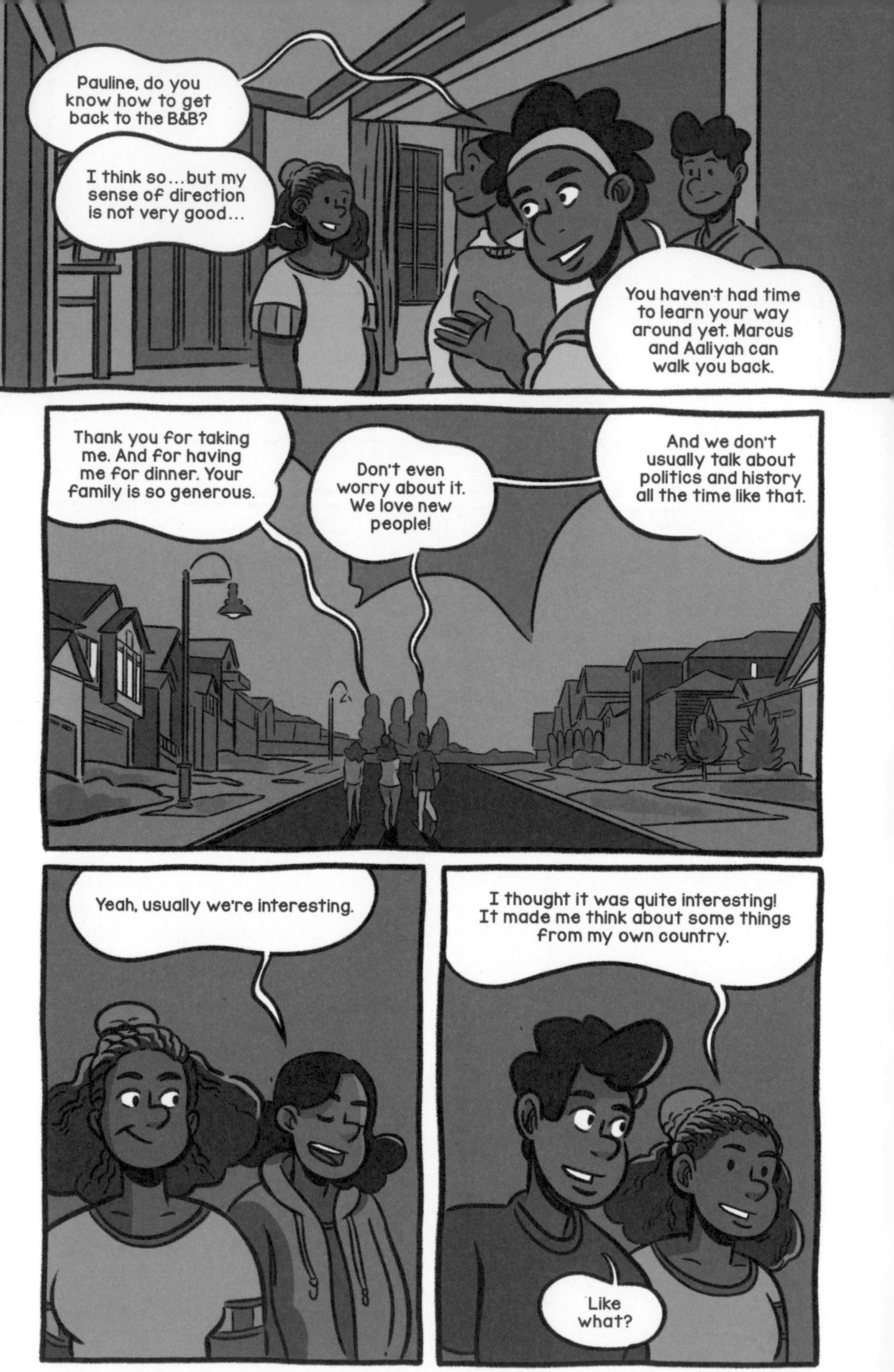
Pauline, do you know how to get back to the B&B?
I think so...but my sense of direction is not very good...
You haven't had time to learn your way around yet. Marcus and Aaliyah can walk you back.
Thank you for taking me. And for having me for dinner. Your family is so generous.
Don't even worry about it. We love new people!
And we don't usually talk about politics and history all the time like that.
Yeah, usually we're interesting.
I thought it was quite interesting! It made me think about some things from my own country.
Like what?

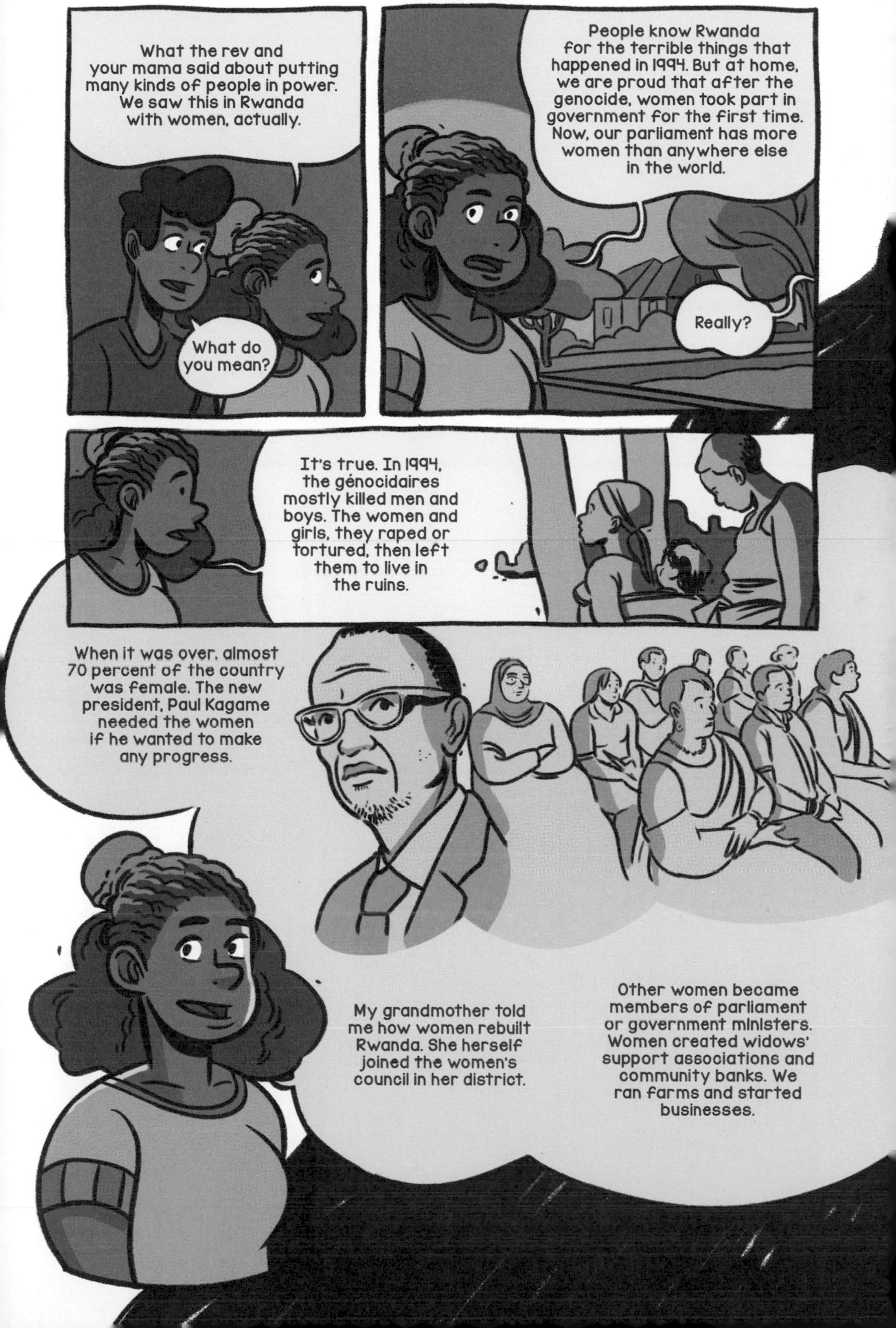
What the rev and your mama said about putting many kinds of people in power. We saw this in Rwanda with women, actually.
What do you mean?
People know Rwanda for the terrible things that happened in 1994. But at home, we are proud that after the genocide, women took part in government for the first time. Now, our parliament has more women than anywhere else in the world.
Really?
It's true. In 1994, the génocidaires mostly killed men and boys. The women and girls, they raped or tortured, then left them to live in the ruins.
When it was over, almost 70 percent of the country was female. The new president, Paul Kagame needed the women if he wanted to make any progress.
My grandmother told me how women rebuilt Rwanda. She herself joined the women's council in her district.
Other women became members of parliament or government ministers. Women created widows' support associations and community banks. We ran farms and started businesses.

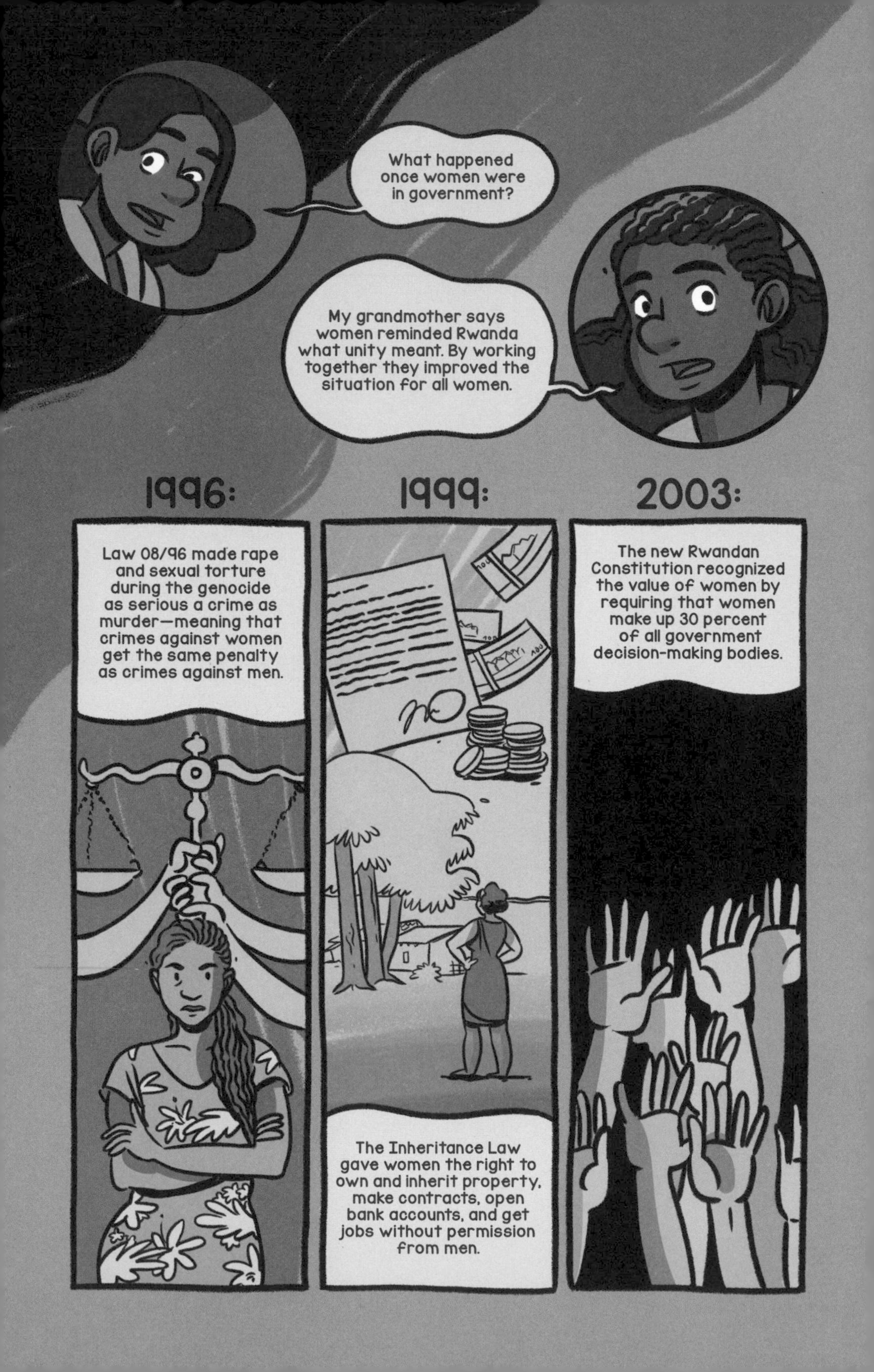
What happened once women were in government?
My grandmother says women reminded Rwanda what unity meant. By working together they improved the situation for all women.
1996:
Law 08/96 made rape and sexual torture during the genocide as serious a crime as murder—meaning that crimes against women get the same penalty as crimes against men.
1999:
The Inheritance Law gave women the right to own and inherit property, make contracts, open bank accounts, and get jobs without permission from men.
2003:
The new Rwandan Constitution recognized the value of women by requiring that women make up 30 percent of all government decision-making bodies.

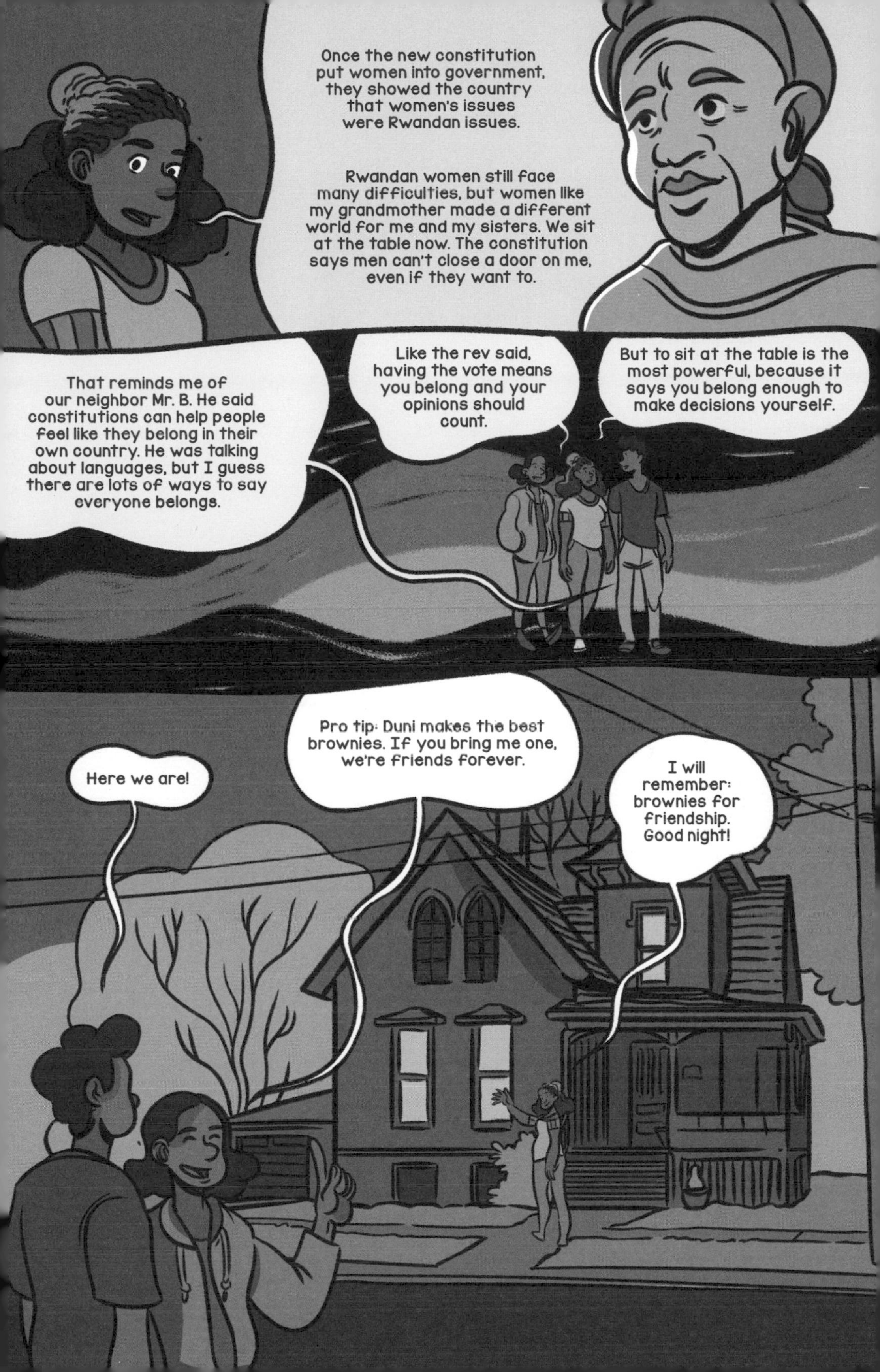
Once the new constitution put women into government, they showed the country that women's issues were Rwandan issues.
Rwandan women still face many difficulties, but women like my grandmother made a different world for me and my sisters. We sit at the table now. The constitution says men can't close a door on me, even if they want to.
That reminds me of our neighbor Mr. B. He said constitutions can help people feel like they belong in their own country. He was talking about languages, but I guess there are lots of ways to say everyone belongs.
Like the rev said, having the vote means you belong and your opinions should count.
But to sit at the table is the most powerful, because it says you belong enough to make decisions yourself.
Here we are!
Pro tip: Duni makes the best brownies. If you bring me one, we're friends forever.
I will remember: brownies for friendship. Good night!

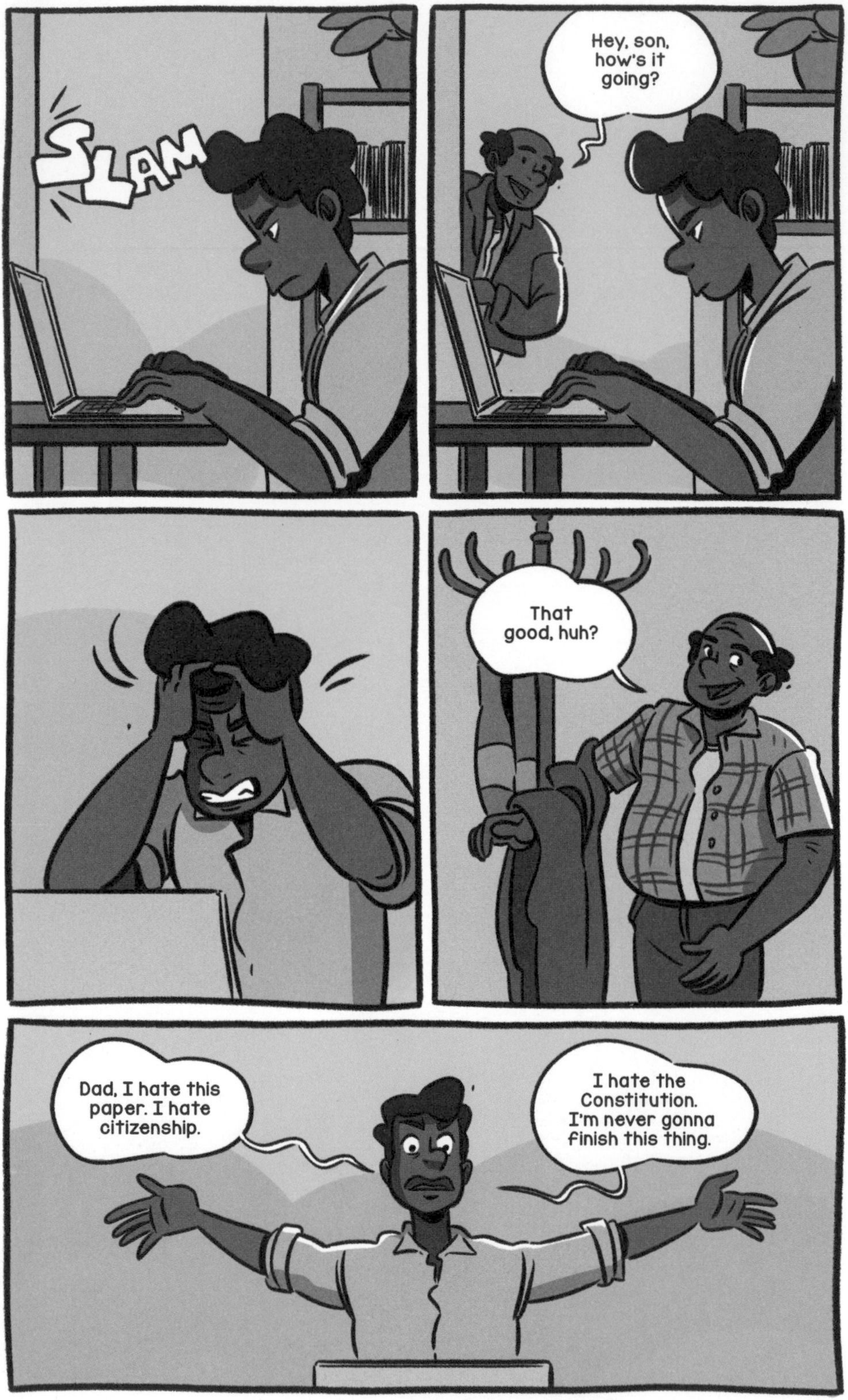
SLAM
Hey, son, how's it going?
That good, huh?
Dad, I hate this paper. I hate citizenship.
I hate the Constitution. I'm never gonna finish this thing.

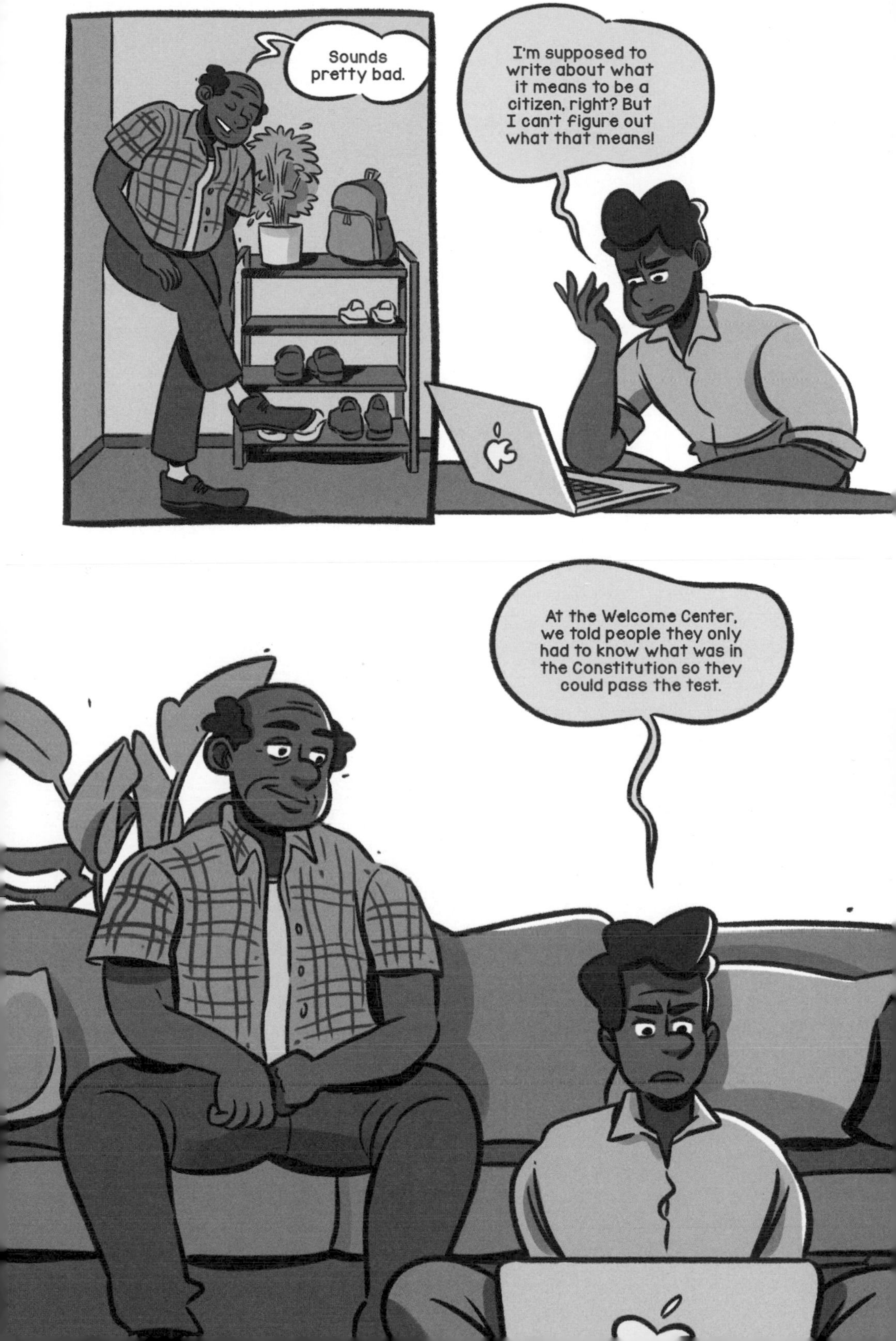
Sounds pretty bad.
I'm supposed to write about what it means to be a citizen, right? But I can't figure out what that means!
At the Welcome Center, we told people they only had to know what was in the Constitution so they could pass the test.

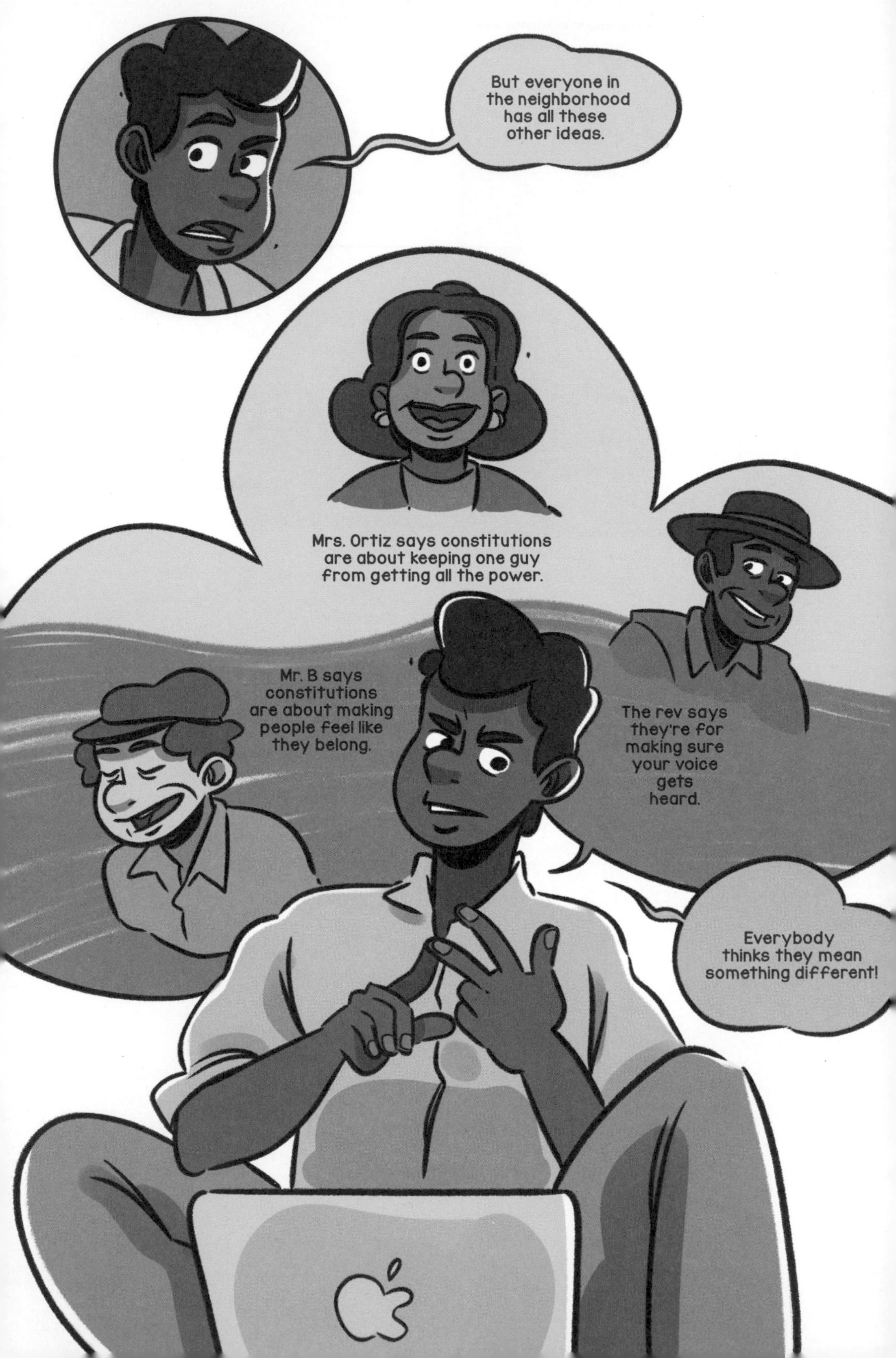
But everyone in the neighborhood has all these other ideas.
Mrs. Ortiz says constitutions are about keeping one guy from getting all the power.
Mr. B says constitutions are about making people feel like they belong.
The rev says they're for making sure your voice gets heard.
Everybody thinks they mean something different!

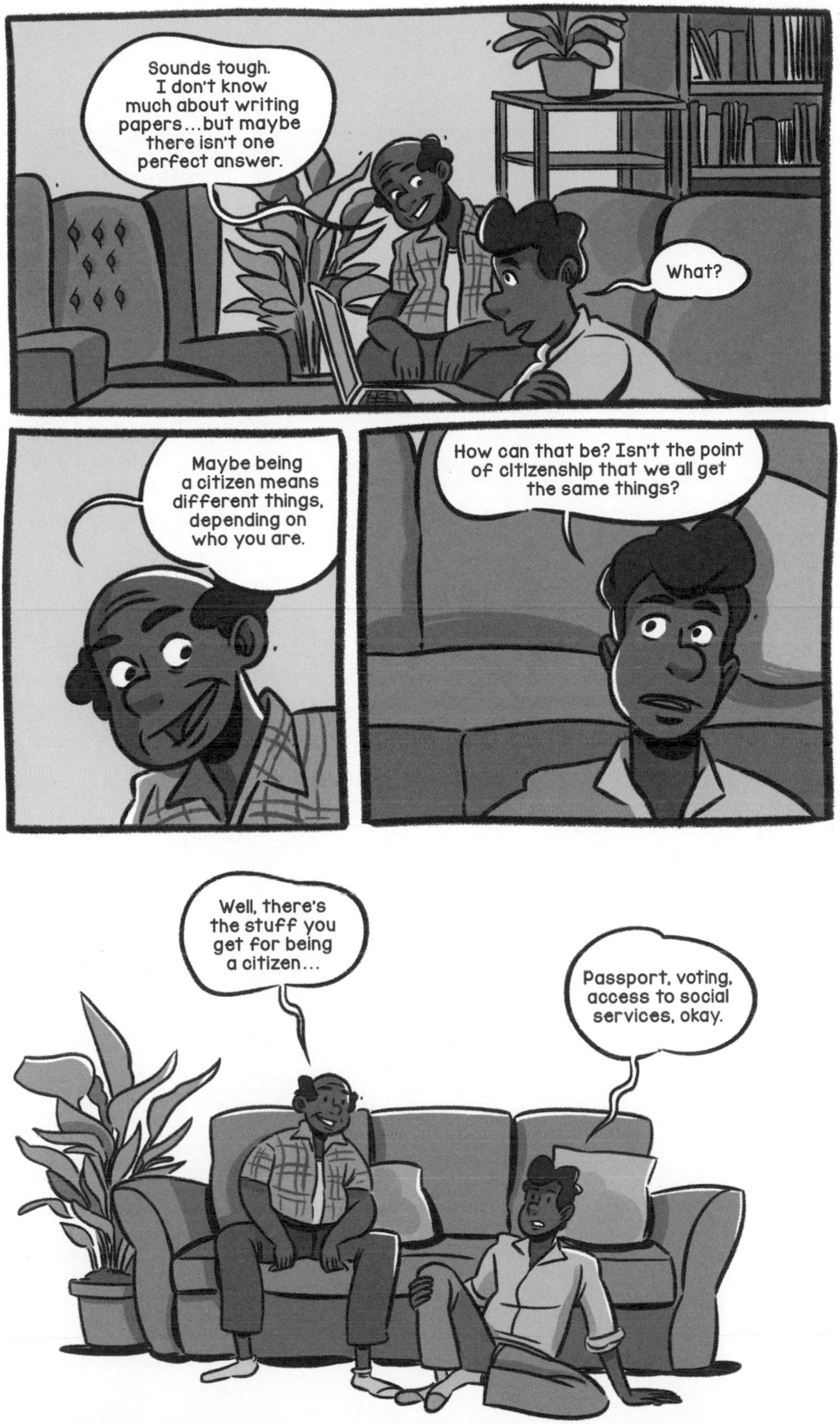
Sounds tough. I don't know much about writing papers...but maybe there isn't one perfect answer.
What?
Maybe being a citizen means different things, depending on who you are.
How can that be? Isn't the point of citizenship that we all get the same things?
Well, there's the stuff you get for being a citizen...
Passport, voting, access to social services, okay.

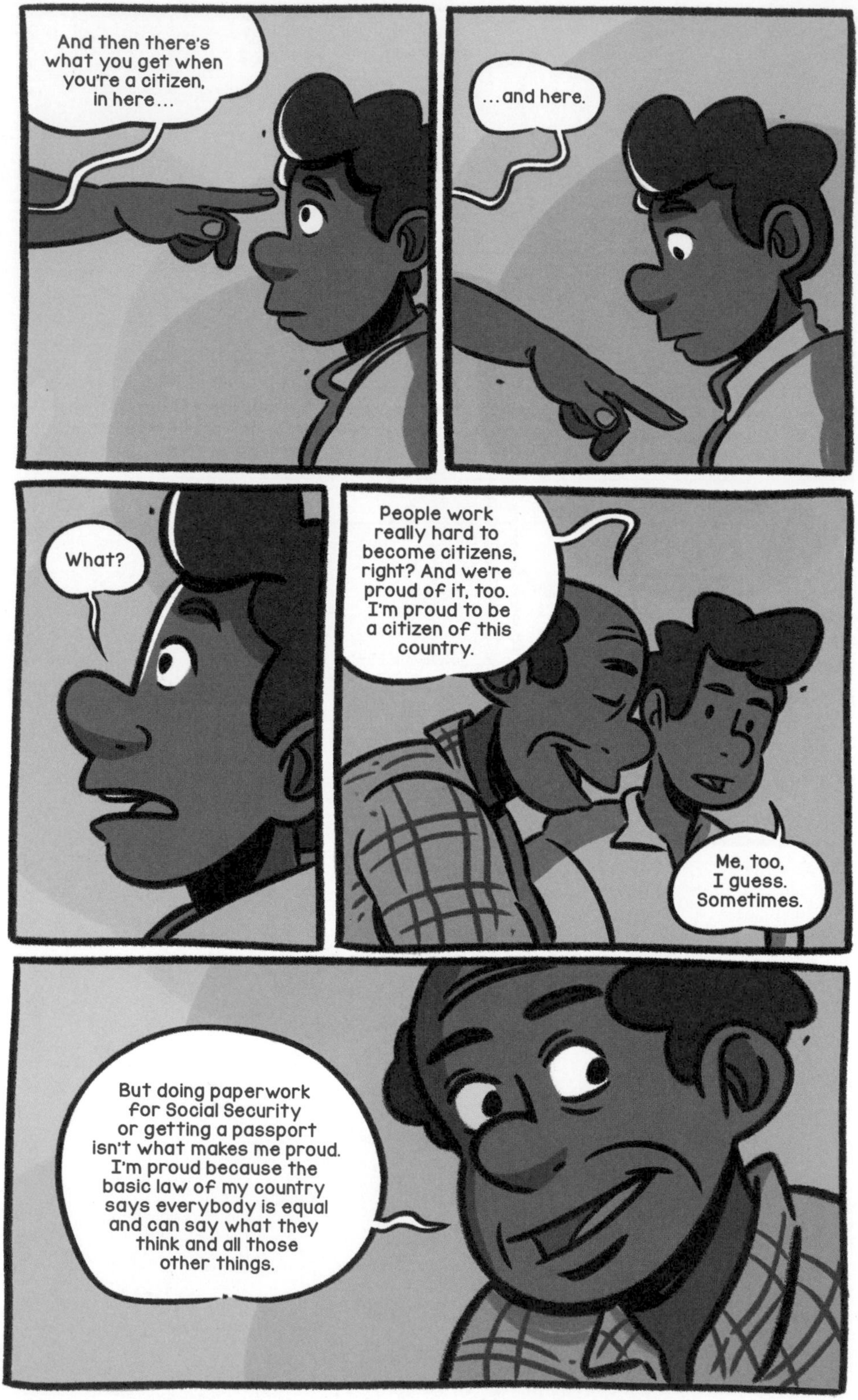
And then there's what you get when you're a citizen, in here...
...and here.
What?
People work really hard to become citizens, right? And we're proud of it, too. I'm proud to be a citizen of this country.
Me, too, I guess. Sometimes.
But doing paperwork for Social Security or getting a passport isn't what makes me proud. I'm proud because the basic law of my country says everybody is equal and can say what they think and all those other things.

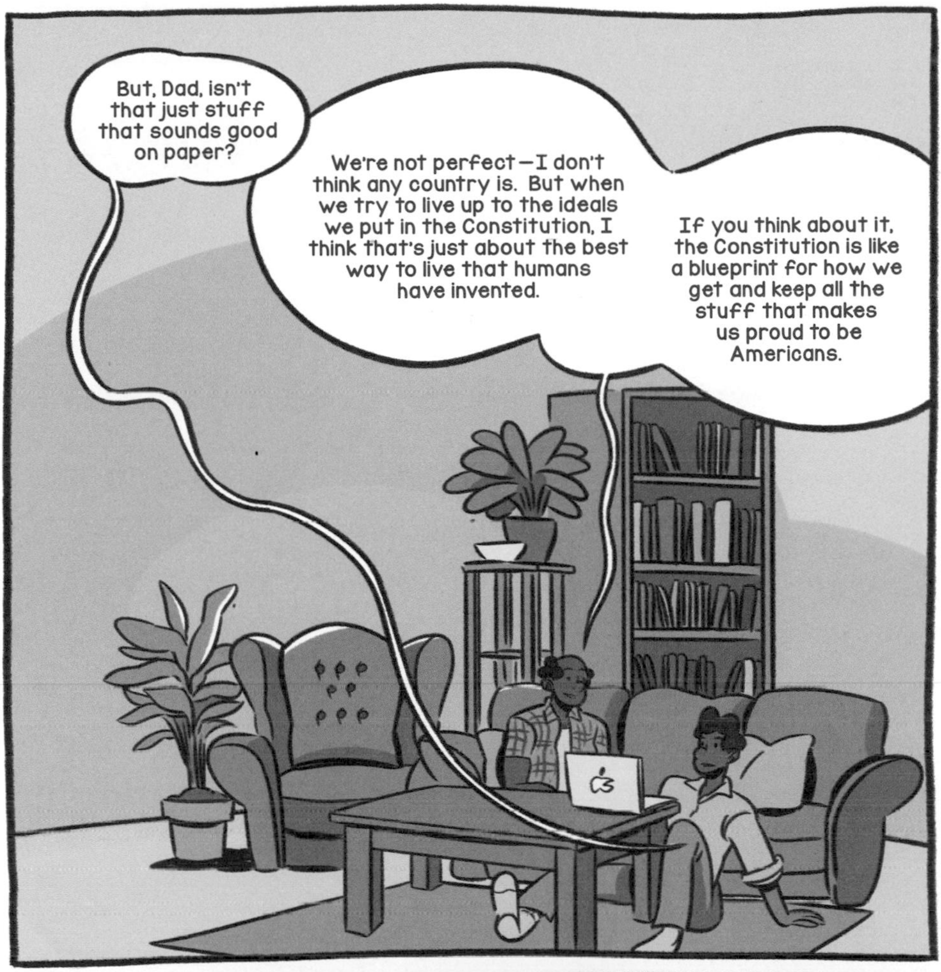
But, Dad, isn't that just stuff that sounds good on paper?
We're not perfect—I don't think any country is. But when we try to live up to the ideals we put in the Constitution, I think that's just about the best way to live that humans have invented.
If you think about it, the Constitution is like a blueprint for how we get and keep all the stuff that makes us proud to be Americans.

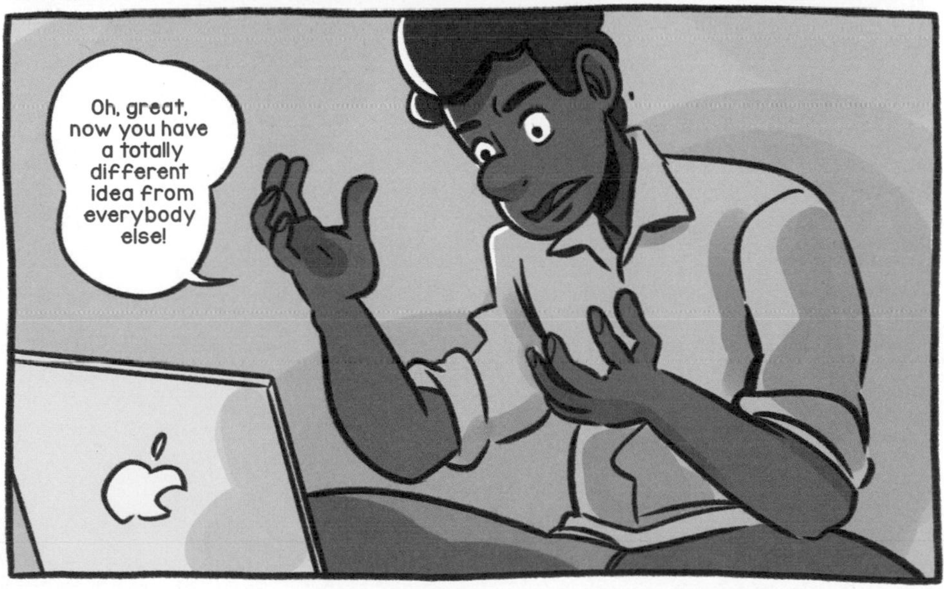
Oh, great, now you have a totally different idea from everybody else!

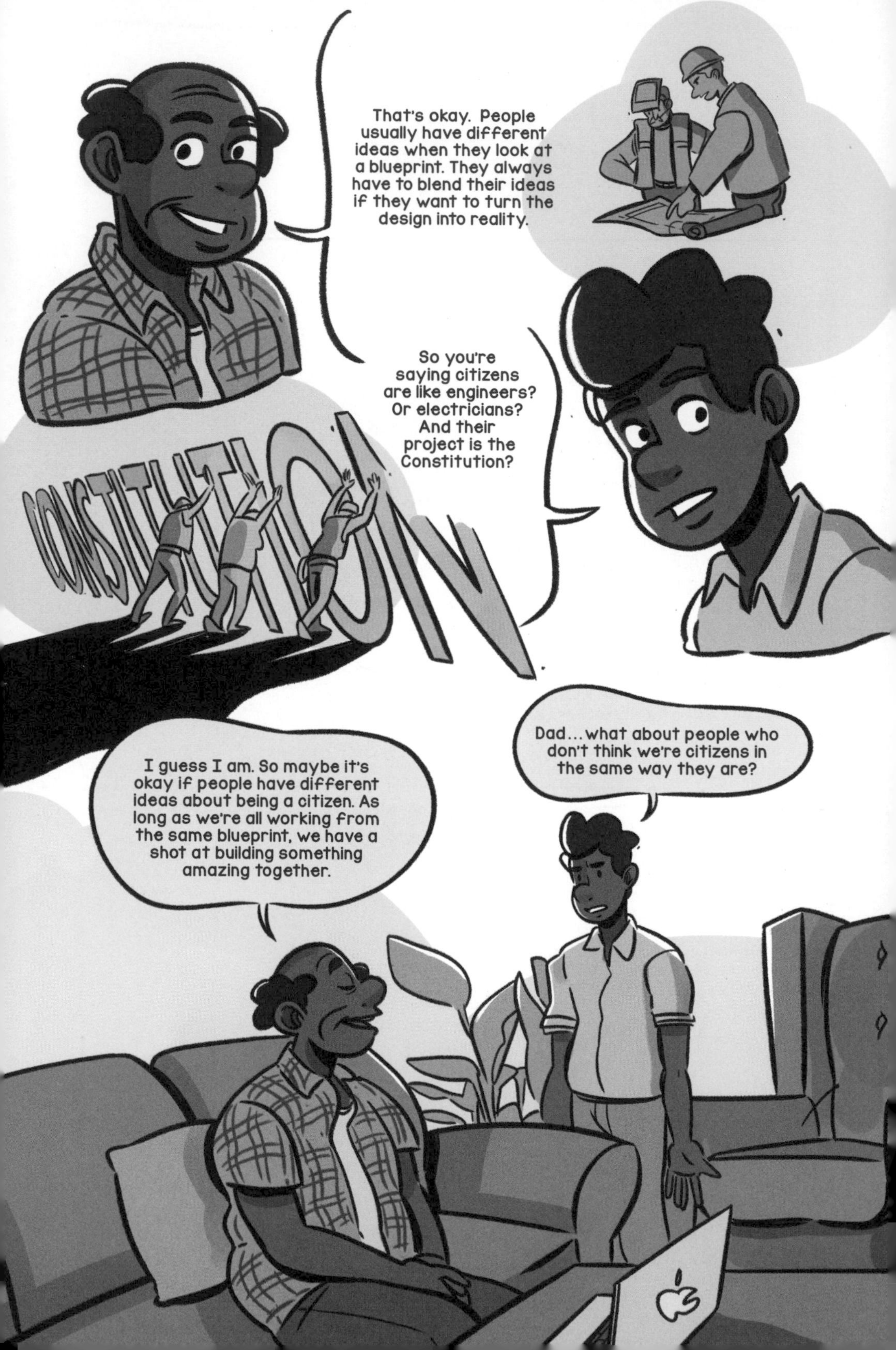
That's okay. People usually have different ideas when they look at a blueprint. They always have to blend their ideas if they want to turn the design into reality.
So you're saying citizens are like engineers? Or electricians? And their project is the Constitution?
CONSTITUTION
I guess I am. So maybe it's okay if people have different ideas about being a citizen. As long as we're all working from the same blueprint, we have a shot at building something amazing together.
Dad... what about people who don't think we're citizens in the same way they are?

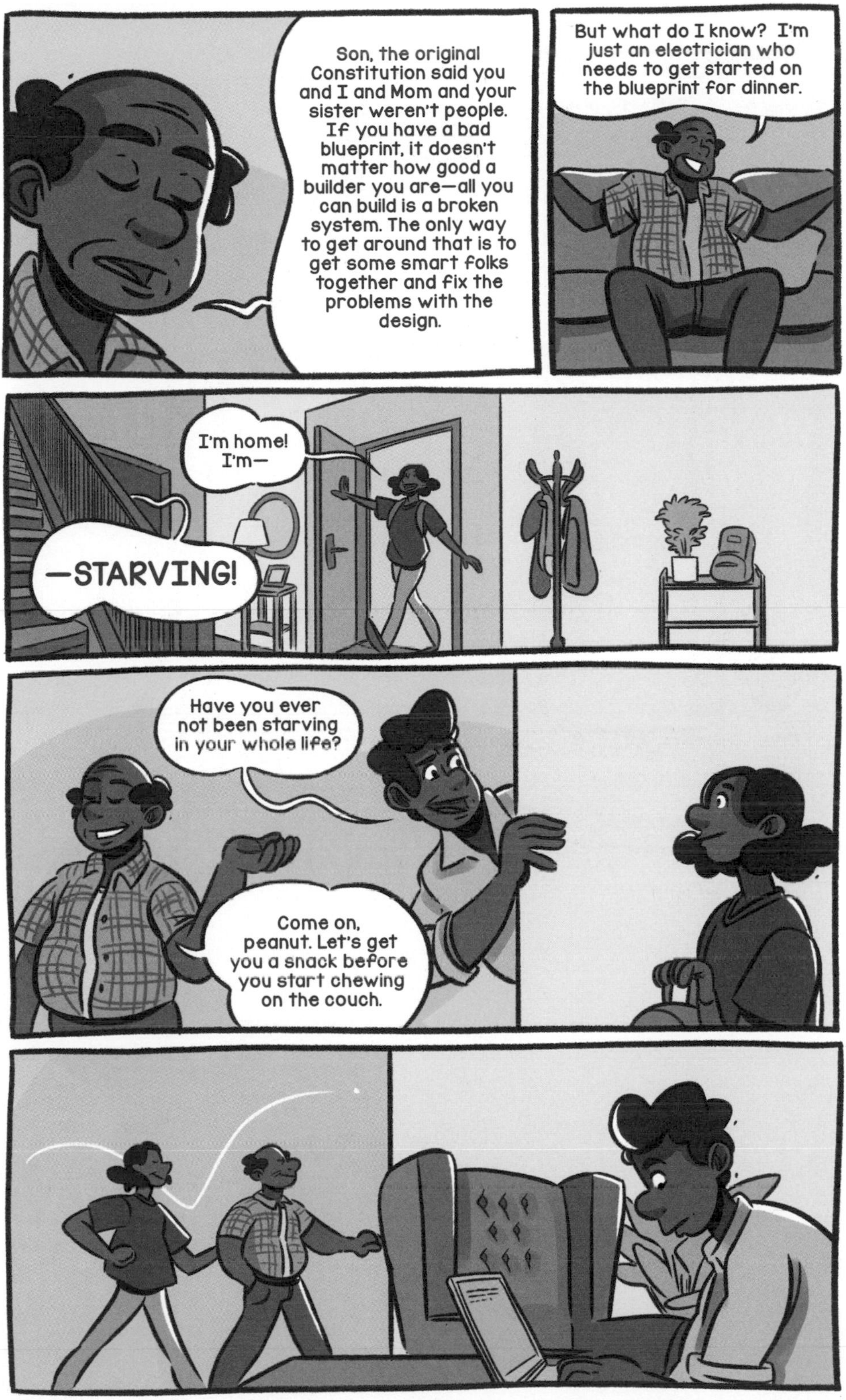
Son, the original Constitution said you and I and Mom and your sister weren't people. If you have a bad blueprint, it doesn't matter how good a builder you are—all you can build is a broken system. The only way to get around that is to get some smart folks together and fix the problems with the design.
But what do I know? I'm just an electrician who needs to get started on the blueprint for dinner.
I'm home! I'm—
—STARVING!
Have you ever not been starving in your whole life?
Come on, peanut. Let's get you a snack before you start chewing on the couch.

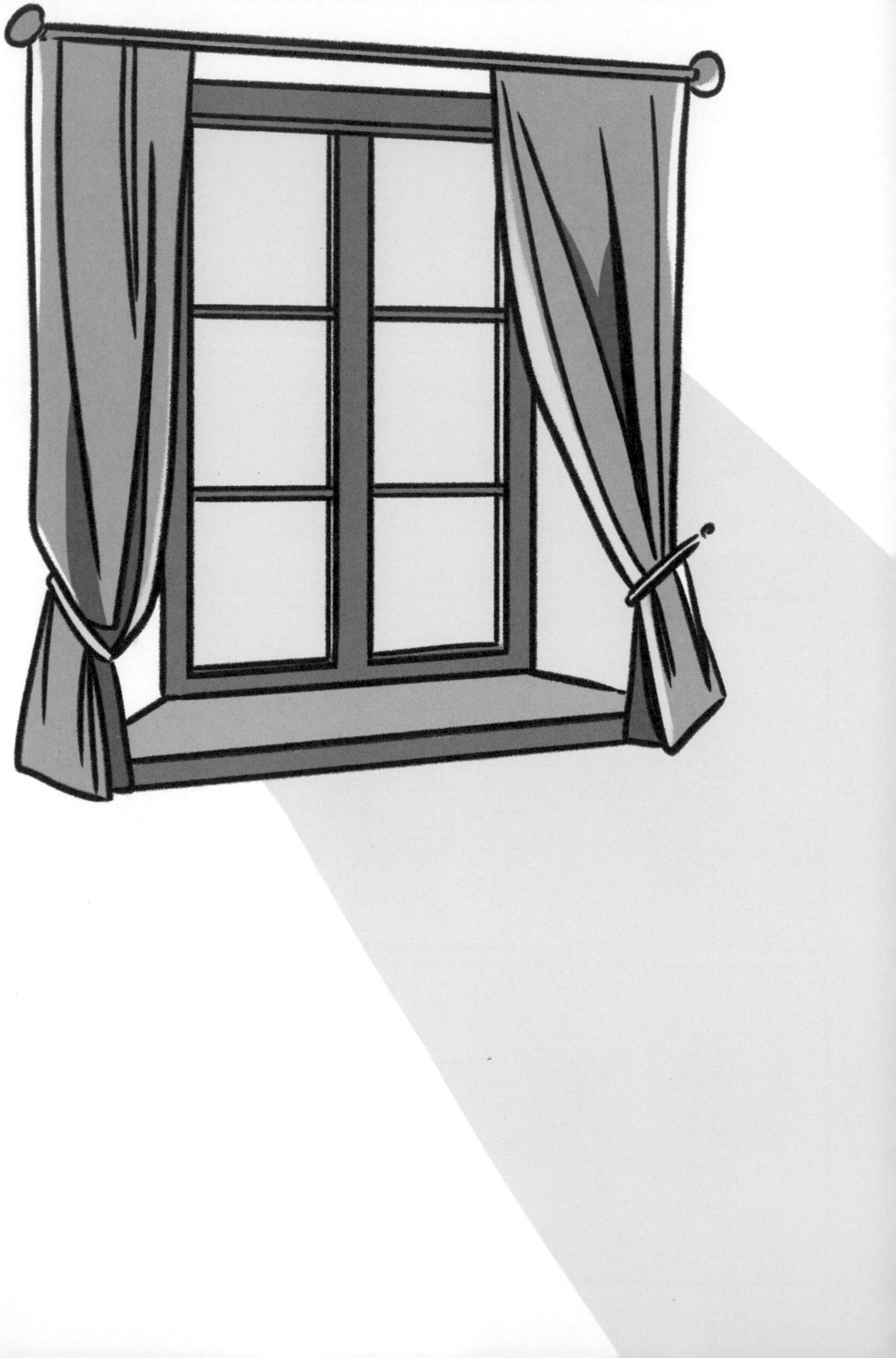

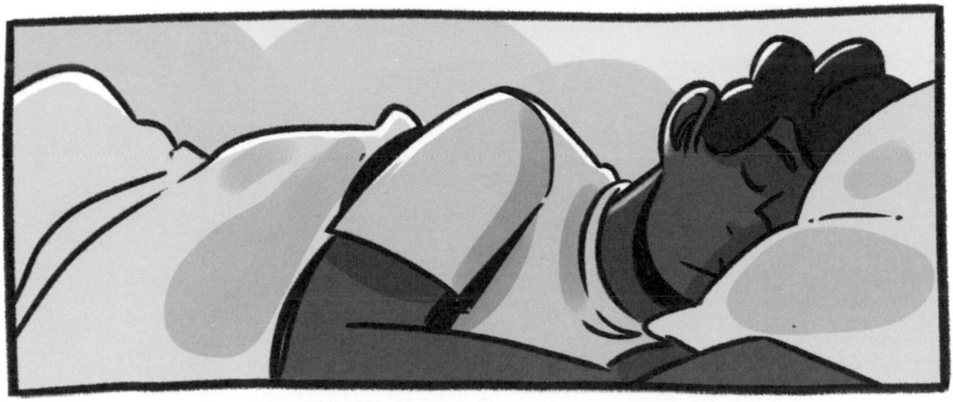

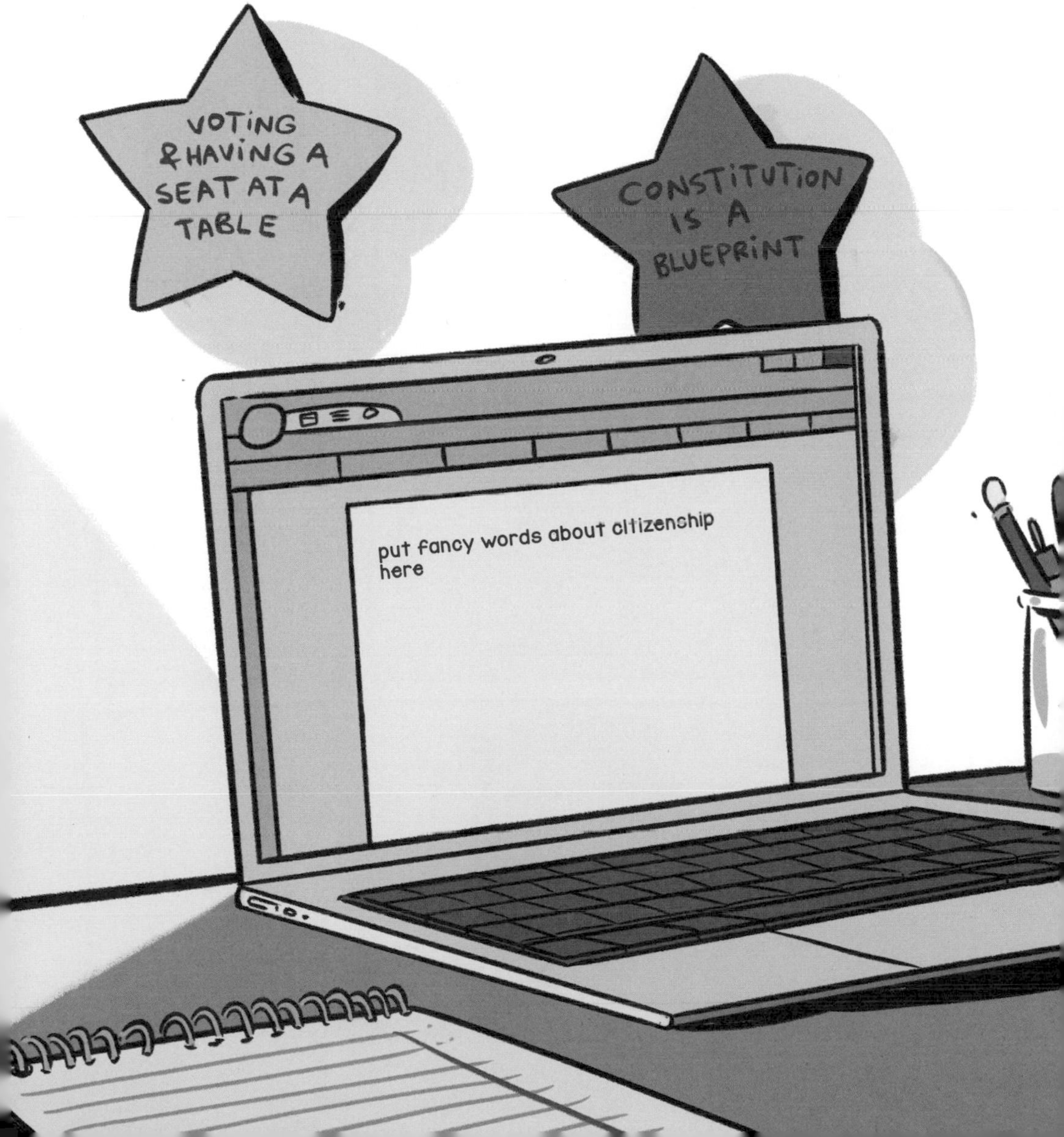
VOTING & HAVING A SEAT AT A TABLE
CONSTITUTION IS A BLUEPRINT
put fancy words about citizenship here

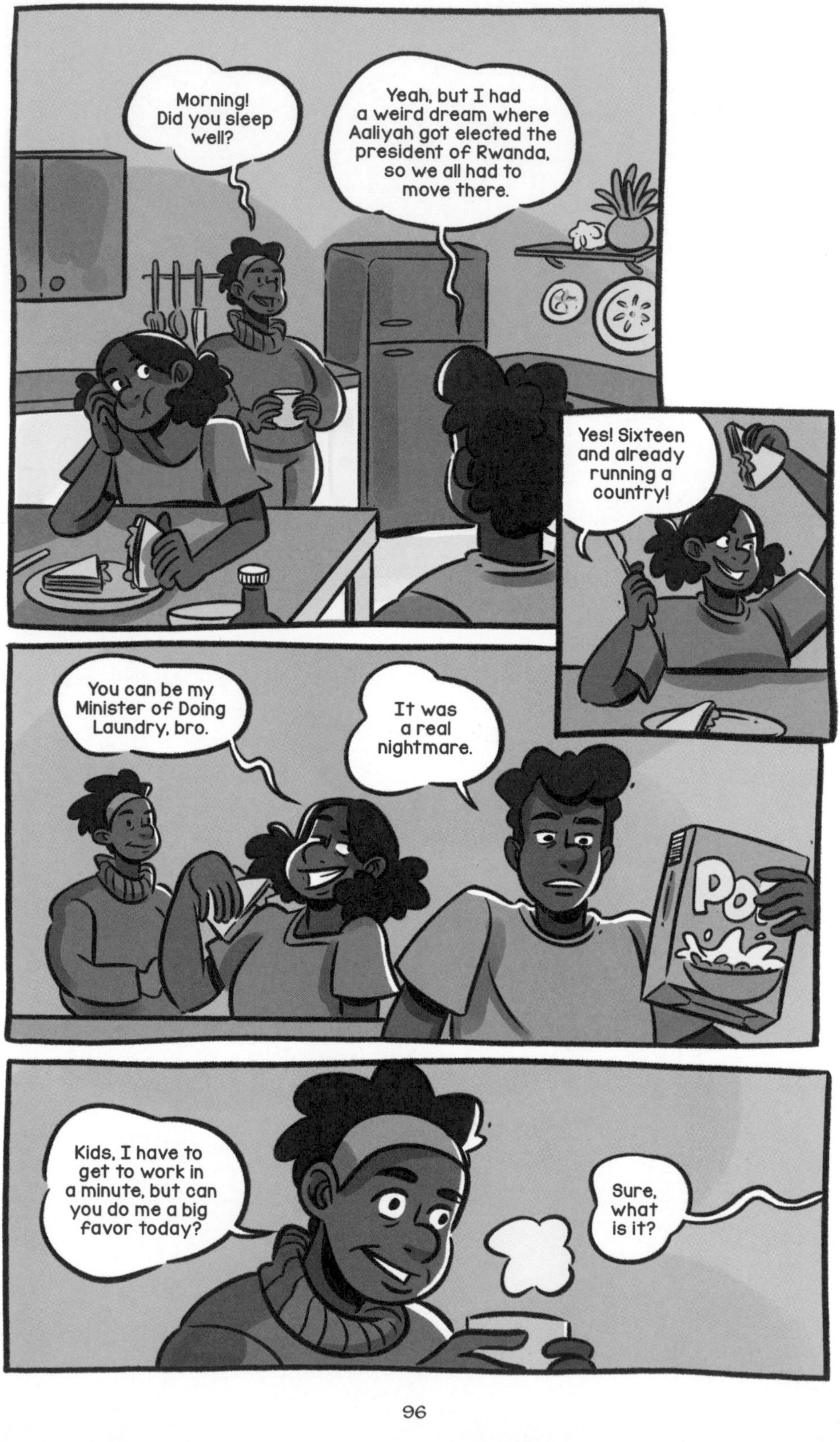
Morning! Did you sleep well?
Yeah, but I had a weird dream where Aaliyah got elected the president of Rwanda, so we all had to move there.
Yes! Sixteen and already running a country!
You can be my Minister of Doing Laundry, bro.
It was a real nightmare.
Kids, I have to get to work in a minute, but can you do me a big favor today?
Sure, what is it?

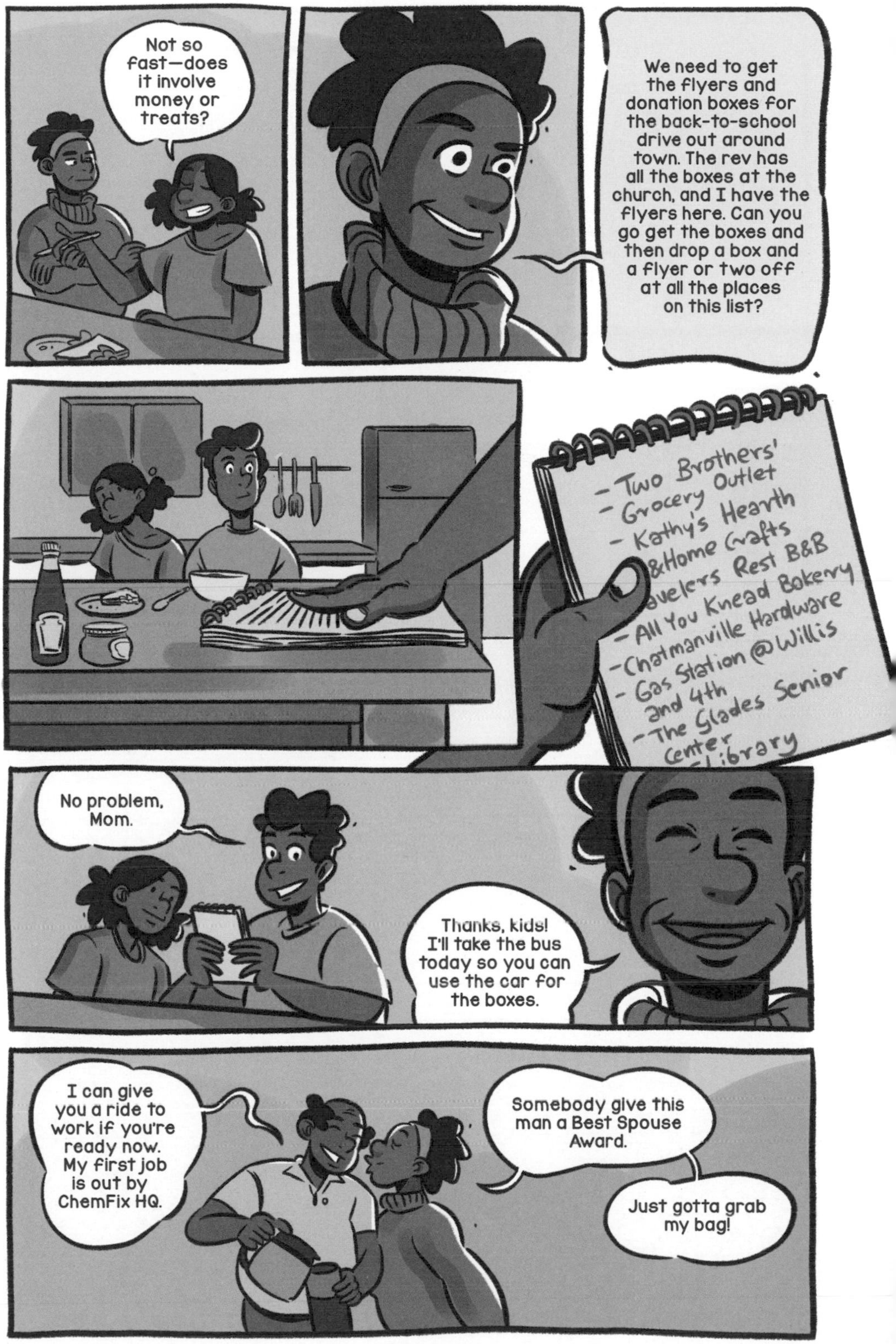

Not so fast—does it involve money or treats?
We need to get the flyers and donation boxes for the back-to-school drive out around town. The rev has all the boxes at the church, and I have the flyers here. Can you go get the boxes and then drop a box and a flyer or two off at all the places on this list?
-Two Brothers' Grocery Outlet
-Kathy's Hearth &Home Crafts
avelers Rest B&B
-All You Knead Bakery
-Chatmanville Hardware
-Gas Station @ Willis and 4th
-The Glades Senior Center
ibrary
No problem, Mom.
Thanks, kids! I'll take the bus today so you can use the car for the boxes.
I can give you a ride to work if you're ready now. My first job is out by ChemFix HQ.
Somebody give this man a Best Spouse Award.
Just gotta grab my bag!

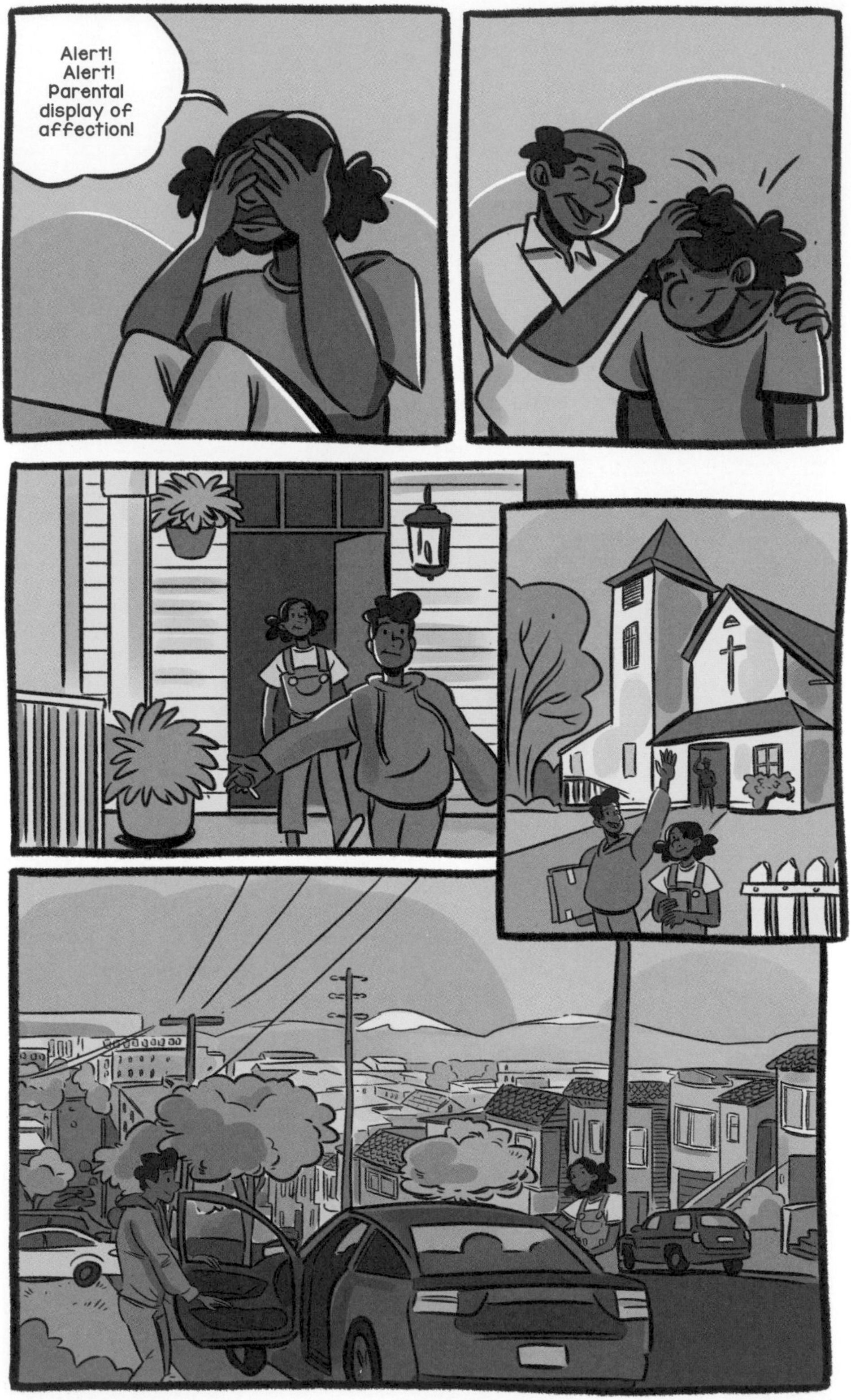
Alert!
Alert!
Parental
display of
affection!

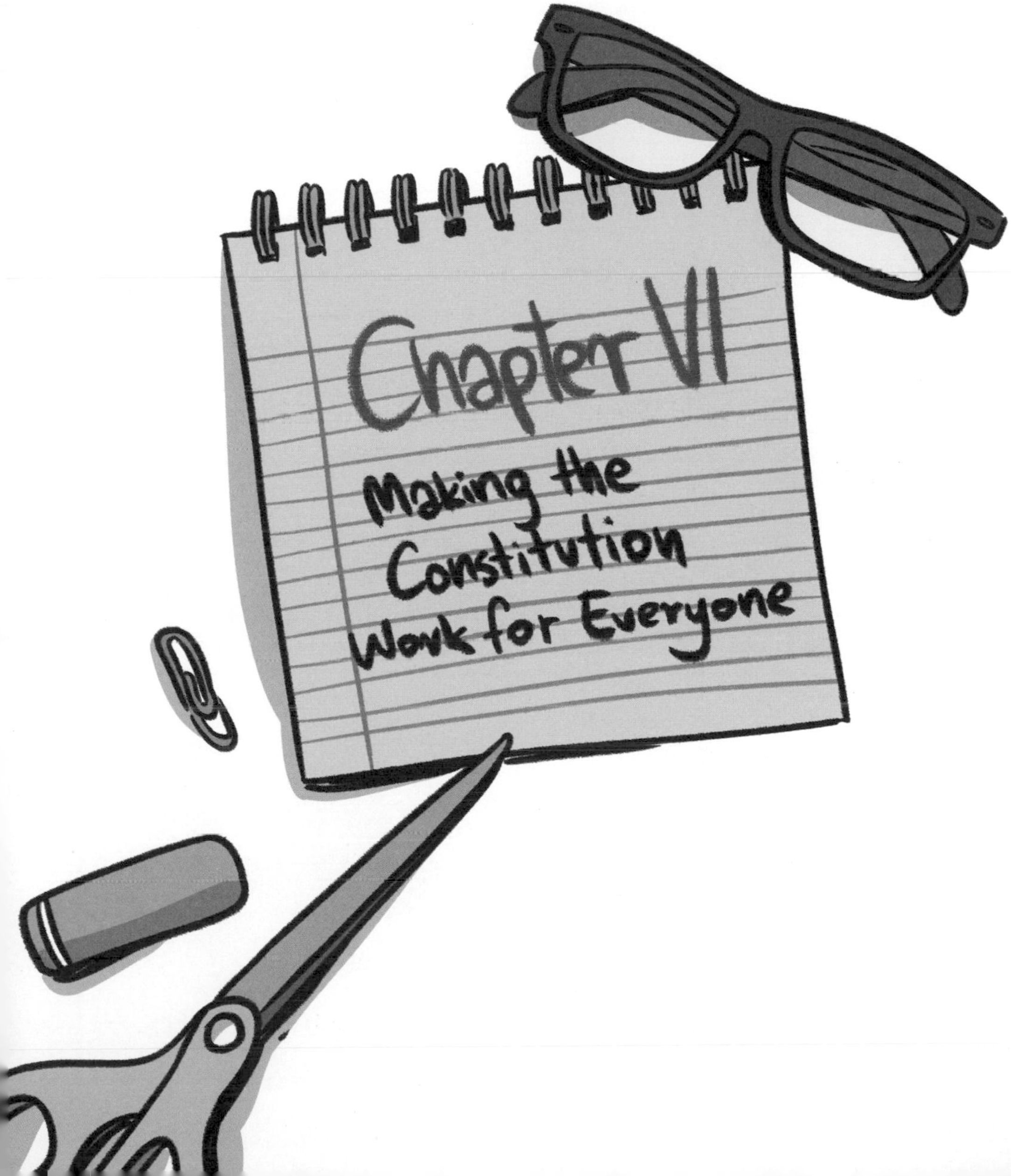
Chapter VI
Making the Constitution Work for Everyone

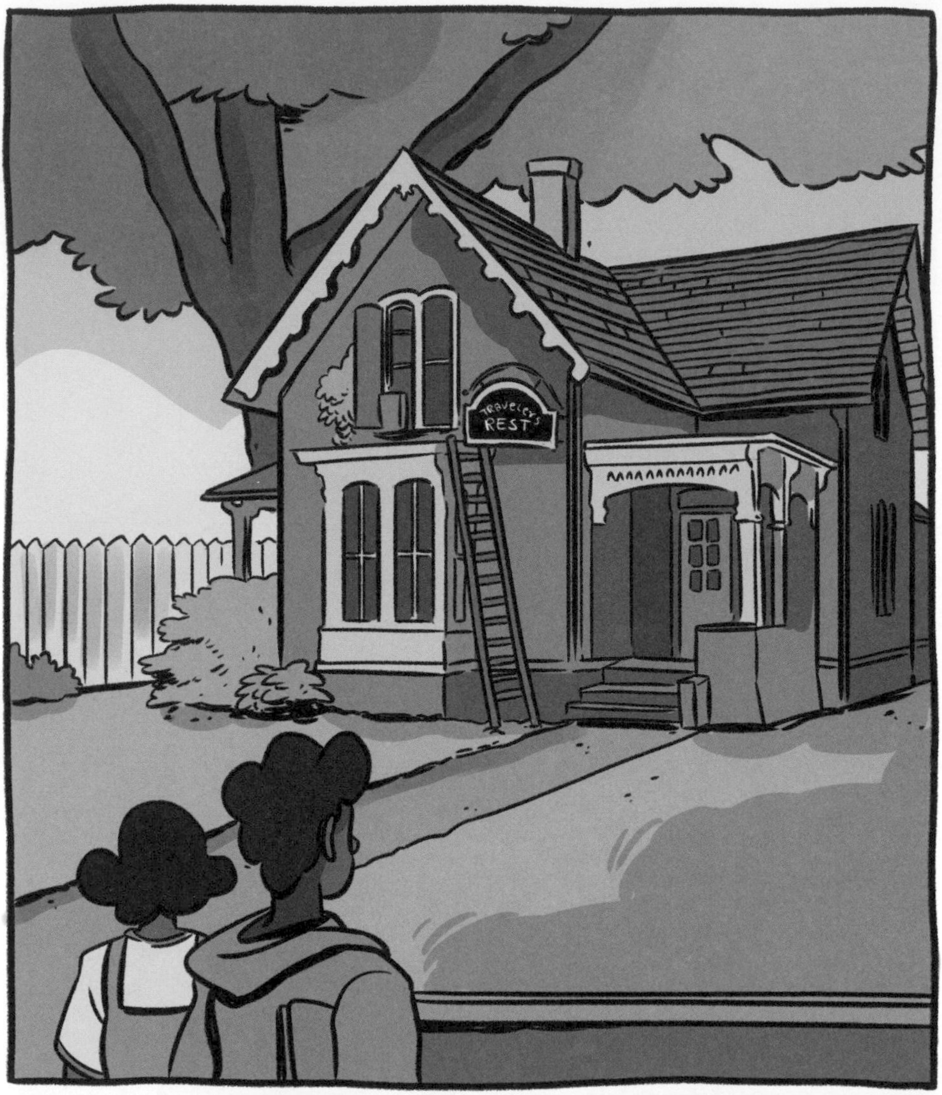
TRAVELER'S
REST

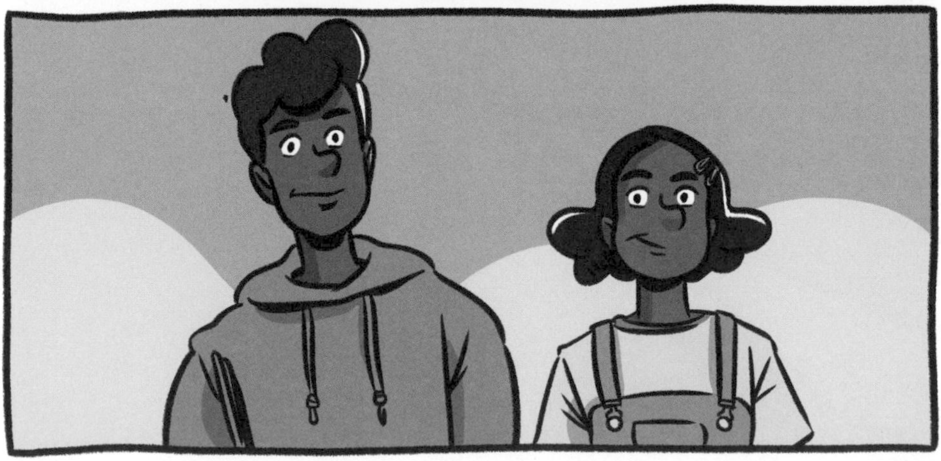

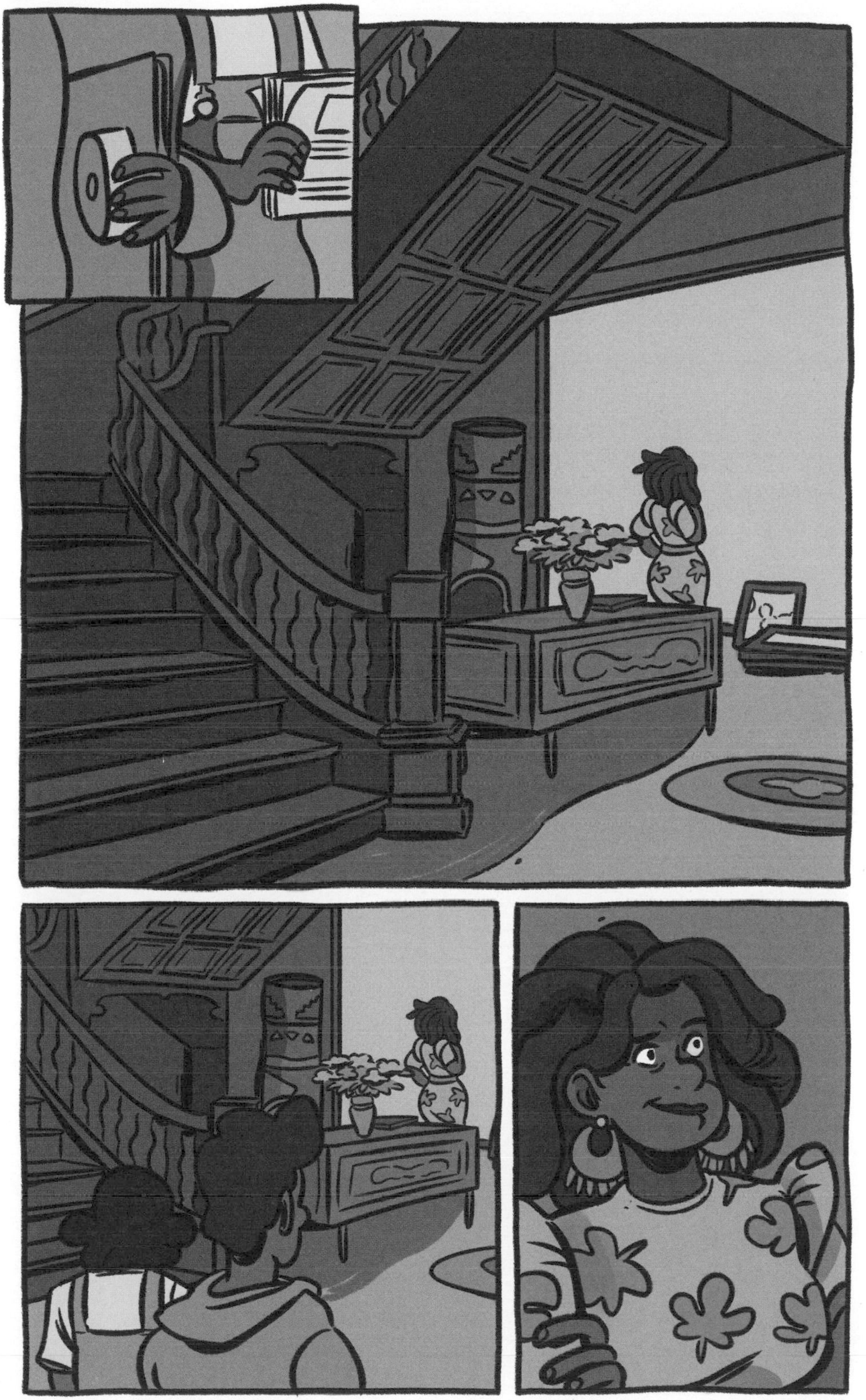

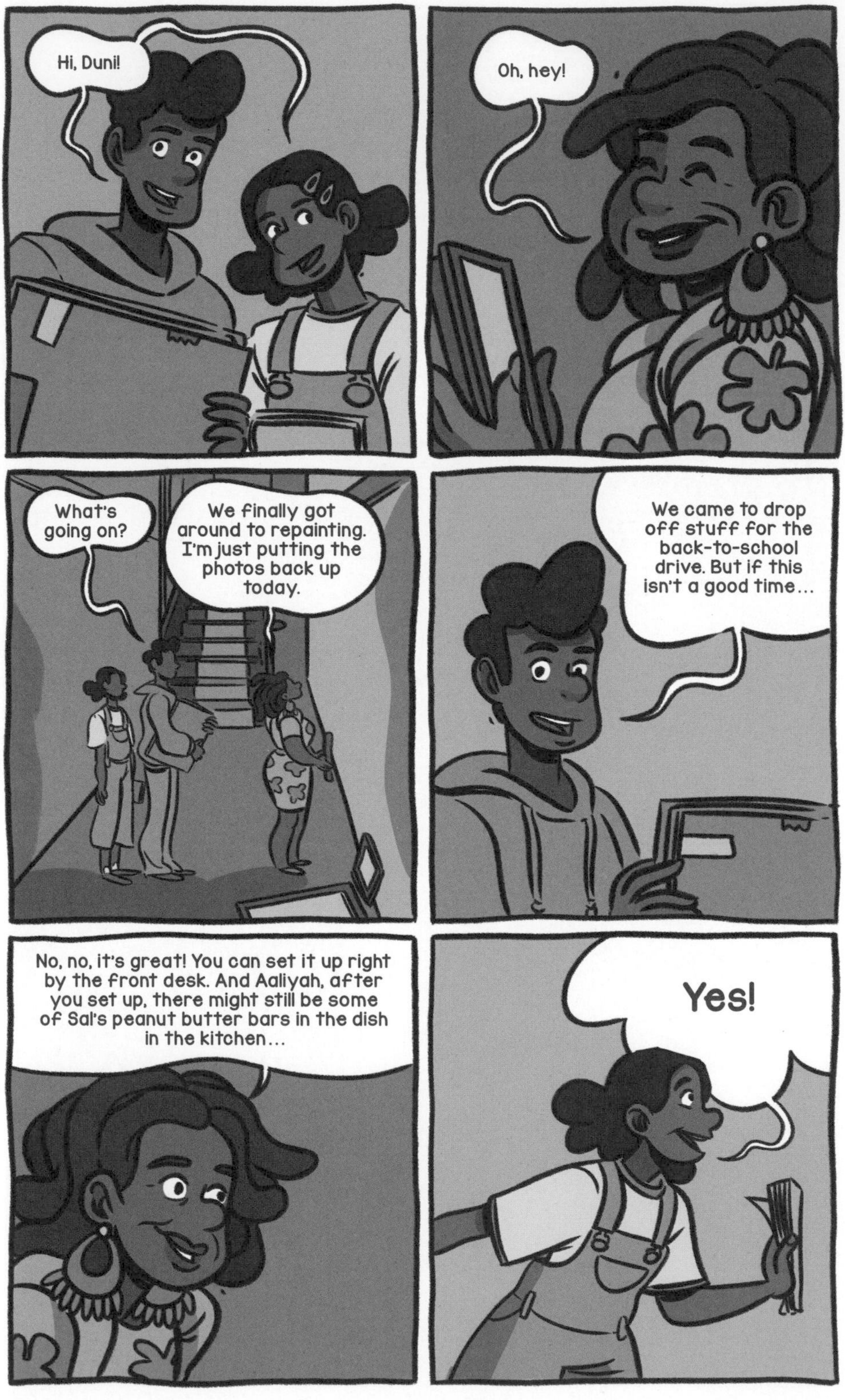
Hi, Duni!
Oh, hey!
What's going on?
We finally got around to repainting. I'm just putting the photos back up today.
We came to drop off stuff for the back-to-school drive. But if this isn't a good time...
No, no, it's great! You can set it up right by the front desk. And Aaliyah, after you set up, there might still be some of Sal's peanut butter bars in the dish in the kitchen...
Yes!

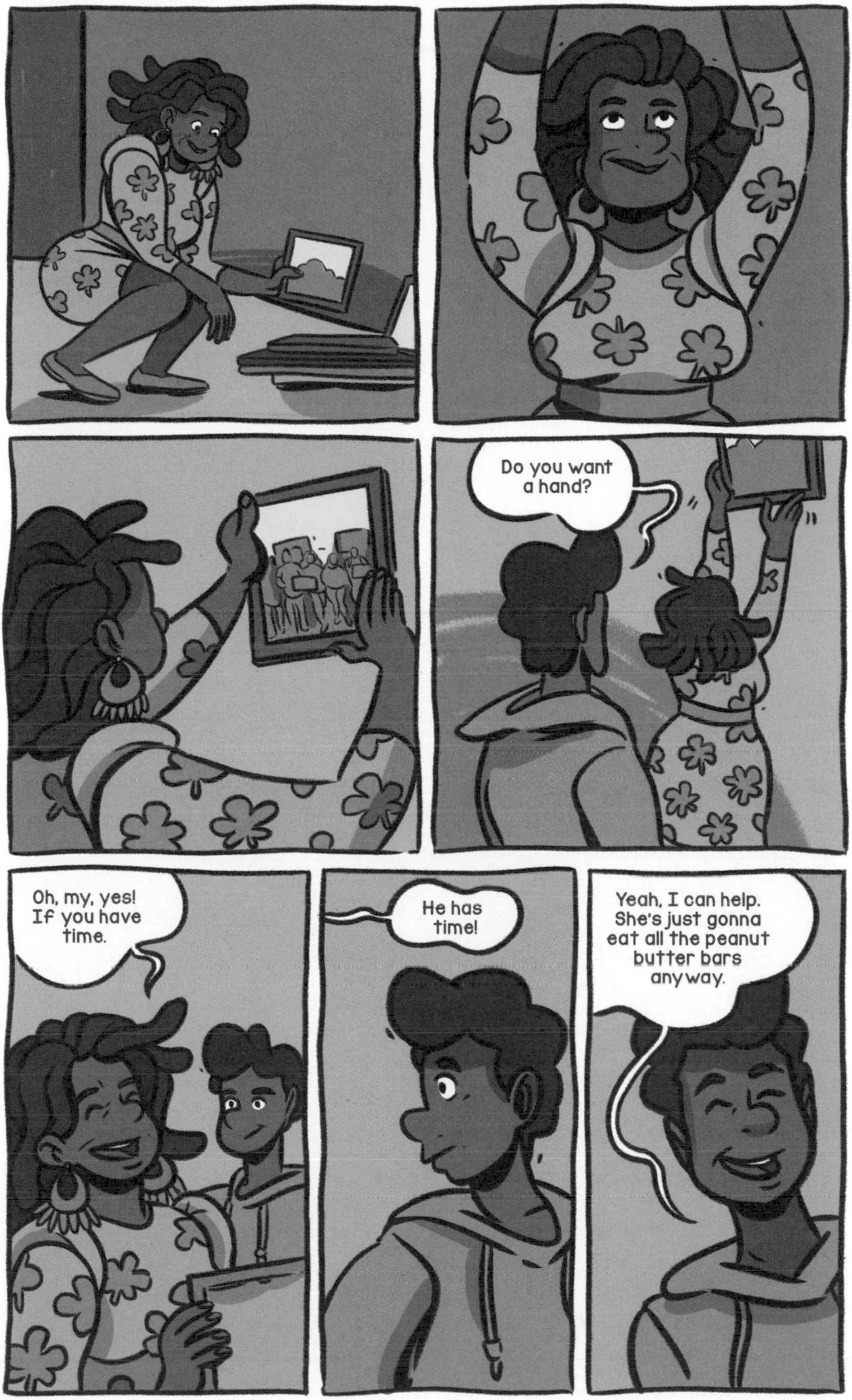
Do you want a hand?
Oh, my, yes! If you have time.
He has time!
Yeah, I can help. She's just gonna eat all the peanut butter bars anyway.

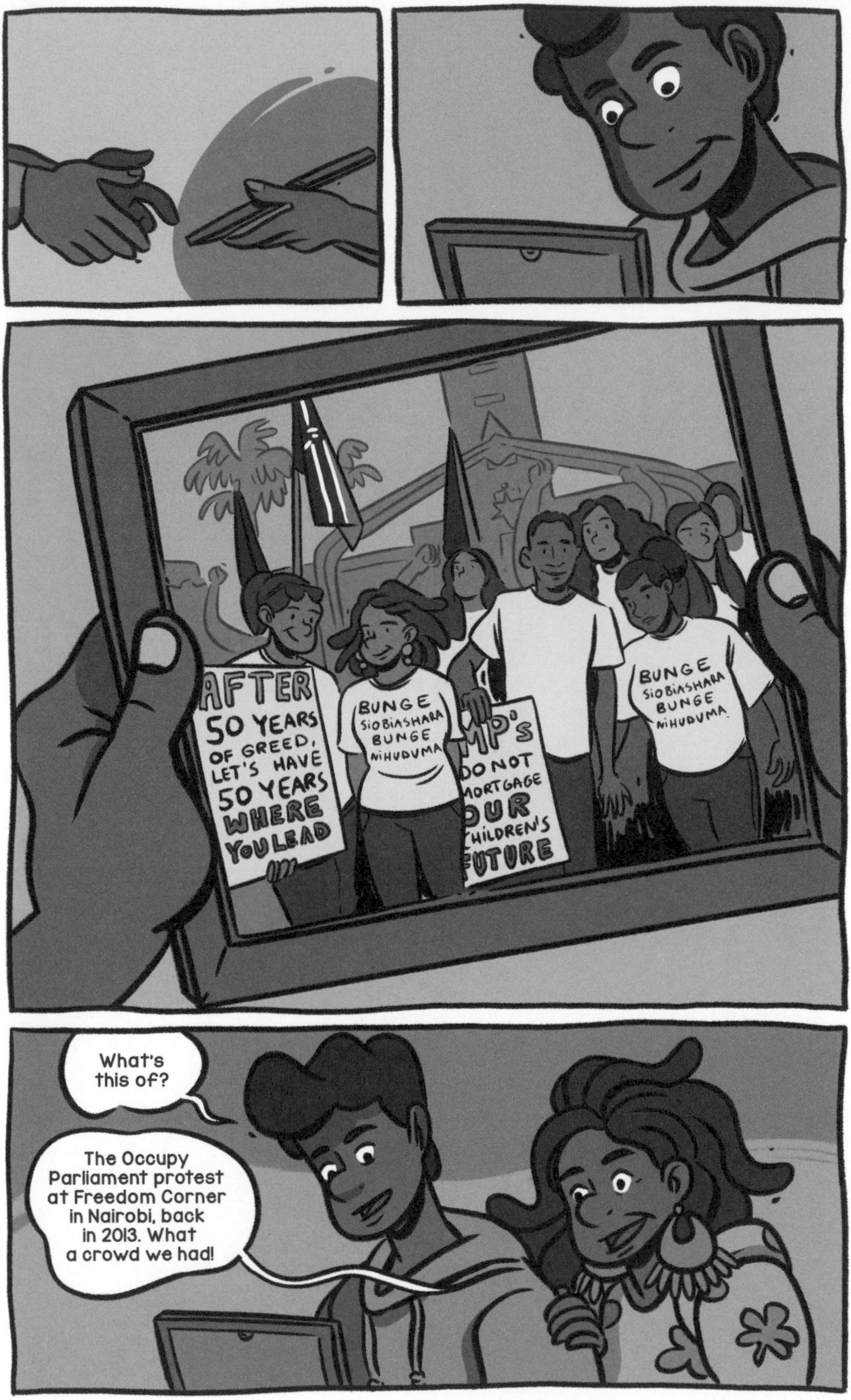
AFTER 50 YEARS OF GREED, LET'S HAVE 50 YEARS WHERE YOU LEAD
BUNGE SIO BIASHARA BUNGE NIHUDUMA
MP's DO NOT MORTGAGE OUR CHILDREN'S FUTURE
BUNGE SIO BIASHARA BUNGE NIHUDUMA
What's this of?
The Occupy Parliament protest at Freedom Corner in Nairobi, back in 2013. What a crowd we had!

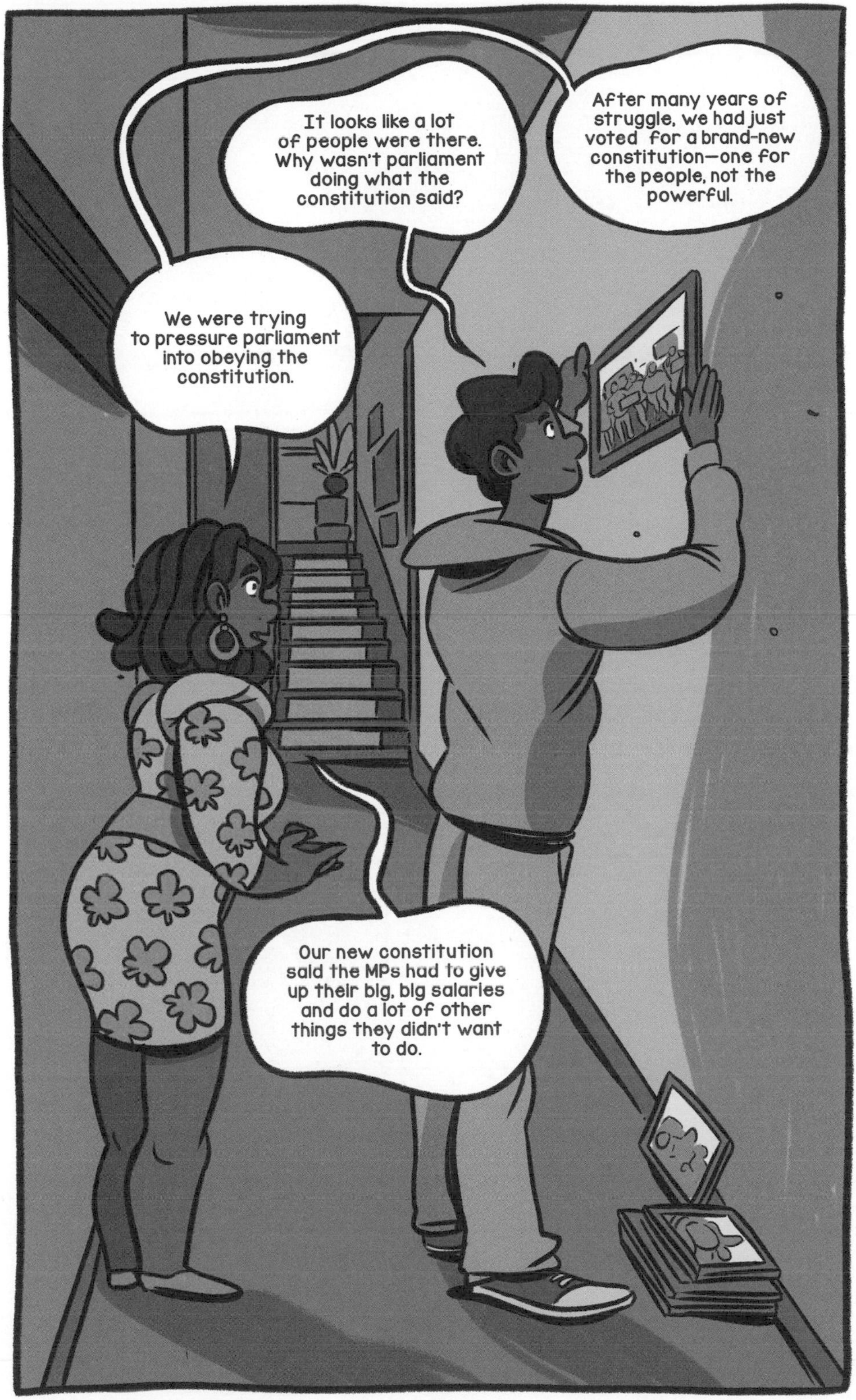
After many years of struggle, we had just voted for a brand-new constitution—one for the people, not the powerful.
It looks like a lot of people were there. Why wasn't parliament doing what the constitution said?
We were trying to pressure parliament into obeying the constitution.
Our new constitution said the MPs had to give up their big, big salaries and do a lot of other things they didn't want to do.

They agreed to a new constitution even though they didn't like what it said?

It was the only way to stop the violence after the 2008 election. But they *thought* it was enough to say nice words about the constitution while still lining their own pockets.

50 YEARS OF GREED, LET'S HAVE 50 YEARS WHERE YOU LEAD

BUNGE SIO BIASHARA BUNGE NIHUDUMA

MP's DO NOT MORTGAGE CHIL FUT

BUNGE SIO BIASHARA BUNGE NIHUDUMA

So we had to make them keep their promises.

How did you get a new constitution in the first place? Doesn't that only happen when a country gets started?

We've had a constitution since independence in Kenya. But from the beginning, the men in charge were only interested in the parts that gave them more power.

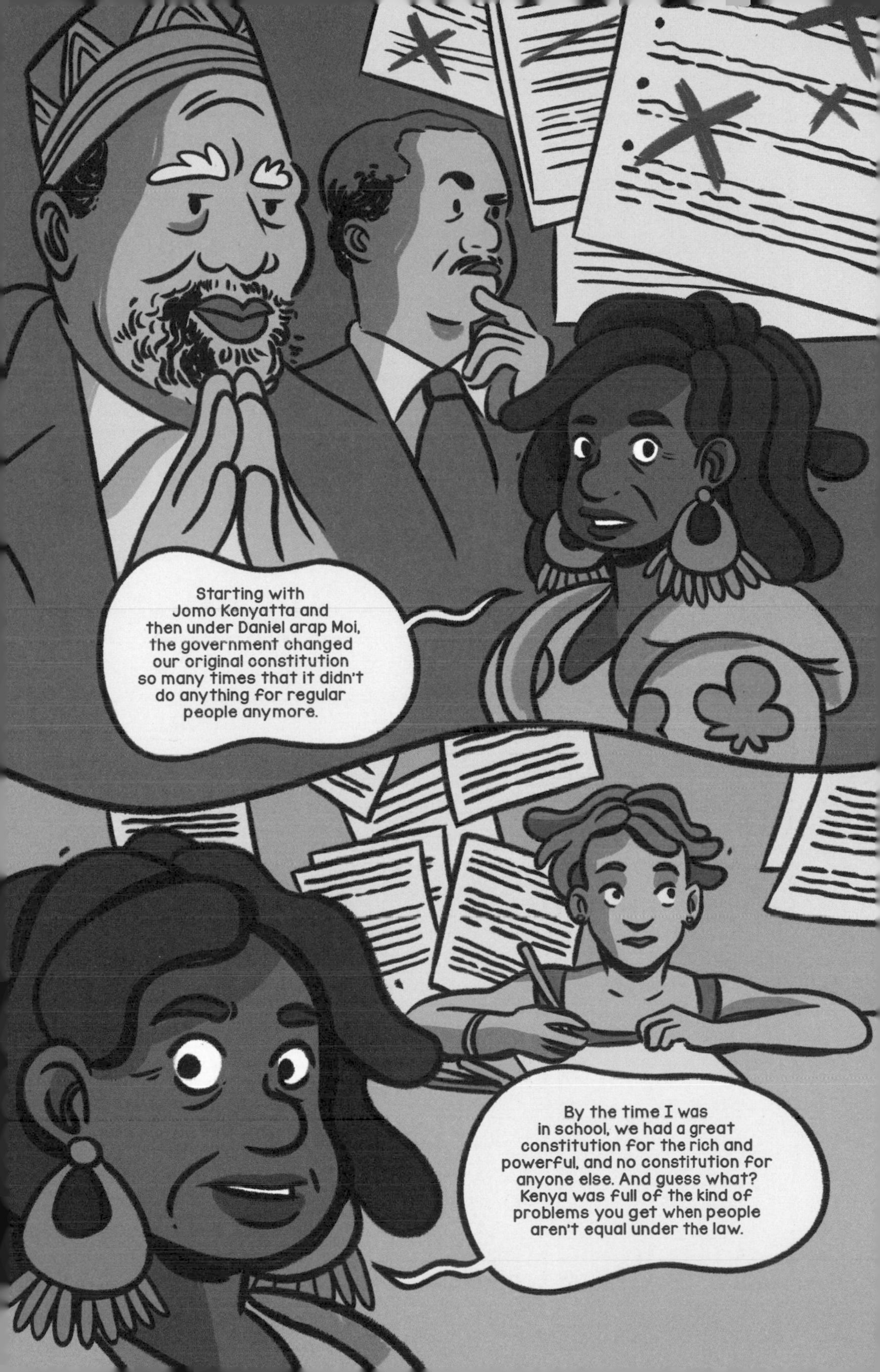
Starting with Jomo Kenyatta and then under Daniel arap Moi, the government changed our original constitution so many times that it didn't do anything for regular people anymore.
By the time I was in school, we had a great constitution for the rich and powerful, and no constitution for anyone else. And guess what? Kenya was full of the kind of problems you get when people aren't equal under the law.

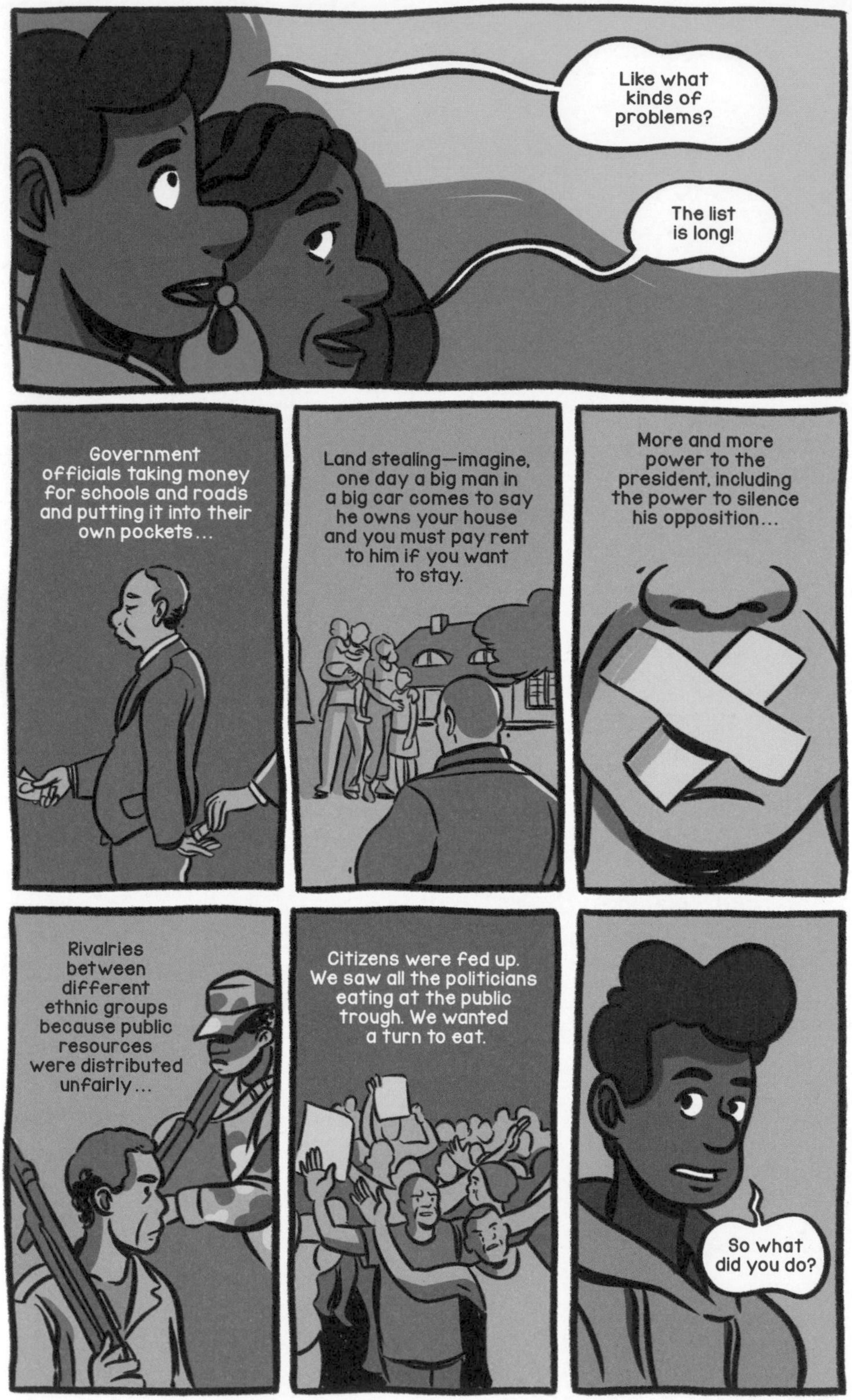
Like what kinds of problems?
The list is long!
Government officials taking money for schools and roads and putting it into their own pockets...
Land stealing—imagine, one day a big man in a big car comes to say he owns your house and you must pay rent to him if you want to stay.
More and more power to the president, including the power to silence his opposition...
Rivalries between different ethnic groups because public resources were distributed unfairly...
Citizens were fed up. We saw all the politicians eating at the public trough. We wanted a turn to eat.
So what did you do?

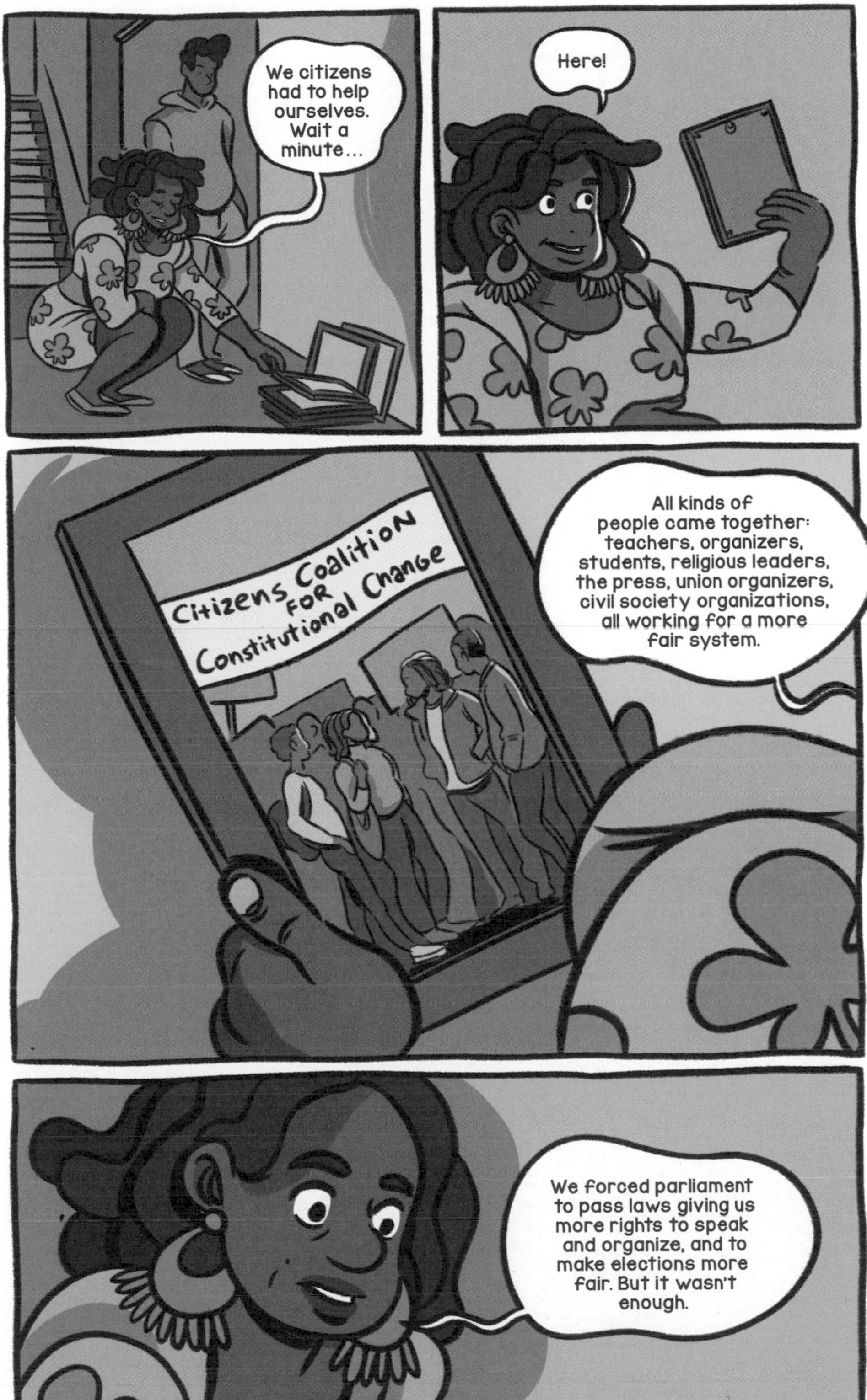
We citizens had to help ourselves. Wait a minute...
Here!
Citizens Coalition for Constitutional Change
All kinds of people came together: teachers, organizers, students, religious leaders, the press, union organizers, civil society organizations, all working for a more fair system.
We forced parliament to pass laws giving us more rights to speak and organize, and to make elections more fair. But it wasn't enough.

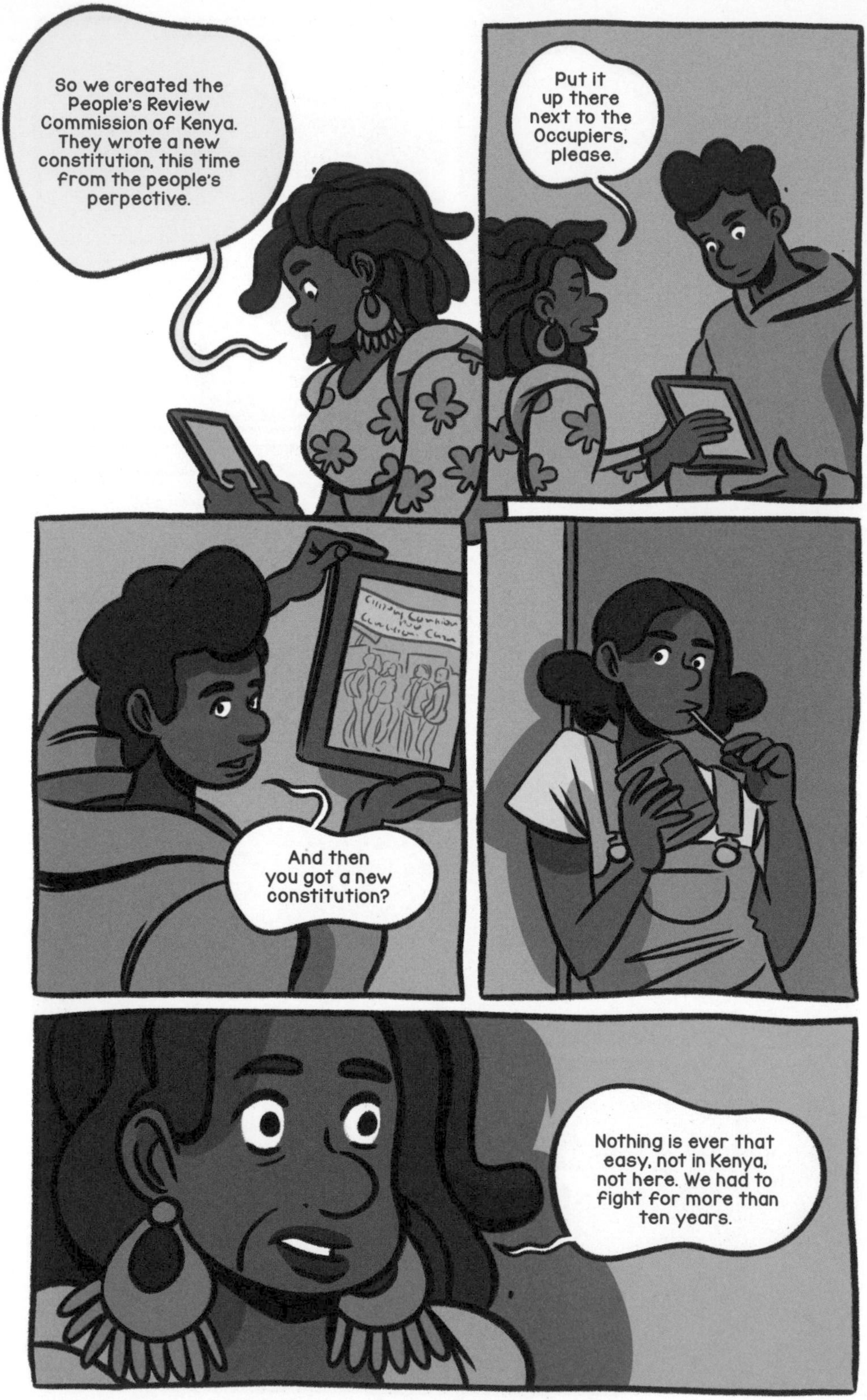
So we created the People's Review Commission of Kenya. They wrote a new constitution, this time from the people's perpective.
Put it up there next to the Occupiers, please.
And then you got a new constitution?
Nothing is ever that easy, not in Kenya, not here. We had to fight for more than ten years.

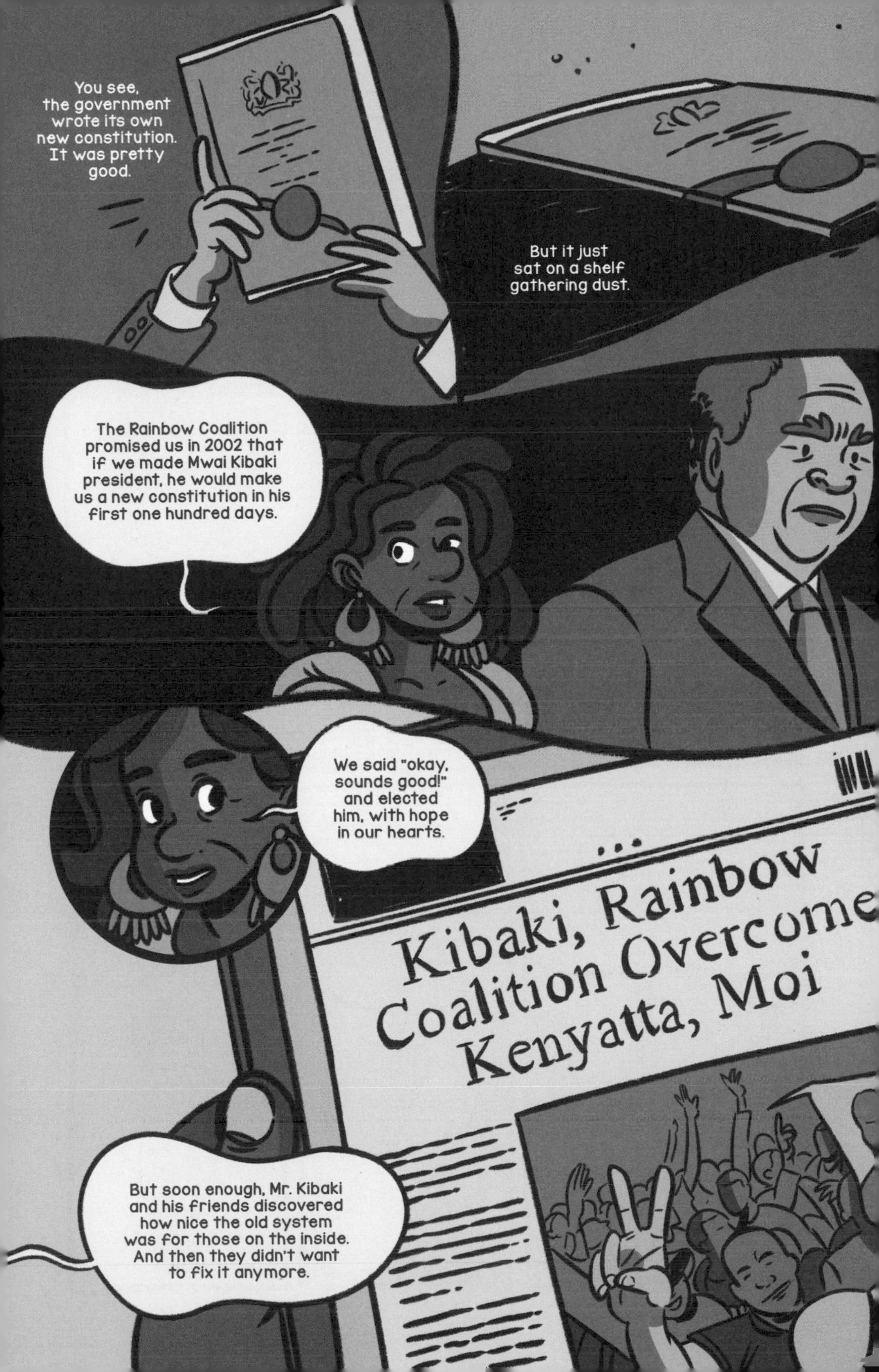

You see, the government wrote its own new constitution. It was pretty good.
But it just sat on a shelf gathering dust.
The Rainbow Coalition promised us in 2002 that if we made Mwai Kibaki president, he would make us a new constitution in his first one hundred days.
We said "okay, sounds good!" and elected him, with hope in our hearts.
Kibaki, Rainbow Coalition Overcome Kenyatta, Moi
But soon enough, Mr. Kibaki and his friends discovered how nice the old system was for those on the inside. And then they didn't want to fix it anymore.

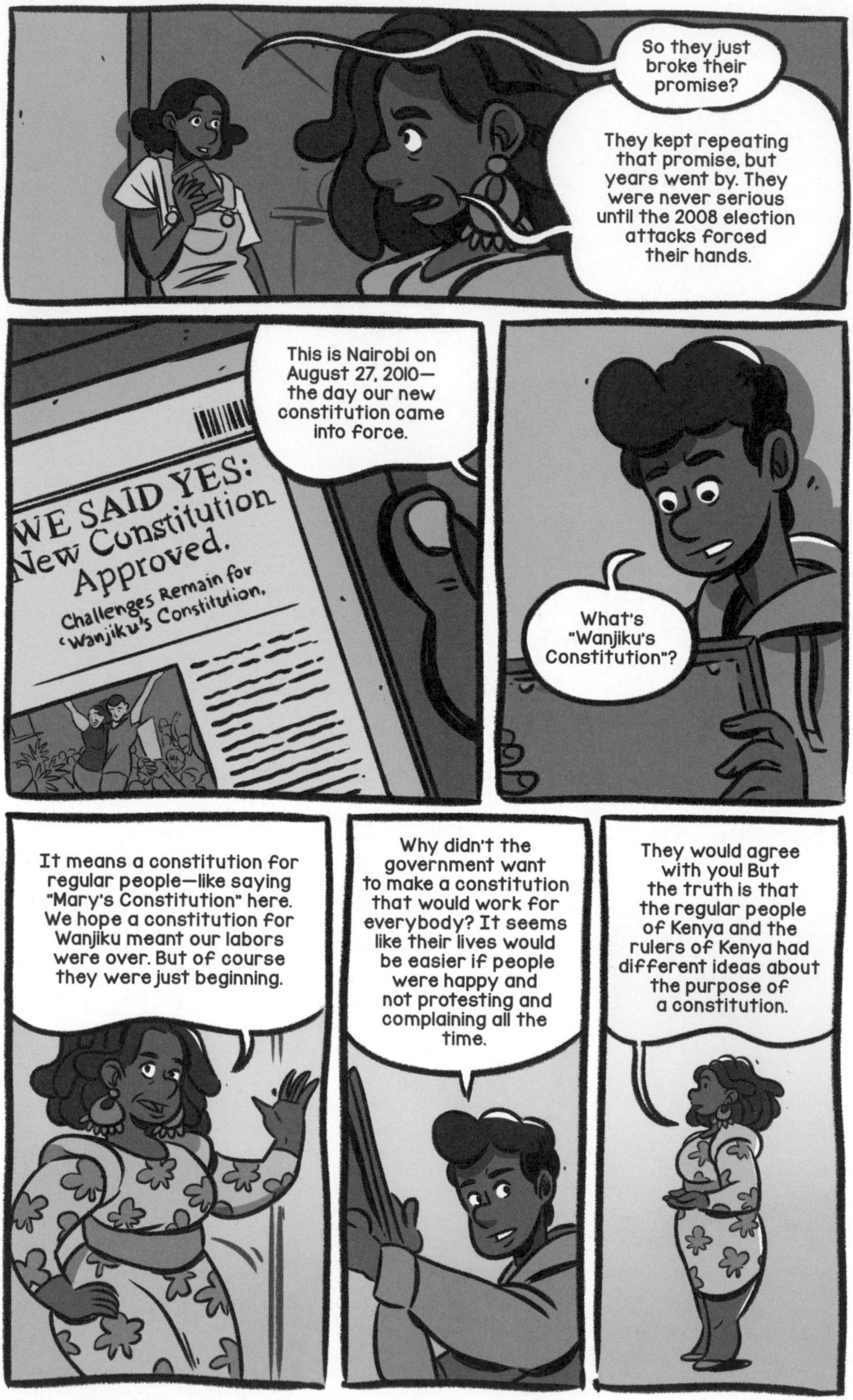
So they just broke their promise?
They kept repeating that promise, but years went by. They were never serious until the 2008 election attacks forced their hands.
This is Nairobi on August 27, 2010—the day our new constitution came into force.
WE SAID YES: New Constitution Approved.
Challenges Remain for 'Wanjiku's Constitution.
What's "Wanjiku's Constitution"?
It means a constitution for regular people—like saying "Mary's Constitution" here. We hope a constitution for Wanjiku meant our labors were over. But of course they were just beginning.
Why didn't the government want to make a constitution that would work for everybody? It seems like their lives would be easier if people were happy and not protesting and complaining all the time.
They would agree with you! But the truth is that the regular people of Kenya and the rulers of Kenya had different ideas about the purpose of a constitution.

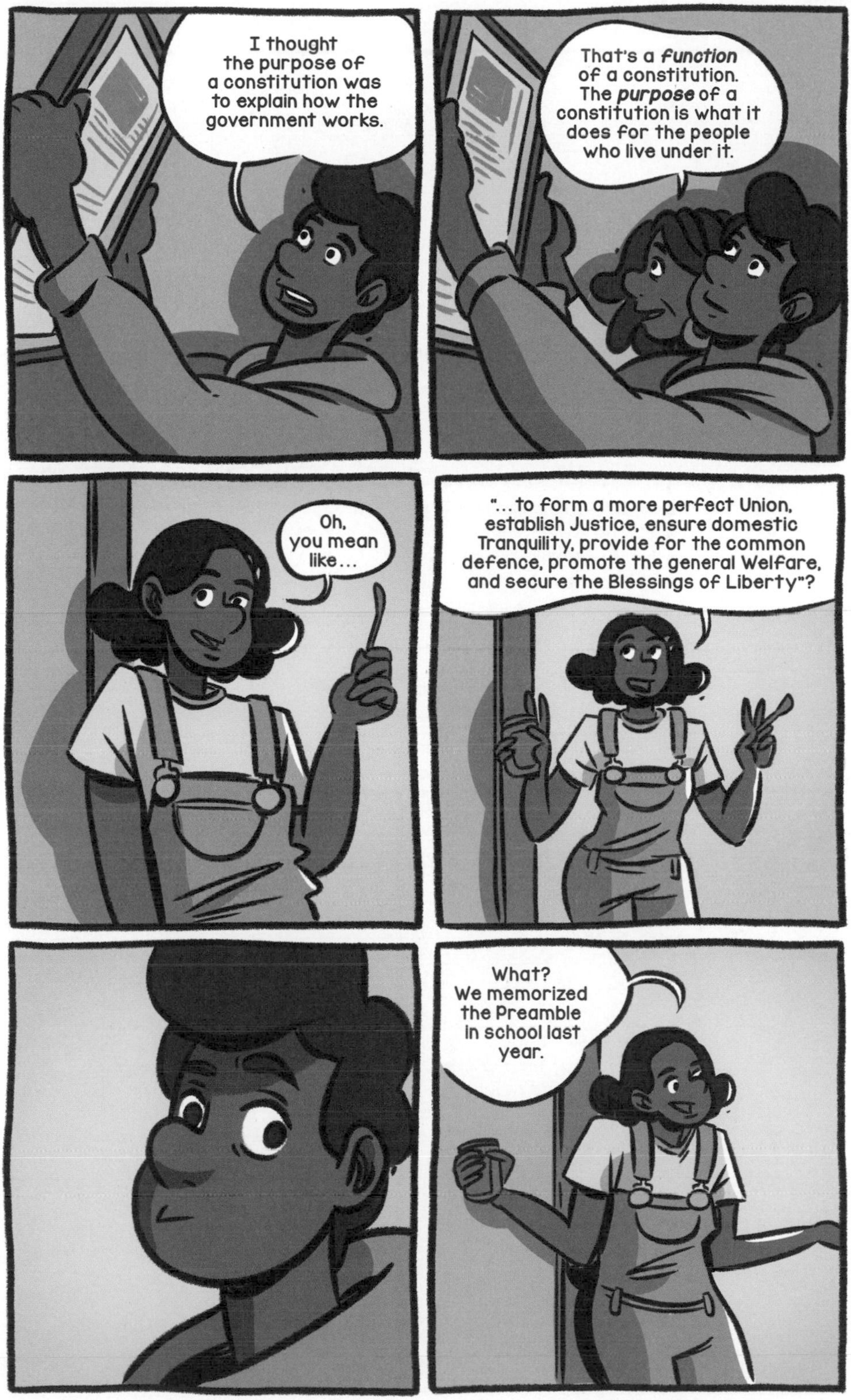

I thought the purpose of a constitution was to explain how the government works.
That's a *function* of a constitution. The *purpose* of a constitution is what it does for the people who live under it.
Oh, you mean like...
"...to form a more perfect Union, establish Justice, ensure domestic Tranquility, provide for the common defence, promote the general Welfare, and secure the Blessings of Liberty"?
What? We memorized the Preamble in school last year.

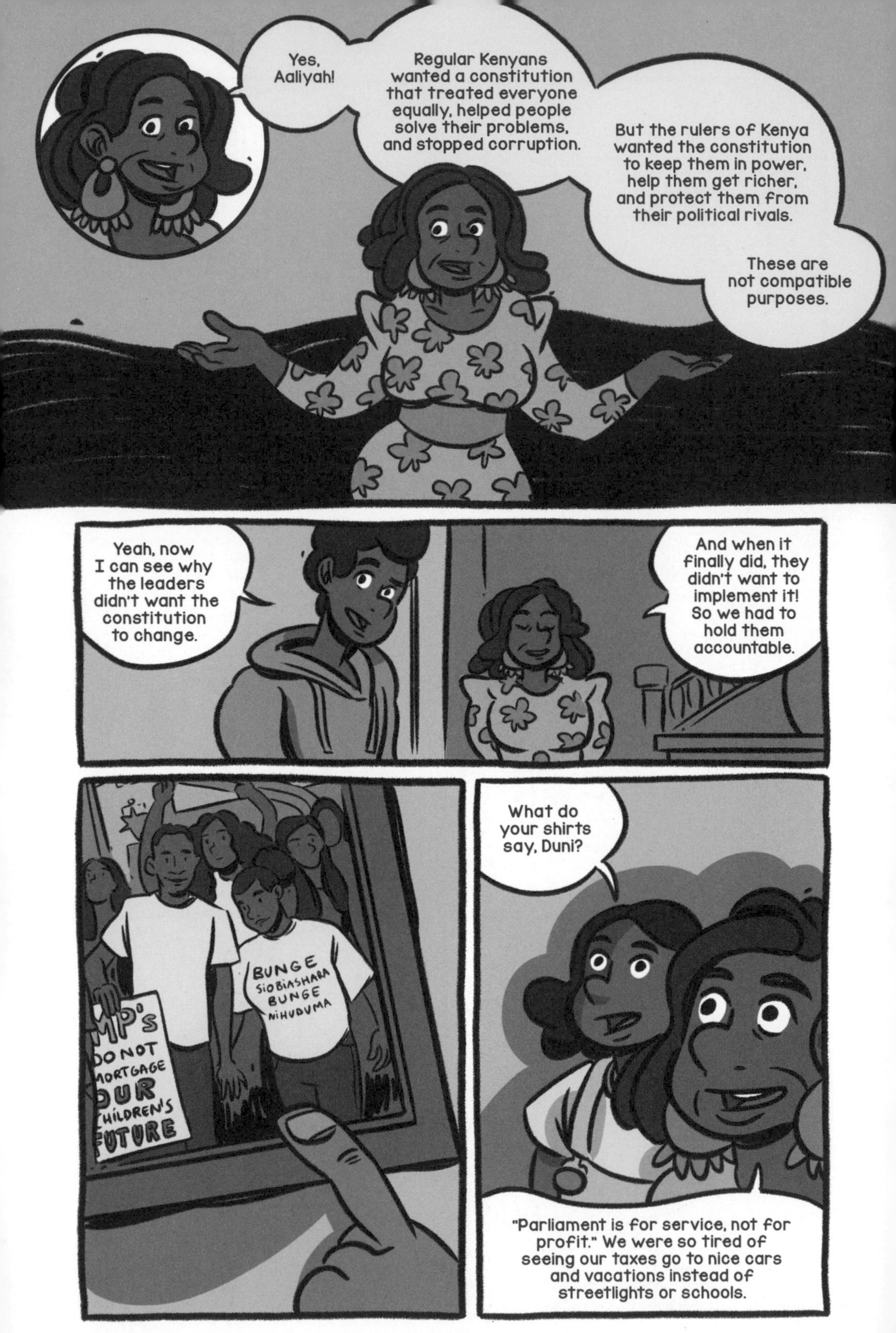
Yes, Aaliyah!
Regular Kenyans wanted a constitution that treated everyone equally, helped people solve their problems, and stopped corruption.
But the rulers of Kenya wanted the constitution to keep them in power, help them get richer, and protect them from their political rivals.
These are not compatible purposes.
Yeah, now I can see why the leaders didn't want the constitution to change.
And when it finally did, they didn't want to implement it! So we had to hold them accountable.
BUNGE SIO BIASHARA BUNGE NI HUDUMA
MP'S DO NOT MORTGAGE OUR CHILDREN'S FUTURE
What do your shirts say, Duni?
"Parliament is for service, not for profit." We were so tired of seeing our taxes go to nice cars and vacations instead of streetlights or schools.

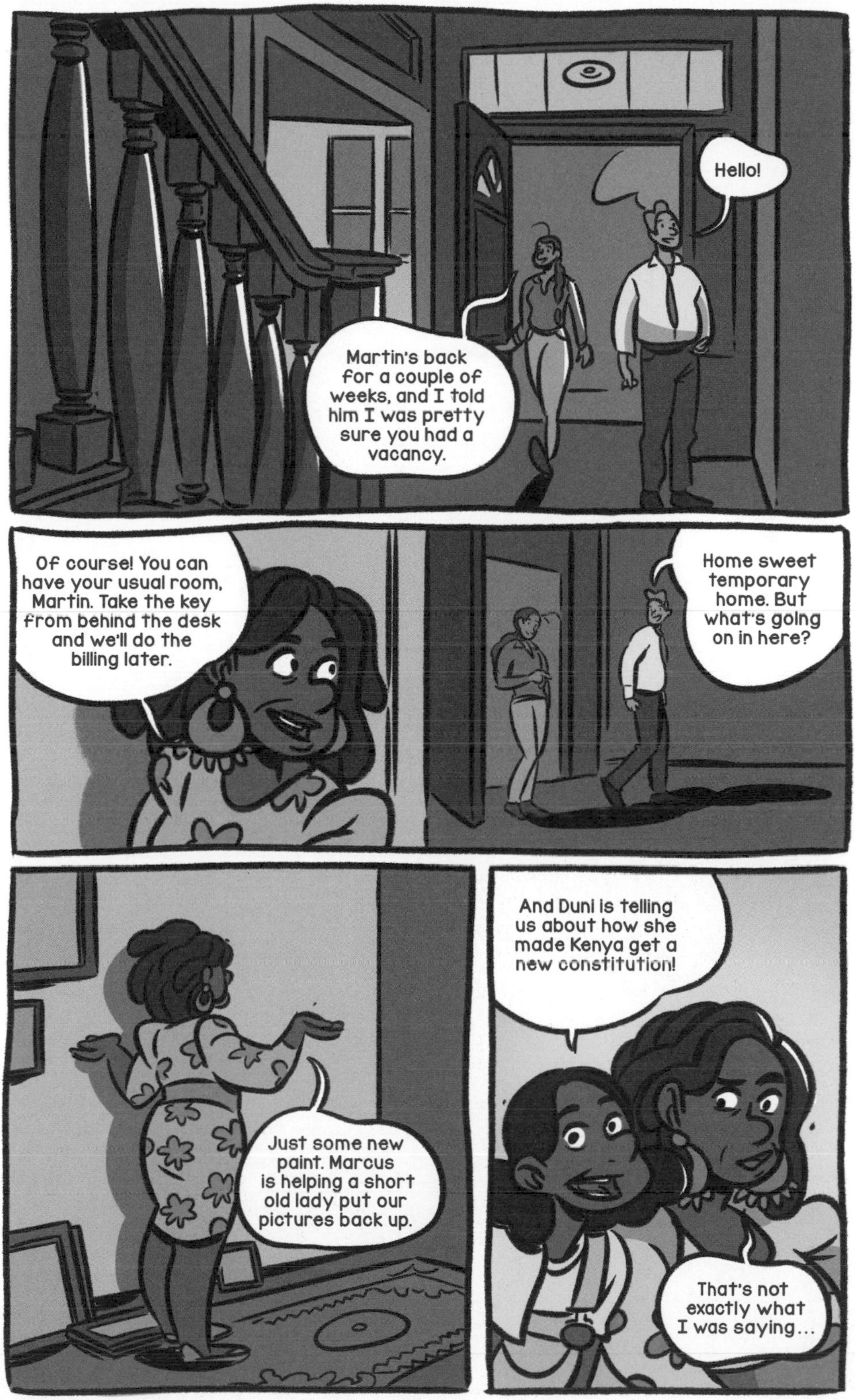
Hello!
Martin's back for a couple of weeks, and I told him I was pretty sure you had a vacancy.
Of course! You can have your usual room, Martin. Take the key from behind the desk and we'll do the billing later.
Home sweet temporary home. But what's going on in here?
Just some new paint. Marcus is helping a short old lady put our pictures back up.
And Duni is telling us about how she made Kenya get a new constitution!
That's not exactly what I was saying...

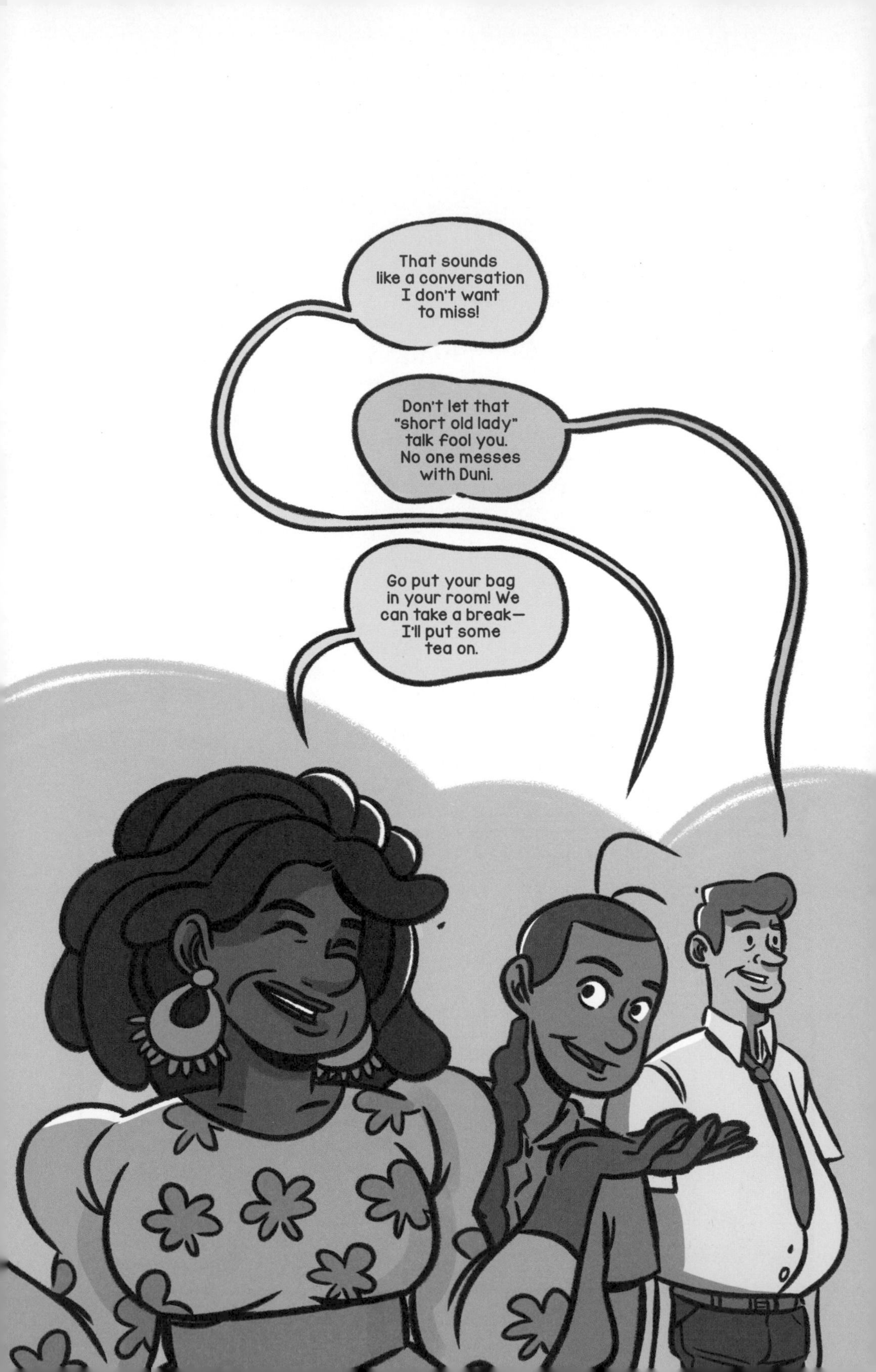
That sounds like a conversation I don't want to miss!
Don't let that "short old lady" talk fool you. No one messes with Duni.
Go put your bag in your room! We can take a break— I'll put some tea on.

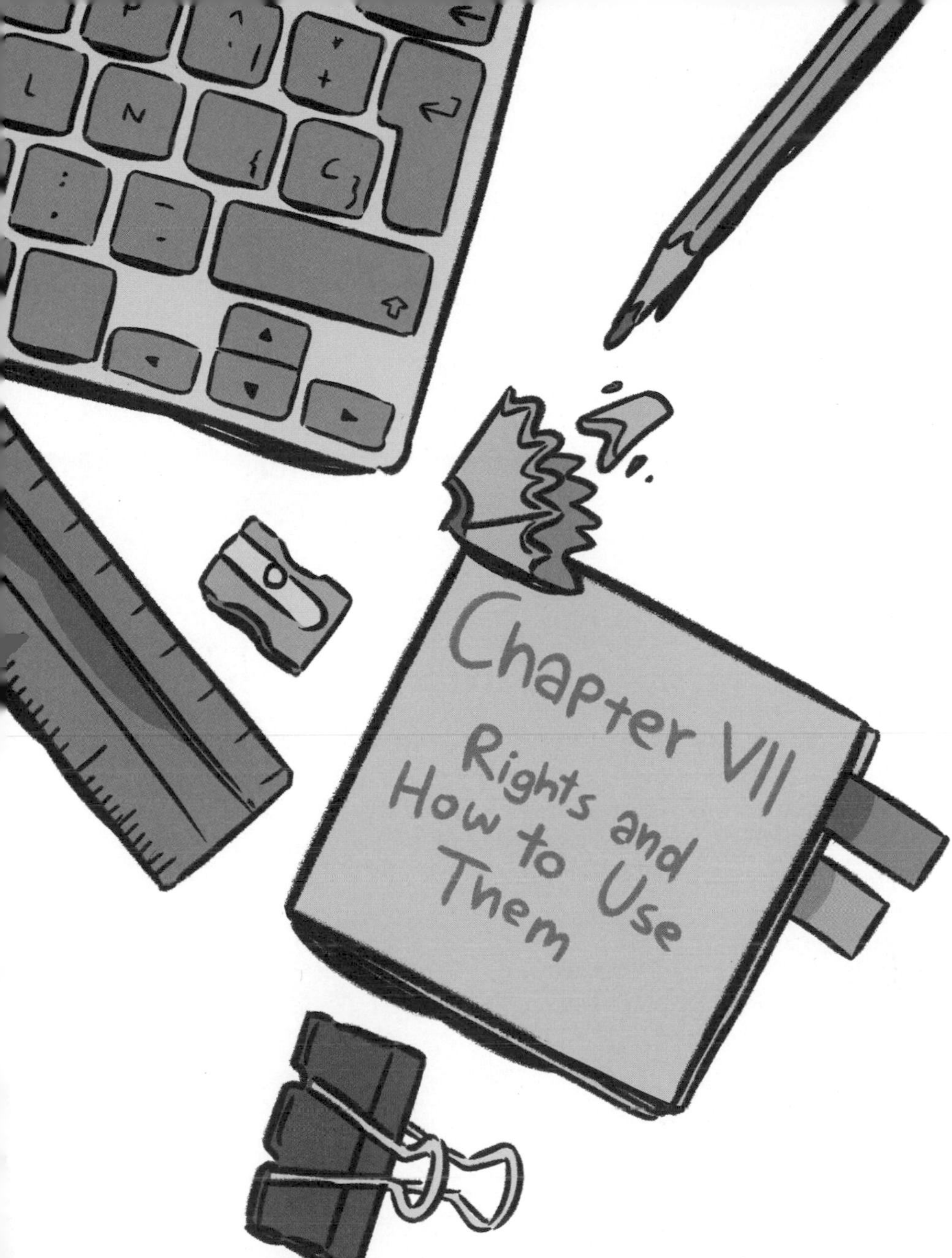
Chapter VII
Rights and How to Use Them

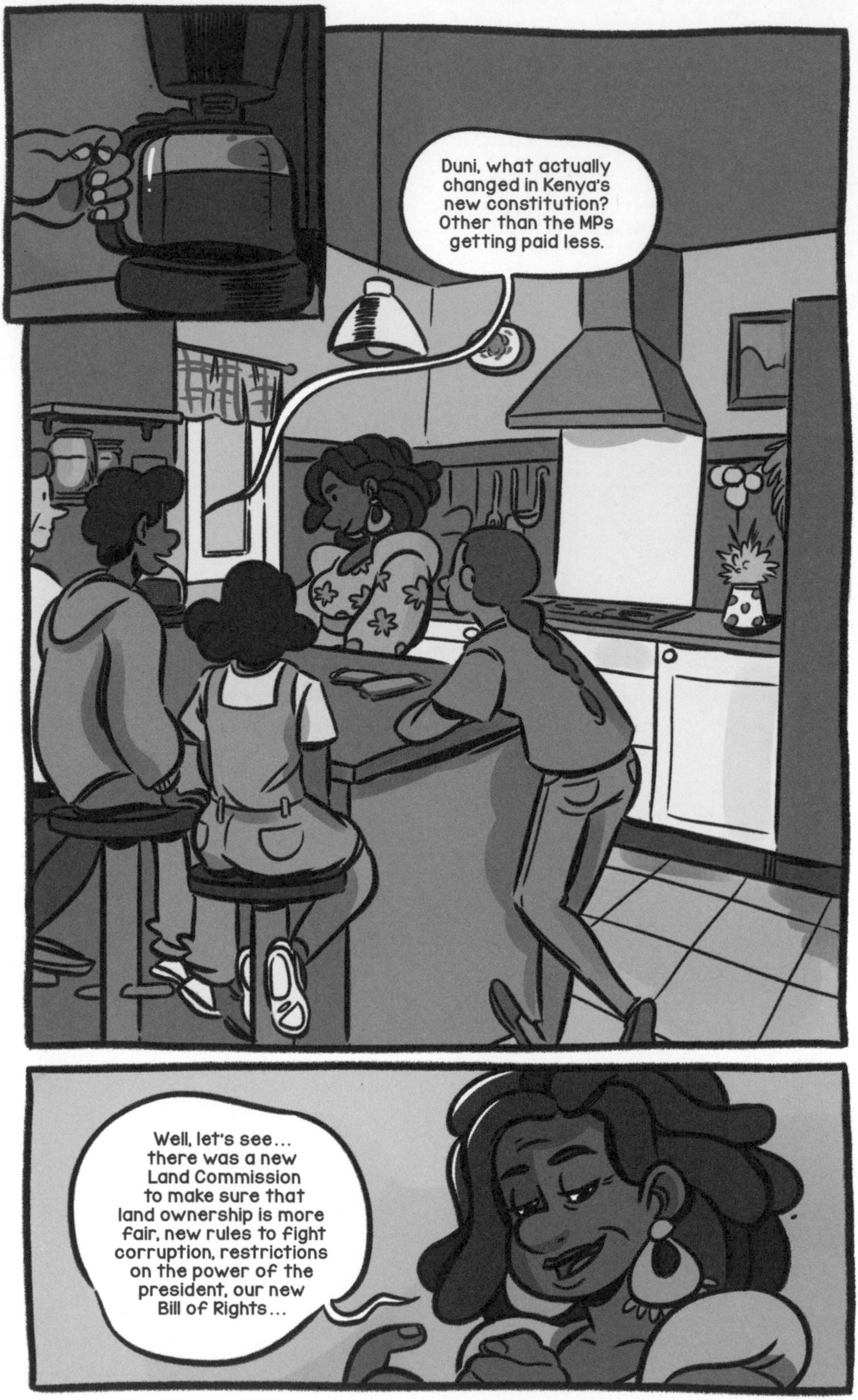
Duni, what actually changed in Kenya's new constitution? Other than the MPs getting paid less.
Well, let's see... there was a new Land Commission to make sure that land ownership is more fair, new rules to fight corruption, restrictions on the power of the president, our new Bill of Rights...

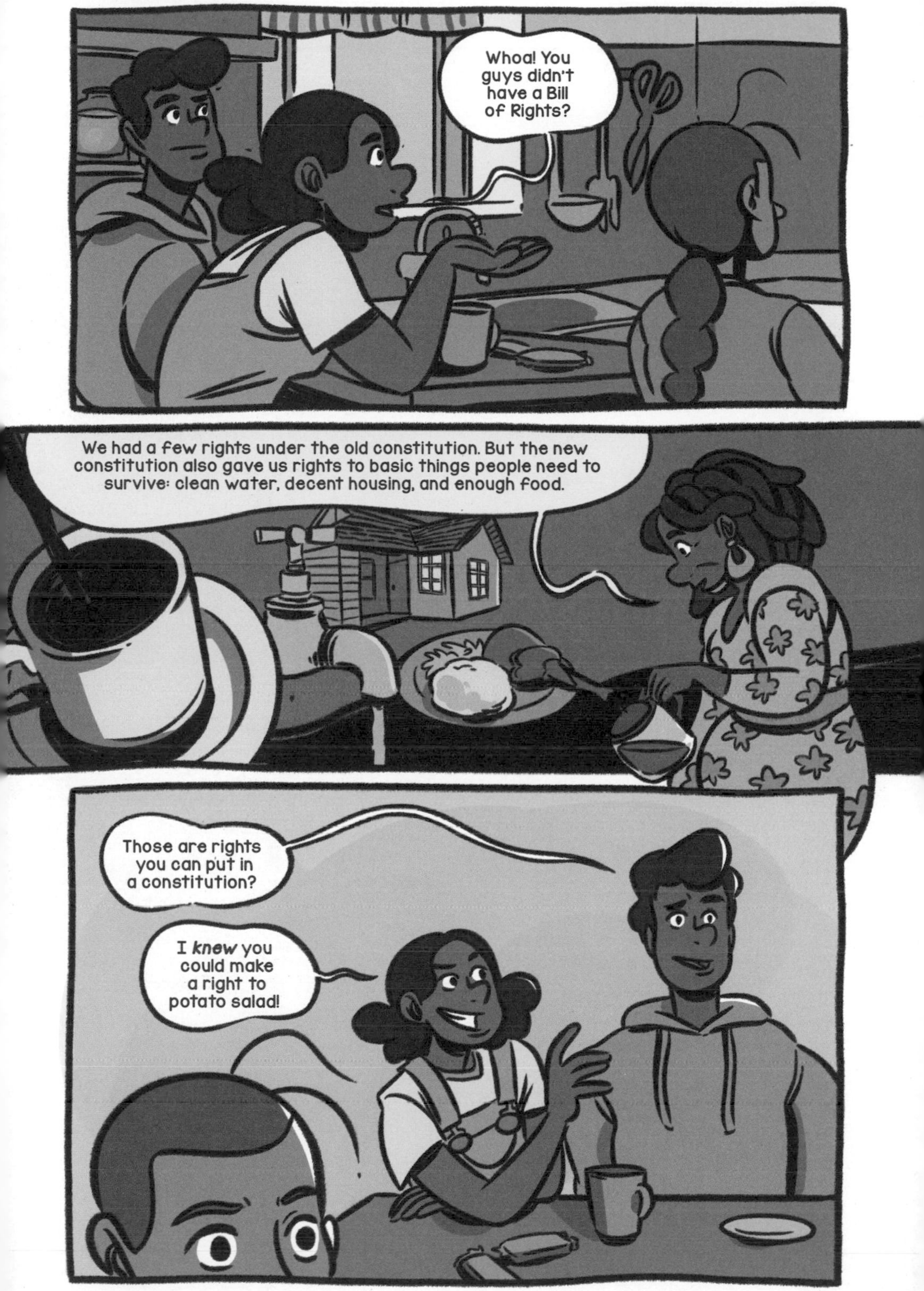
Whoa! You guys didn't have a Bill of Rights?
We had a few rights under the old constitution. But the new constitution also gave us rights to basic things people need to survive: clean water, decent housing, and enough food.
Those are rights you can put in a constitution?
I *knew* you could make a right to potato salad!

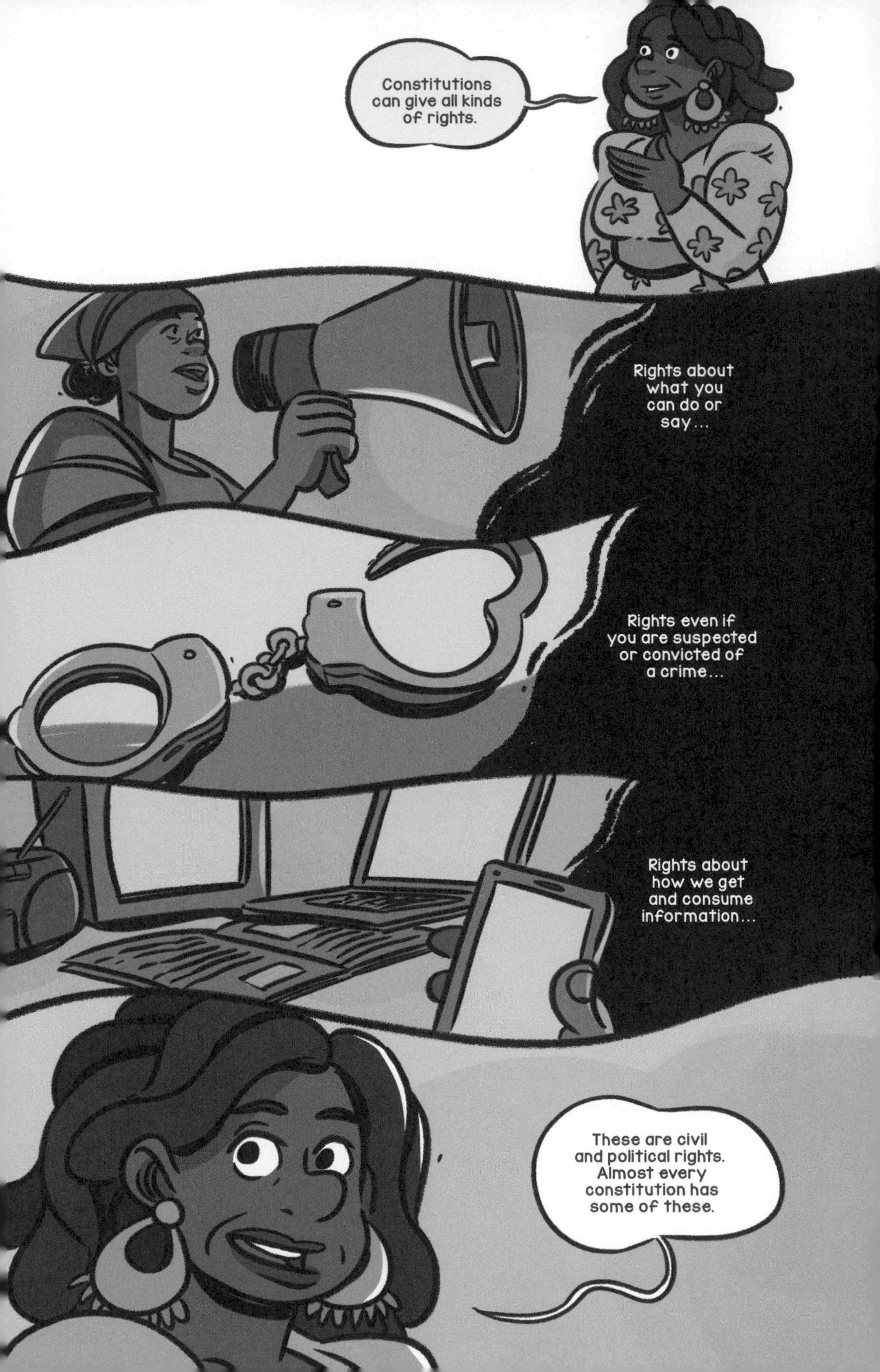
Constitutions can give all kinds of rights.
Rights about what you can do or say...
Rights even if you are suspected or convicted of a crime...
Rights about how we get and consume information...
These are civil and political rights. Almost every constitution has some of these.

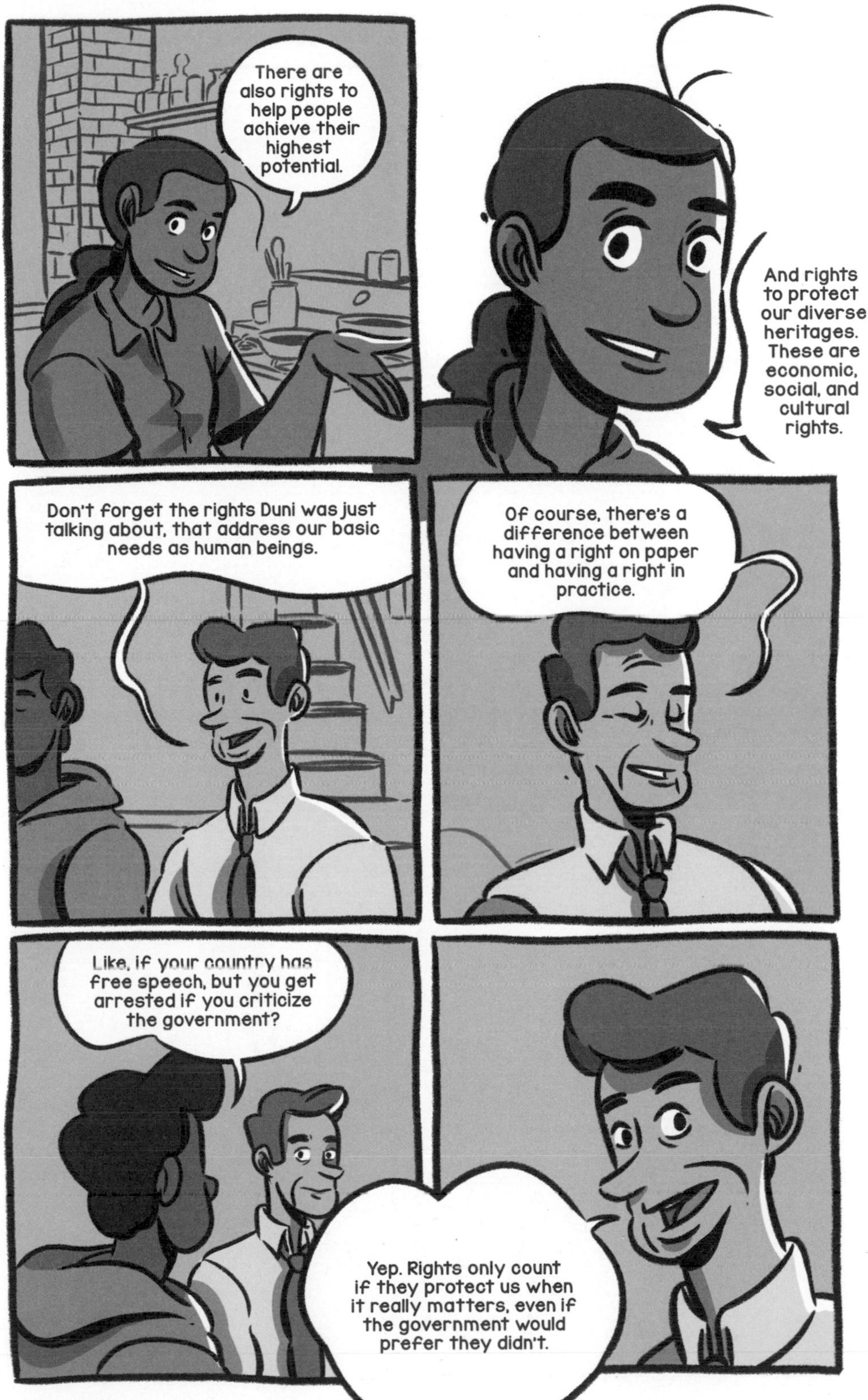
There are also rights to help people achieve their highest potential.
And rights to protect our diverse heritages. These are economic, social, and cultural rights.
Don't forget the rights Duni was just talking about, that address our basic needs as human beings.
Of course, there's a difference between having a right on paper and having a right in practice.
Like, if your country has free speech, but you get arrested if you criticize the government?
Yep. Rights only count if they protect us when it really matters, even if the government would prefer they didn't.

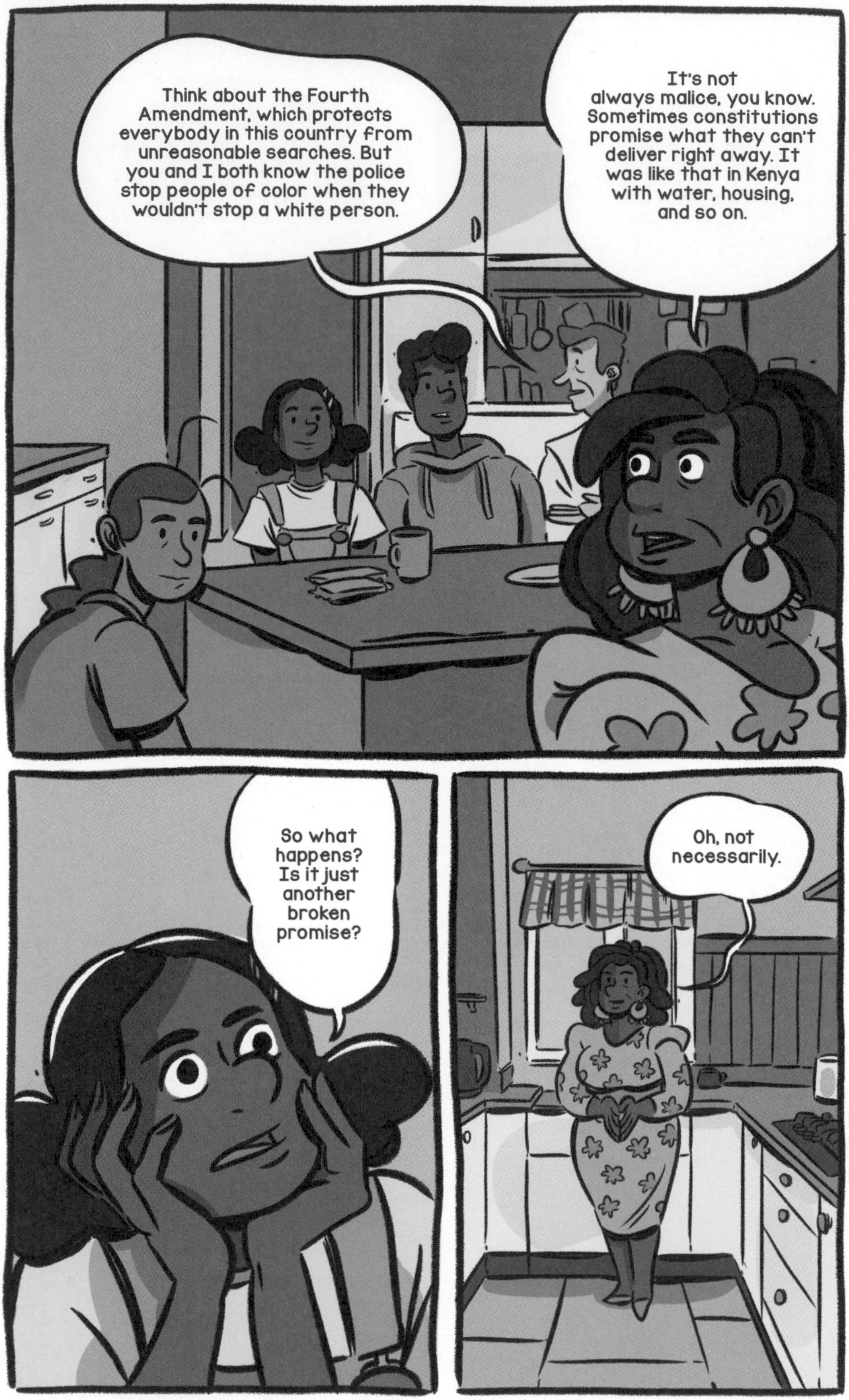

Think about the Fourth Amendment, which protects everybody in this country from unreasonable searches. But you and I both know the police stop people of color when they wouldn't stop a white person.
It's not always malice, you know. Sometimes constitutions promise what they can't deliver right away. It was like that in Kenya with water, housing, and so on.
So what happens? Is it just another broken promise?
Oh, not necessarily.

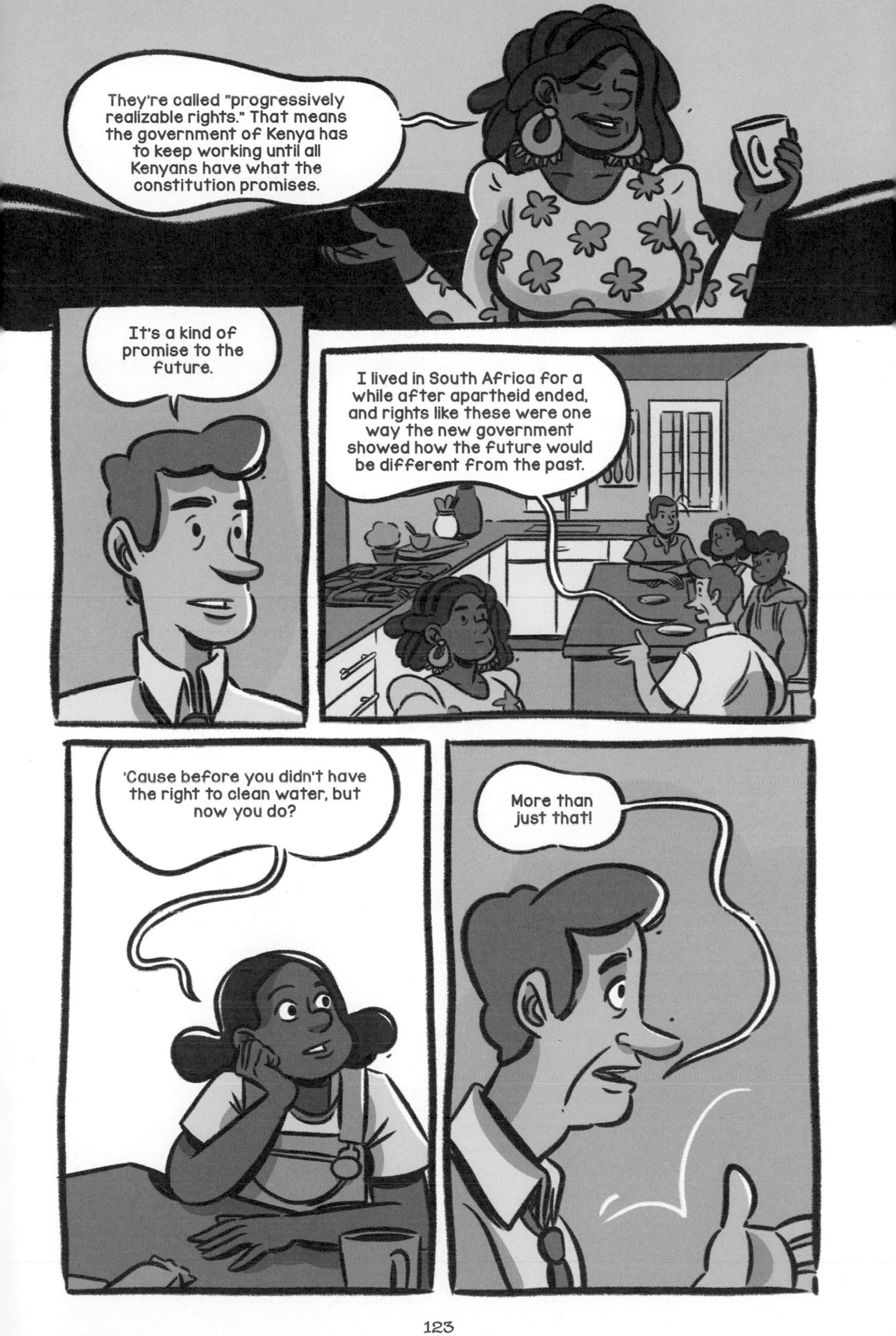
They're called "progressively realizable rights." That means the government of Kenya has to keep working until all Kenyans have what the constitution promises.
It's a kind of promise to the future.
I lived in South Africa for a while after apartheid ended, and rights like these were one way the new government showed how the future would be different from the past.
'Cause before you didn't have the right to clean water, but now you do?
More than just that!

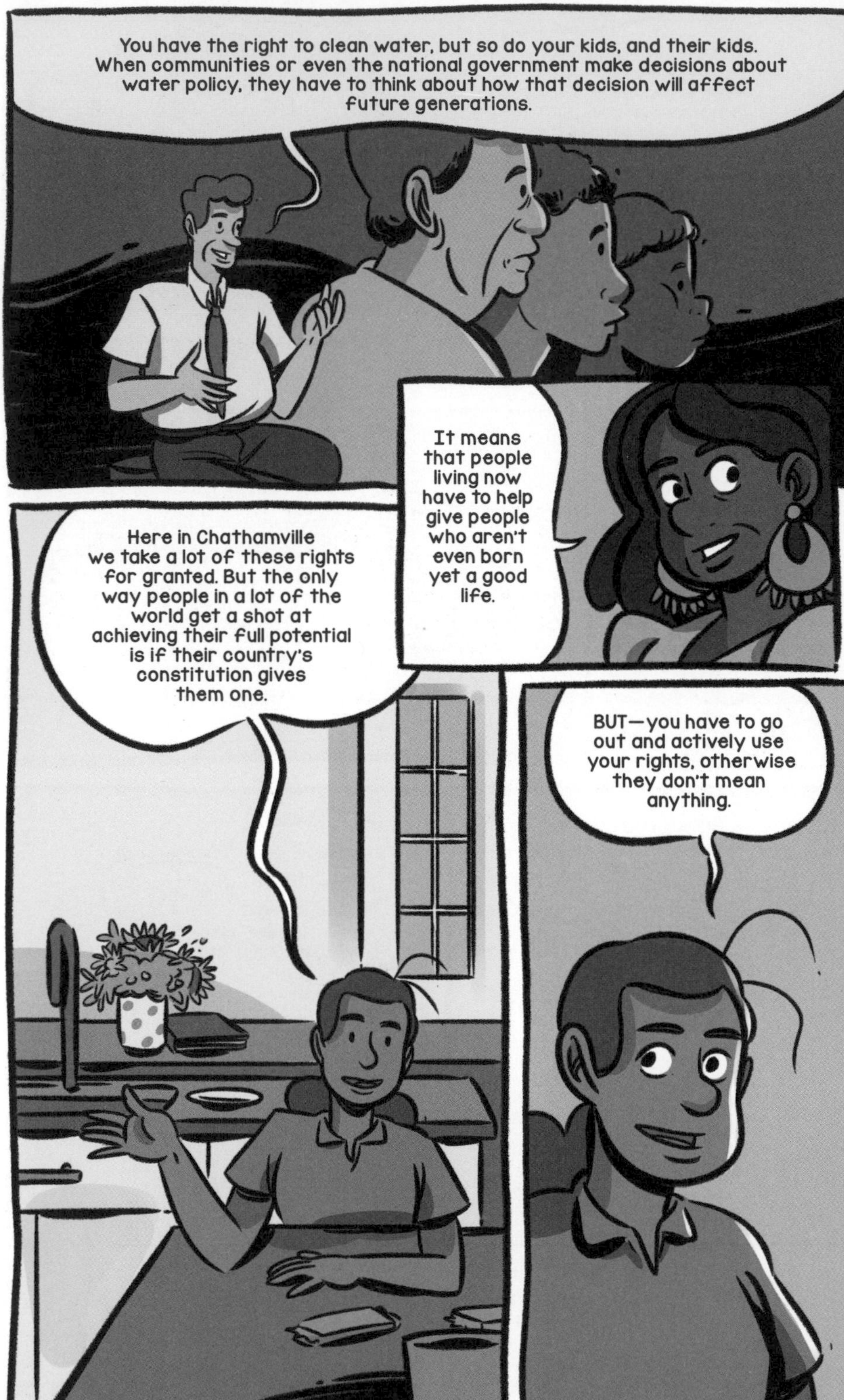
You have the right to clean water, but so do your kids, and their kids. When communities or even the national government make decisions about water policy, they have to think about how that decision will affect future generations.
It means that people living now have to help give people who aren't even born yet a good life.
Here in Chathamville we take a lot of these rights for granted. But the only way people in a lot of the world get a shot at achieving their full potential is if their country's constitution gives them one.
BUT—you have to go out and actively use your rights, otherwise they don't mean anything.

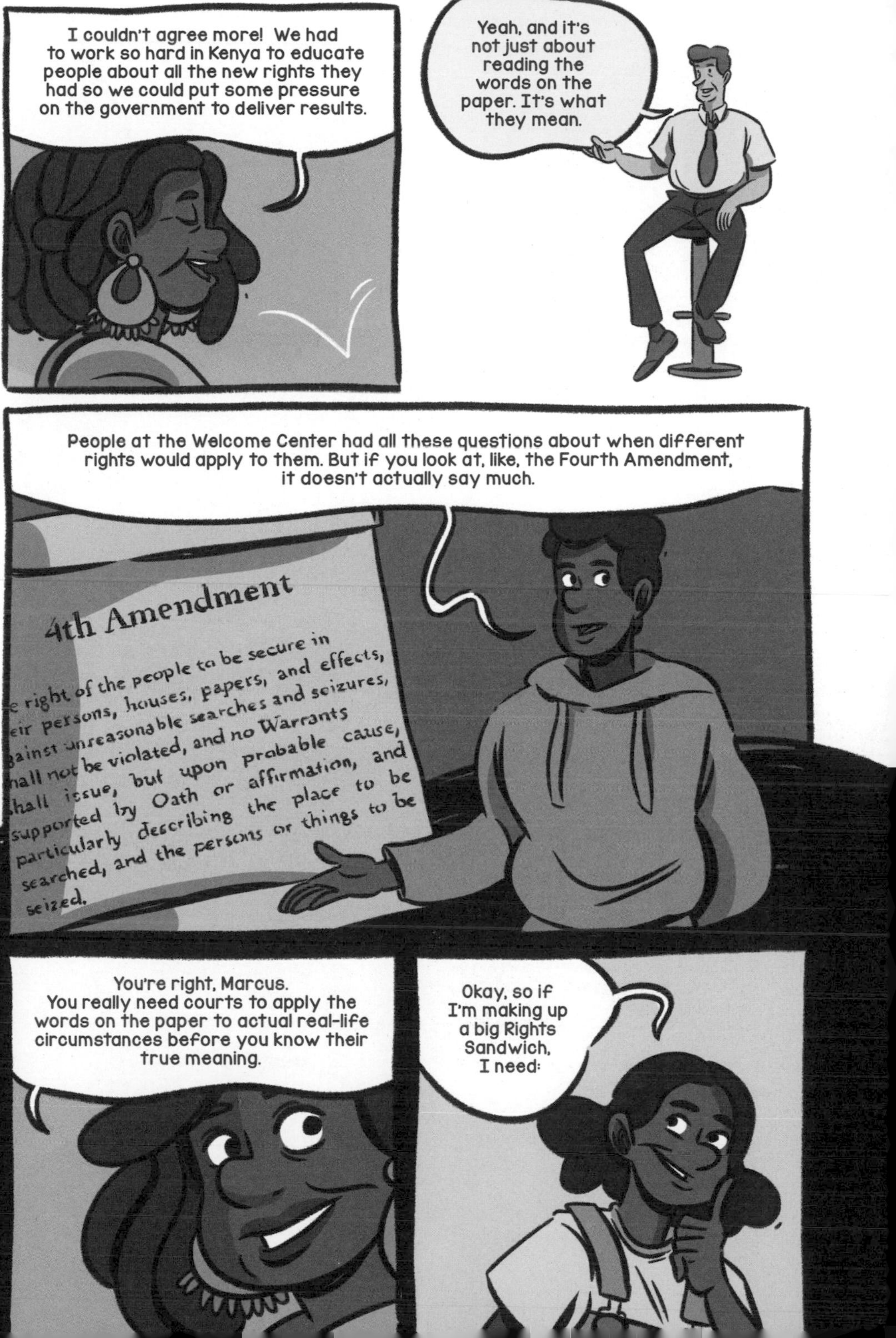
I couldn't agree more! We had to work so hard in Kenya to educate people about all the new rights they had so we could put some pressure on the government to deliver results.
Yeah, and it's not just about reading the words on the paper. It's what they mean.
People at the Welcome Center had all these questions about when different rights would apply to them. But if you look at, like, the Fourth Amendment, it doesn't actually say much.
4th Amendment
e right of the people to be secure in eir persons, houses, papers, and effects, gainst unreasonable searches and seizures, hall not be violated, and no Warrants hall issue, but upon probable cause, supported by Oath or affirmation, and particularly describing the place to be searched, and the persons or things to be seized.
You're right, Marcus. You really need courts to apply the words on the paper to actual real-life circumstances before you know their true meaning.
Okay, so if I'm making up a big Rights Sandwich, I need:

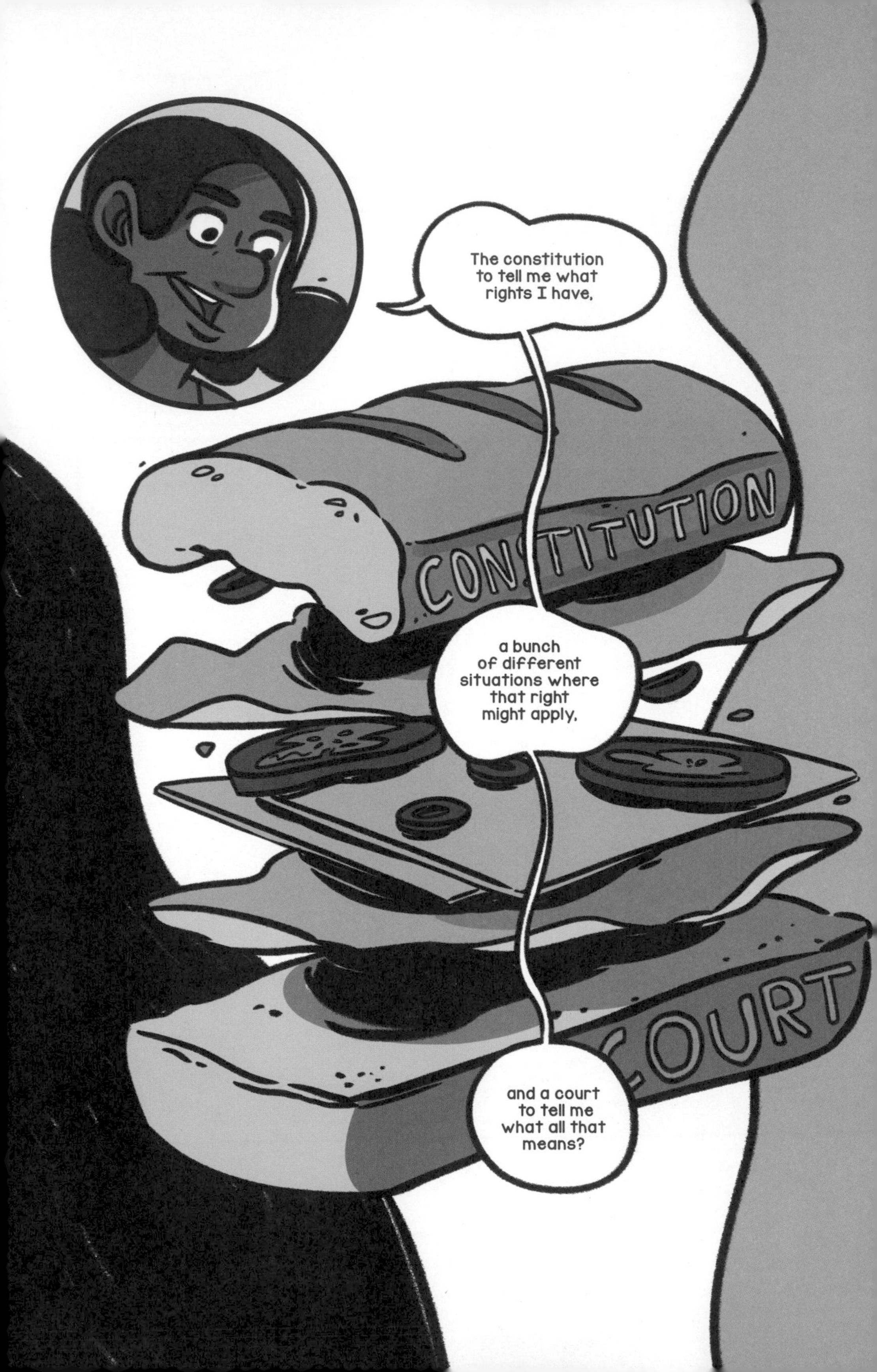
The constitution to tell me what rights I have,
CONSTITUTION
a bunch of different situations where that right might apply,
COURT
and a court to tell me what all that means?

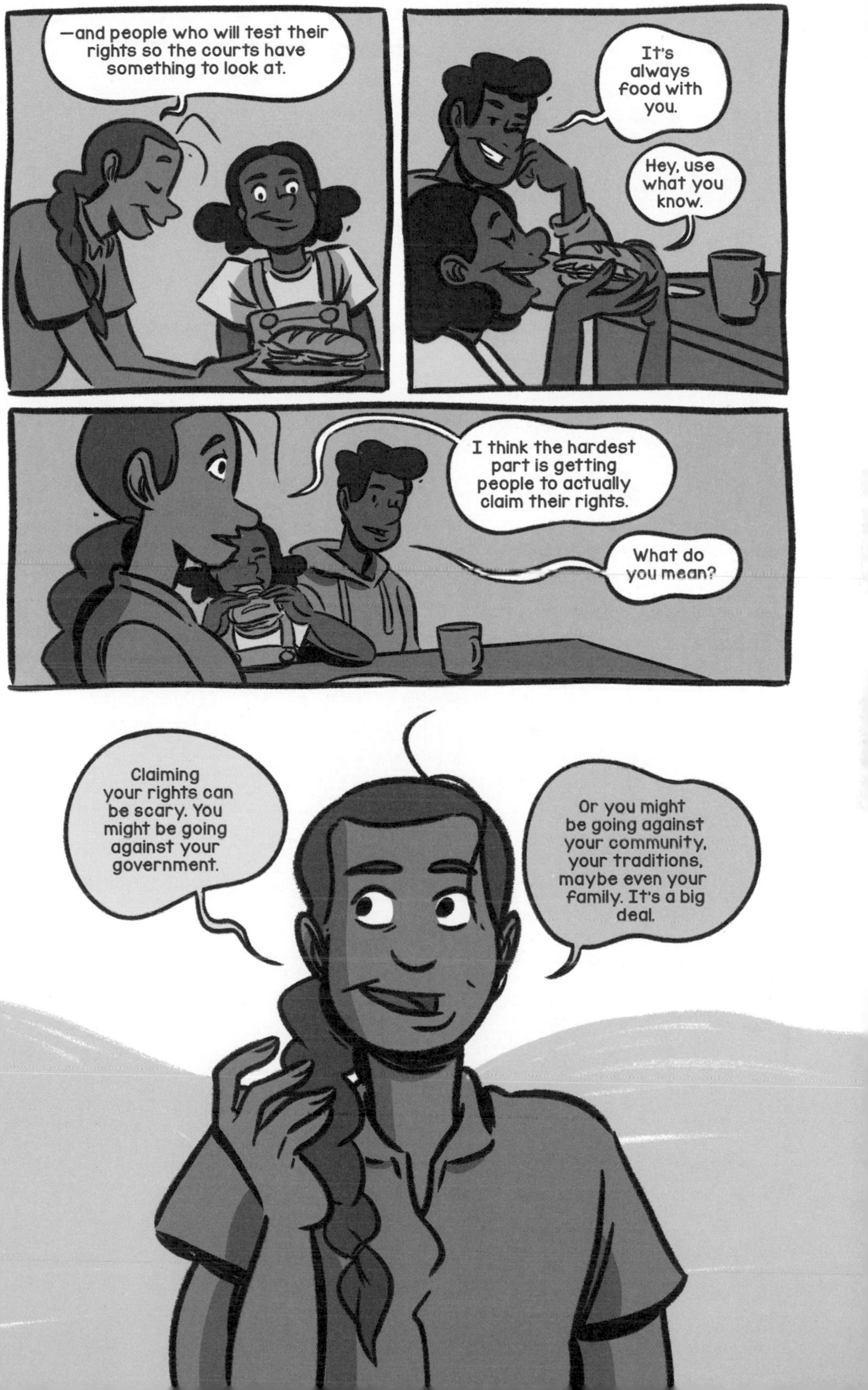
—and people who will test their rights so the courts have something to look at.
It's always food with you.
Hey, use what you know.
I think the hardest part is getting people to actually claim their rights.
What do you mean?
Claiming your rights can be scary. You might be going against your government.
Or you might be going against your community, your traditions, maybe even your family. It's a big deal.

What kind of family wouldn't want you to have your rights?

Even people who love you can be afraid if you decide to push the envelope.

You guys know I grew up in northern India, right? My hometown is a pretty tiny village in Uttar Pradesh.

My village was so small we didn't even have a school! We had to walk to the next village over. Plus we had to pay to be a student— school wasn't free.

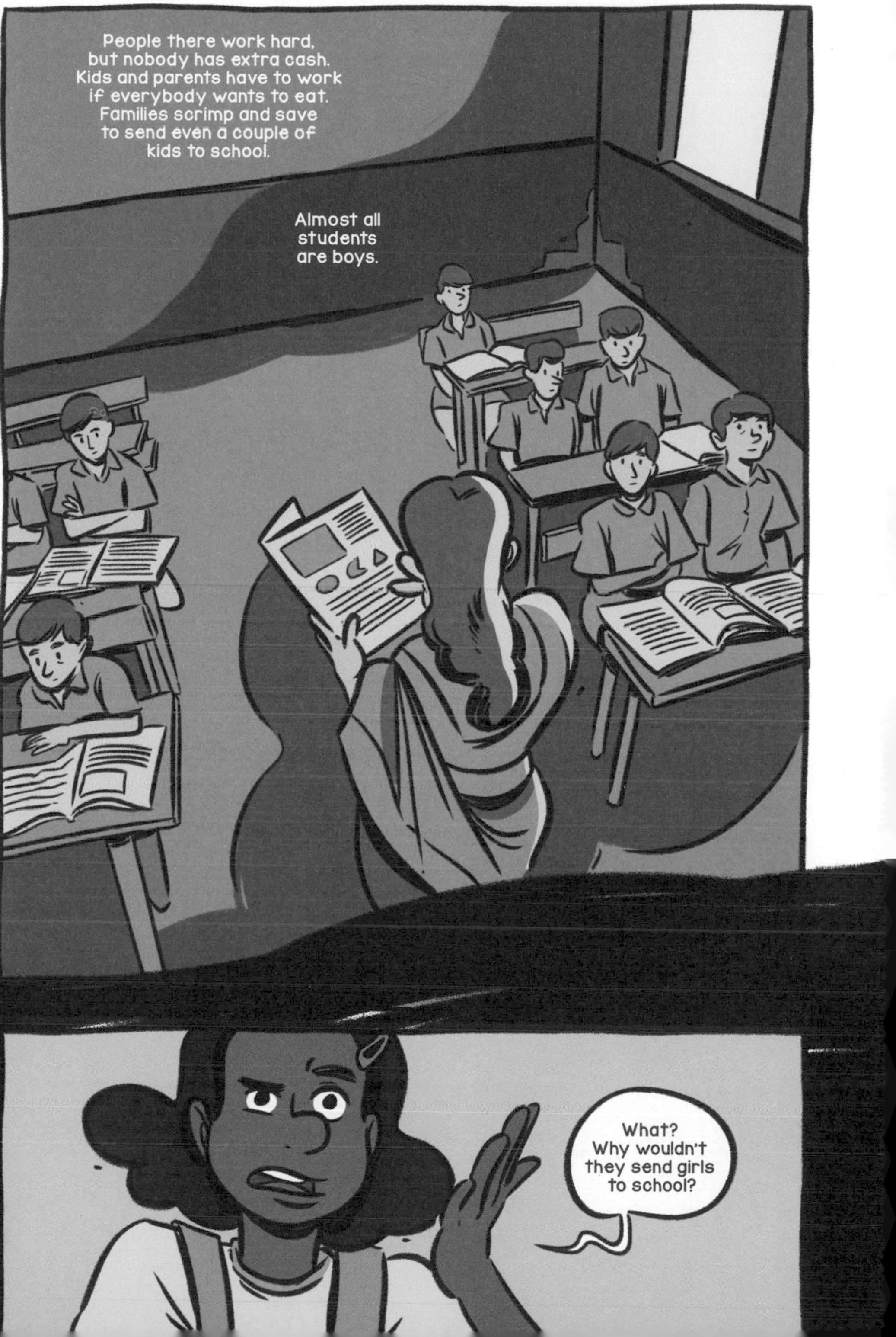
People there work hard, but nobody has extra cash. Kids and parents have to work if everybody wants to eat. Families scrimp and save to send even a couple of kids to school.
Almost all students are boys.
What? Why wouldn't they send girls to school?

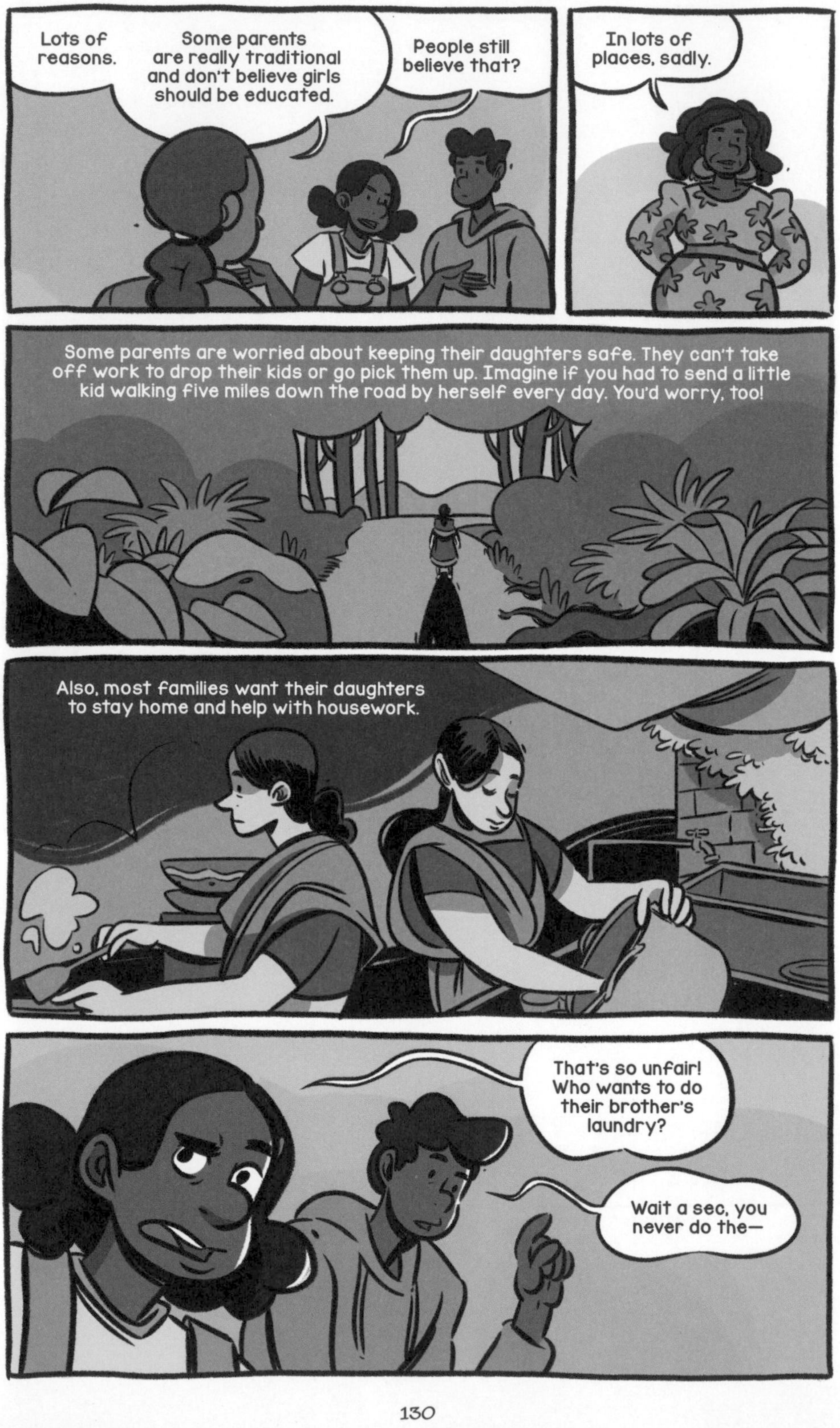
Lots of reasons.
Some parents are really traditional and don't believe girls should be educated.
People still believe that?
In lots of places, sadly.
Some parents are worried about keeping their daughters safe. They can't take off work to drop their kids or go pick them up. Imagine if you had to send a little kid walking five miles down the road by herself every day. You'd worry, too!
Also, most families want their daughters to stay home and help with housework.
That's so unfair! Who wants to do their brother's laundry?
Wait a sec, you never do the—

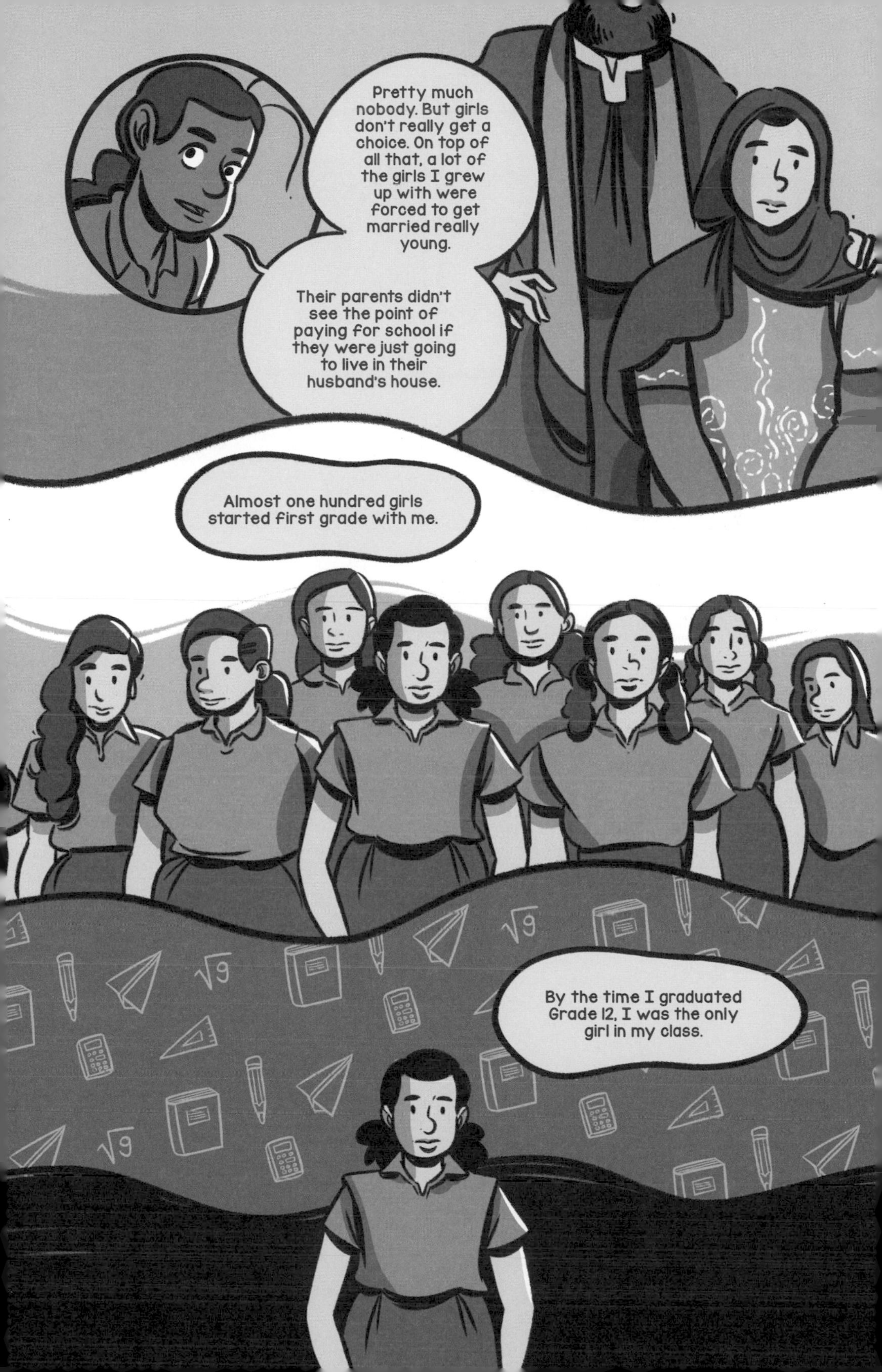
Pretty much nobody. But girls don't really get a choice. On top of all that, a lot of the girls I grew up with were forced to get married really young.
Their parents didn't see the point of paying for school if they were just going to live in their husband's house.
Almost one hundred girls started first grade with me.
By the time I graduated Grade 12, I was the only girl in my class.

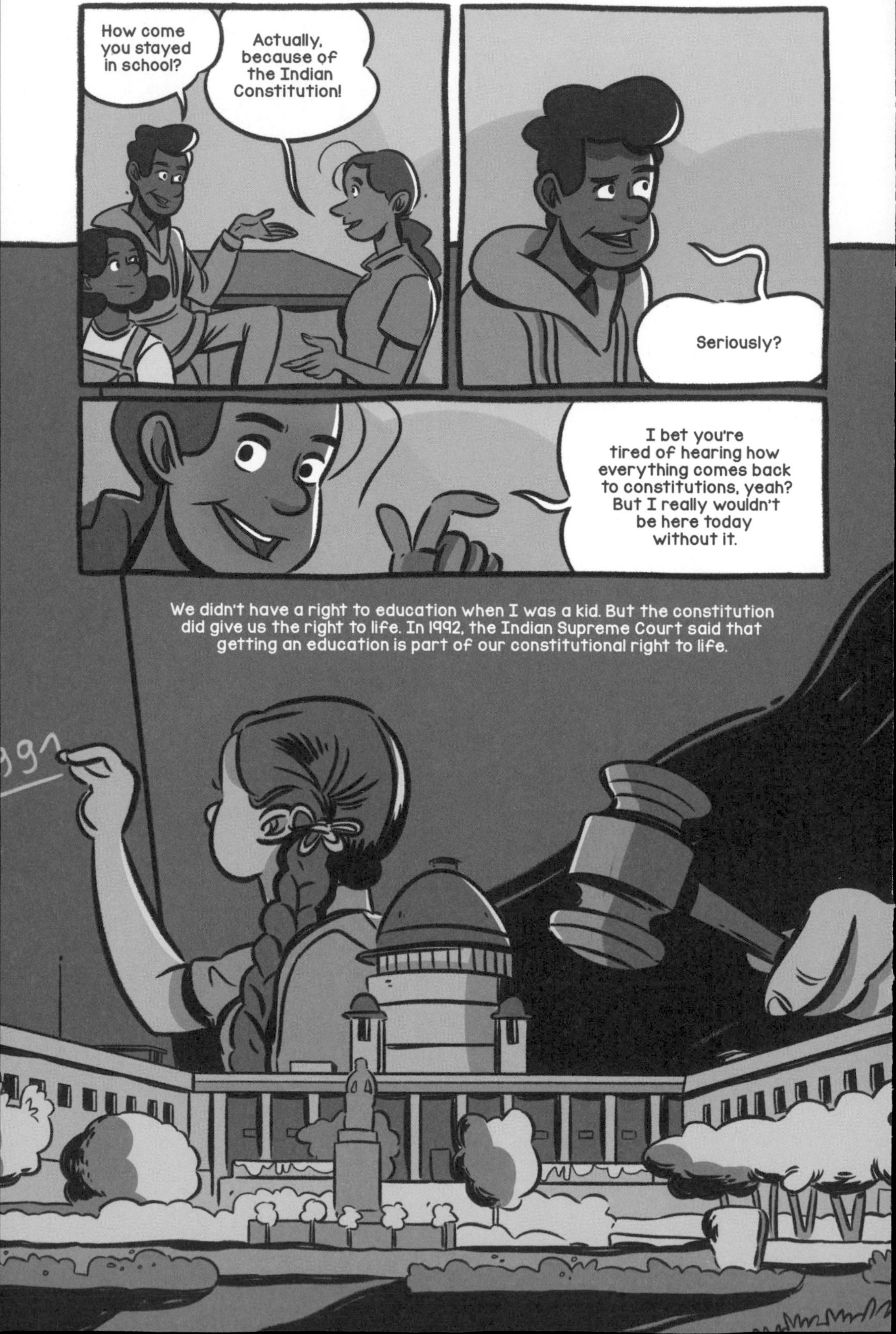
How come you stayed in school?
Actually, because of the Indian Constitution!
Seriously?
I bet you're tired of hearing how everything comes back to constitutions, yeah? But I really wouldn't be here today without it.
We didn't have a right to education when I was a kid. But the constitution did give us the right to life. In 1992, the Indian Supreme Court said that getting an education is part of our constitutional right to life.

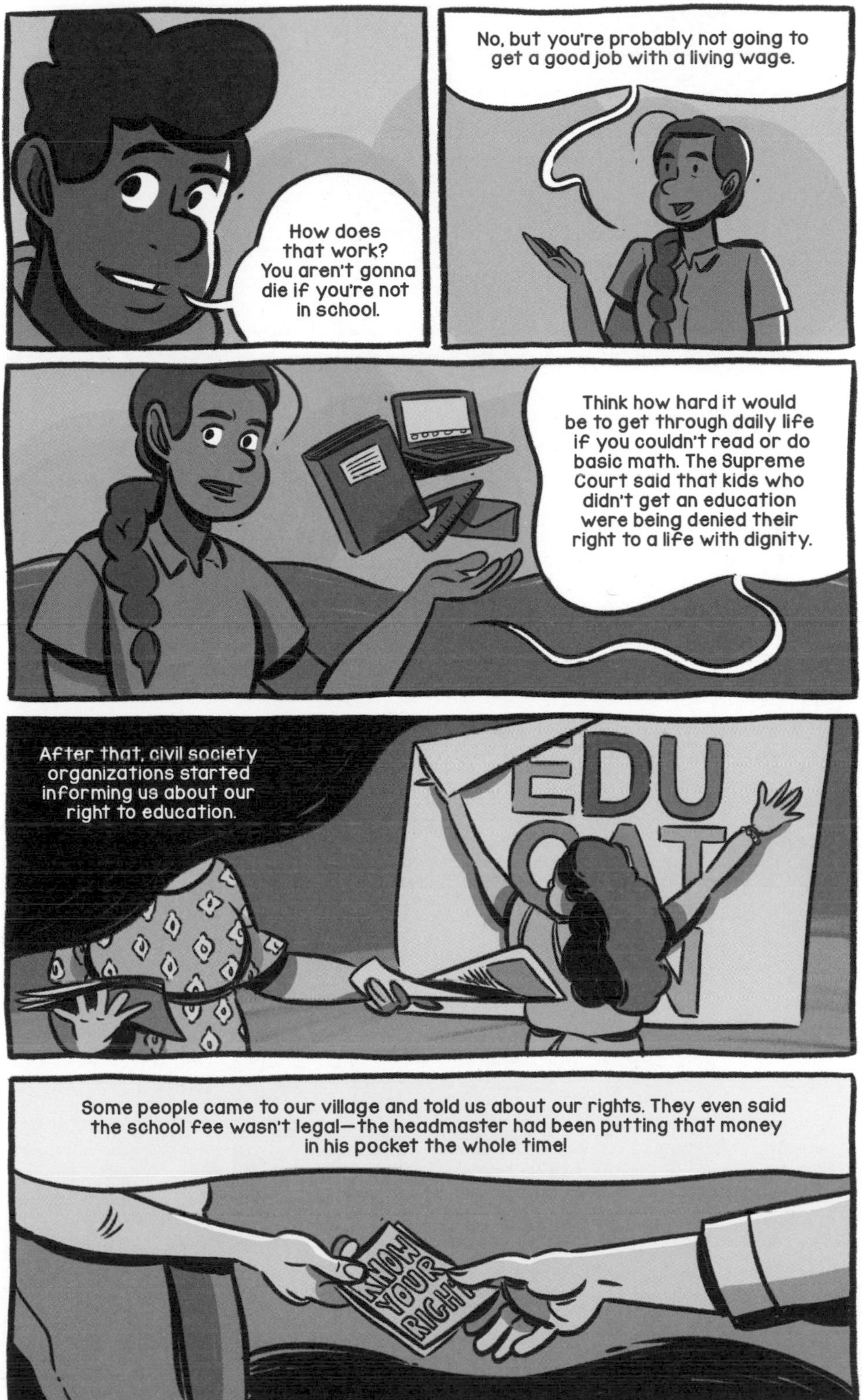
How does that work? You aren't gonna die if you're not in school.
No, but you're probably not going to get a good job with a living wage.
Think how hard it would be to get through daily life if you couldn't read or do basic math. The Supreme Court said that kids who didn't get an education were being denied their right to a life with dignity.
After that, civil society organizations started informing us about our right to education.
EDU
Some people came to our village and told us about our rights. They even said the school fee wasn't legal—the headmaster had been putting that money in his pocket the whole time!
KNOW YOUR RIGHT

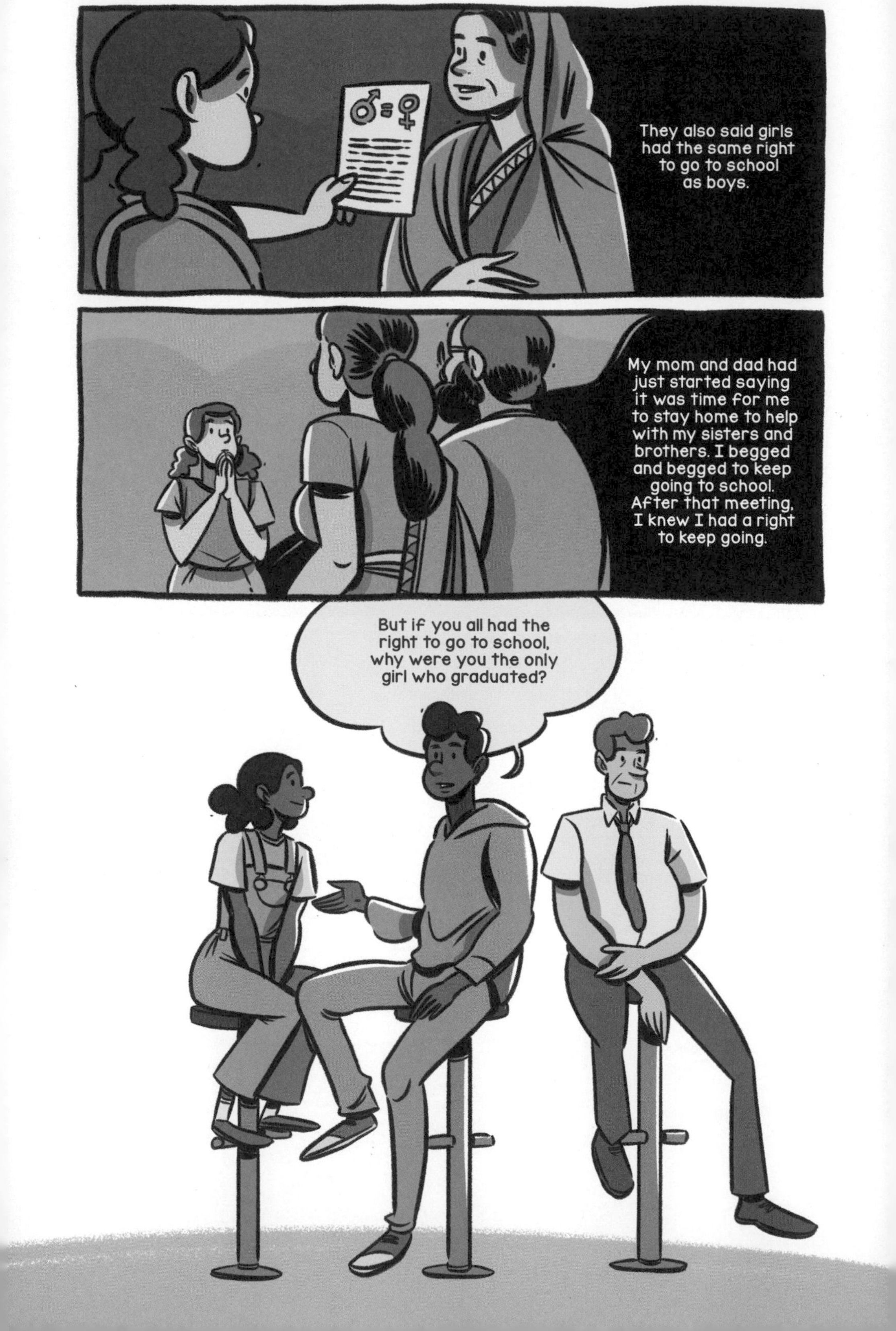
They also said girls had the same right to go to school as boys.
My mom and dad had just started saying it was time for me to stay home to help with my sisters and brothers. I begged and begged to keep going to school. After that meeting, I knew I had a right to keep going.
But if you all had the right to go to school, why were you the only girl who graduated?

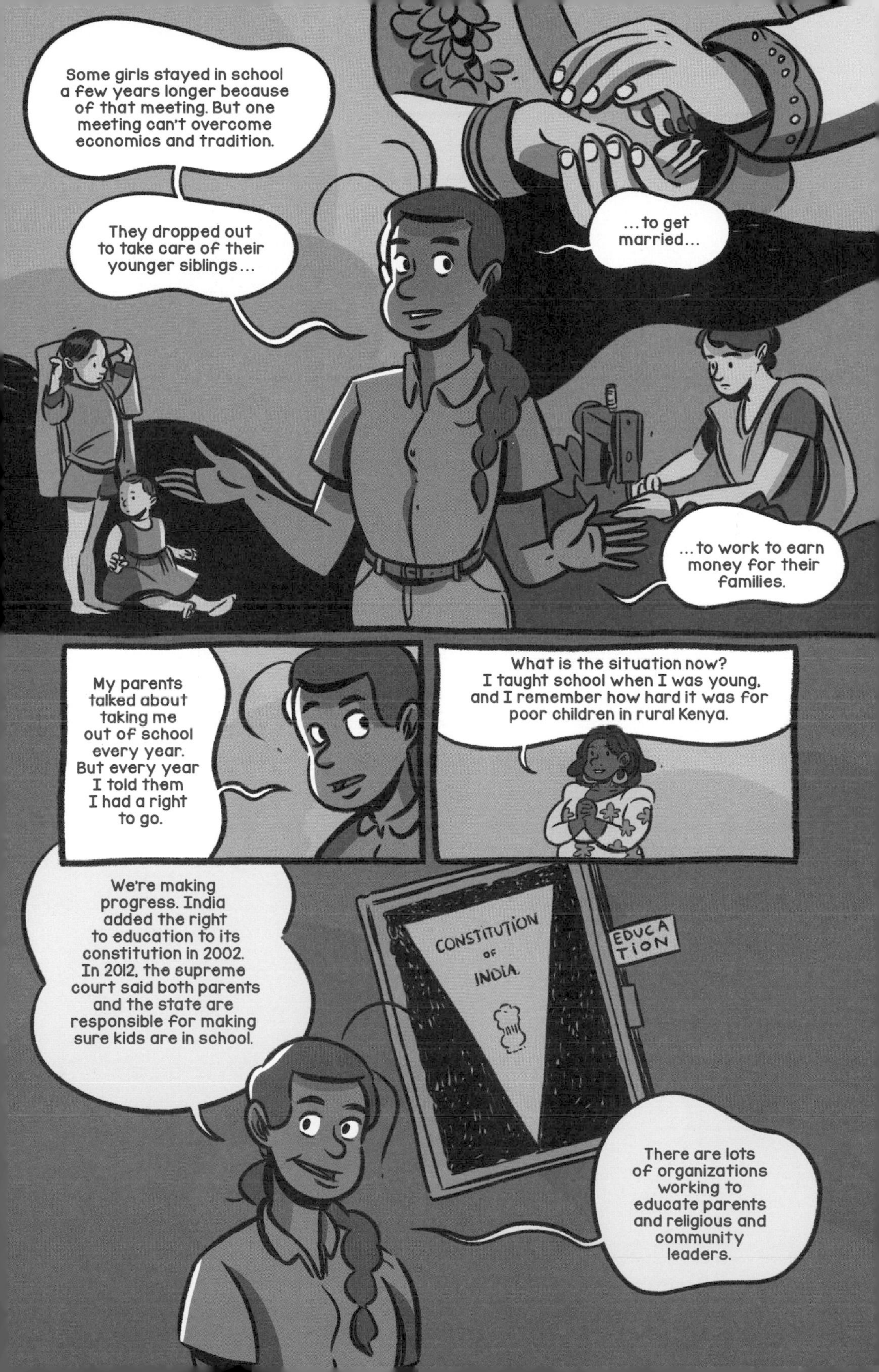

Some girls stayed in school a few years longer because of that meeting. But one meeting can't overcome economics and tradition.
They dropped out to take care of their younger siblings...
...to get married...
...to work to earn money for their families.
My parents talked about taking me out of school every year. But every year I told them I had a right to go.
What is the situation now? I taught school when I was young, and I remember how hard it was for poor children in rural Kenya.
We're making progress. India added the right to education to its constitution in 2002. In 2012, the supreme court said both parents and the state are responsible for making sure kids are in school.
CONSTITUTION OF INDIA
EDUCA TION
There are lots of organizations working to educate parents and religious and community leaders.

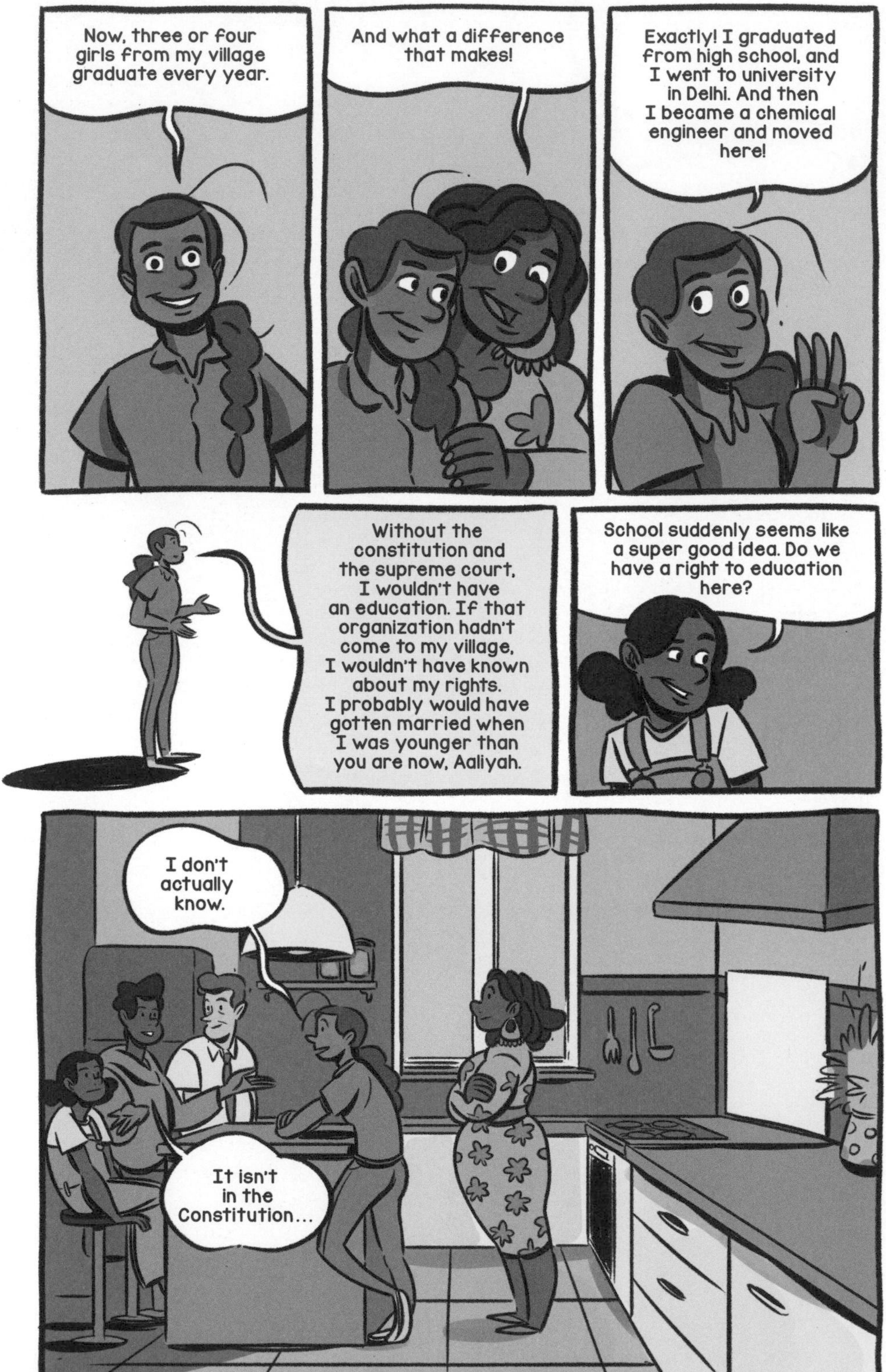
Now, three or four girls from my village graduate every year.
And what a difference that makes!
Exactly! I graduated from high school, and I went to university in Delhi. And then I became a chemical engineer and moved here!
Without the constitution and the supreme court, I wouldn't have an education. If that organization hadn't come to my village, I wouldn't have known about my rights. I probably would have gotten married when I was younger than you are now, Aaliyah.
School suddenly seems like a super good idea. Do we have a right to education here?
I don't actually know.
It isn't in the Constitution...

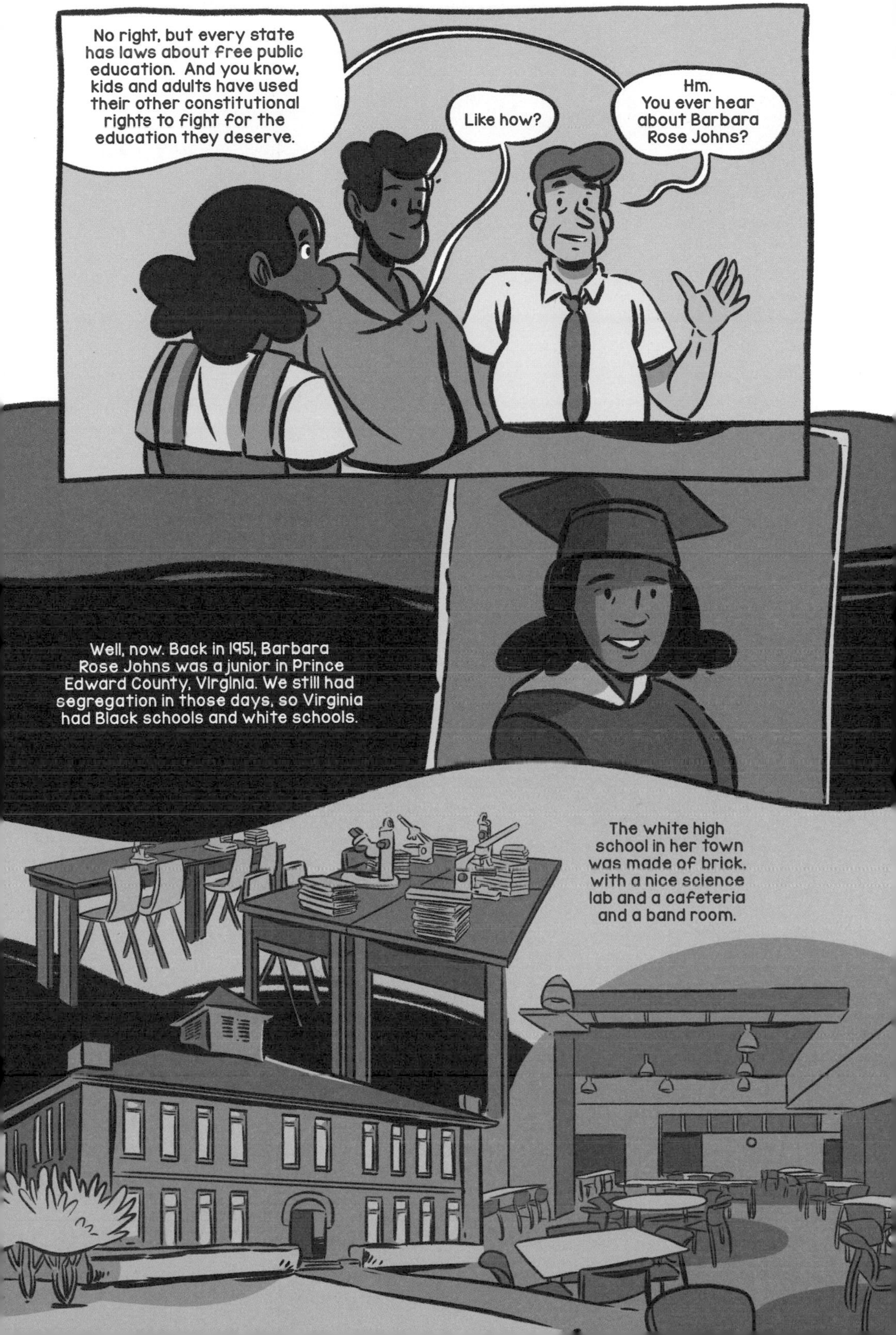
No right, but every state has laws about free public education. And you know, kids and adults have used their other constitutional rights to fight for the education they deserve.
Like how?
Hm. You ever hear about Barbara Rose Johns?
Well, now. Back in 1951, Barbara Rose Johns was a junior in Prince Edward County, Virginia. We still had segregation in those days, so Virginia had Black schools and white schools.
The white high school in her town was made of brick, with a nice science lab and a cafeteria and a band room.

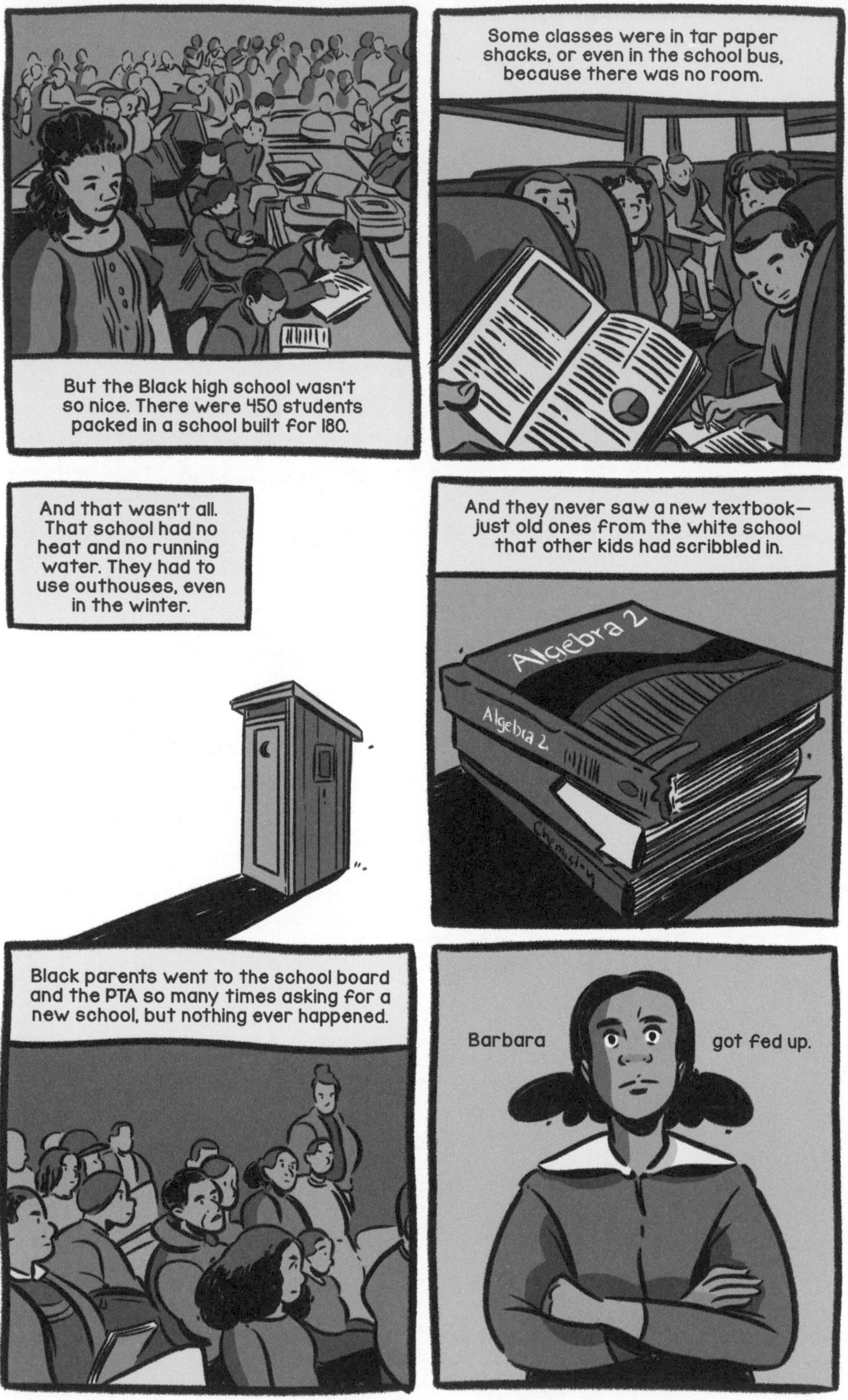
But the Black high school wasn't so nice. There were 450 students packed in a school built for 180.
Some classes were in tar paper shacks, or even in the school bus, because there was no room.
And that wasn't all. That school had no heat and no running water. They had to use outhouses, even in the winter.
And they never saw a new textbook—just old ones from the white school that other kids had scribbled in.
Algebra 2
Algebra 2.
Chemistry
Black parents went to the school board and the PTA so many times asking for a new school, but nothing ever happened.
Barbara
got fed up.

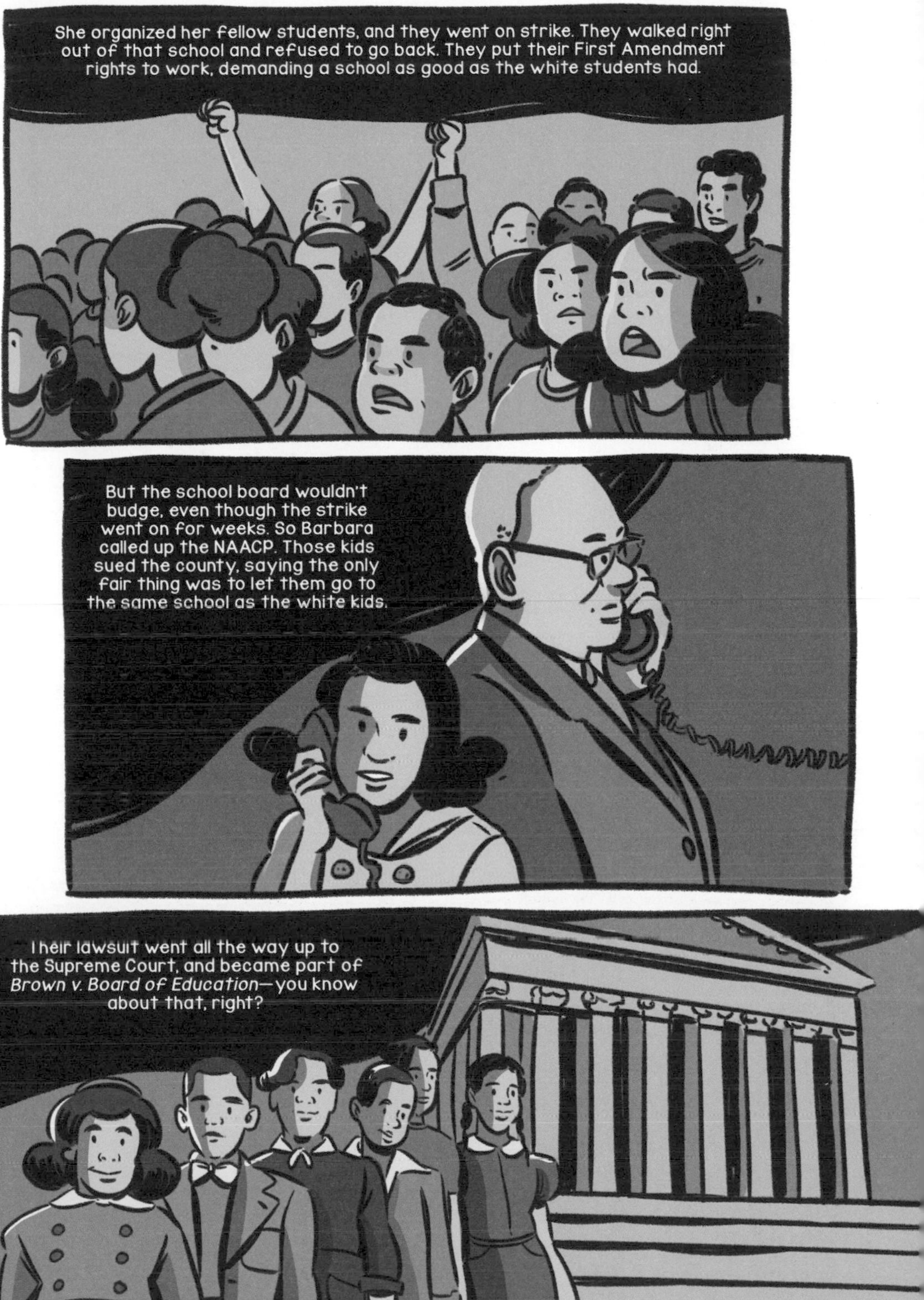

She organized her fellow students, and they went on strike. They walked right out of that school and refused to go back. They put their First Amendment rights to work, demanding a school as good as the white students had.
But the school board wouldn't budge, even though the strike went on for weeks. So Barbara called up the NAACP. Those kids sued the county, saying the only fair thing was to let them go to the same school as the white kids.
Their lawsuit went all the way up to the Supreme Court, and became part of *Brown v. Board of Education*—you know about that, right?

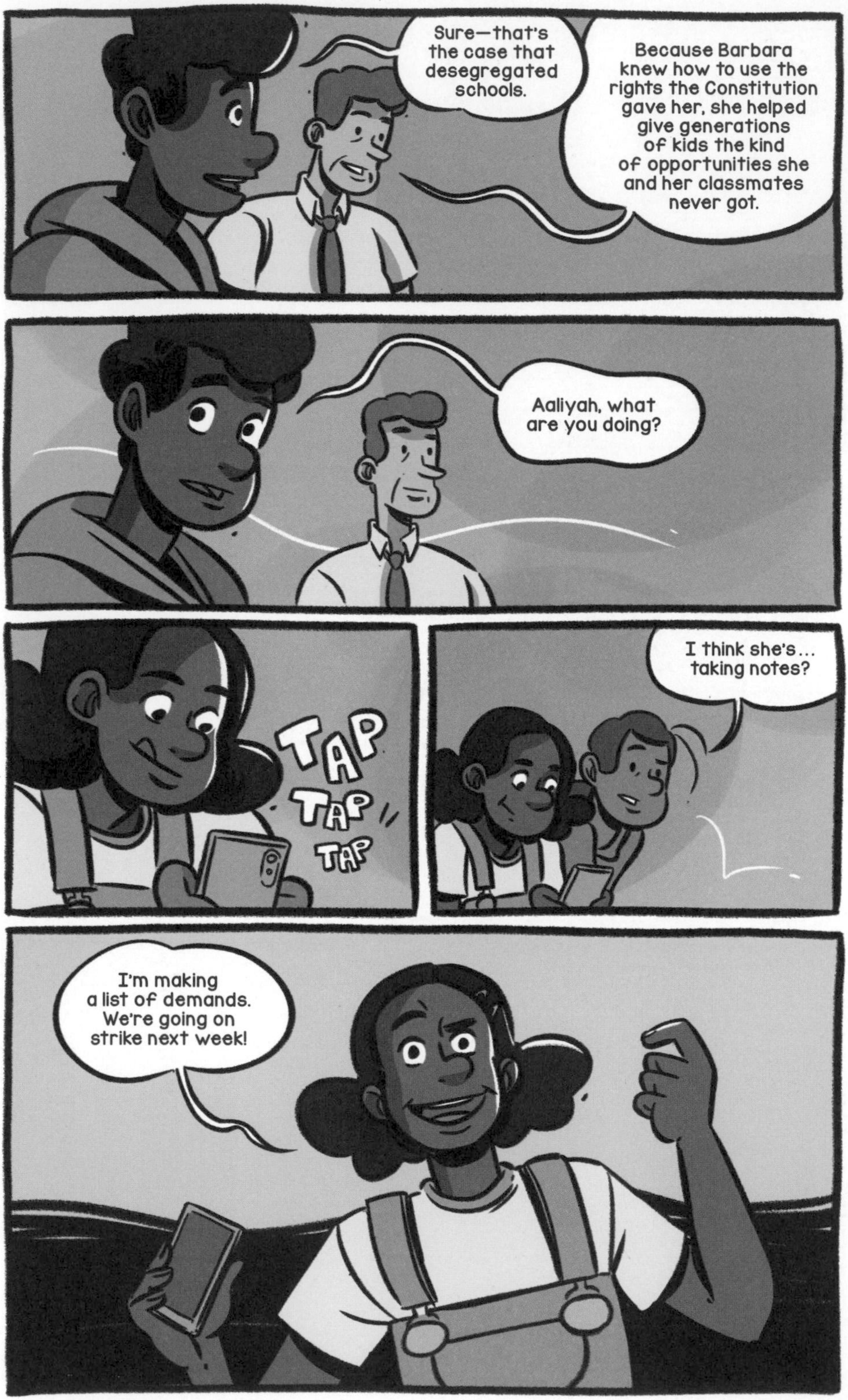
Sure—that's the case that desegregated schools.
Because Barbara knew how to use the rights the Constitution gave her, she helped give generations of kids the kind of opportunities she and her classmates never got.
Aaliyah, what are you doing?
TAP TAP TAP
I think she's... taking notes?
I'm making a list of demands. We're going on strike next week!

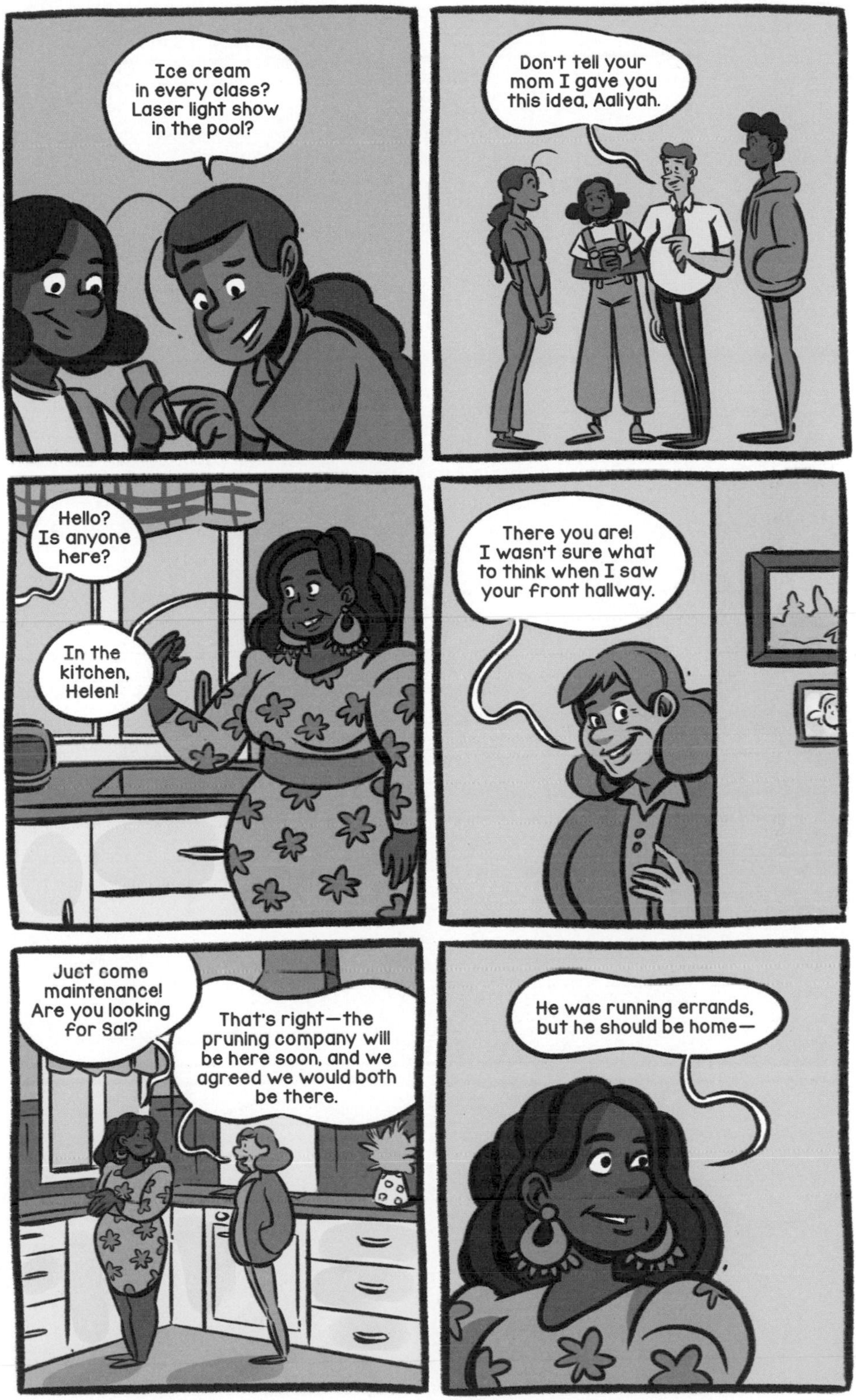
Ice cream in every class? Laser light show in the pool?
Don't tell your mom I gave you this idea, Aaliyah.
Hello? Is anyone here?
In the kitchen, Helen!
There you are! I wasn't sure what to think when I saw your front hallway.
Just some maintenance! Are you looking for Sal?
That's right—the pruning company will be here soon, and we agreed we would both be there.
He was running errands, but he should be home—

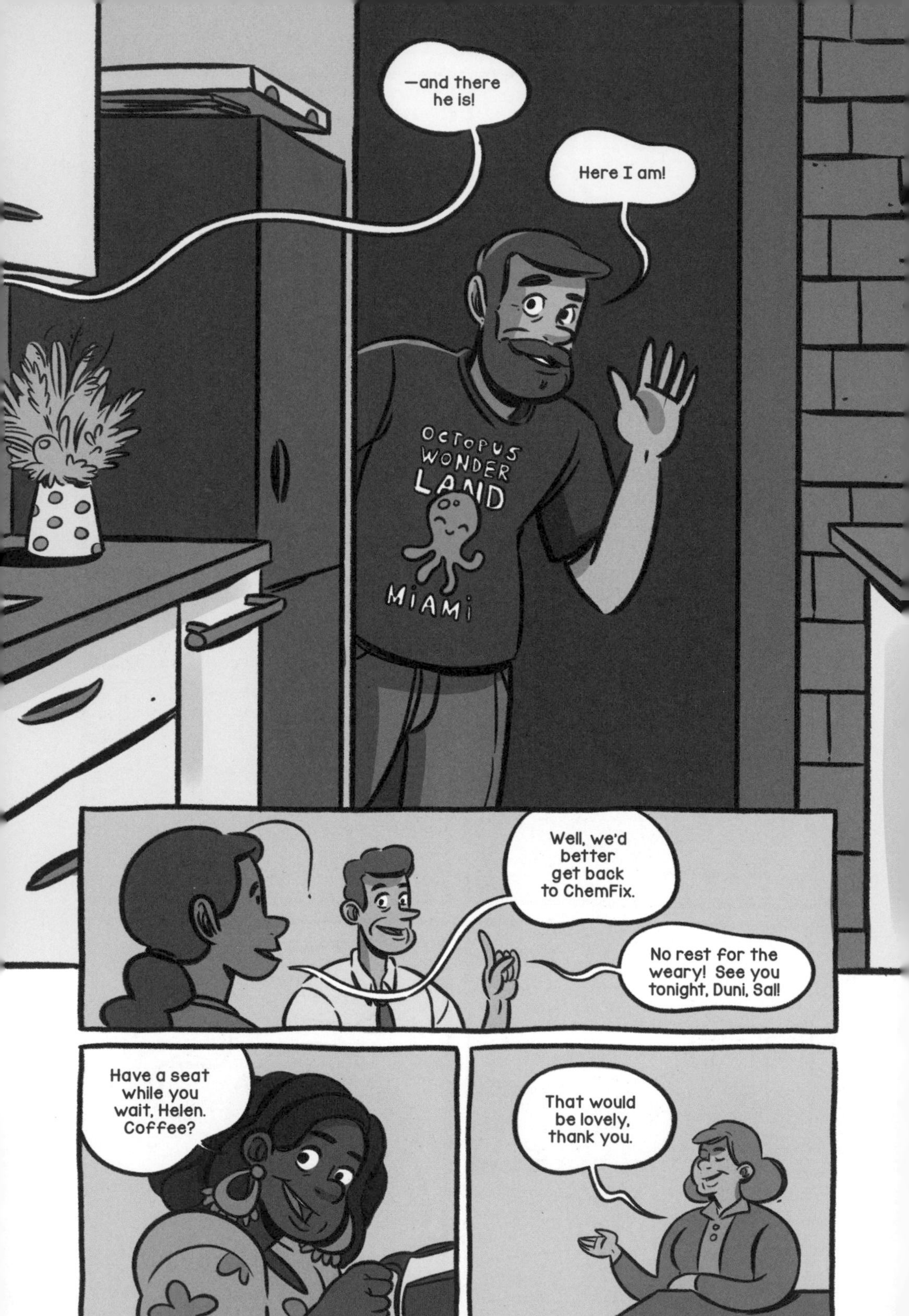
—and there he is!
Here I am!
OCTOPUS WONDER LAND
MIAMI
Well, we'd better get back to ChemFix.
No rest for the weary! See you tonight, Duni, Sal!
Have a seat while you wait, Helen. Coffee?
That would be lovely, thank you.

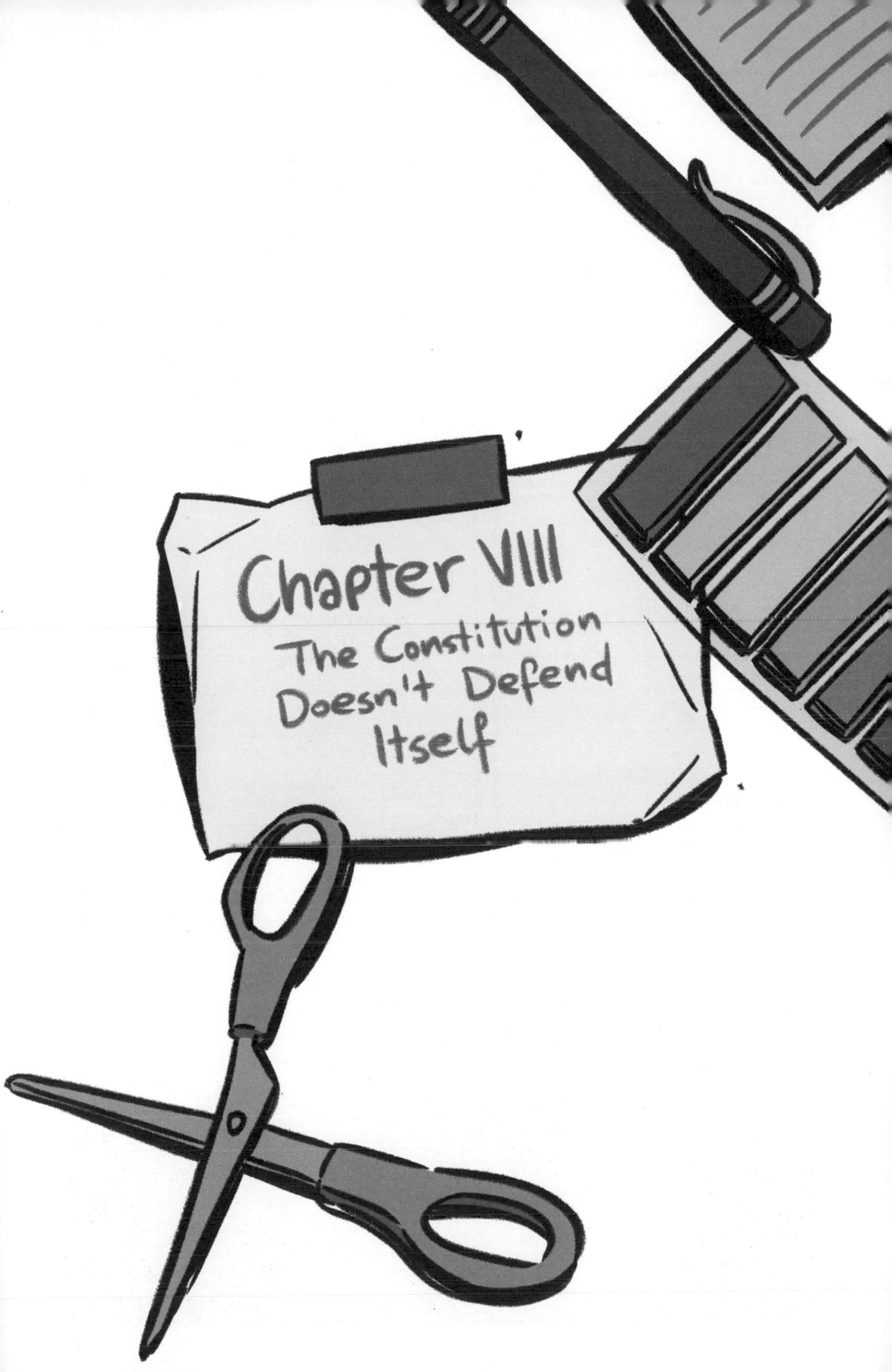
Chapter VIII
The Constitution
Doesn't Defend
Itself

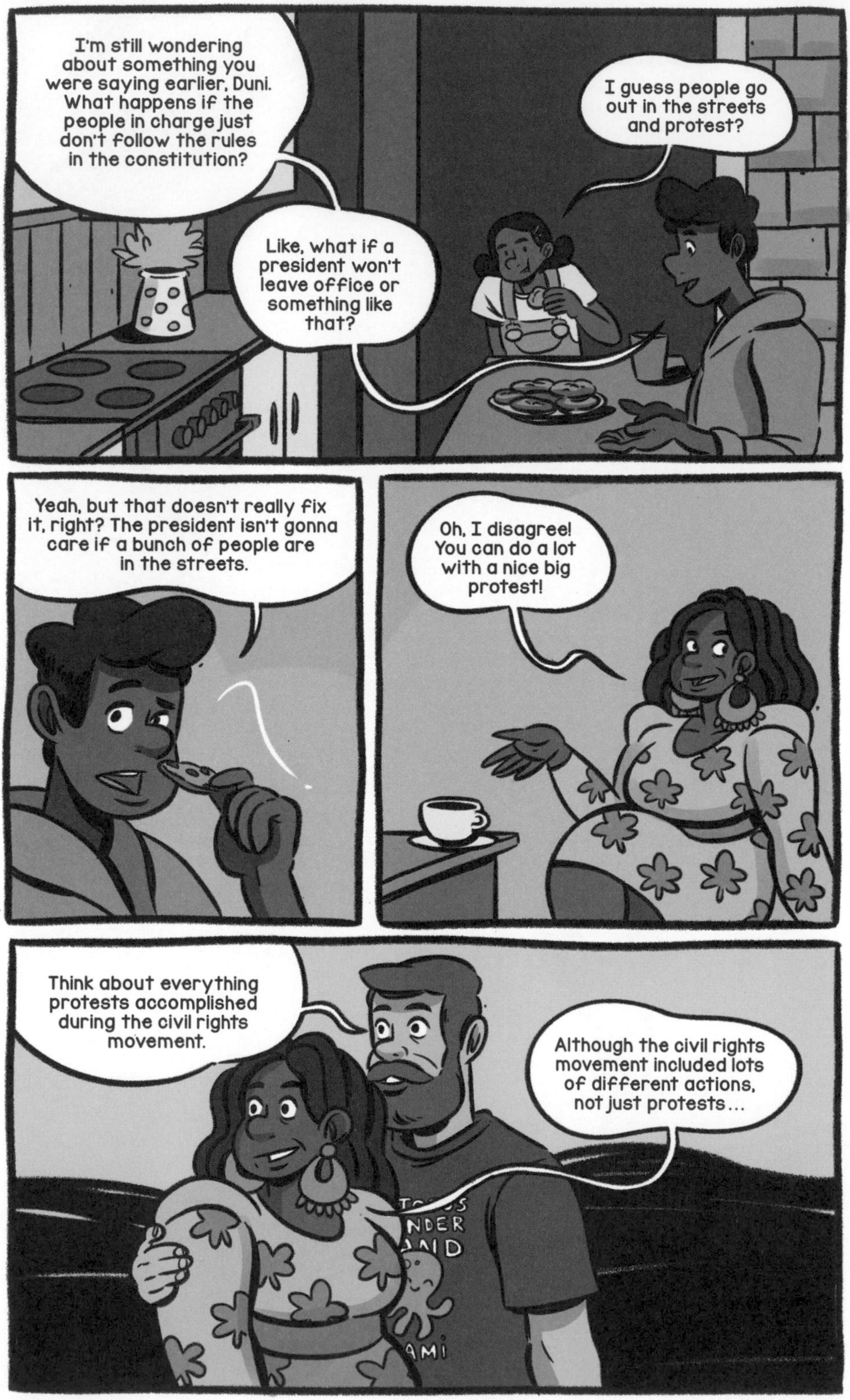

I'm still wondering about something you were saying earlier, Duni. What happens if the people in charge just don't follow the rules in the constitution?
Like, what if a president won't leave office or something like that?
I guess people go out in the streets and protest?
Yeah, but that doesn't really fix it, right? The president isn't gonna care if a bunch of people are in the streets.
Oh, I disagree! You can do a lot with a nice big protest!
Think about everything protests accomplished during the civil rights movement.
Although the civil rights movement included lots of different actions, not just protests...

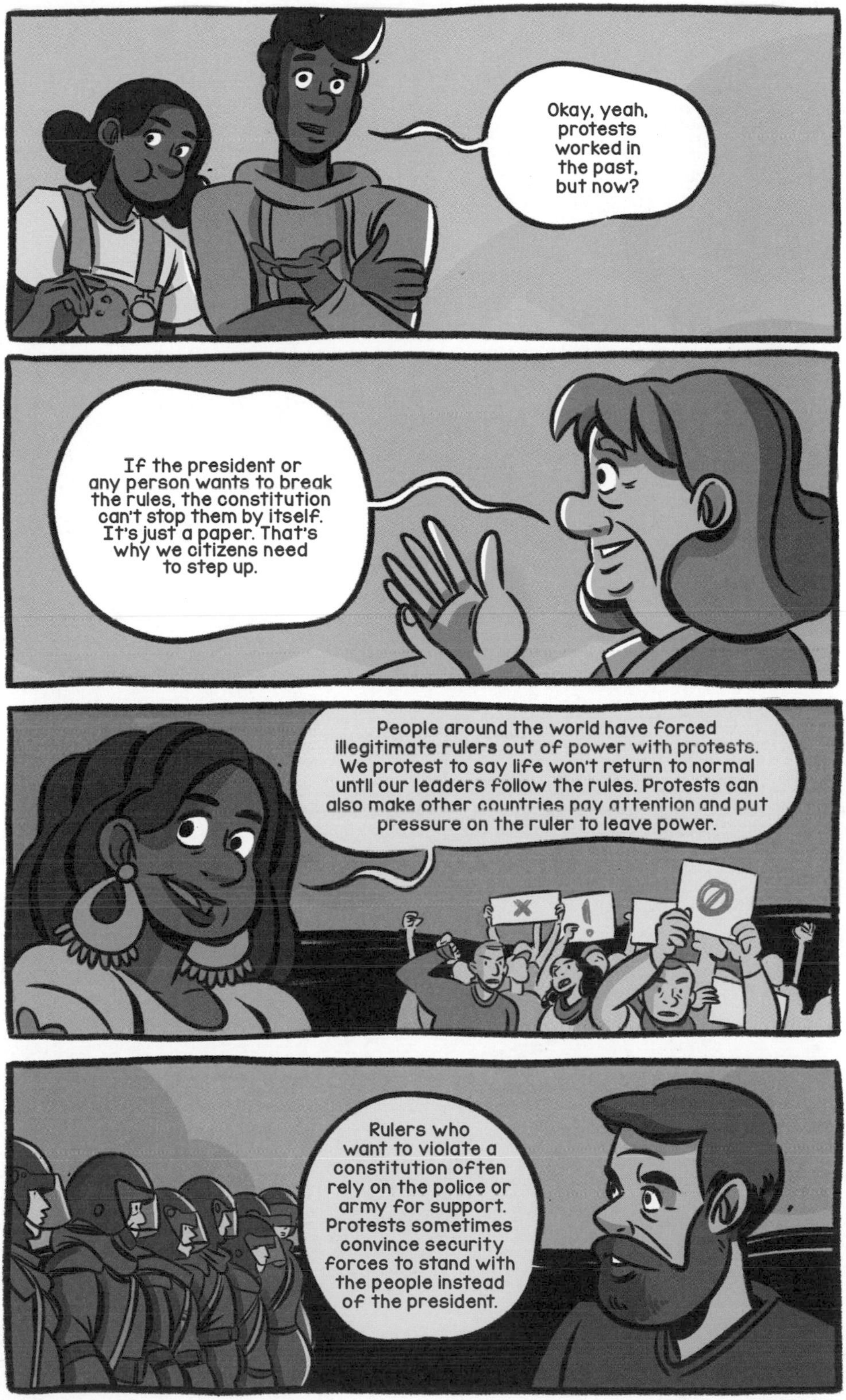
Okay, yeah, protests worked in the past, but now?
If the president or any person wants to break the rules, the constitution can't stop them by itself. It's just a paper. That's why we citizens need to step up.
People around the world have forced illegitimate rulers out of power with protests. We protest to say life won't return to normal until our leaders follow the rules. Protests can also make other countries pay attention and put pressure on the ruler to leave power.
Rulers who want to violate a constitution often rely on the police or army for support. Protests sometimes convince security forces to stand with the people instead of the president.

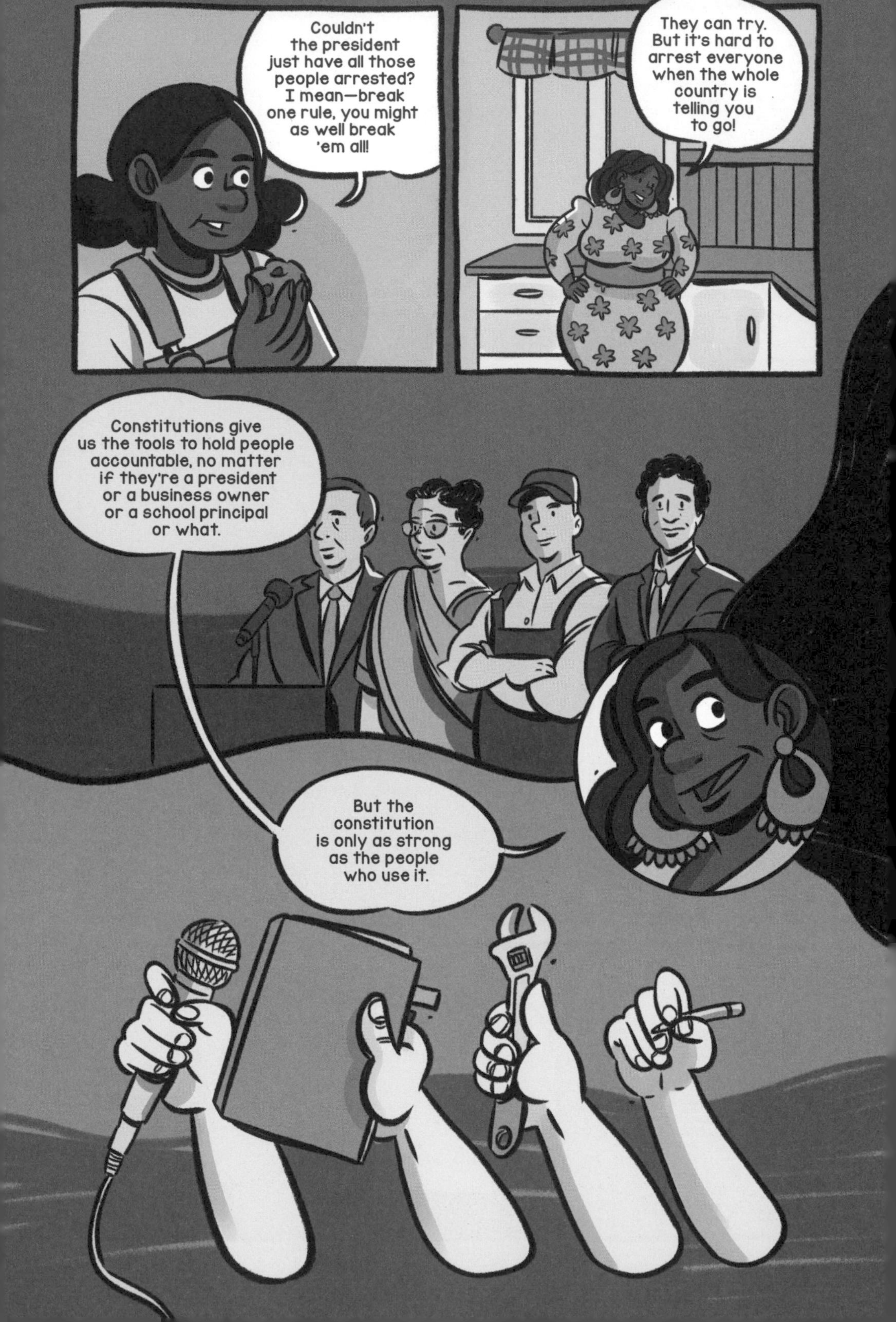
Couldn't the president just have all those people arrested? I mean—break one rule, you might as well break 'em all!
They can try. But it's hard to arrest everyone when the whole country is telling you to go!
Constitutions give us the tools to hold people accountable, no matter if they're a president or a business owner or a school principal or what.
But the constitution is only as strong as the people who use it.

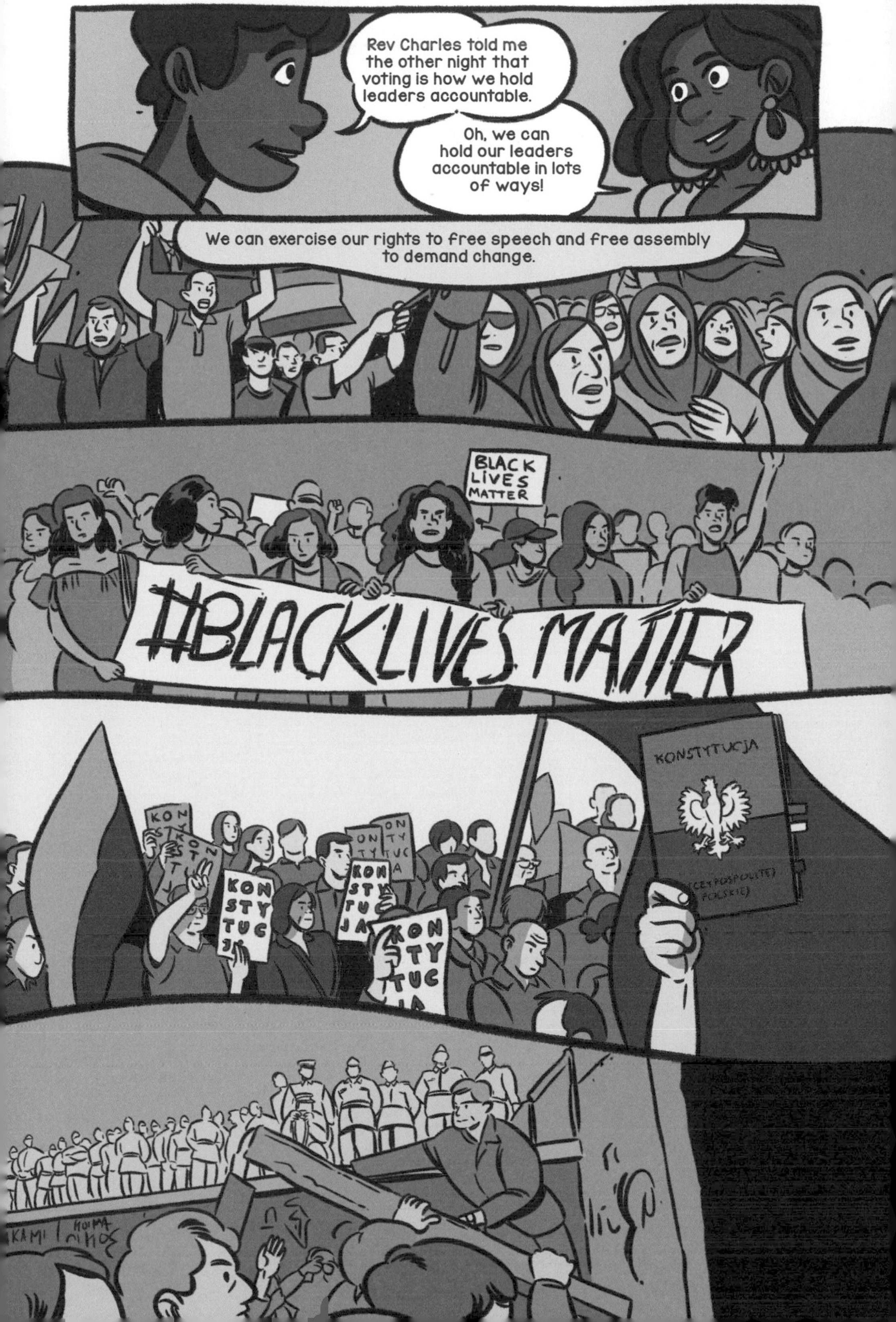

Rev Charles told me the other night that voting is how we hold leaders accountable.
Oh, we can hold our leaders accountable in lots of ways!
We can exercise our rights to free speech and free assembly to demand change.
BLACK LIVES MATTER
#BLACKLIVESMATTER
KONSTYTUCJA
KON STY TUC JA

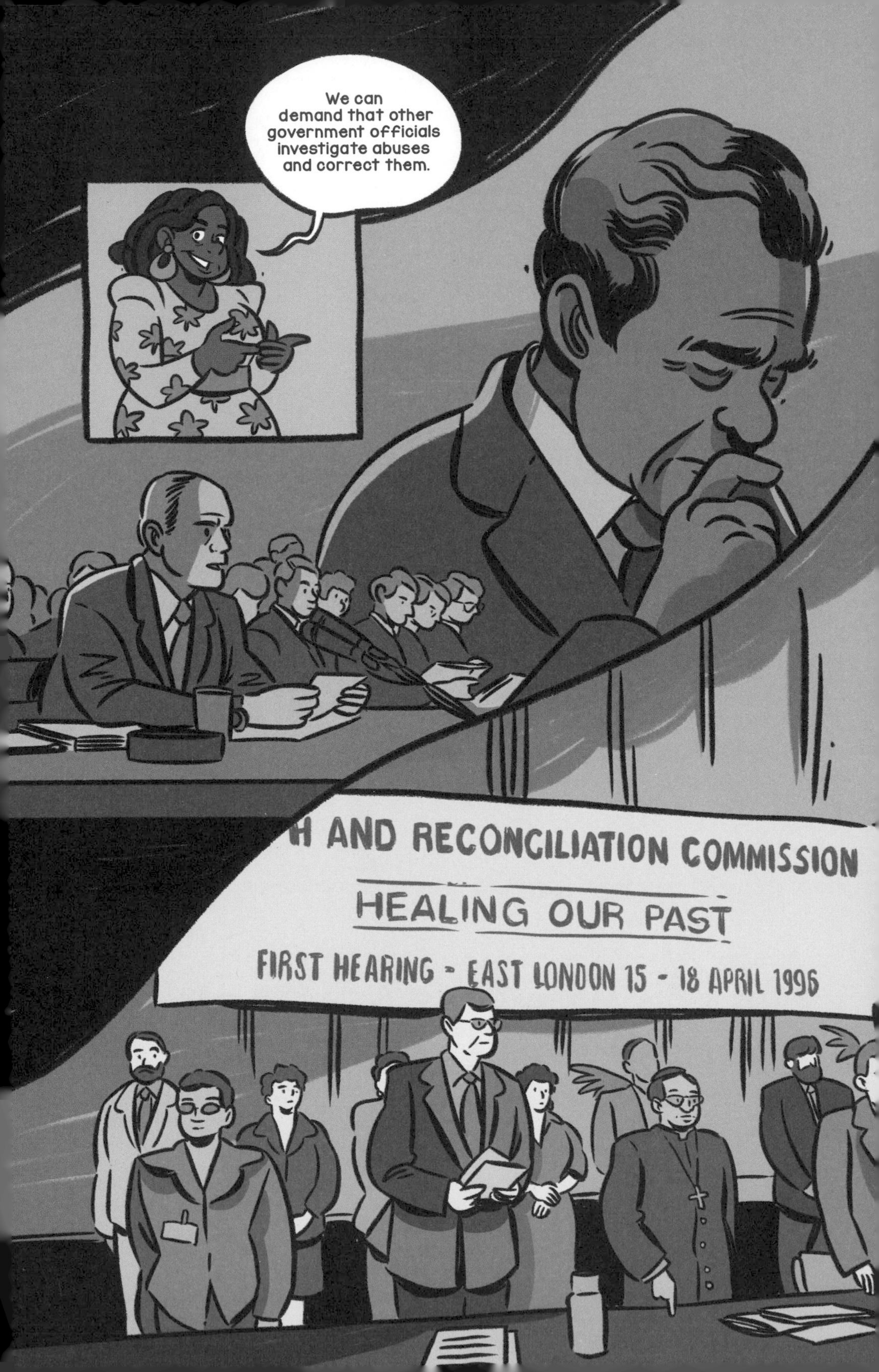

We can demand that other government officials investigate abuses and correct them.
H AND RECONCILIATION COMMISSION
HEALING OUR PAST
FIRST HEARING - EAST LONDON 15 - 18 APRIL 1996

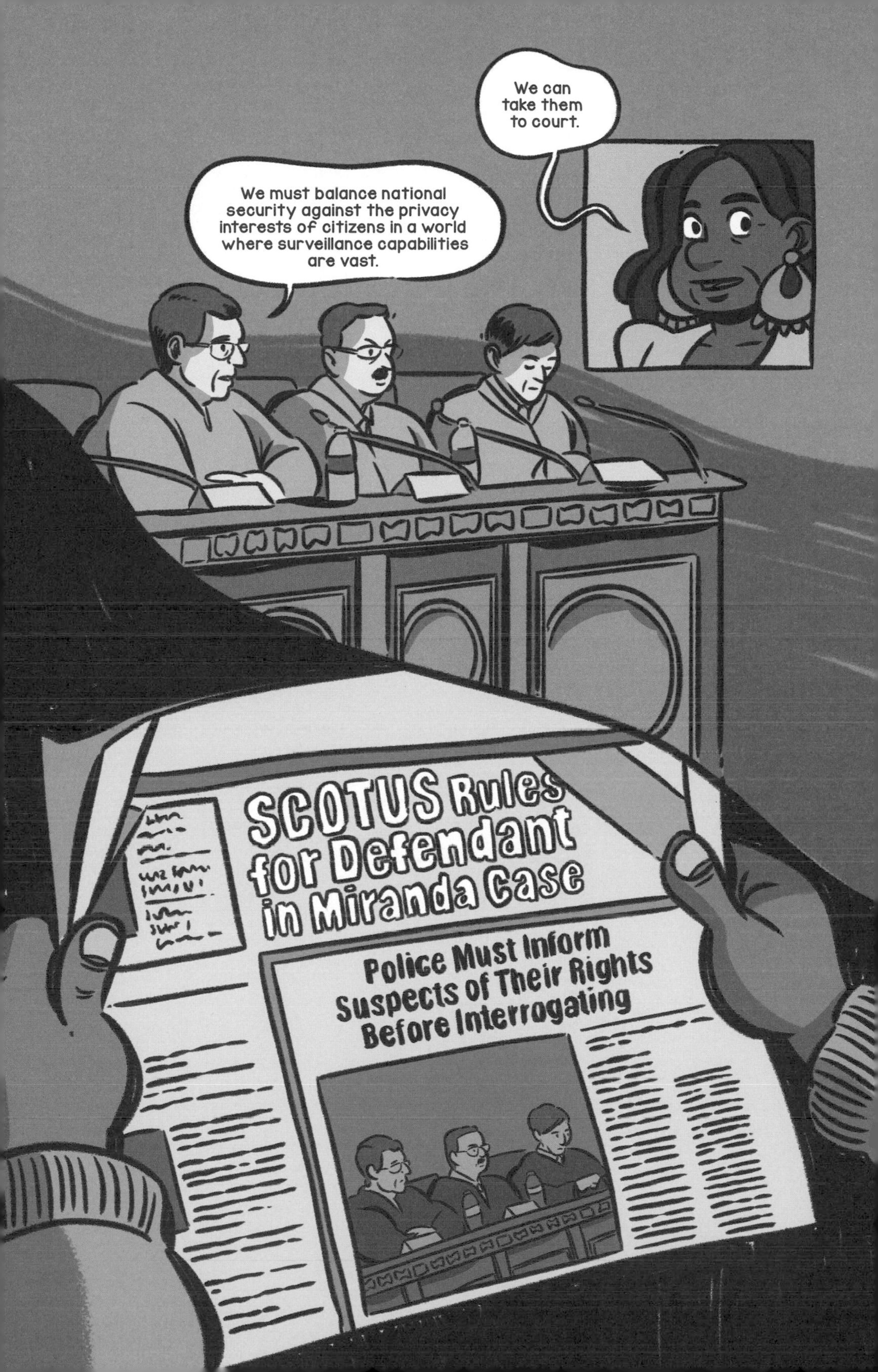

We must balance national security against the privacy interests of citizens in a world where surveillance capabilities are vast.
We can take them to court.
SCOTUS Rules for Defendant in Miranda Case
Police Must Inform Suspects of Their Rights Before Interrogating

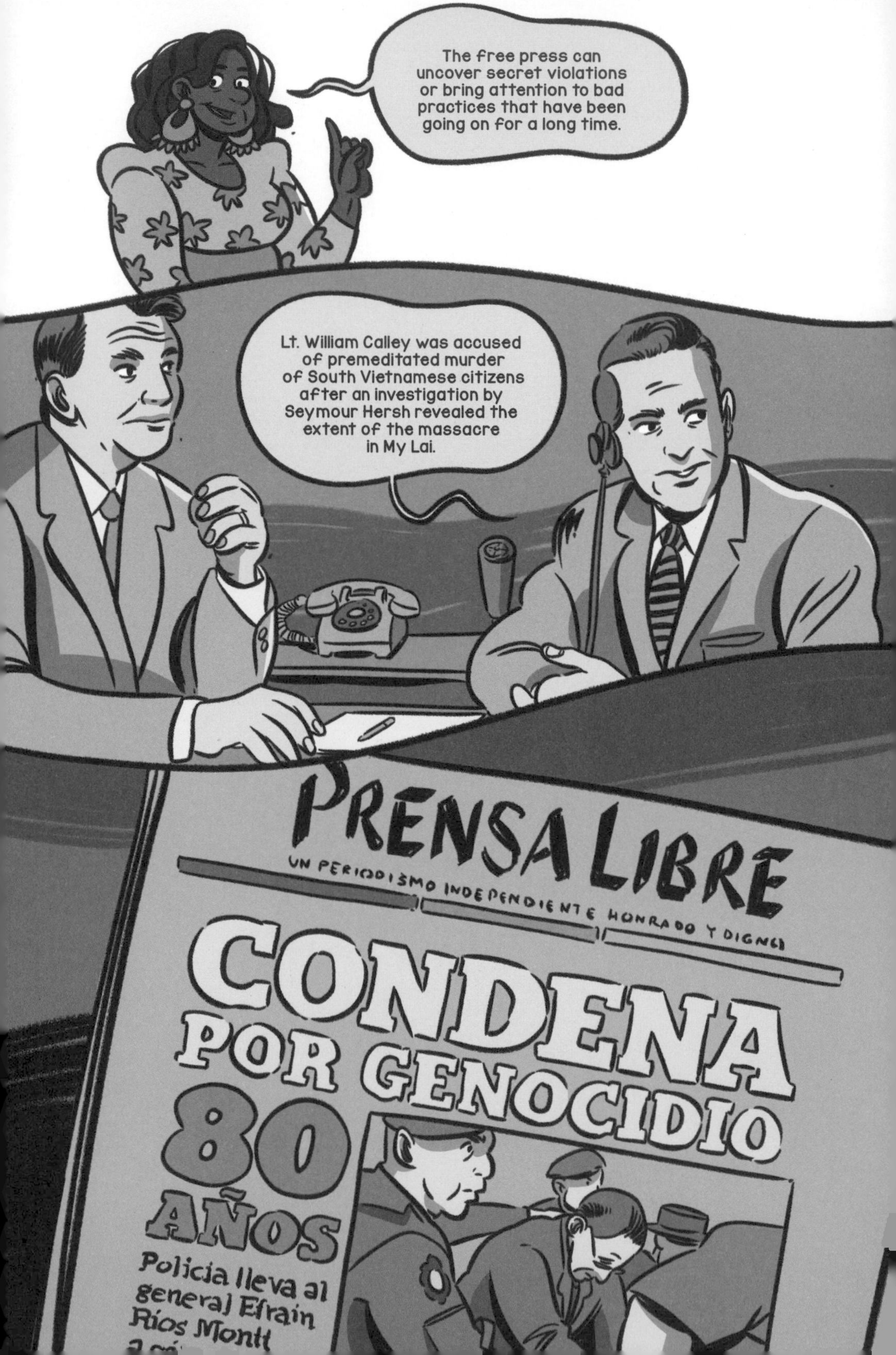
The free press can uncover secret violations or bring attention to bad practices that have been going on for a long time.
Lt. William Calley was accused of premeditated murder of South Vietnamese citizens after an investigation by Seymour Hersh revealed the extent of the massacre in My Lai.
PRENSA LIBRE
UN PERIODISMO INDEPENDIENTE HONRADO Y DIGNO
CONDENA POR GENOCIDIO
80 AÑOS
Policia lleva al general Efrain Ríos Montt

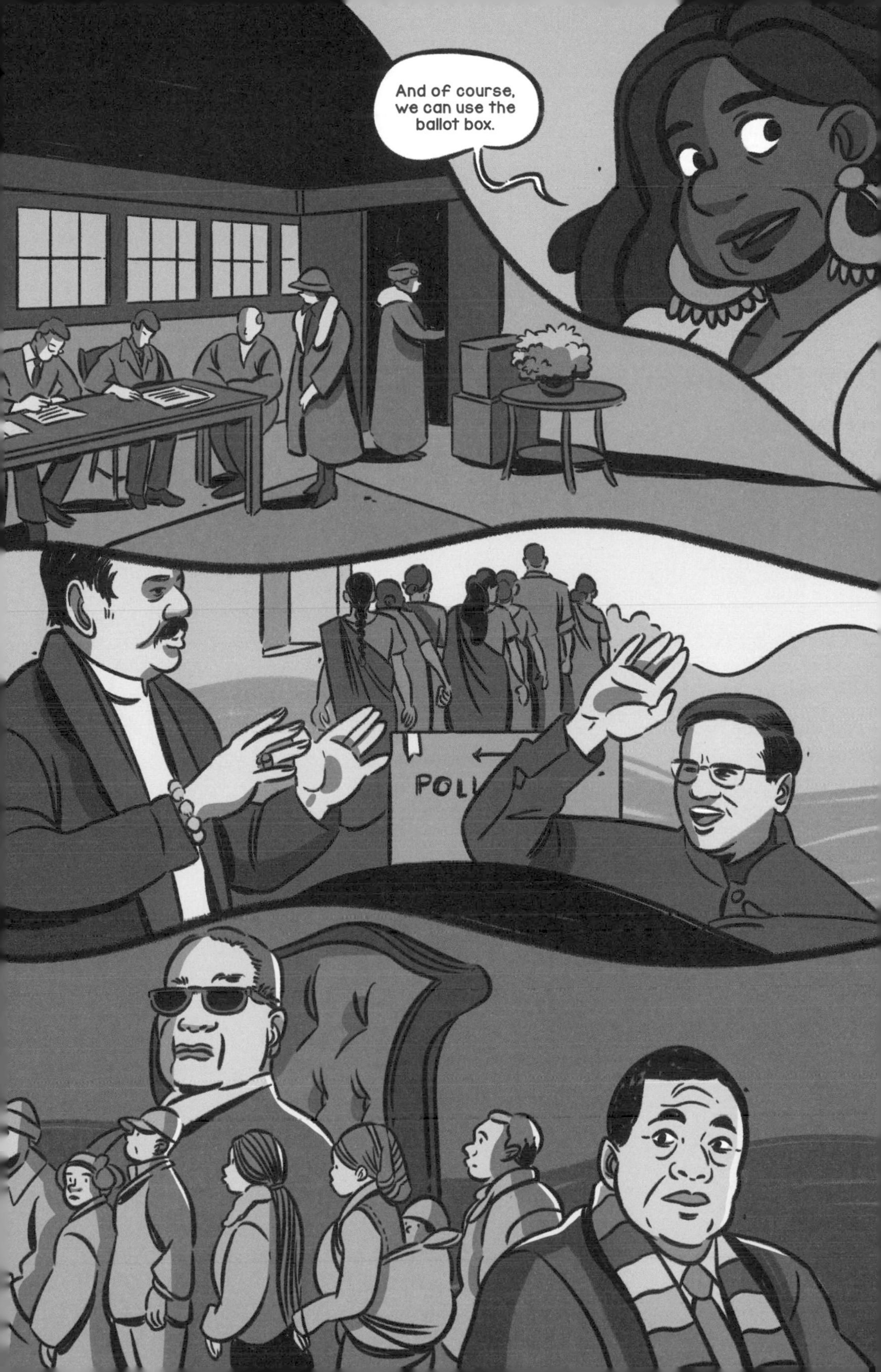
And of course, we can use the ballot box.
POLL

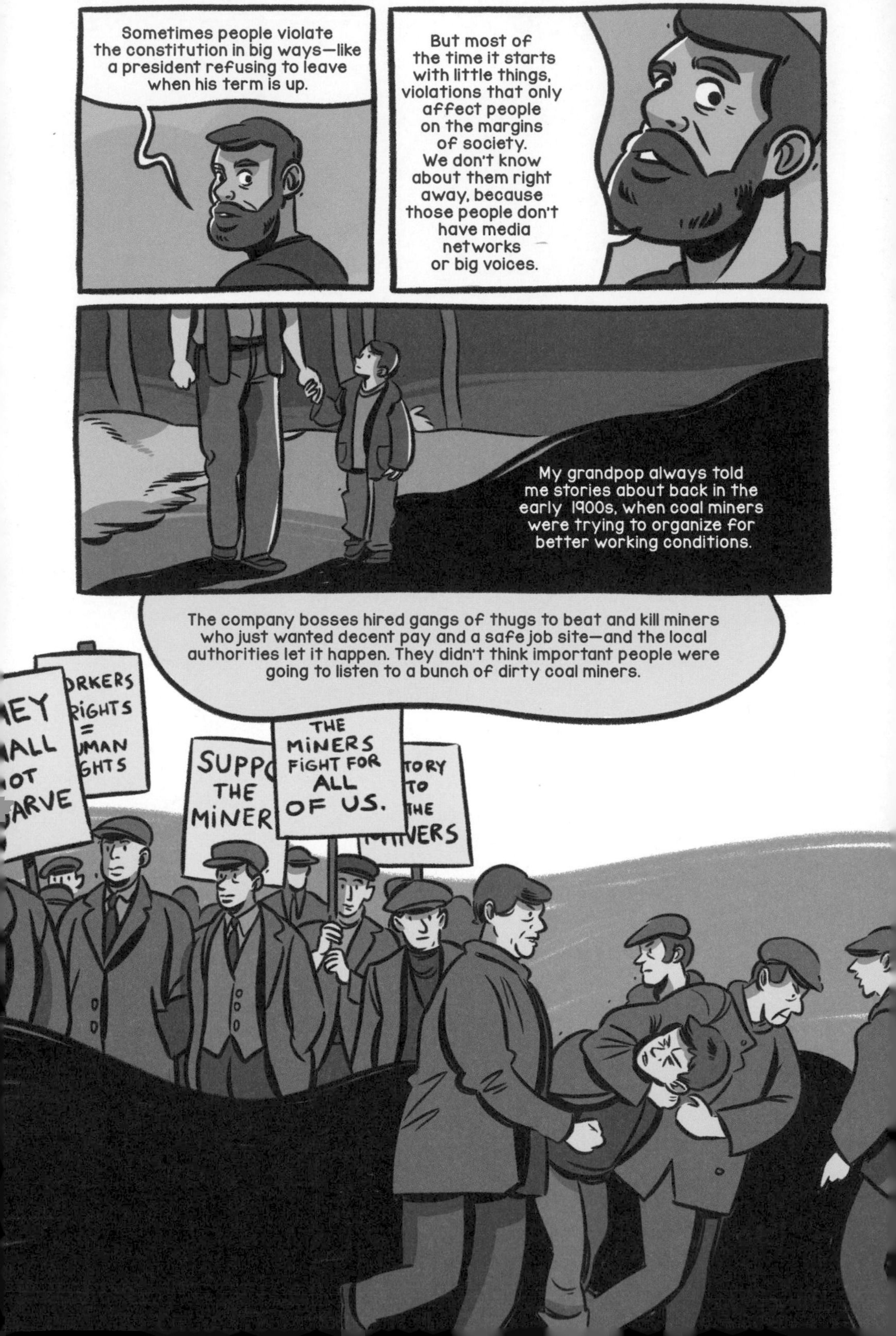
Sometimes people violate the constitution in big ways—like a president refusing to leave when his term is up.
But most of the time it starts with little things, violations that only affect people on the margins of society. We don't know about them right away, because those people don't have media networks or big voices.
My grandpop always told me stories about back in the early 1900s, when coal miners were trying to organize for better working conditions.
The company bosses hired gangs of thugs to beat and kill miners who just wanted decent pay and a safe job site—and the local authorities let it happen. They didn't think important people were going to listen to a bunch of dirty coal miners.
THE MINERS FIGHT FOR ALL OF US.

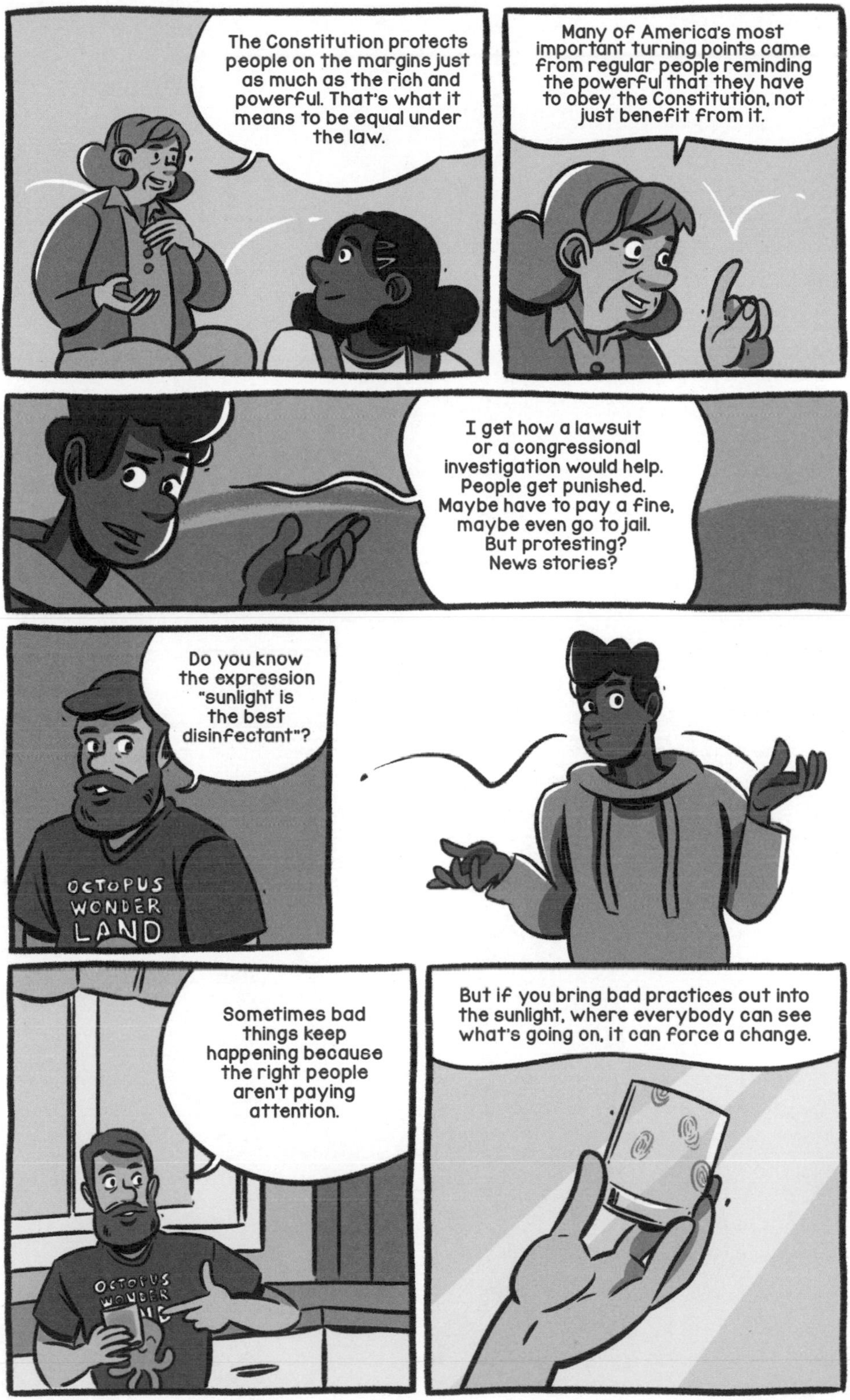
The Constitution protects people on the margins just as much as the rich and powerful. That's what it means to be equal under the law.
Many of America's most important turning points came from regular people reminding the powerful that they have to obey the Constitution, not just benefit from it.
I get how a lawsuit or a congressional investigation would help. People get punished. Maybe have to pay a fine, maybe even go to jail. But protesting? News stories?
Do you know the expression "sunlight is the best disinfectant"?
OCTOPUS WONDER LAND
Sometimes bad things keep happening because the right people aren't paying attention.
But if you bring bad practices out into the sunlight, where everybody can see what's going on, it can force a change.

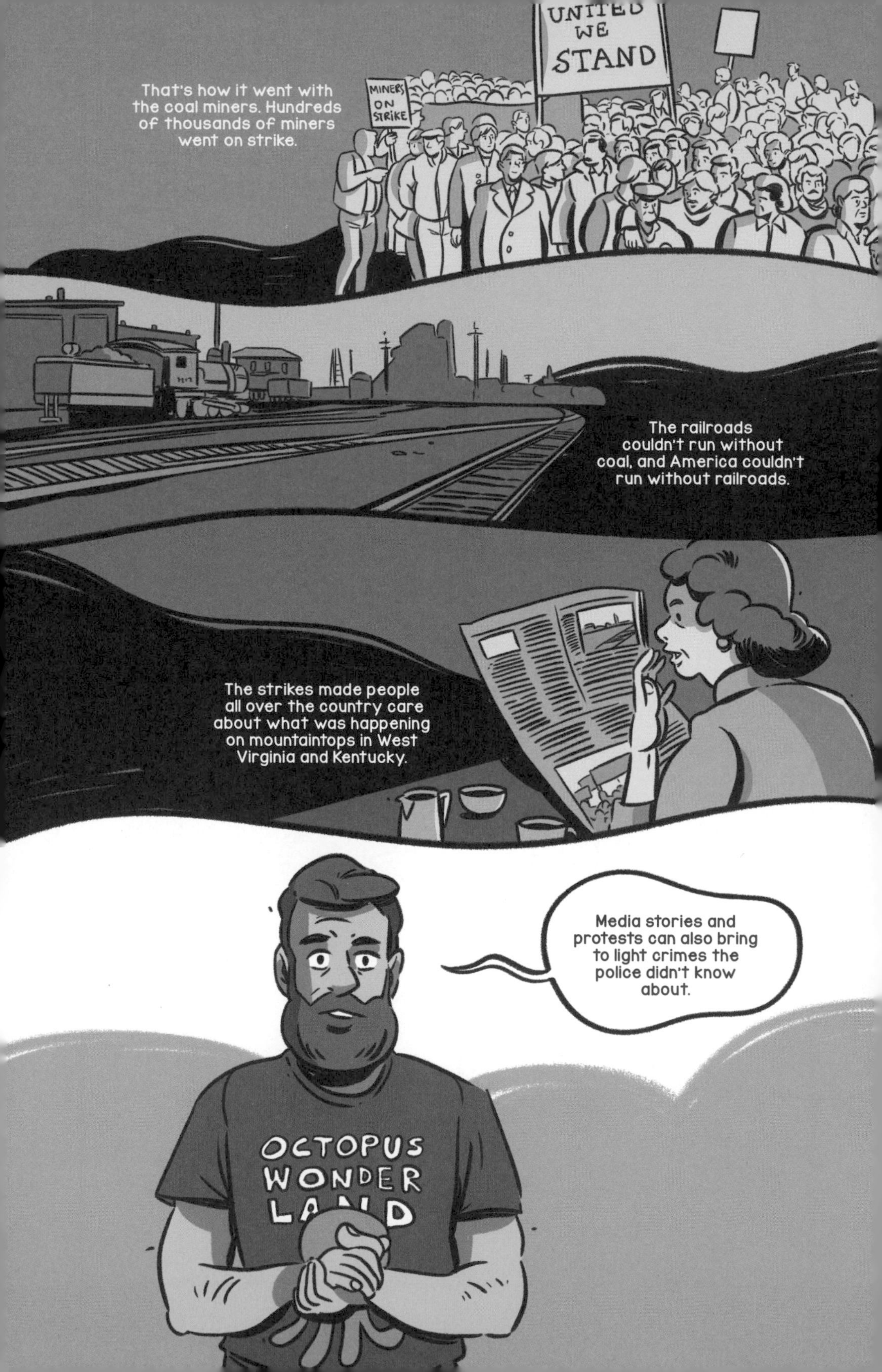
UNITED WE STAND
MINERS ON STRIKE
That's how it went with the coal miners. Hundreds of thousands of miners went on strike.
The railroads couldn't run without coal, and America couldn't run without railroads.
The strikes made people all over the country care about what was happening on mountaintops in West Virginia and Kentucky.
Media stories and protests can also bring to light crimes the police didn't know about.
OCTOPUS WONDER LAND

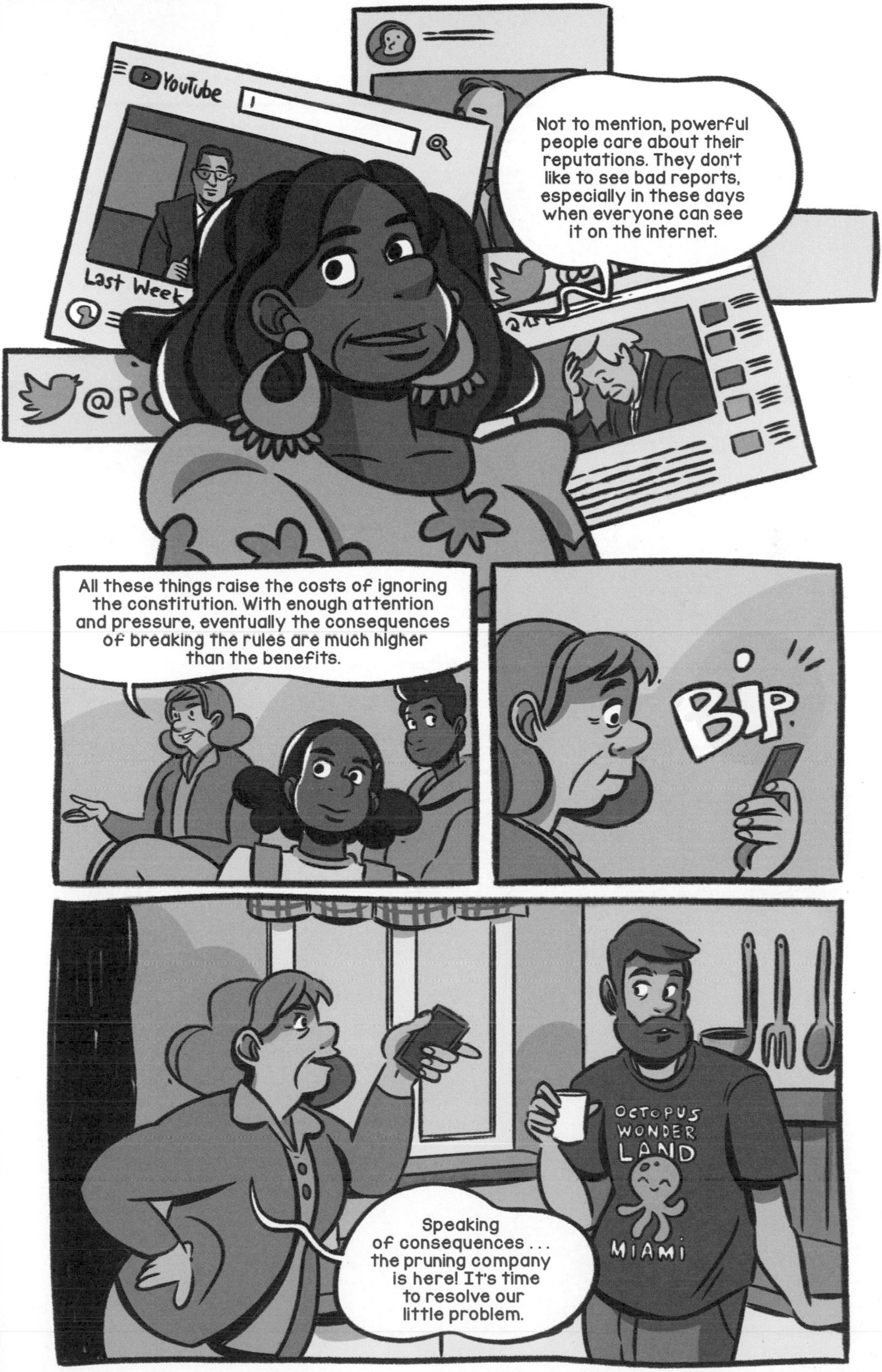
YouTube
Last Week
@PO
Not to mention, powerful people care about their reputations. They don't like to see bad reports, especially in these days when everyone can see it on the internet.
All these things raise the costs of ignoring the constitution. With enough attention and pressure, eventually the consequences of breaking the rules are much higher than the benefits.
BIP.
OCTOPUS WONDER LAND
MIAMI
Speaking of consequences . . . the pruning company is here! It's time to resolve our little problem.

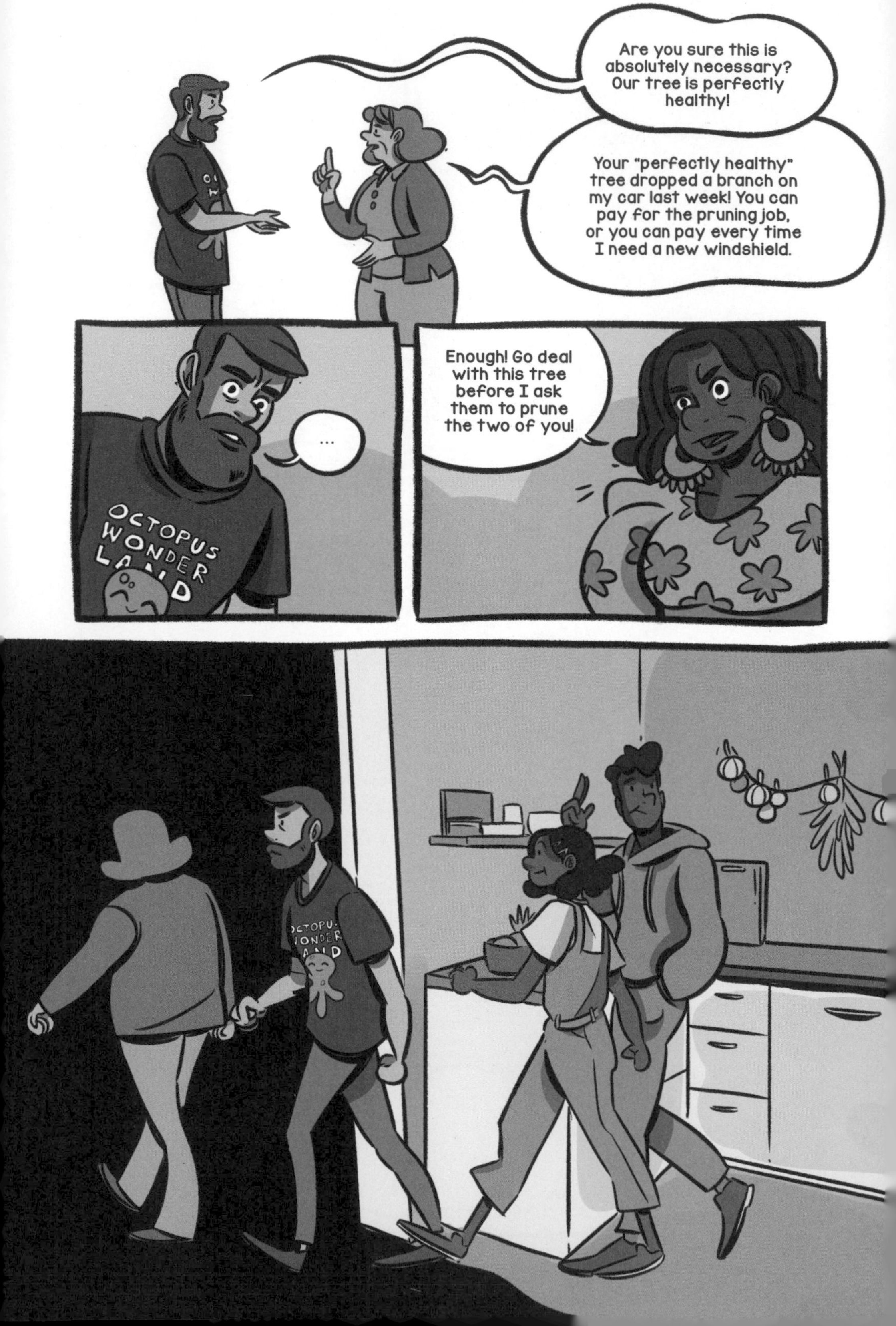
Are you sure this is absolutely necessary? Our tree is perfectly healthy!
Your "perfectly healthy" tree dropped a branch on my car last week! You can pay for the pruning job, or you can pay every time I need a new windshield.
...
OCTOPUS WONDER LAND
Enough! Go deal with this tree before I ask them to prune the two of you!

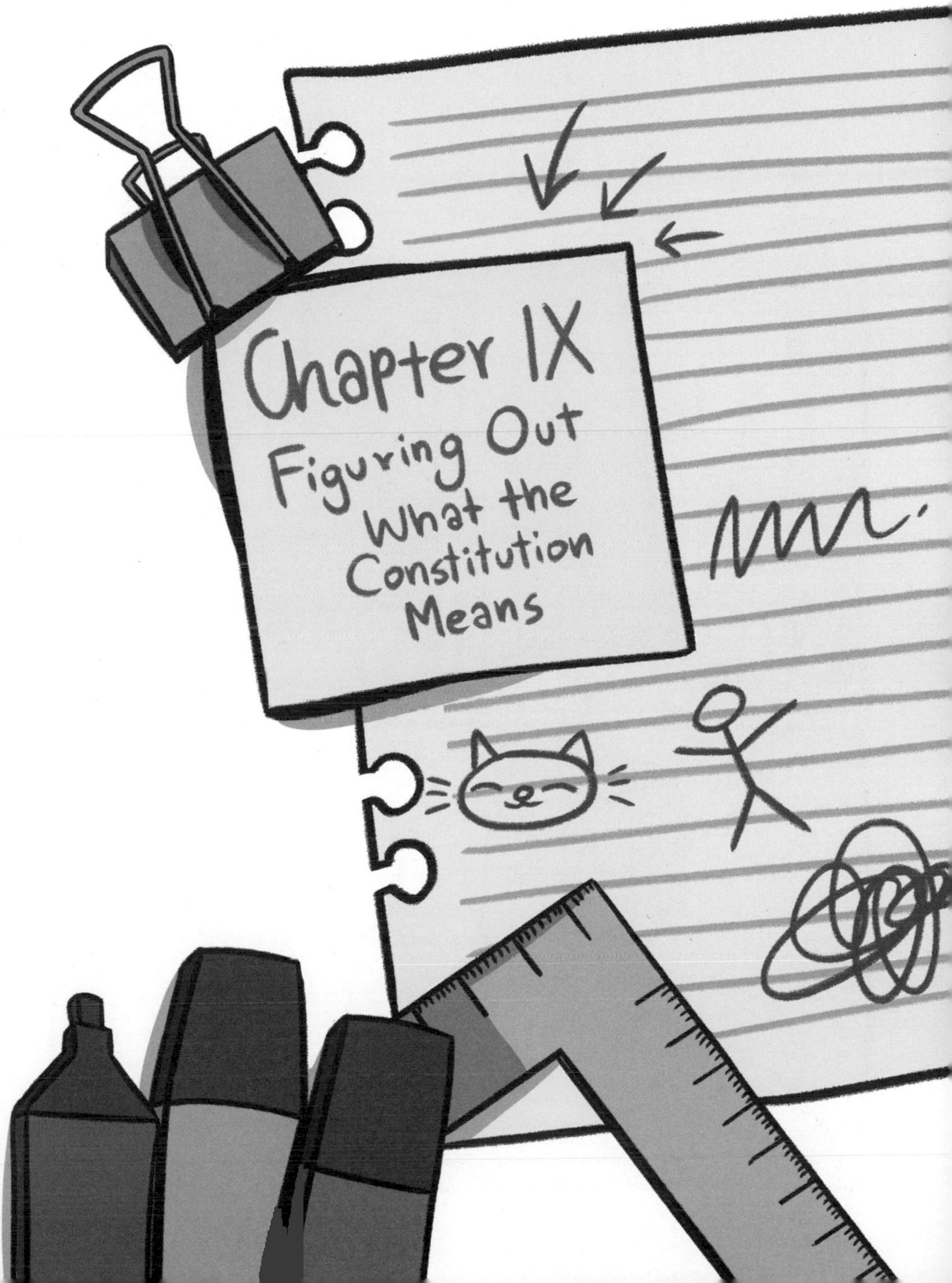
Chapter IX
Figuring Out What the Constitution Means

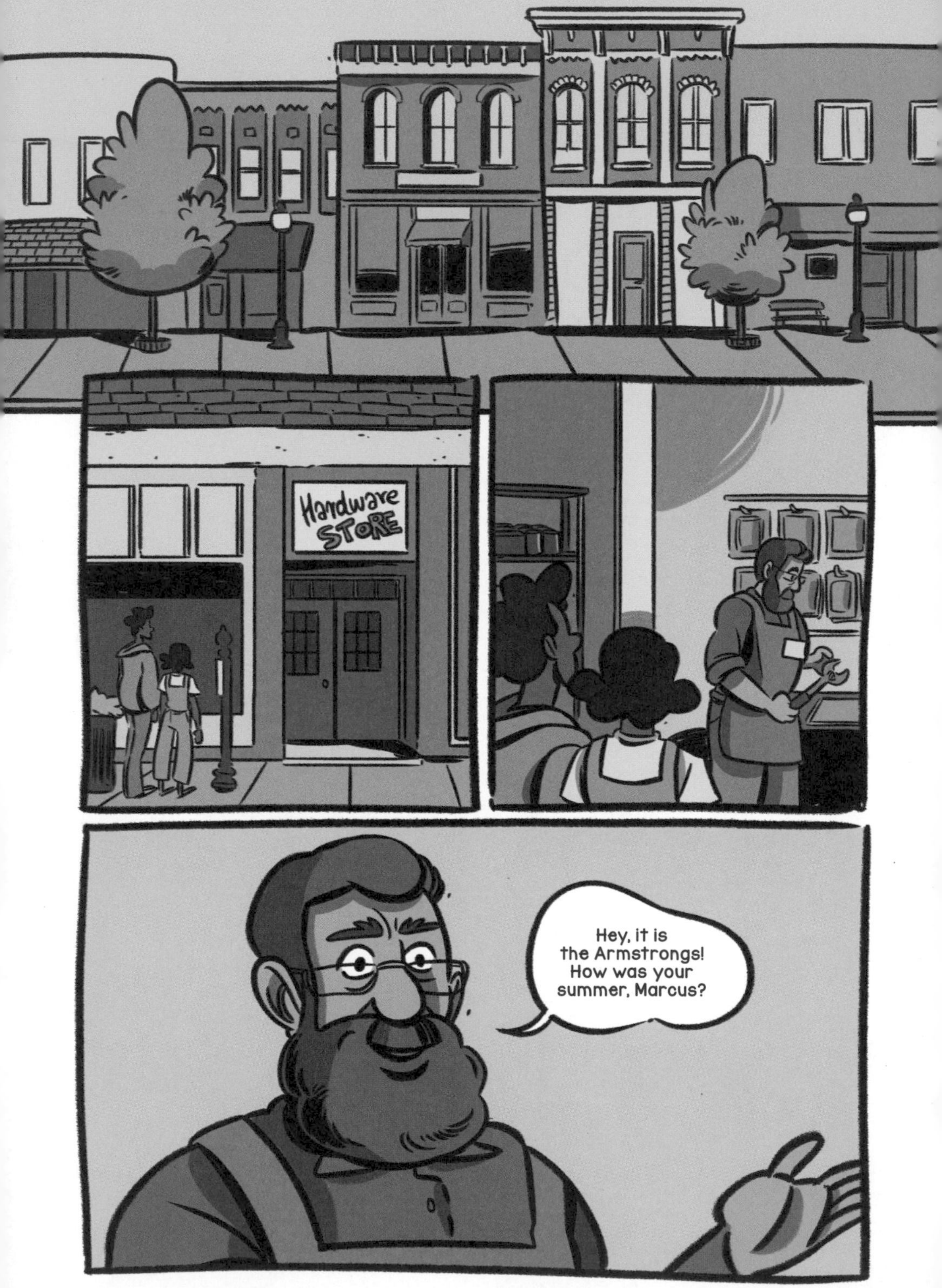
Hardware STORE
Hey, it is the Armstrongs! How was your summer, Marcus?

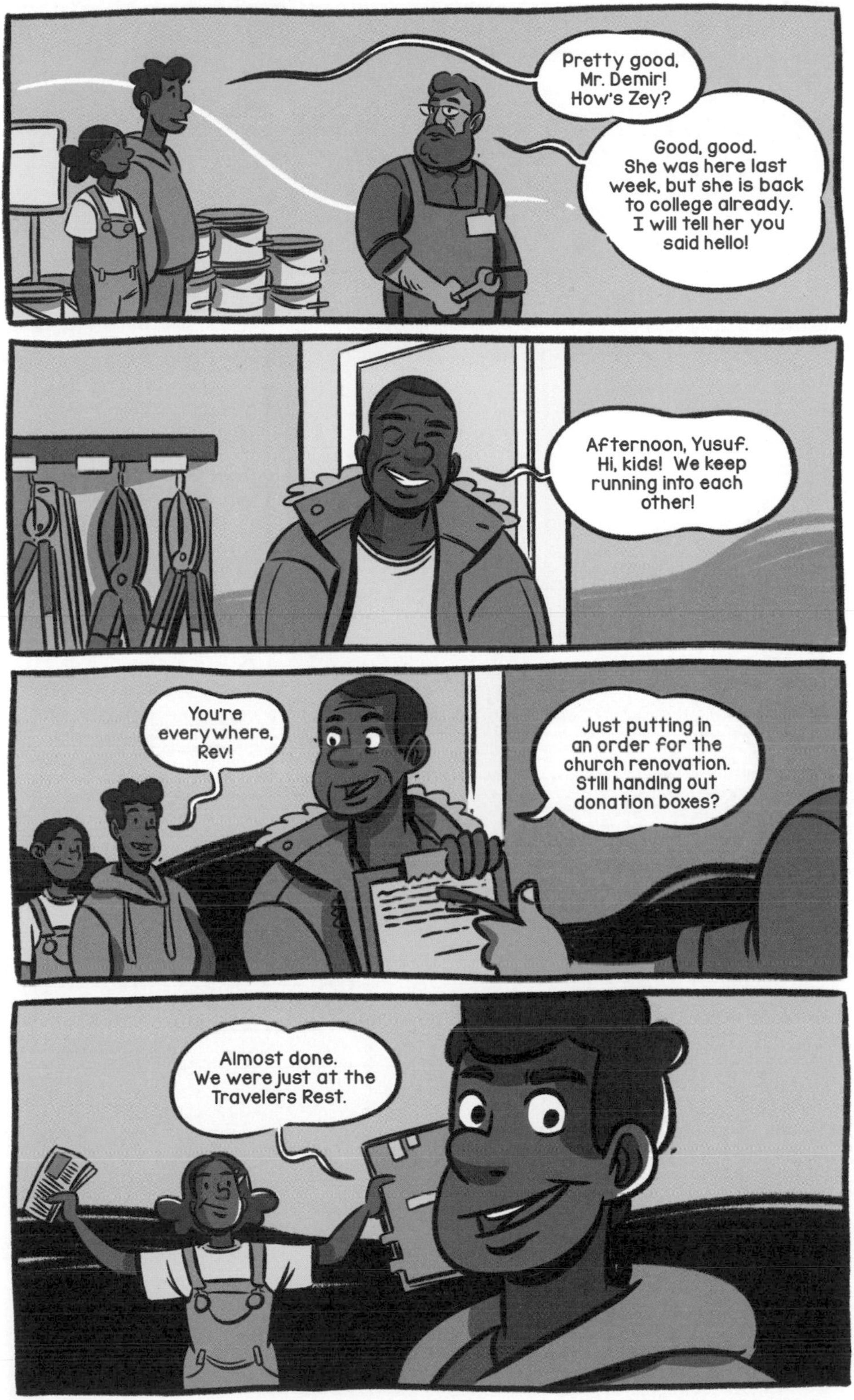

Pretty good, Mr. Demir! How's Zey?
Good, good. She was here last week, but she is back to college already. I will tell her you said hello!
Afternoon, Yusuf. Hi, kids! We keep running into each other!
You're everywhere, Rev!
Just putting in an order for the church renovation. Still handing out donation boxes?
Almost done. We were just at the Travelers Rest.

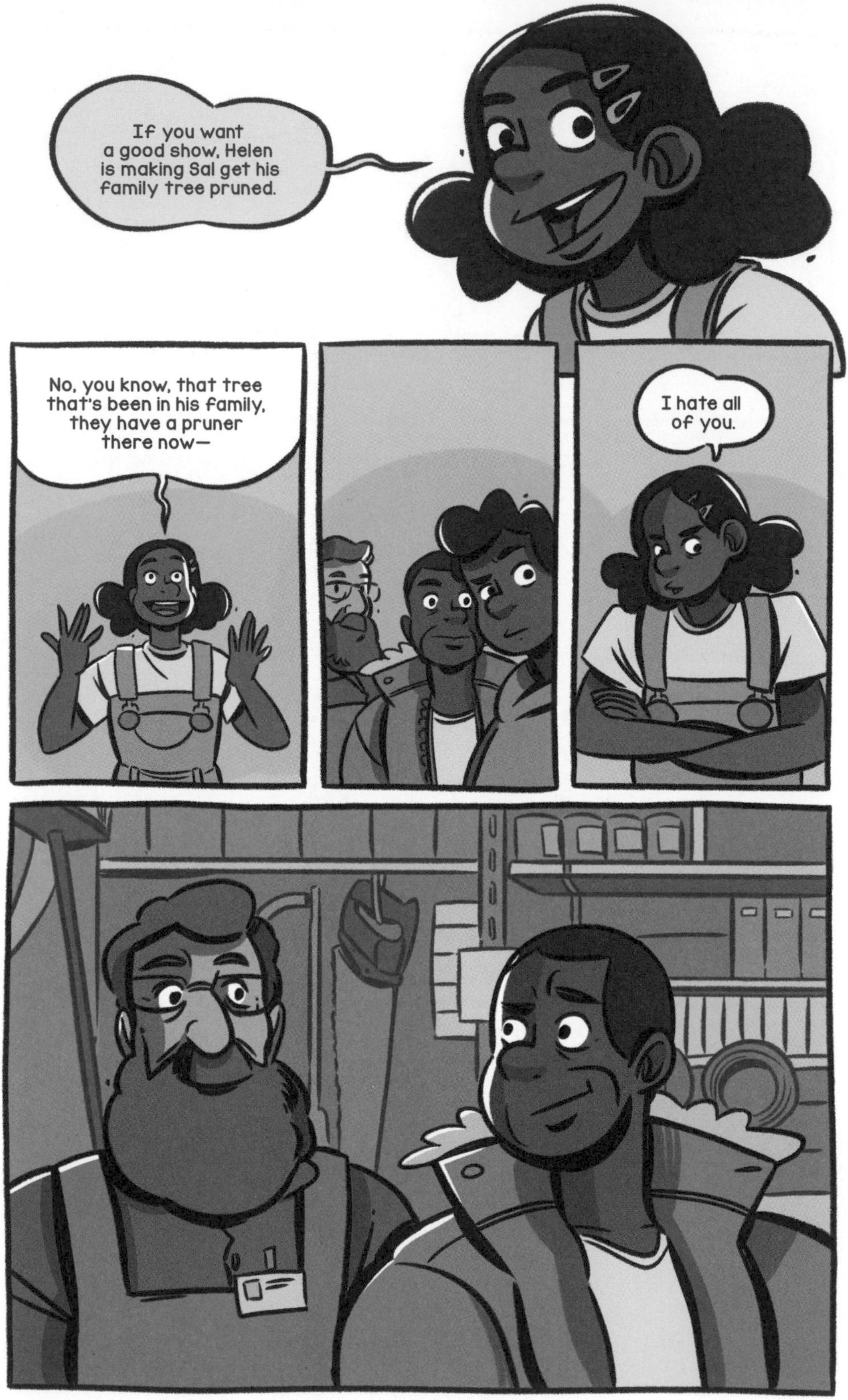
If you want a good show, Helen is making Sal get his family tree pruned.
No, you know, that tree that's been in his family, they have a pruner there now—
I hate all of you.

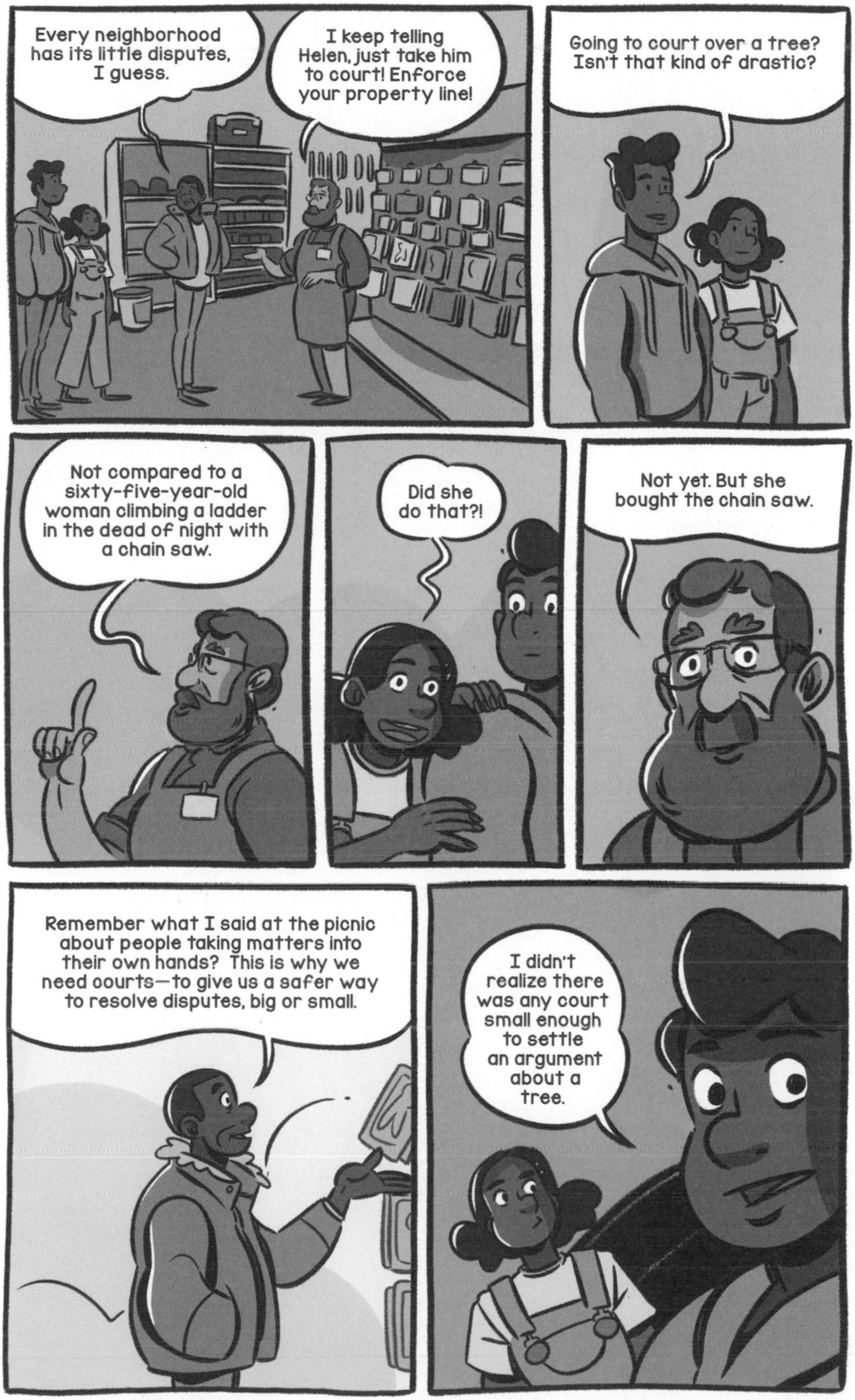
Every neighborhood has its little disputes, I guess.
I keep telling Helen, just take him to court! Enforce your property line!
Going to court over a tree? Isn't that kind of drastic?
Not compared to a sixty-five-year-old woman climbing a ladder in the dead of night with a chain saw.
Did she do that?!
Not yet. But she bought the chain saw.
Remember what I said at the picnic about people taking matters into their own hands? This is why we need courts—to give us a safer way to resolve disputes, big or small.
I didn't realize there was any court small enough to settle an argument about a tree.

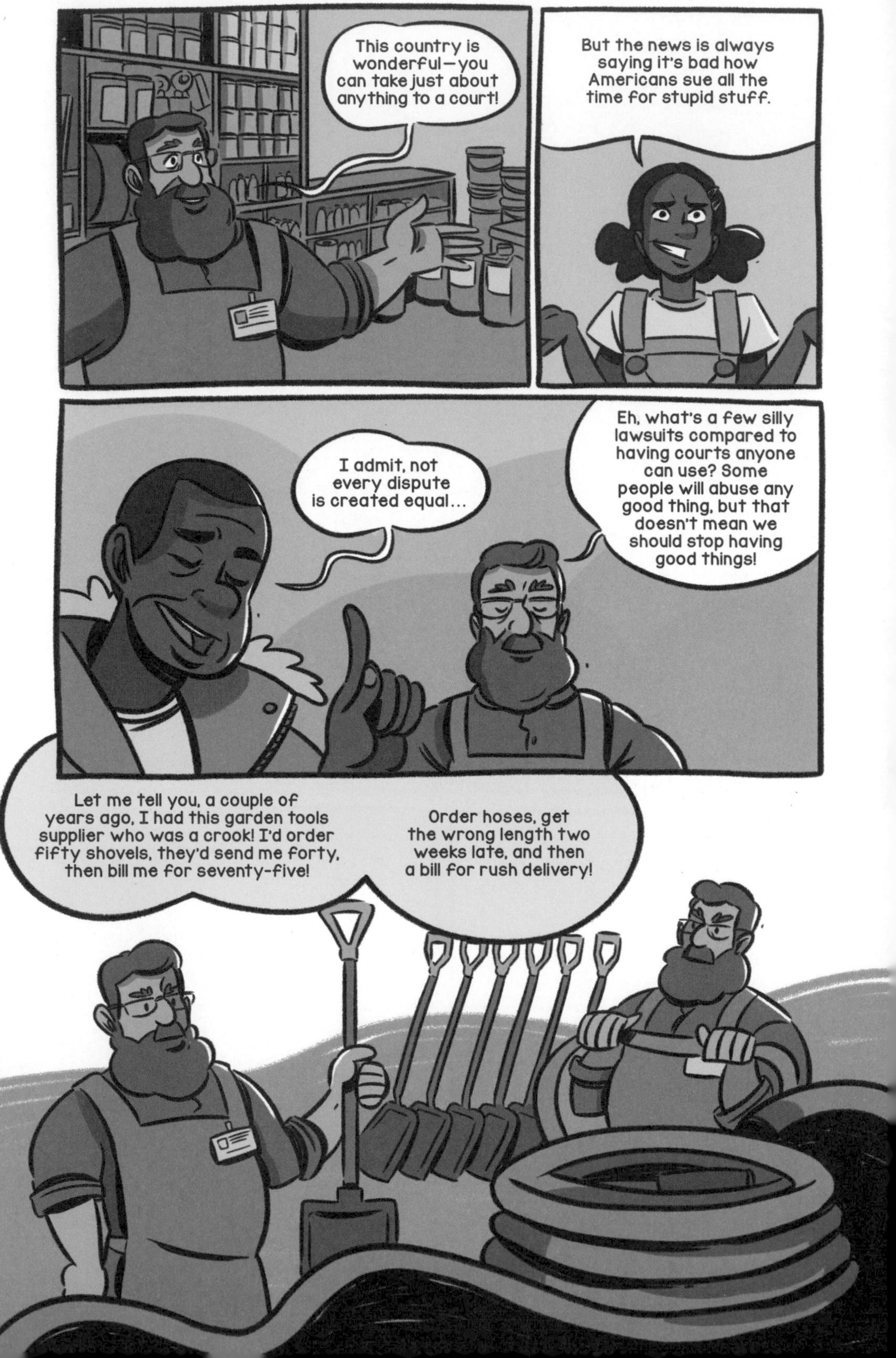
This country is wonderful—you can take just about anything to a court!
But the news is always saying it's bad how Americans sue all the time for stupid stuff.
I admit, not every dispute is created equal...
Eh, what's a few silly lawsuits compared to having courts anyone can use? Some people will abuse any good thing, but that doesn't mean we should stop having good things!
Let me tell you, a couple of years ago, I had this garden tools supplier who was a crook! I'd order fifty shovels, they'd send me forty, then bill me for seventy-five!
Order hoses, get the wrong length two weeks late, and then a bill for rush delivery!

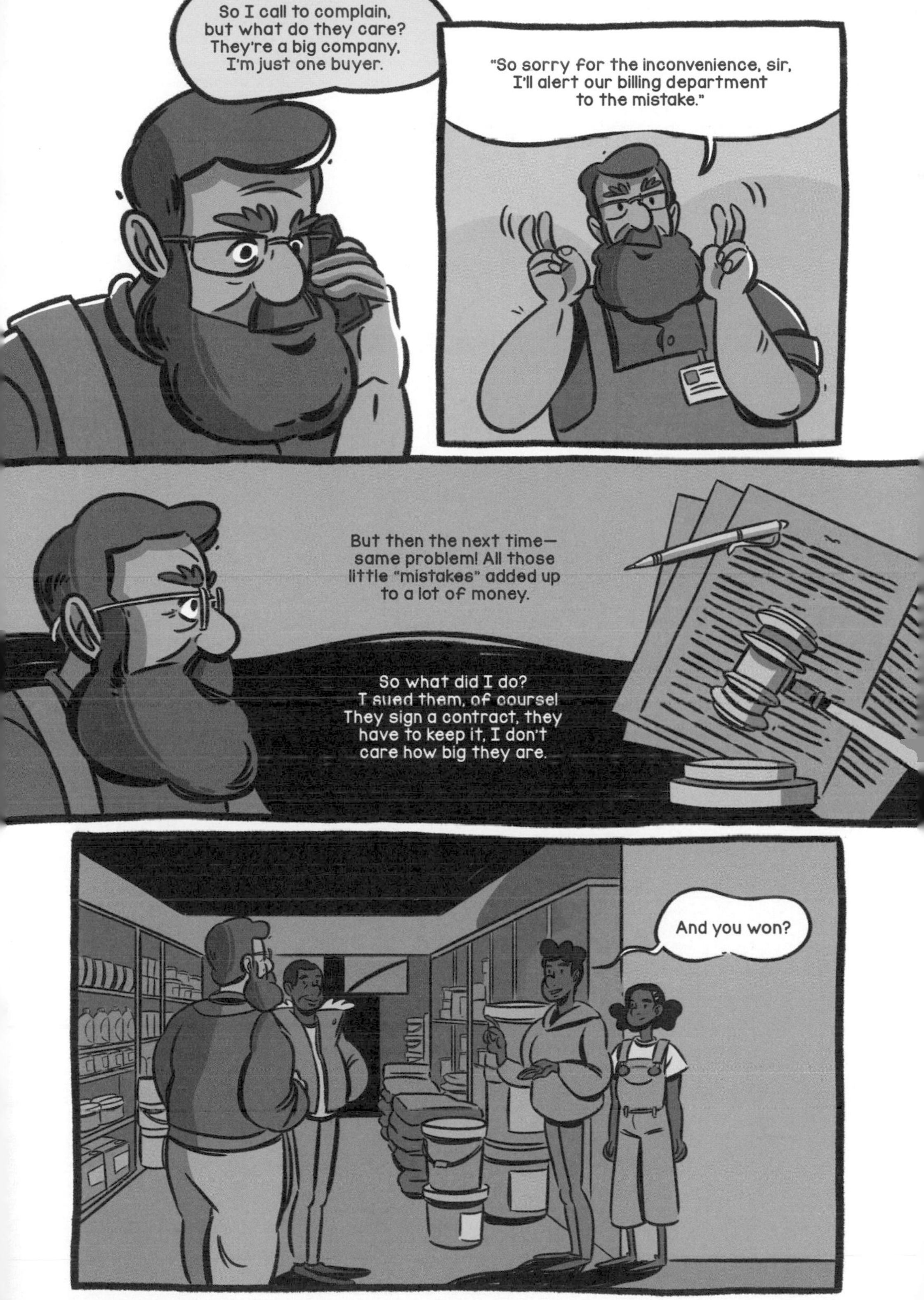
So I call to complain, but what do they care? They're a big company, I'm just one buyer.
"So sorry for the inconvenience, sir, I'll alert our billing department to the mistake."
But then the next time— same problem! All those little "mistakes" added up to a lot of money.
So what did I do? I sued them, of course! They sign a contract, they have to keep it, I don't care how big they are.
And you won?

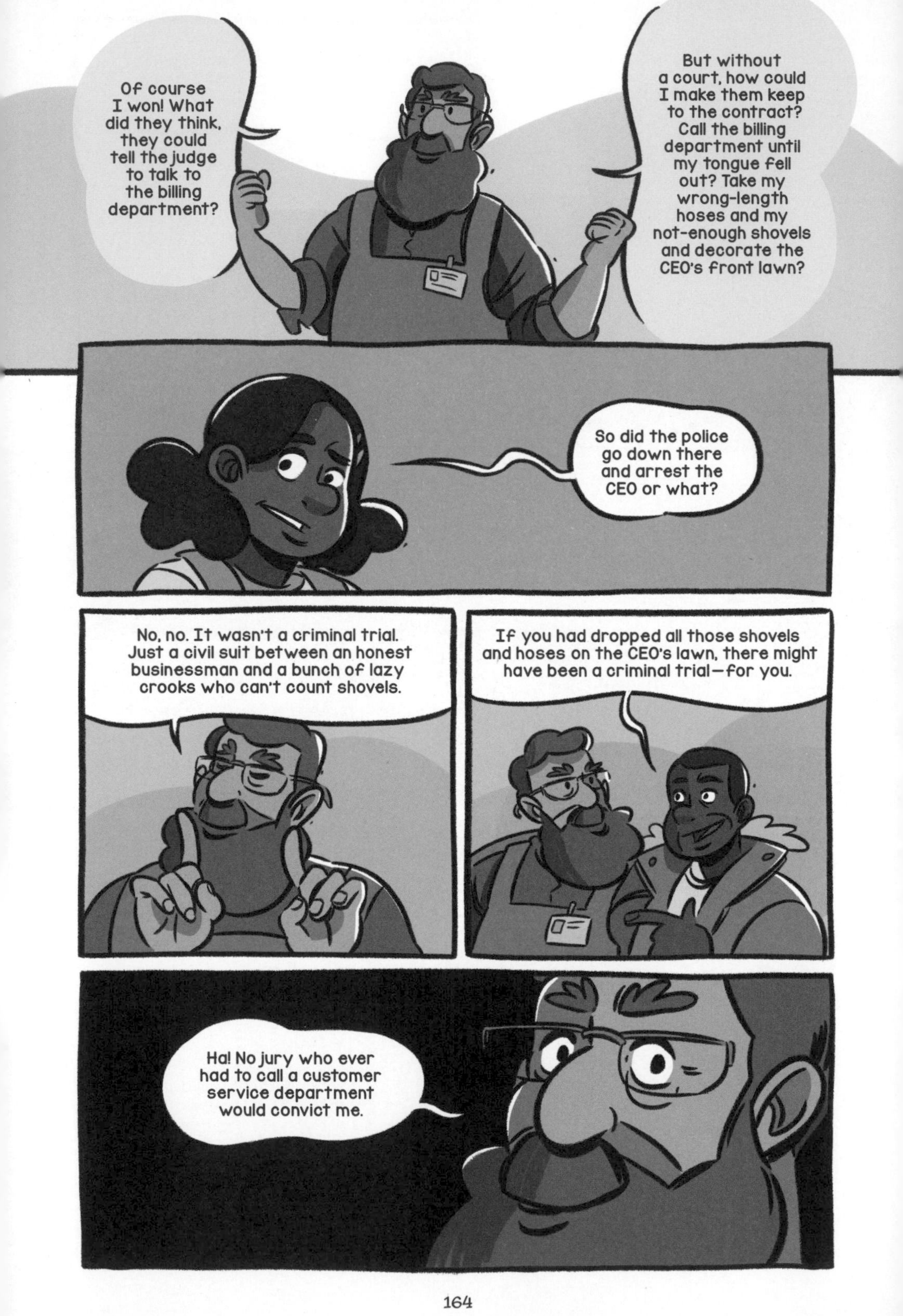
Of course I won! What did they think, they could tell the judge to talk to the billing department?
But without a court, how could I make them keep to the contract? Call the billing department until my tongue fell out? Take my wrong-length hoses and my not-enough shovels and decorate the CEO's front lawn?
So did the police go down there and arrest the CEO or what?
No, no. It wasn't a criminal trial. Just a civil suit between an honest businessman and a bunch of lazy crooks who can't count shovels.
If you had dropped all those shovels and hoses on the CEO's lawn, there might have been a criminal trial—for you.
Ha! No jury who ever had to call a customer service department would convict me.

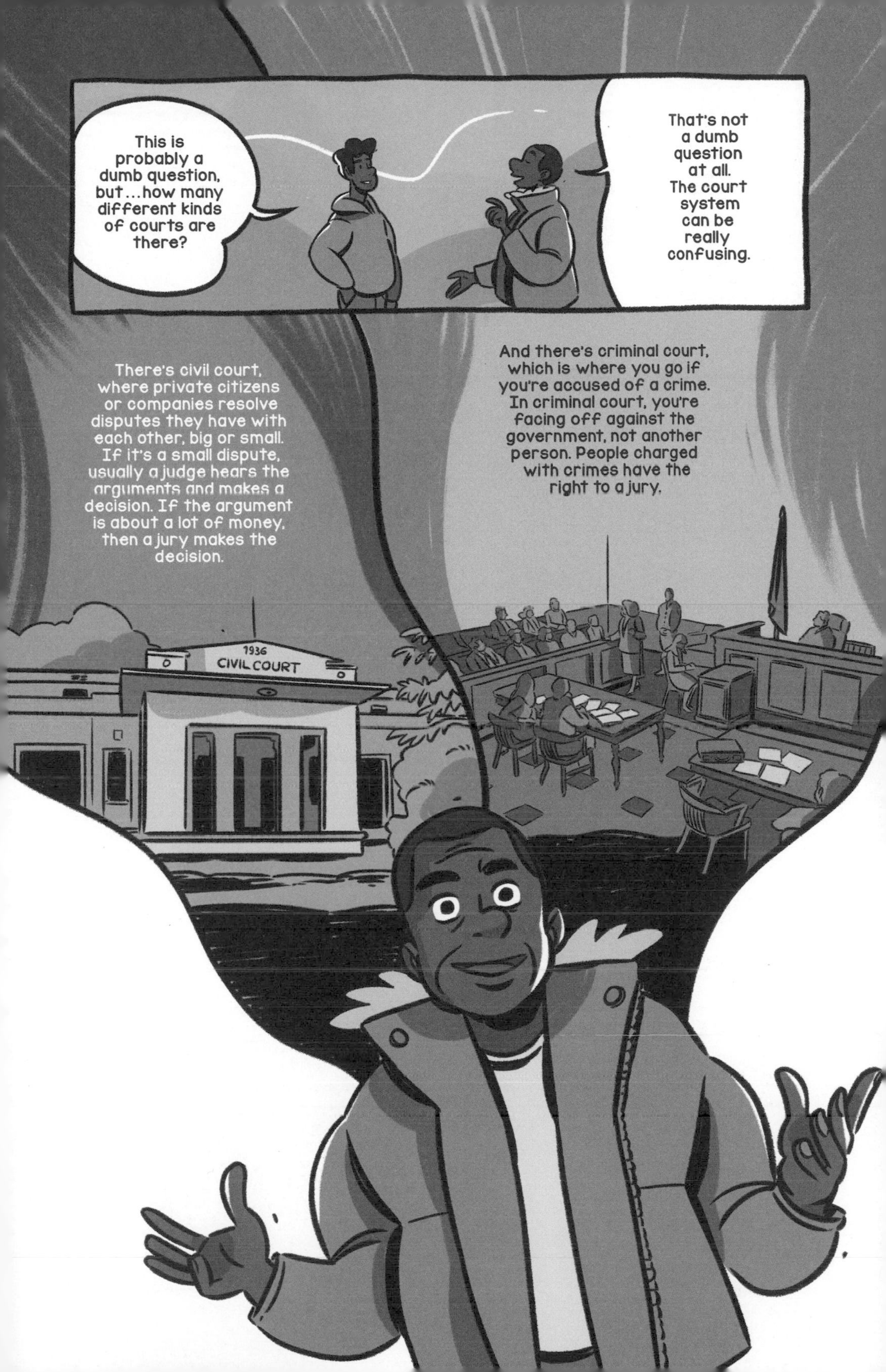
This is probably a dumb question, but...how many different kinds of courts are there?
That's not a dumb question at all. The court system can be really confusing.
There's civil court, where private citizens or companies resolve disputes they have with each other, big or small. If it's a small dispute, usually a judge hears the arguments and makes a decision. If the argument is about a lot of money, then a jury makes the decision.
1936
CIVIL COURT
And there's criminal court, which is where you go if you're accused of a crime. In criminal court, you're facing off against the government, not another person. People charged with crimes have the right to a jury.

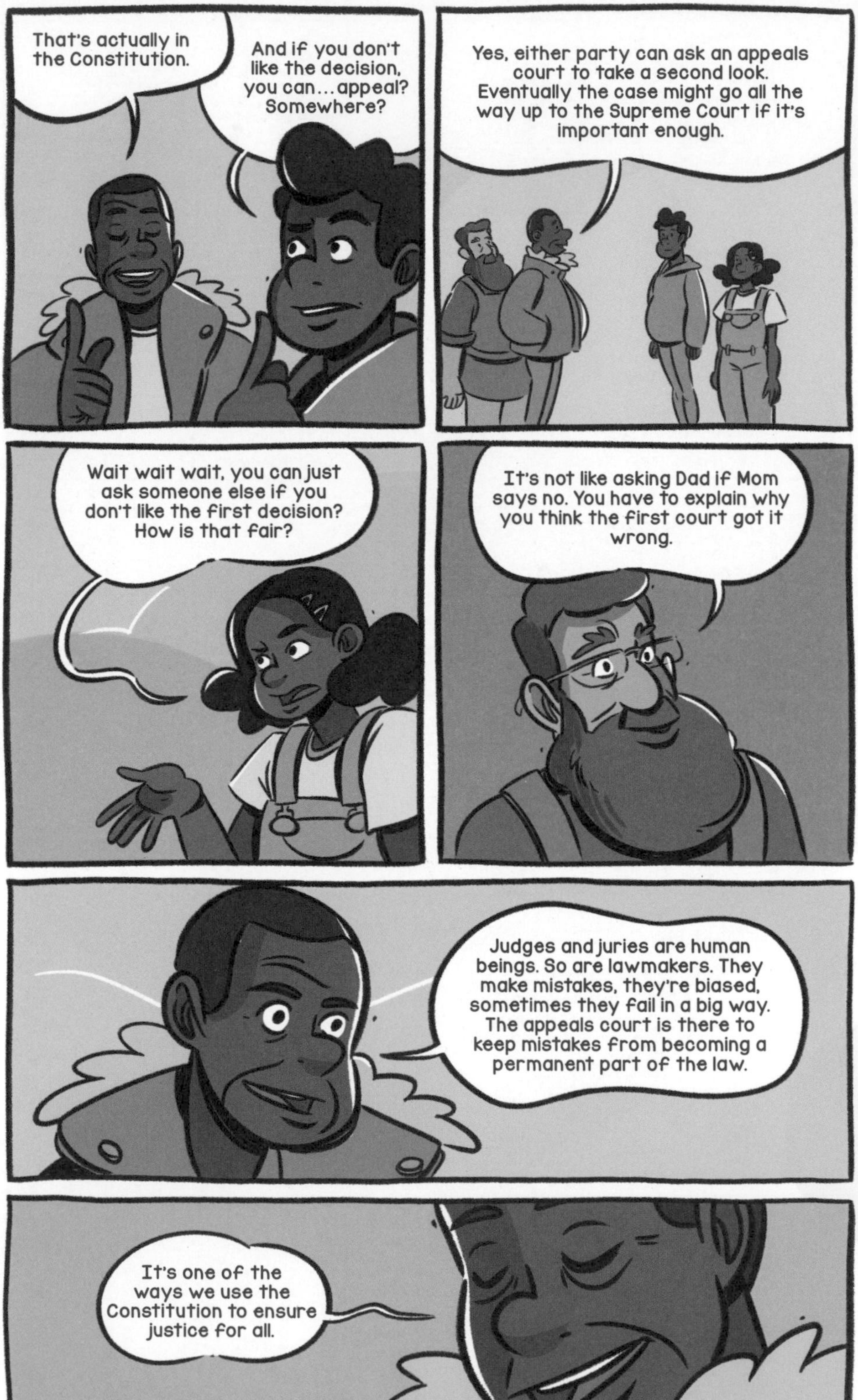

That's actually in the Constitution.
And if you don't like the decision, you can...appeal? Somewhere?
Yes, either party can ask an appeals court to take a second look. Eventually the case might go all the way up to the Supreme Court if it's important enough.
Wait wait wait, you can just ask someone else if you don't like the first decision? How is that fair?
It's not like asking Dad if Mom says no. You have to explain why you think the first court got it wrong.
Judges and juries are human beings. So are lawmakers. They make mistakes, they're biased, sometimes they fail in a big way. The appeals court is there to keep mistakes from becoming a permanent part of the law.
It's one of the ways we use the Constitution to ensure justice for all.

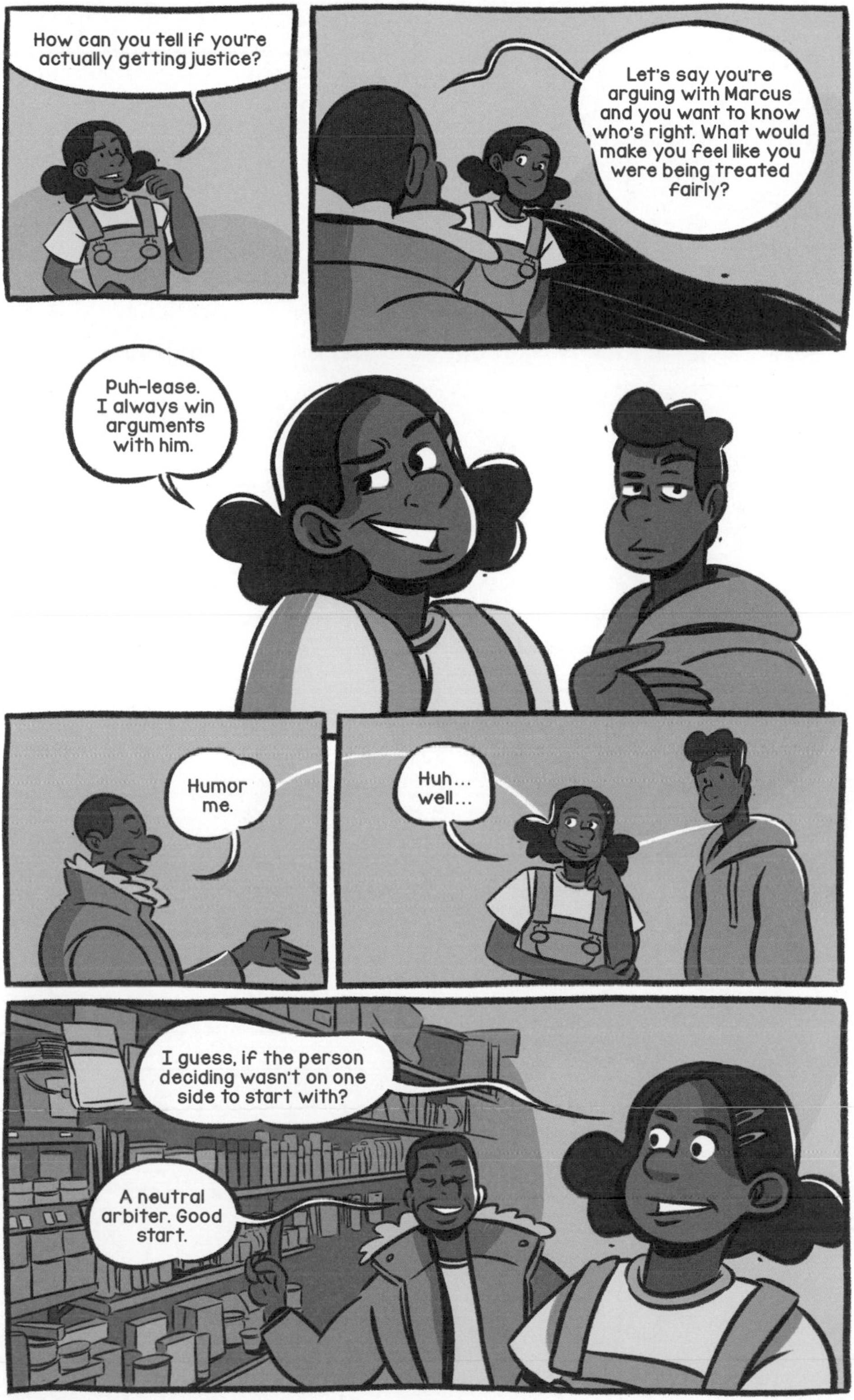
How can you tell if you're actually getting justice?
Let's say you're arguing with Marcus and you want to know who's right. What would make you feel like you were being treated fairly?
Puh-lease. I always win arguments with him.
Humor me.
Huh... well...
I guess, if the person deciding wasn't on one side to start with?
A neutral arbiter. Good start.

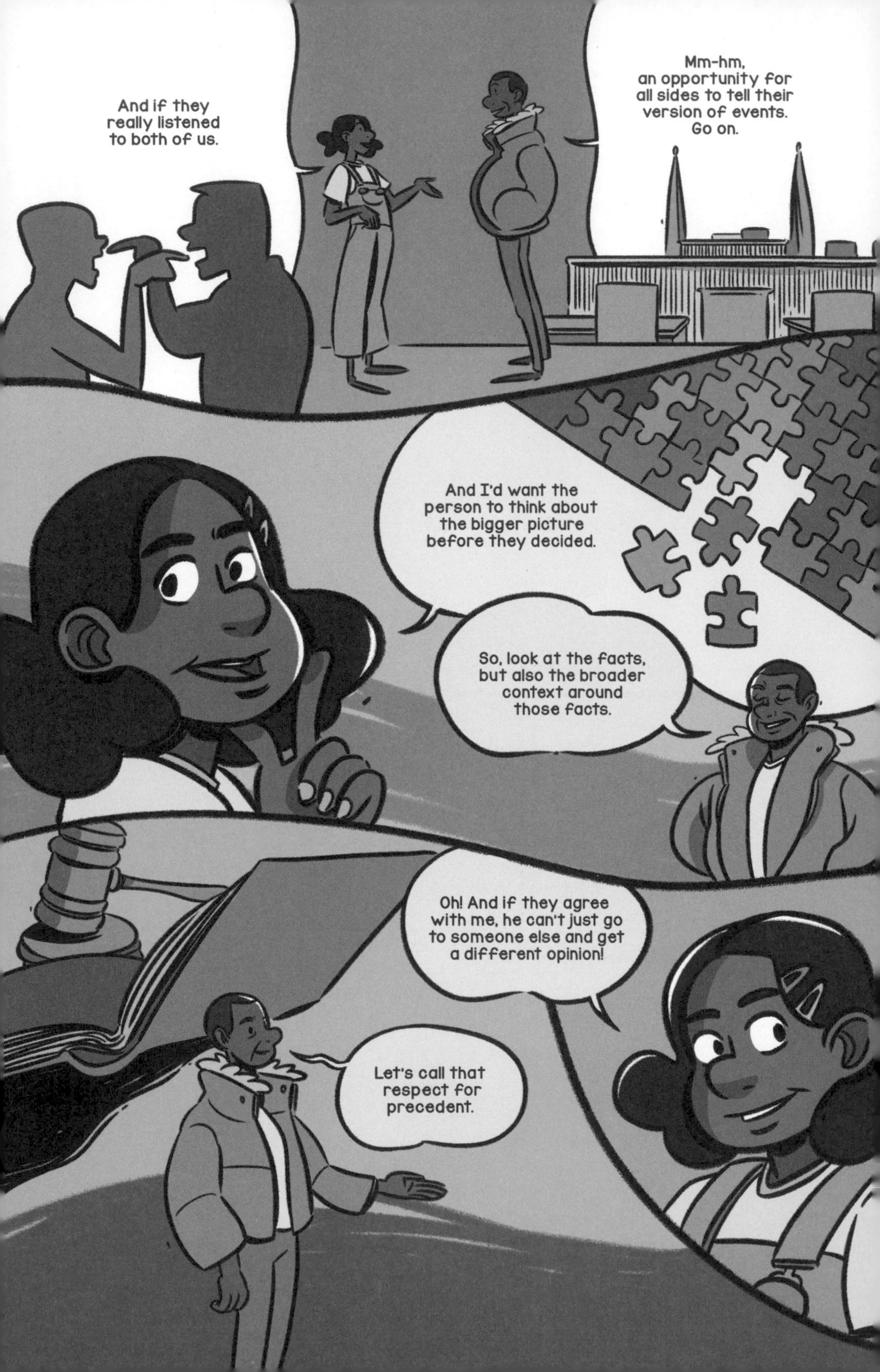
And if they really listened to both of us.
Mm-hm, an opportunity for all sides to tell their version of events. Go on.
And I'd want the person to think about the bigger picture before they decided.
So, look at the facts, but also the broader context around those facts.
Oh! And if they agree with me, he can't just go to someone else and get a different opinion!
Let's call that respect for precedent.

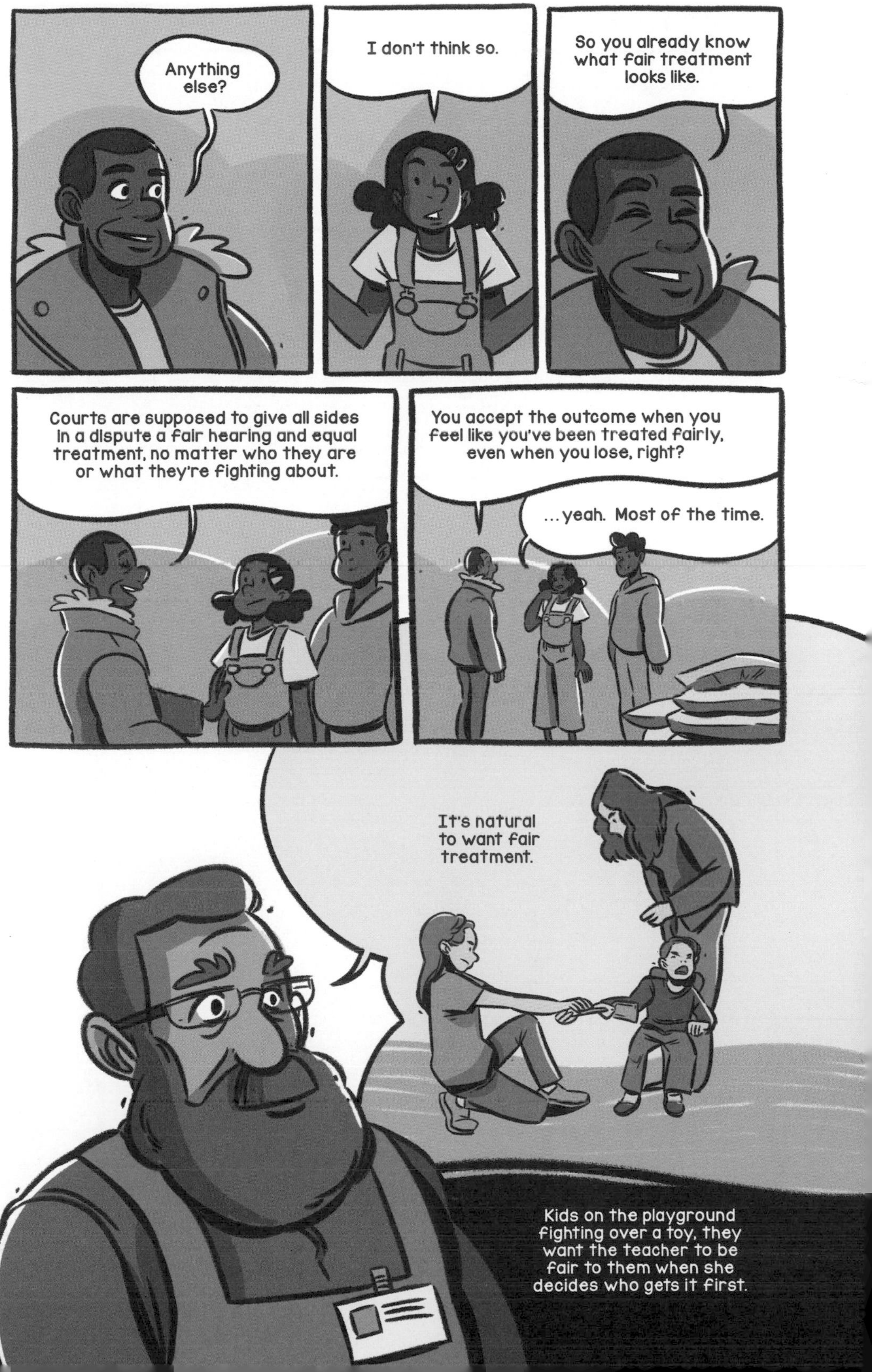
Anything else?
I don't think so.
So you already know what fair treatment looks like.
Courts are supposed to give all sides in a dispute a fair hearing and equal treatment, no matter who they are or what they're fighting about.
You accept the outcome when you feel like you've been treated fairly, even when you lose, right?
...yeah. Most of the time.
It's natural to want fair treatment.
Kids on the playground fighting over a toy, they want the teacher to be fair to them when she decides who gets it first.

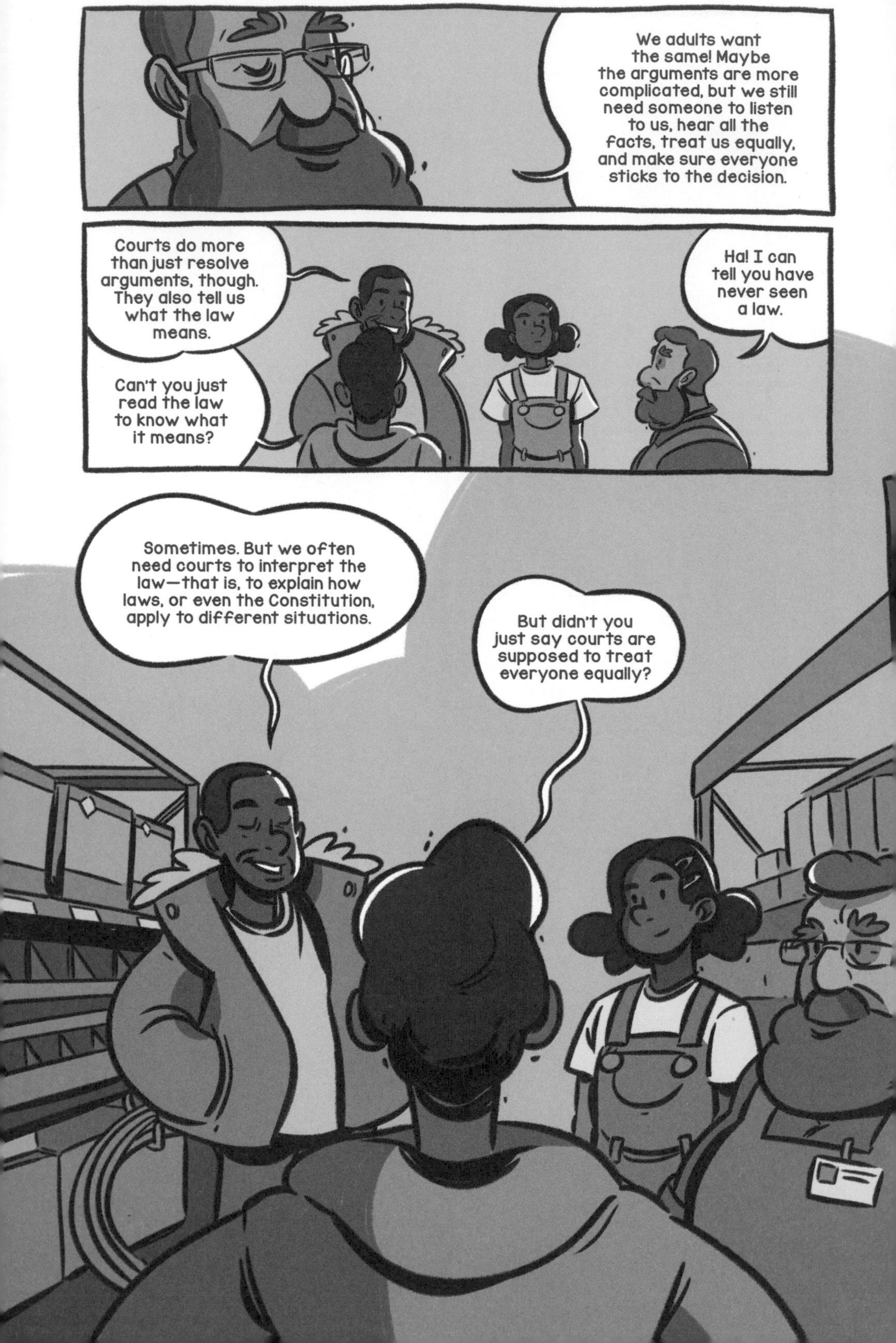
We adults want the same! Maybe the arguments are more complicated, but we still need someone to listen to us, hear all the facts, treat us equally, and make sure everyone sticks to the decision.
Courts do more than just resolve arguments, though. They also tell us what the law means.
Ha! I can tell you have never seen a law.
Can't you just read the law to know what it means?
Sometimes. But we often need courts to interpret the law—that is, to explain how laws, or even the Constitution, apply to different situations.
But didn't you just say courts are supposed to treat everyone equally?

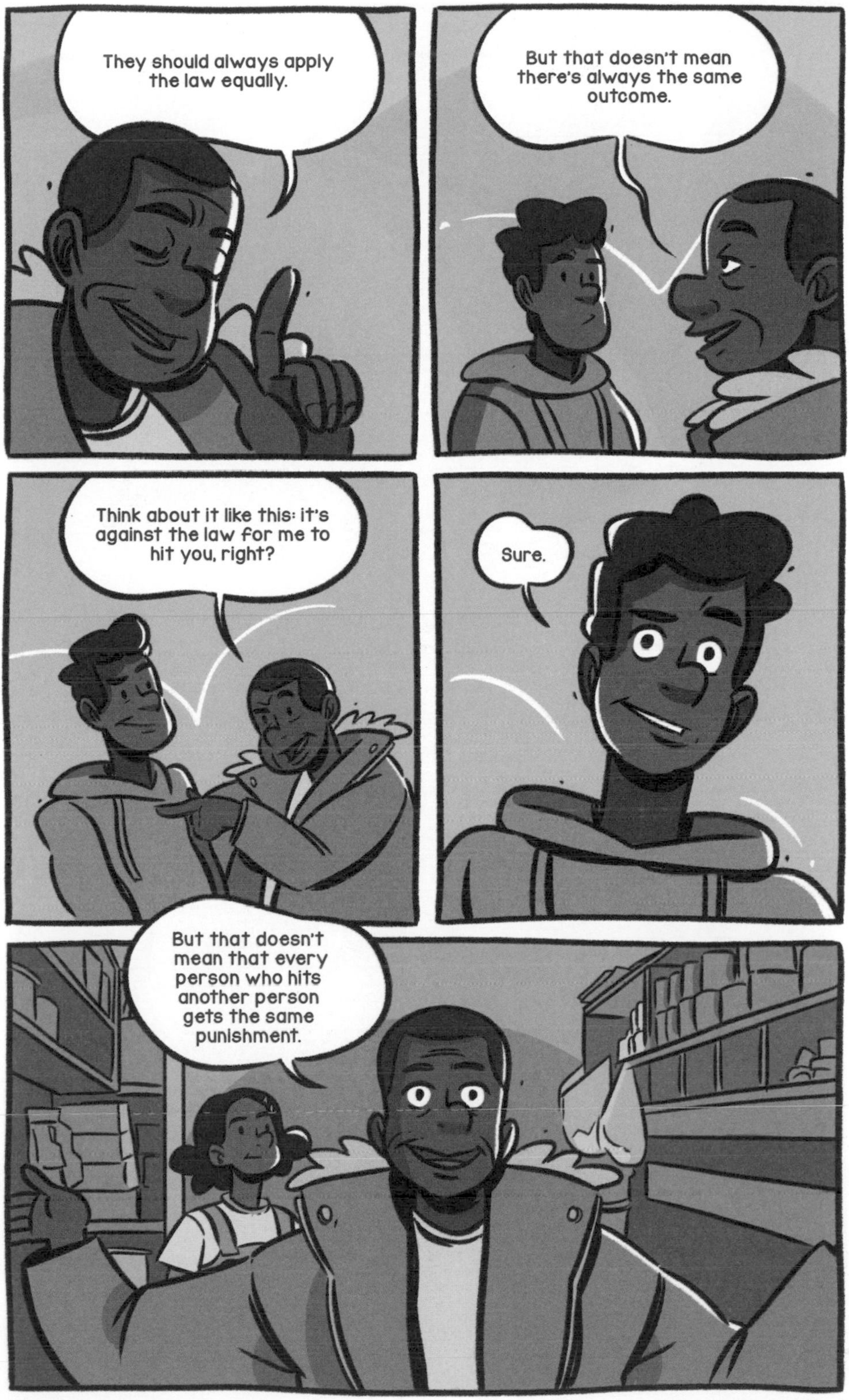
They should always apply the law equally.
But that doesn't mean there's always the same outcome.
Think about it like this: it's against the law for me to hit you, right?
Sure.
But that doesn't mean that every person who hits another person gets the same punishment.

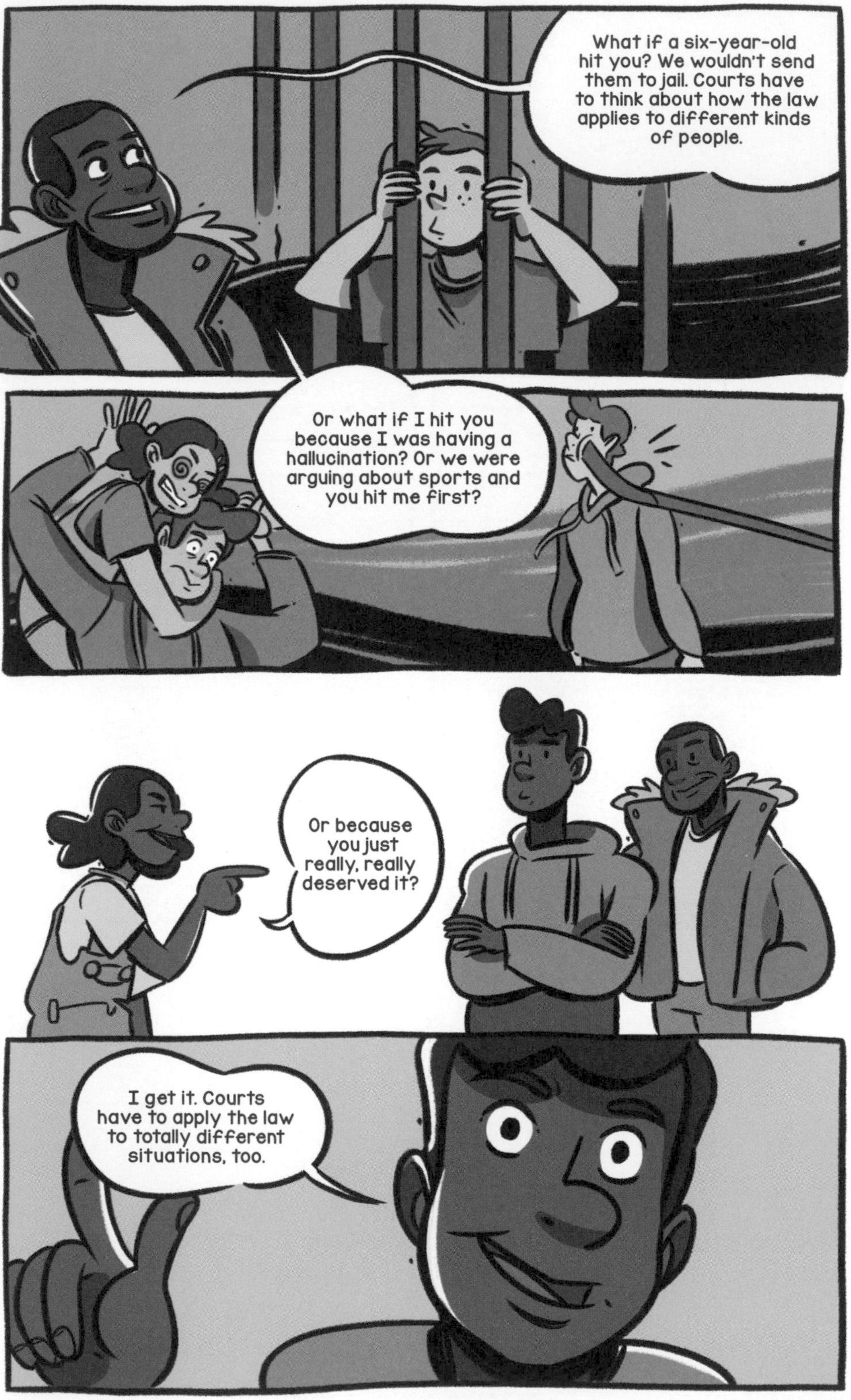
What if a six-year-old hit you? We wouldn't send them to jail. Courts have to think about how the law applies to different kinds of people.
Or what if I hit you because I was having a hallucination? Or we were arguing about sports and you hit me first?
Or because you just really, really deserved it?
I get it. Courts have to apply the law to totally different situations, too.

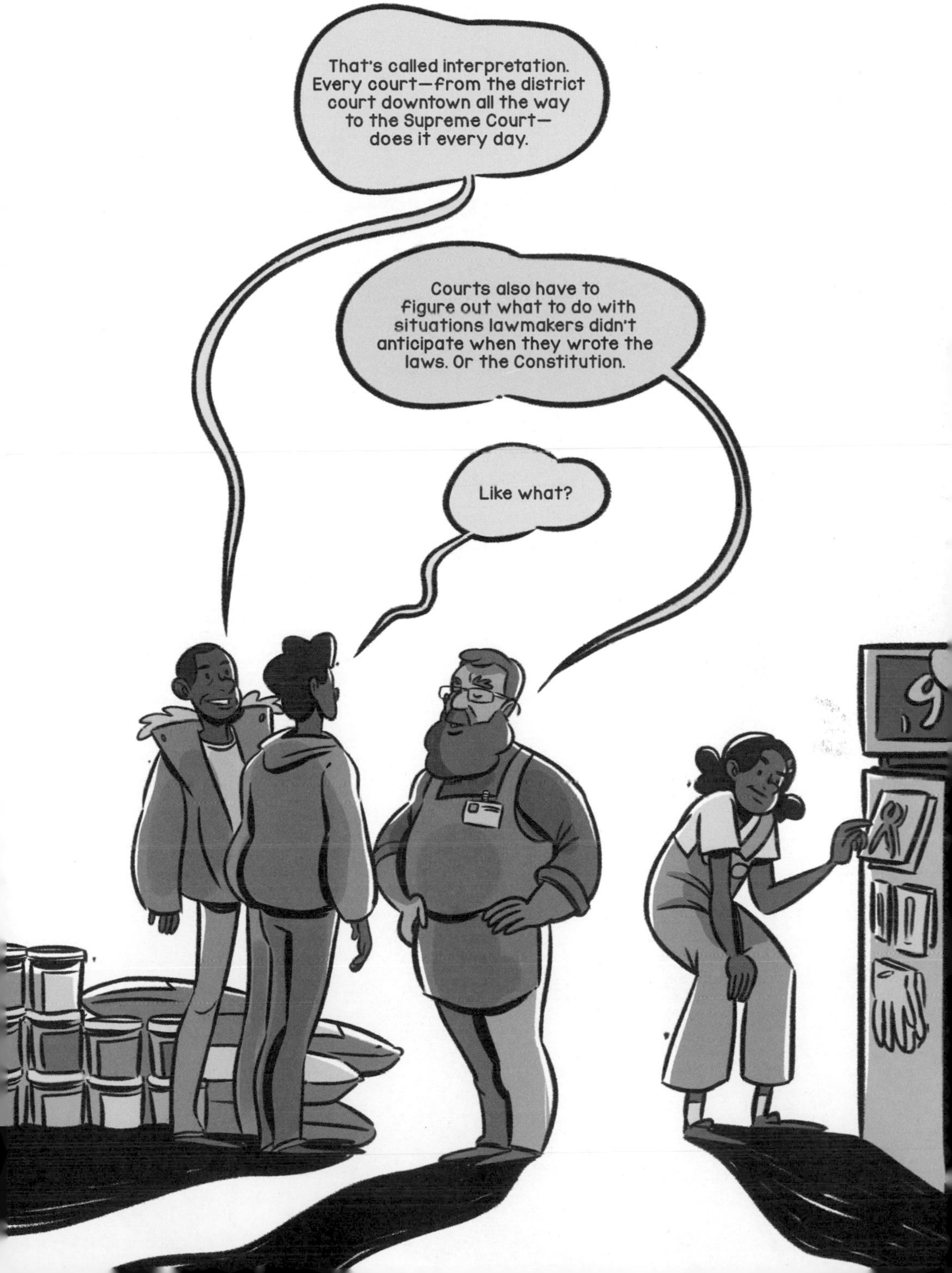
That's called interpretation. Every court—from the district court downtown all the way to the Supreme Court—does it every day.
Courts also have to figure out what to do with situations lawmakers didn't anticipate when they wrote the laws. Or the Constitution.
Like what?

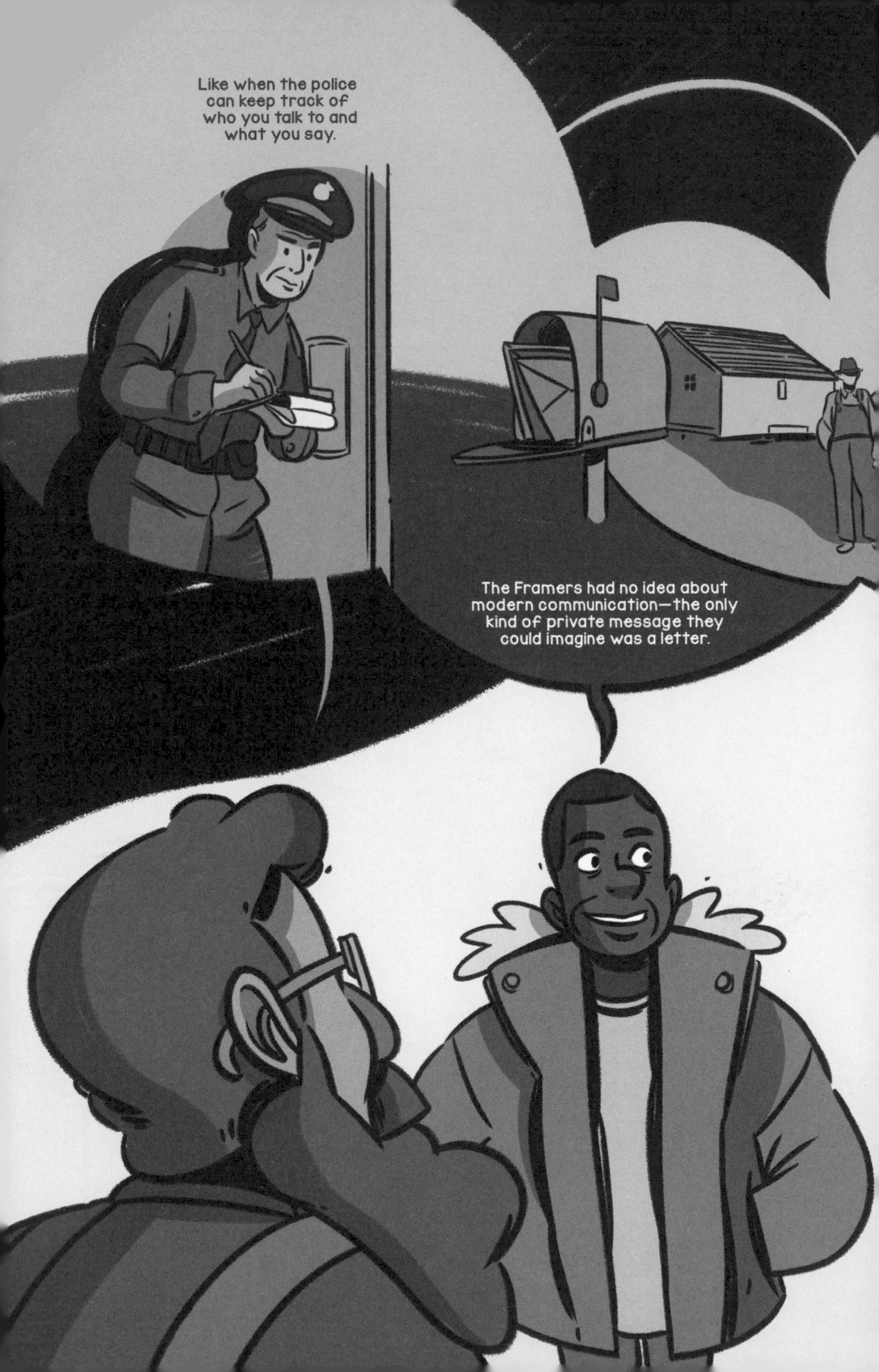
Like when the police can keep track of who you talk to and what you say.
The Framers had no idea about modern communication—the only kind of private message they could imagine was a letter.

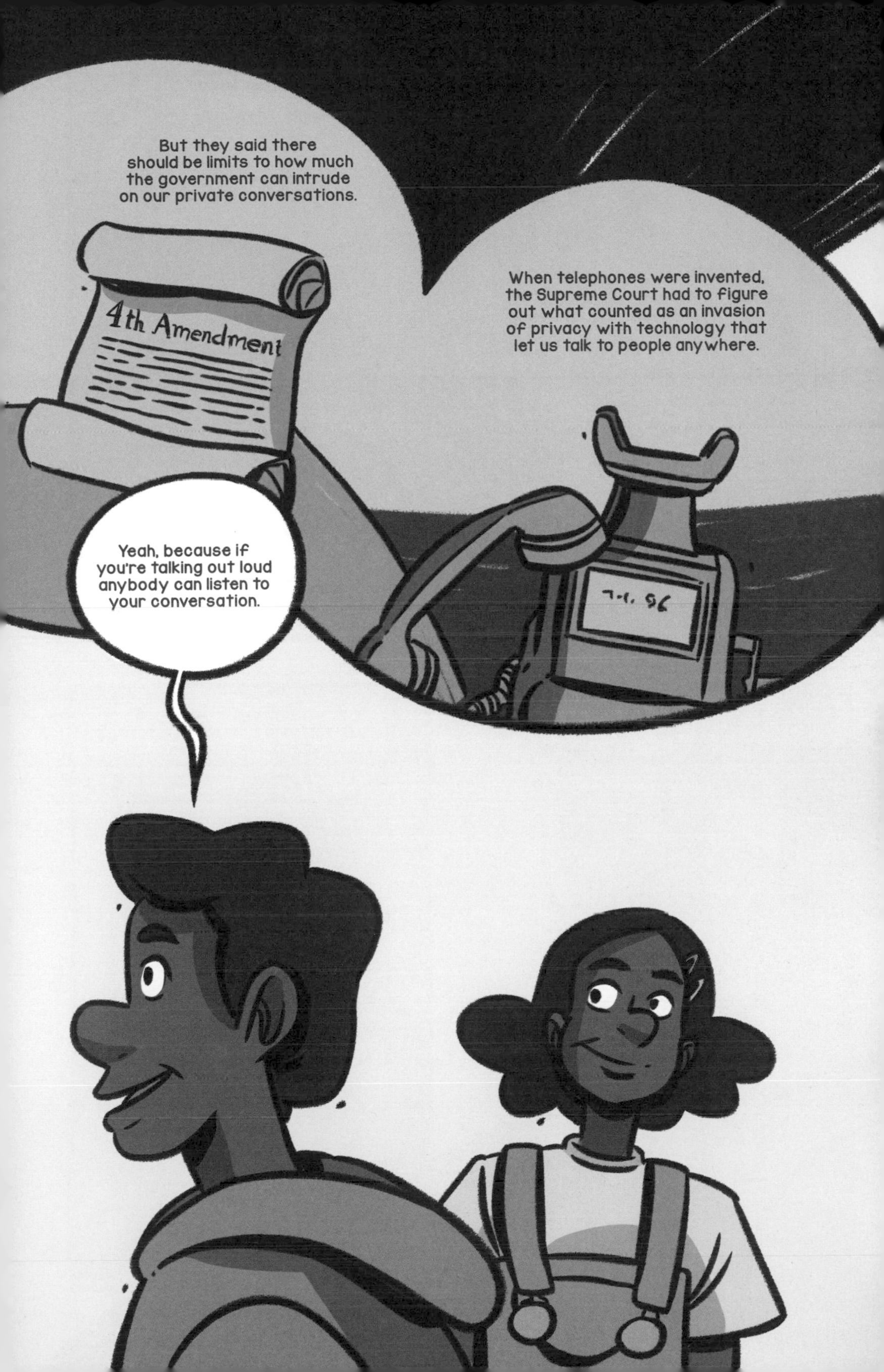
But they said there should be limits to how much the government can intrude on our private conversations.
4th Amendment
When telephones were invented, the Supreme Court had to figure out what counted as an invasion of privacy with technology that let us talk to people anywhere.
7-1, 96
Yeah, because if you're talking out loud anybody can listen to your conversation.

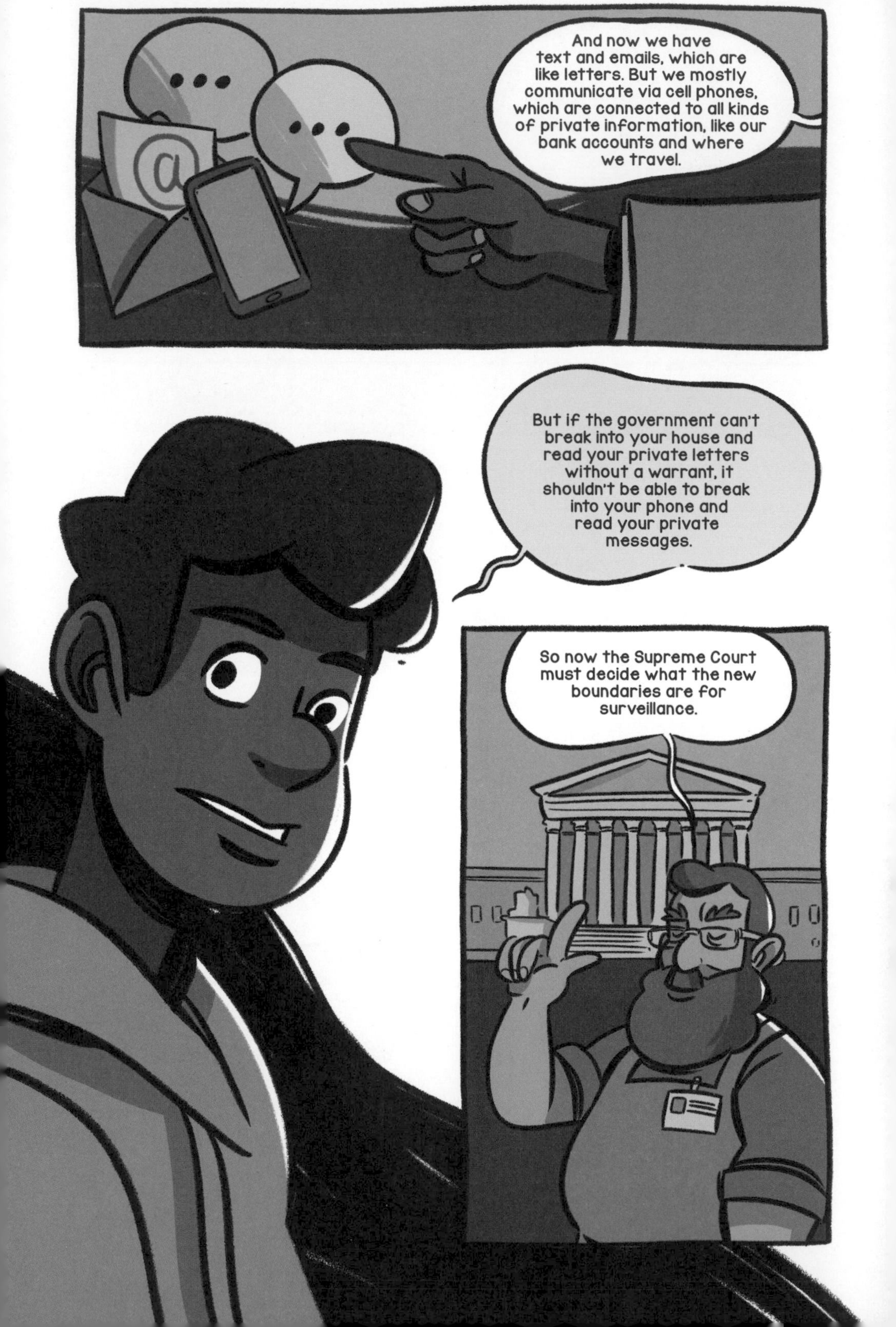
And now we have text and emails, which are like letters. But we mostly communicate via cell phones, which are connected to all kinds of private information, like our bank accounts and where we travel.
But if the government can't break into your house and read your private letters without a warrant, it shouldn't be able to break into your phone and read your private messages.
So now the Supreme Court must decide what the new boundaries are for surveillance.

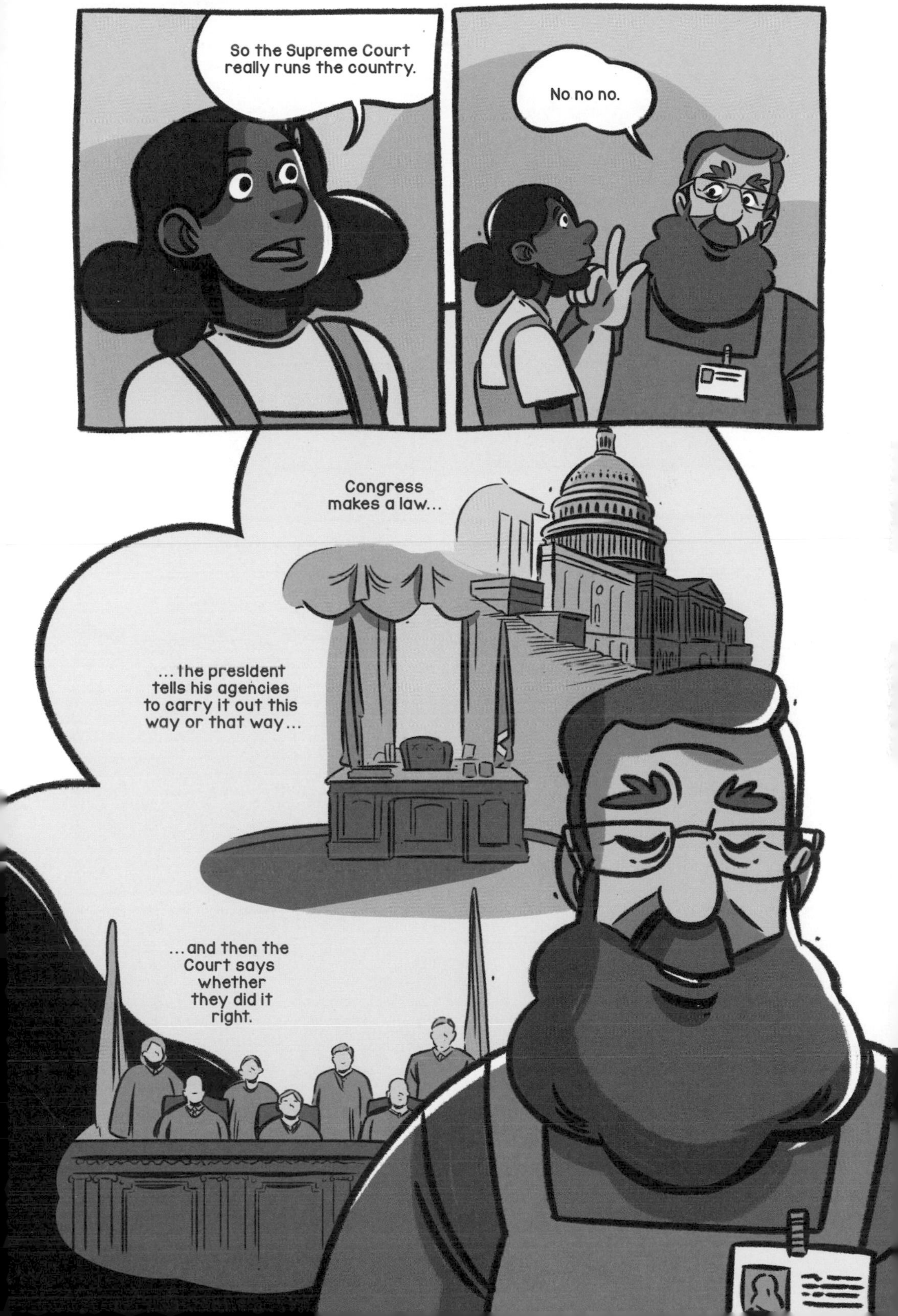
So the Supreme Court really runs the country.
No no no.
Congress makes a law...
... the president tells his agencies to carry it out this way or that way...
...and then the Court says whether they did it right.

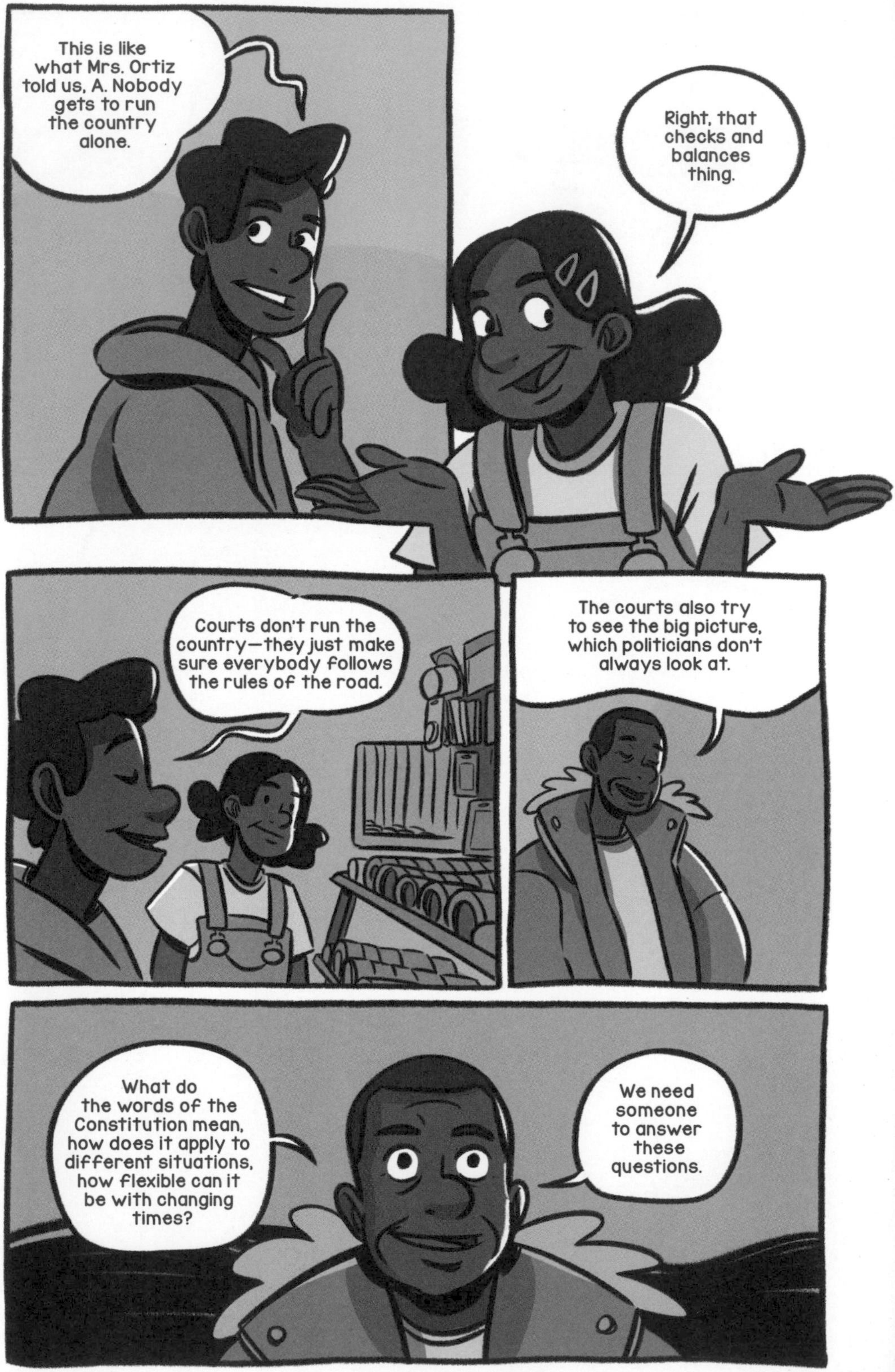
This is like what Mrs. Ortiz told us, A. Nobody gets to run the country alone.
Right, that checks and balances thing.
Courts don't run the country—they just make sure everybody follows the rules of the road.
The courts also try to see the big picture, which politicians don't always look at.
What do the words of the Constitution mean, how does it apply to different situations, how flexible can it be with changing times?
We need someone to answer these questions.

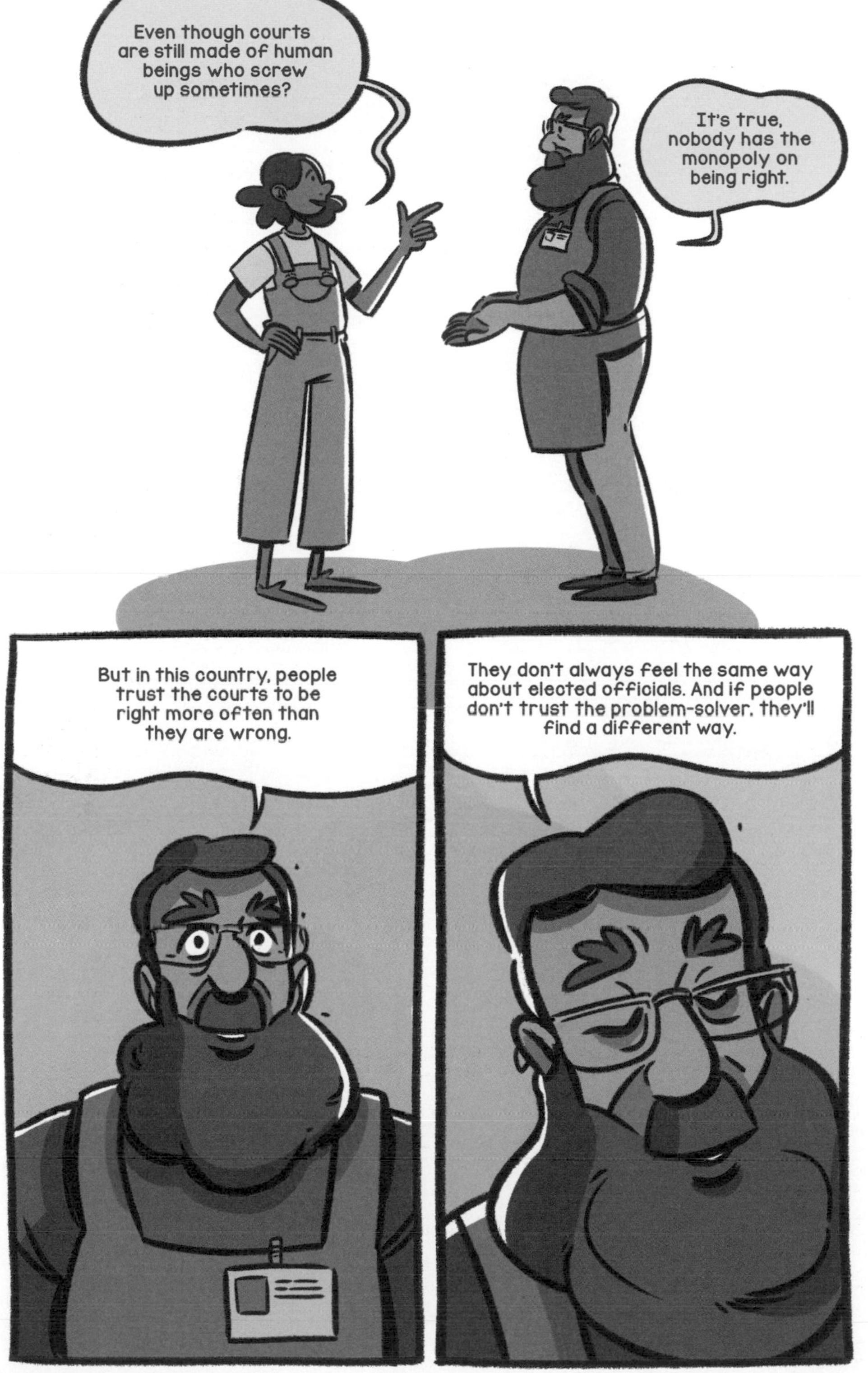
Even though courts are still made of human beings who screw up sometimes?
It's true, nobody has the monopoly on being right.
But in this country, people trust the courts to be right more often than they are wrong.
They don't always feel the same way about elected officials. And if people don't trust the problem-solver, they'll find a different way.

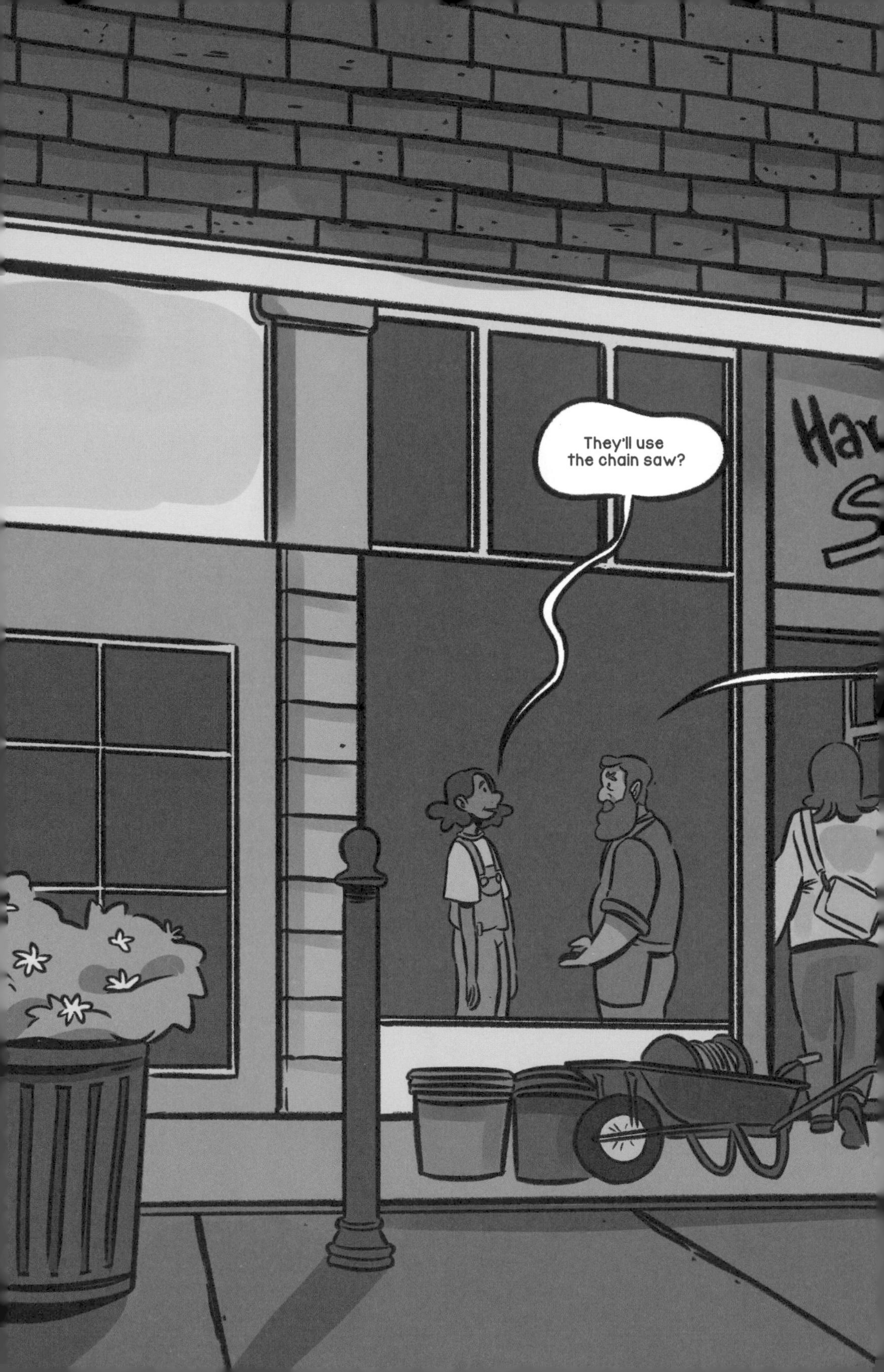
They'll use the chain saw?

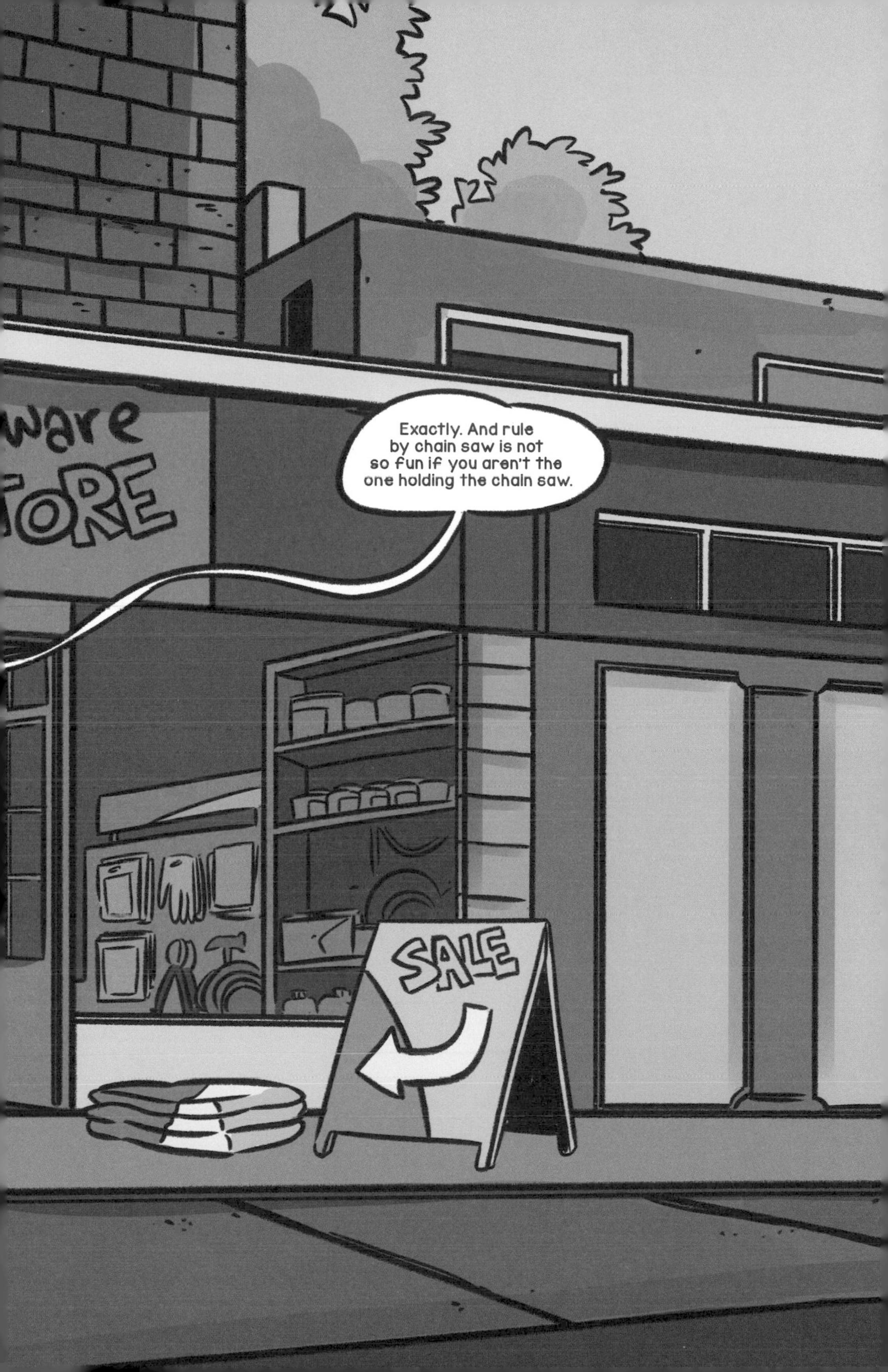
ware
TORE
Exactly. And rule by chain saw is not so fun if you aren't the one holding the chain saw.
SALE

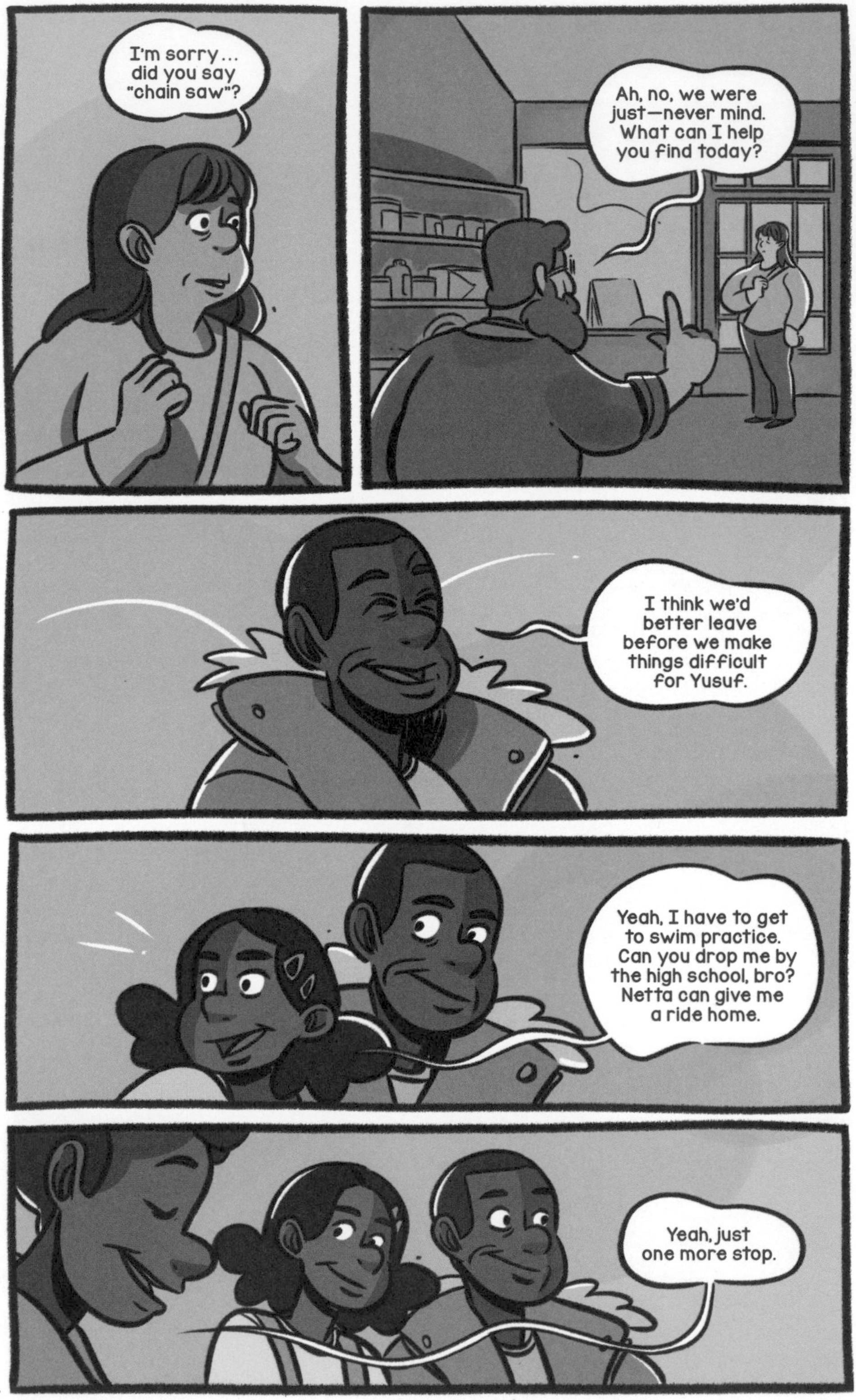
I'm sorry...
did you say
"chain saw"?
Ah, no, we were
just—never mind.
What can I help
you find today?
I think we'd
better leave
before we make
things difficult
for Yusuf.
Yeah, I have to get
to swim practice.
Can you drop me by
the high school, bro?
Netta can give me
a ride home.
Yeah, just
one more stop.

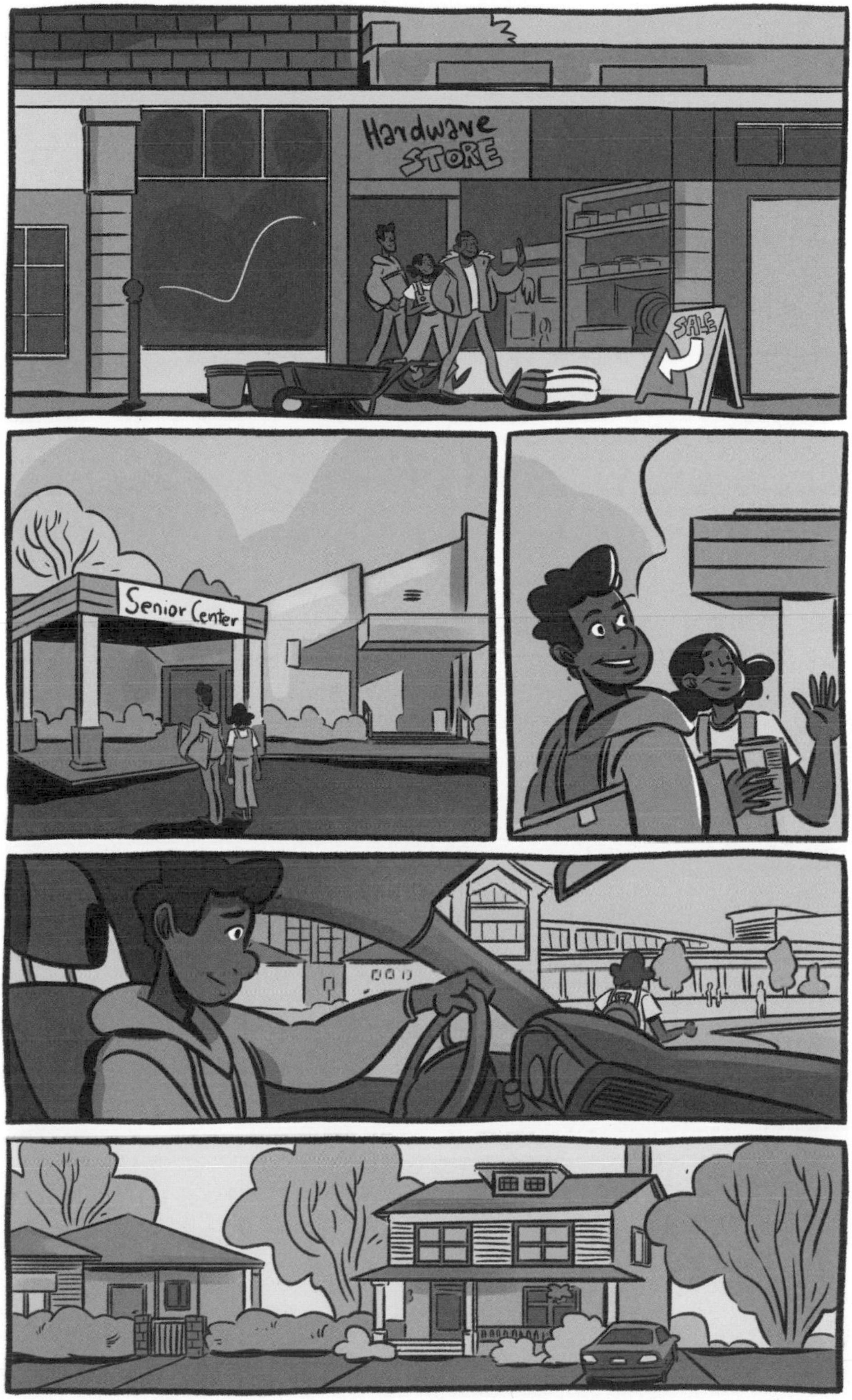
Hardware STORE
SALE
Senior Center

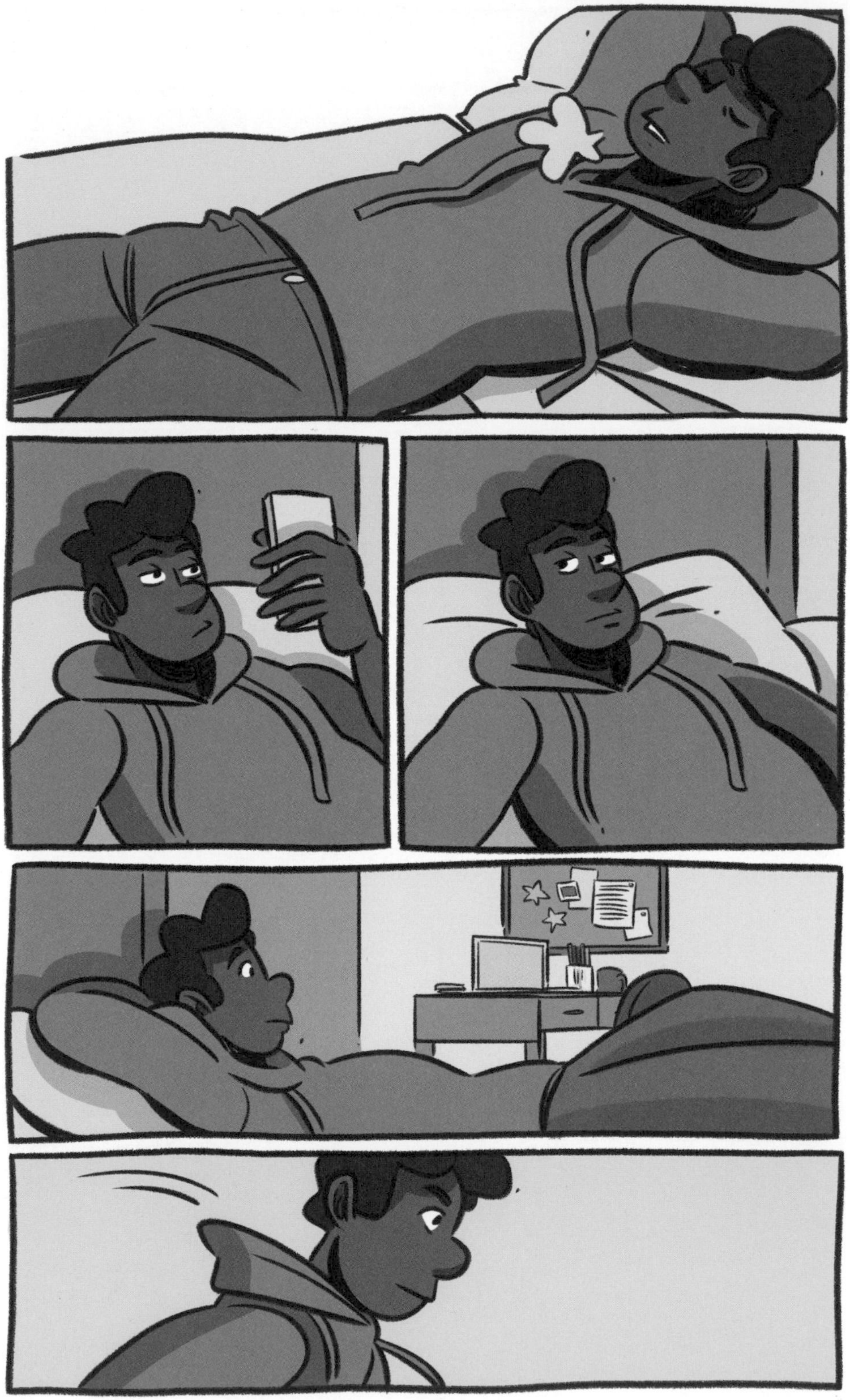

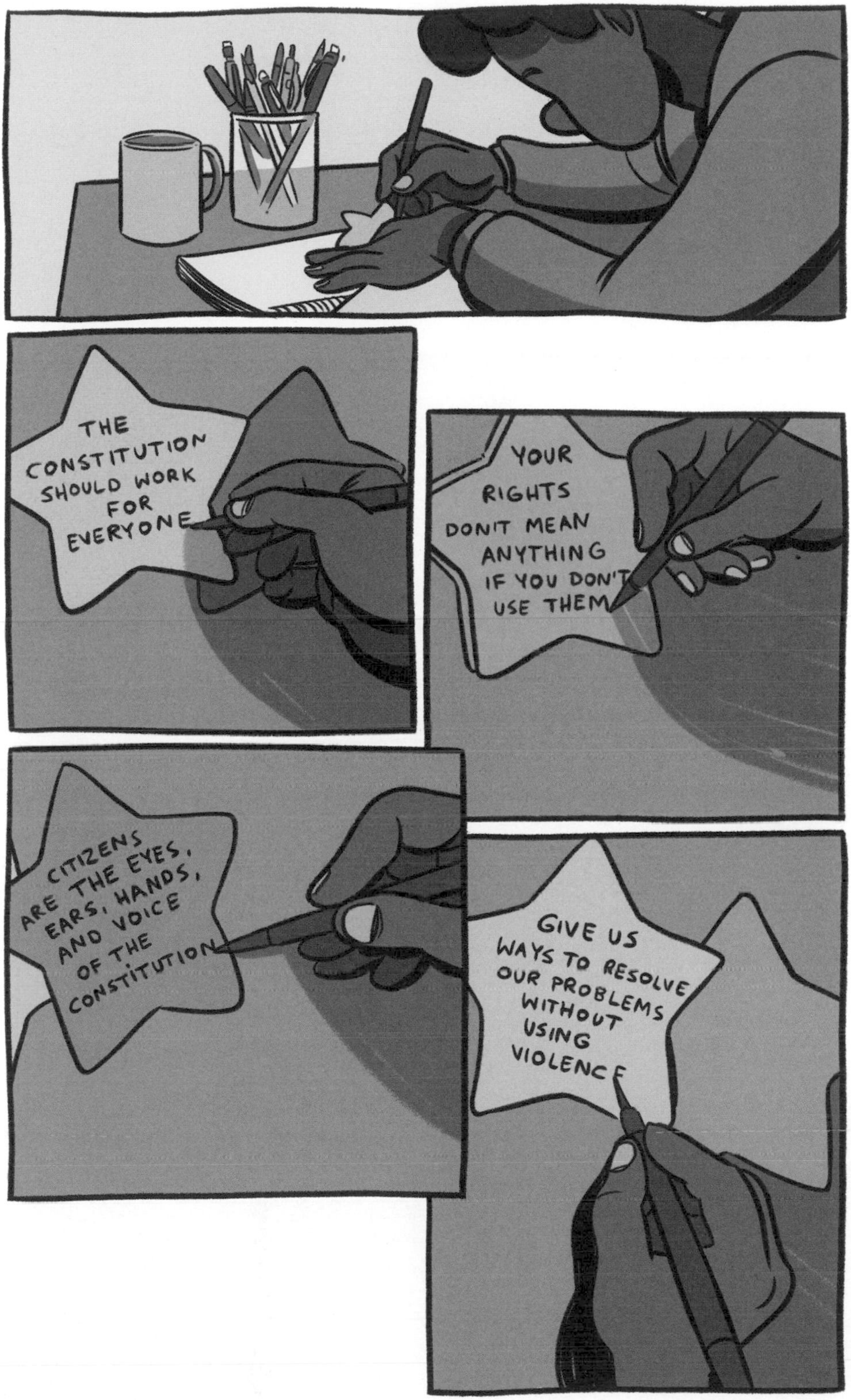
THE CONSTITUTION SHOULD WORK FOR EVERYONE
YOUR RIGHTS DON'T MEAN ANYTHING IF YOU DON'T USE THEM
CITIZENS ARE THE EYES, EARS, HANDS, AND VOICE OF THE CONSTITUTION
GIVE US WAYS TO RESOLVE OUR PROBLEMS WITHOUT USING VIOLENCE

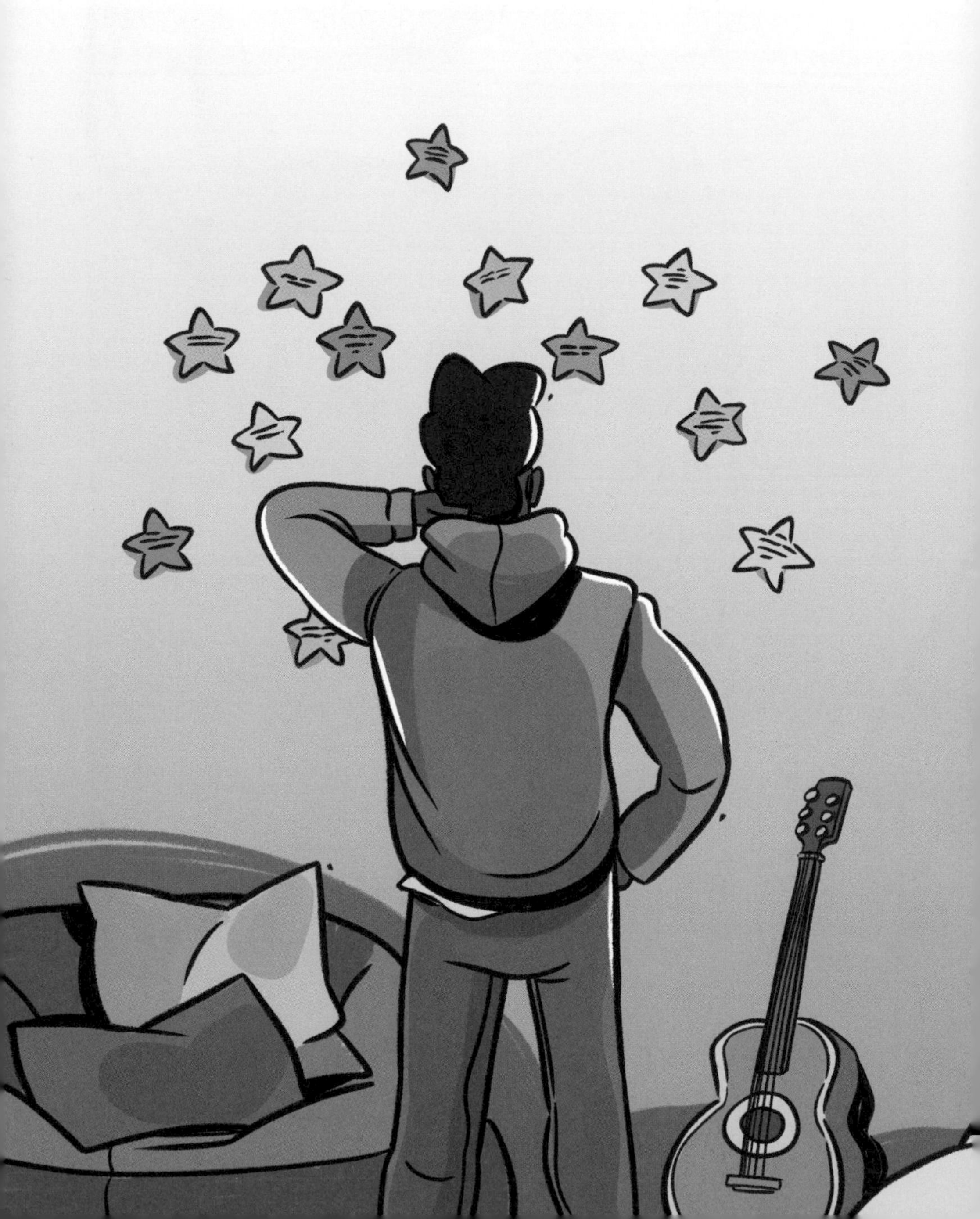

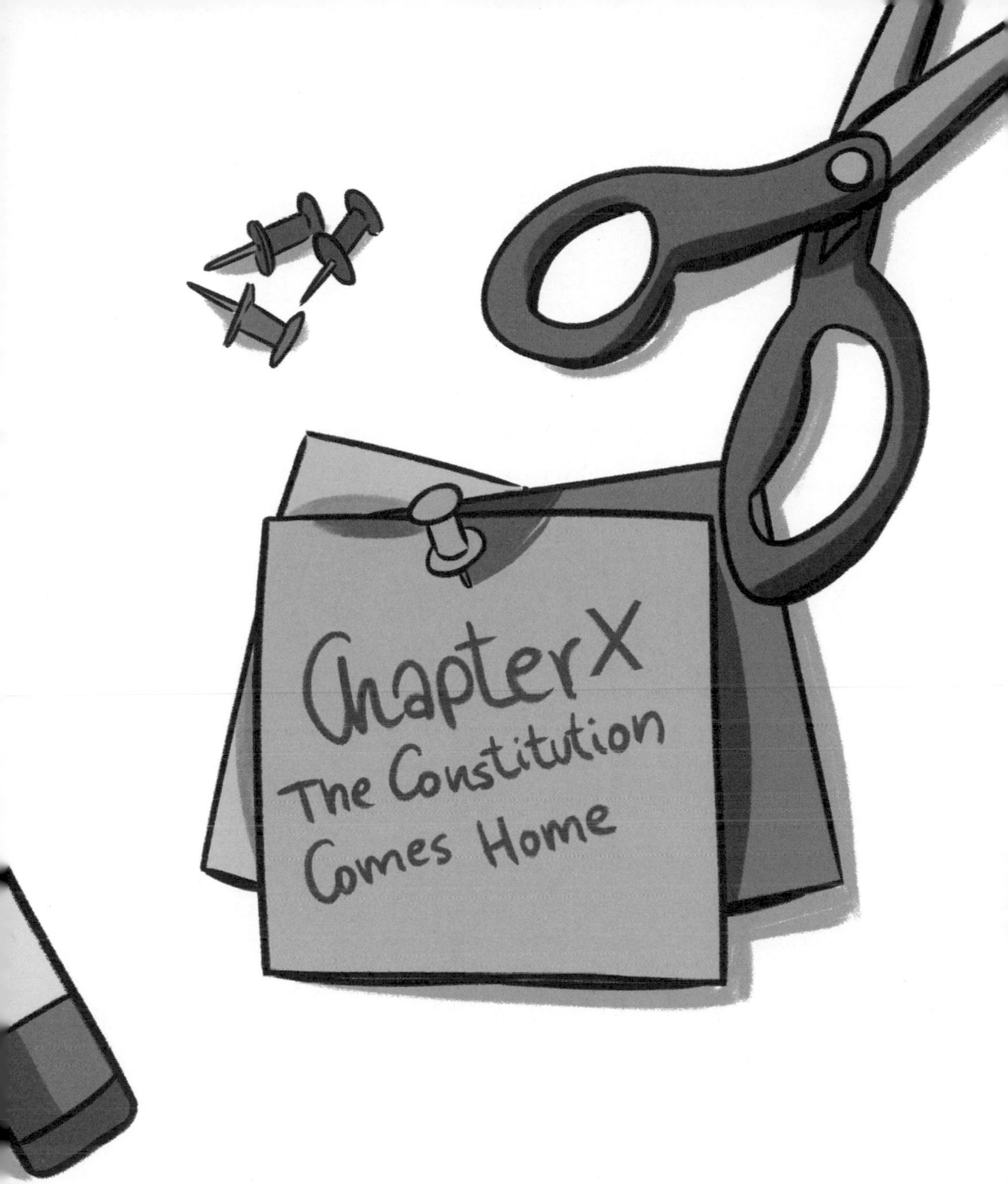
Chapter X
The Constitution
Comes Home

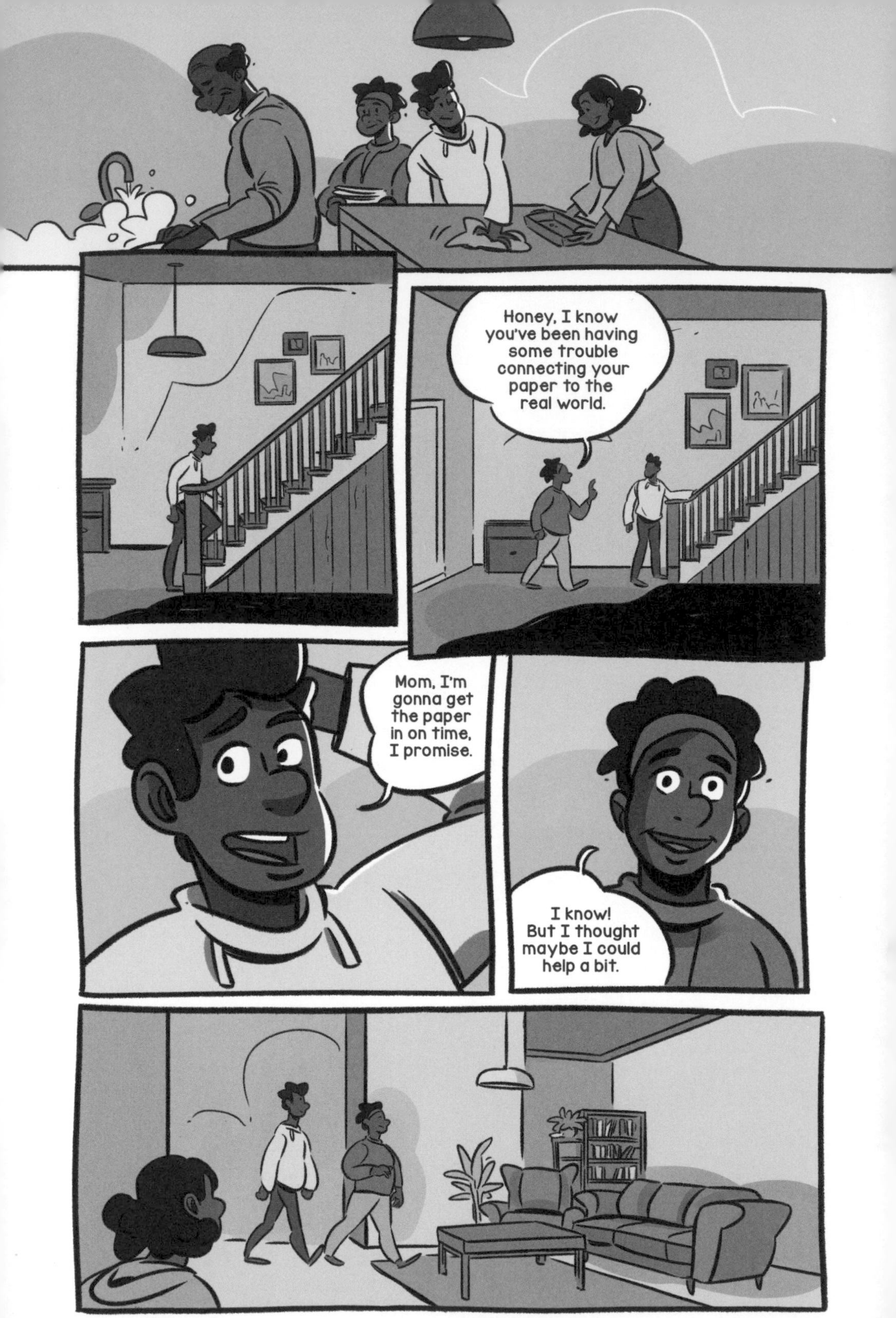
Honey, I know you've been having some trouble connecting your paper to the real world.
Mom, I'm gonna get the paper in on time, I promise.
I know! But I thought maybe I could help a bit.

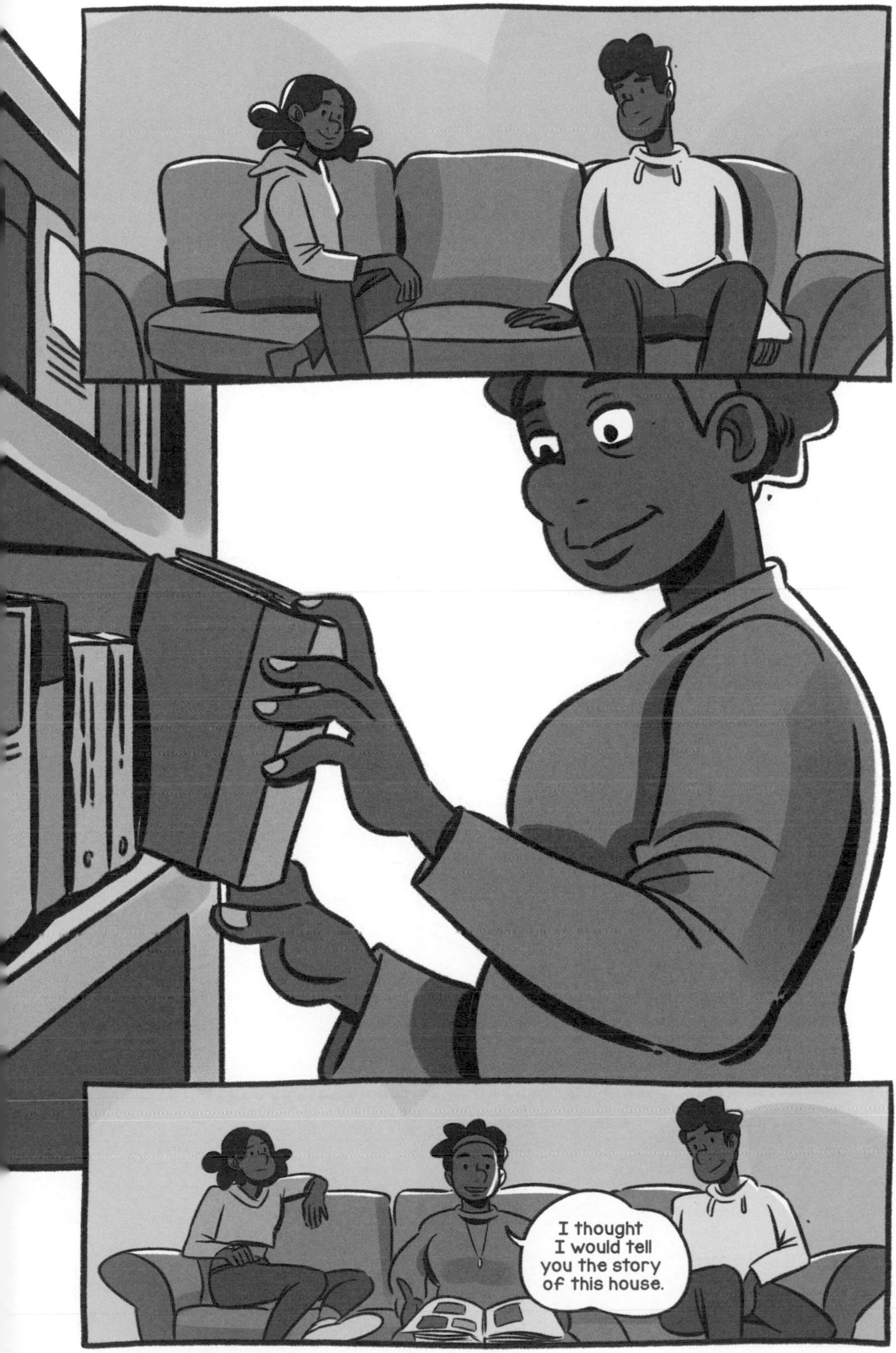
I thought I would tell you the story of this house.

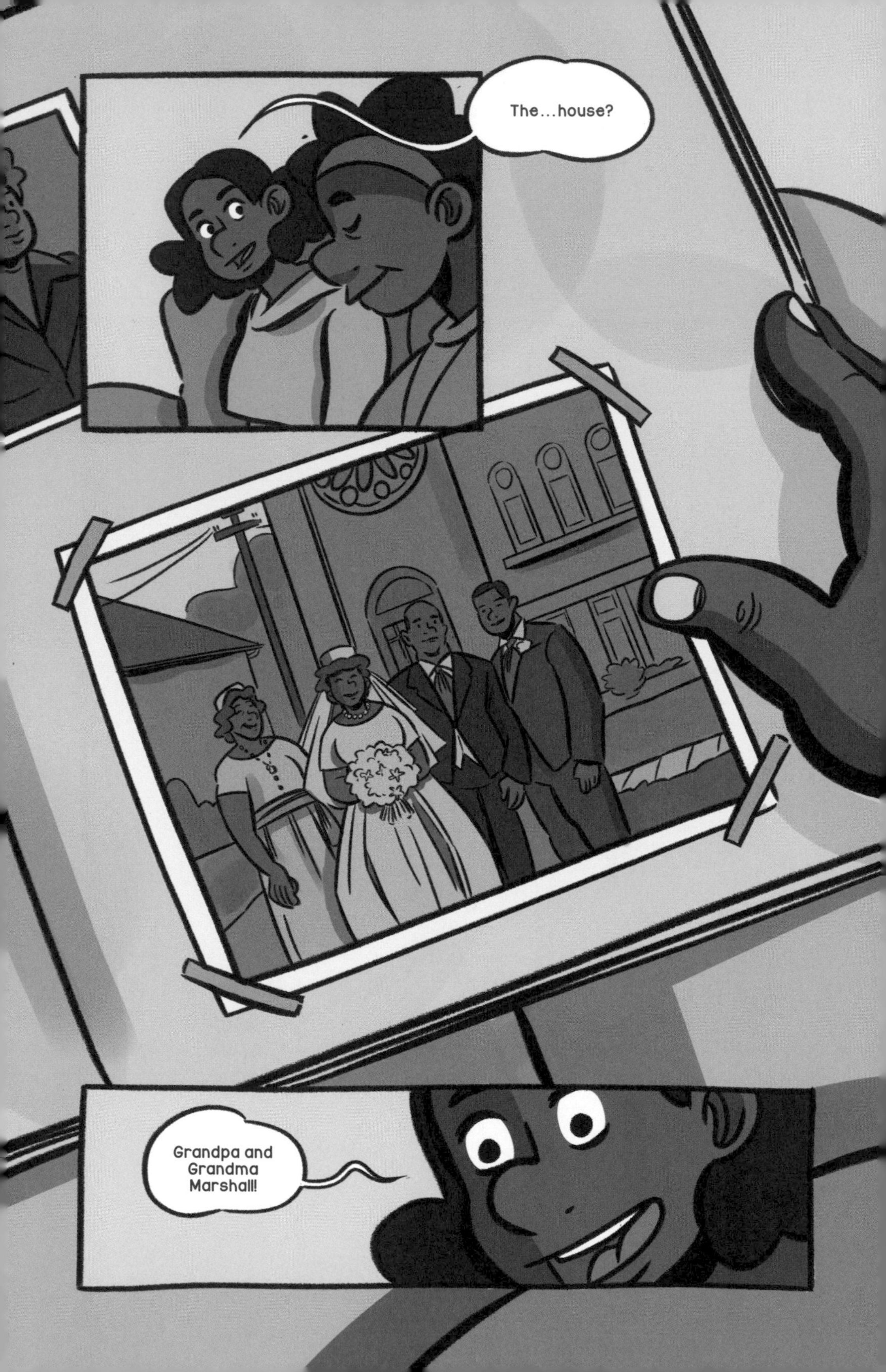
The...house?
Grandpa and Grandma Marshall!

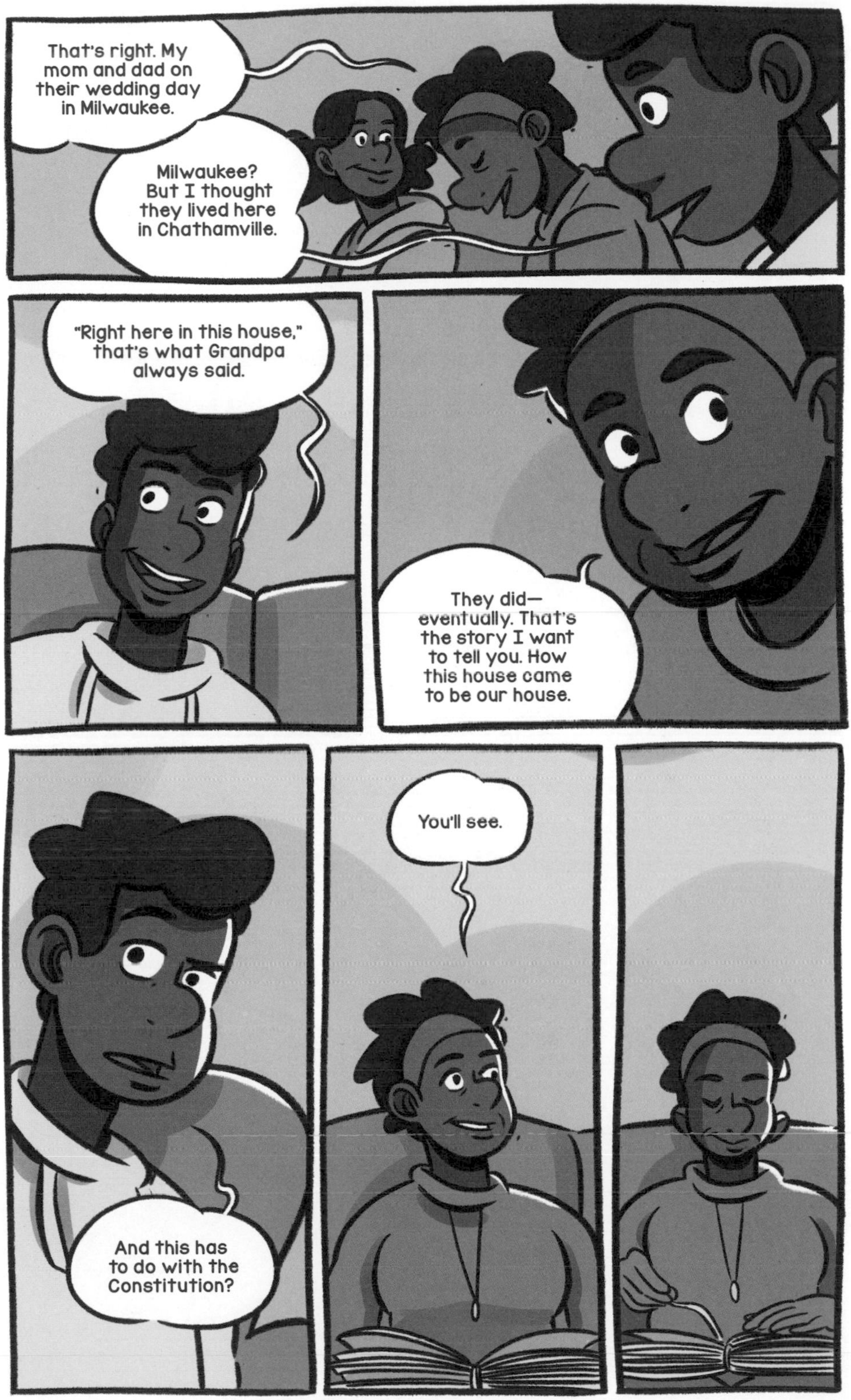
That's right. My mom and dad on their wedding day in Milwaukee.
Milwaukee? But I thought they lived here in Chathamville.
"Right here in this house," that's what Grandpa always said.
They did—eventually. That's the story I want to tell you. How this house came to be our house.
And this has to do with the Constitution?
You'll see.

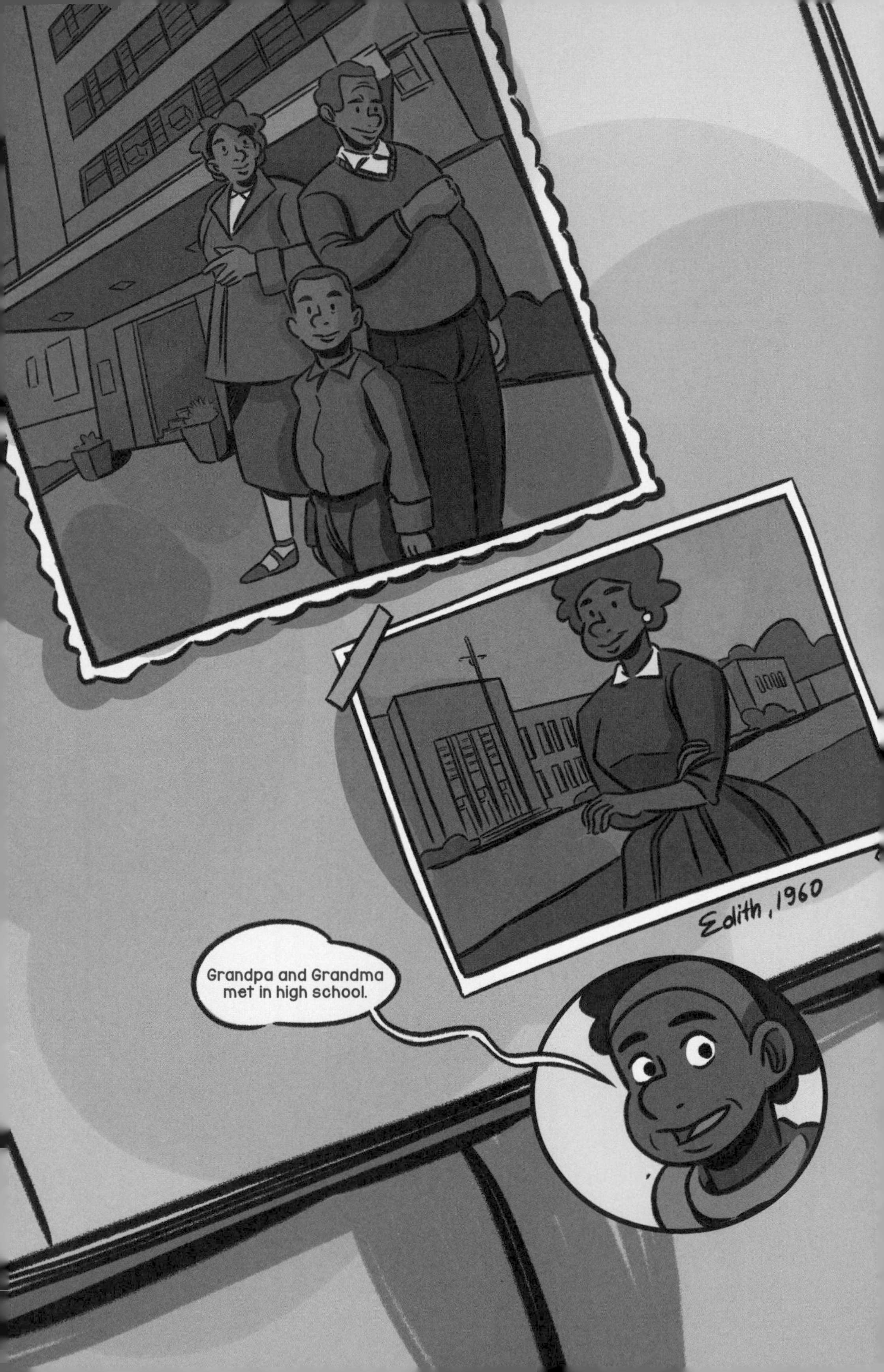
Edith, 1960
Grandpa and Grandma met in high school.

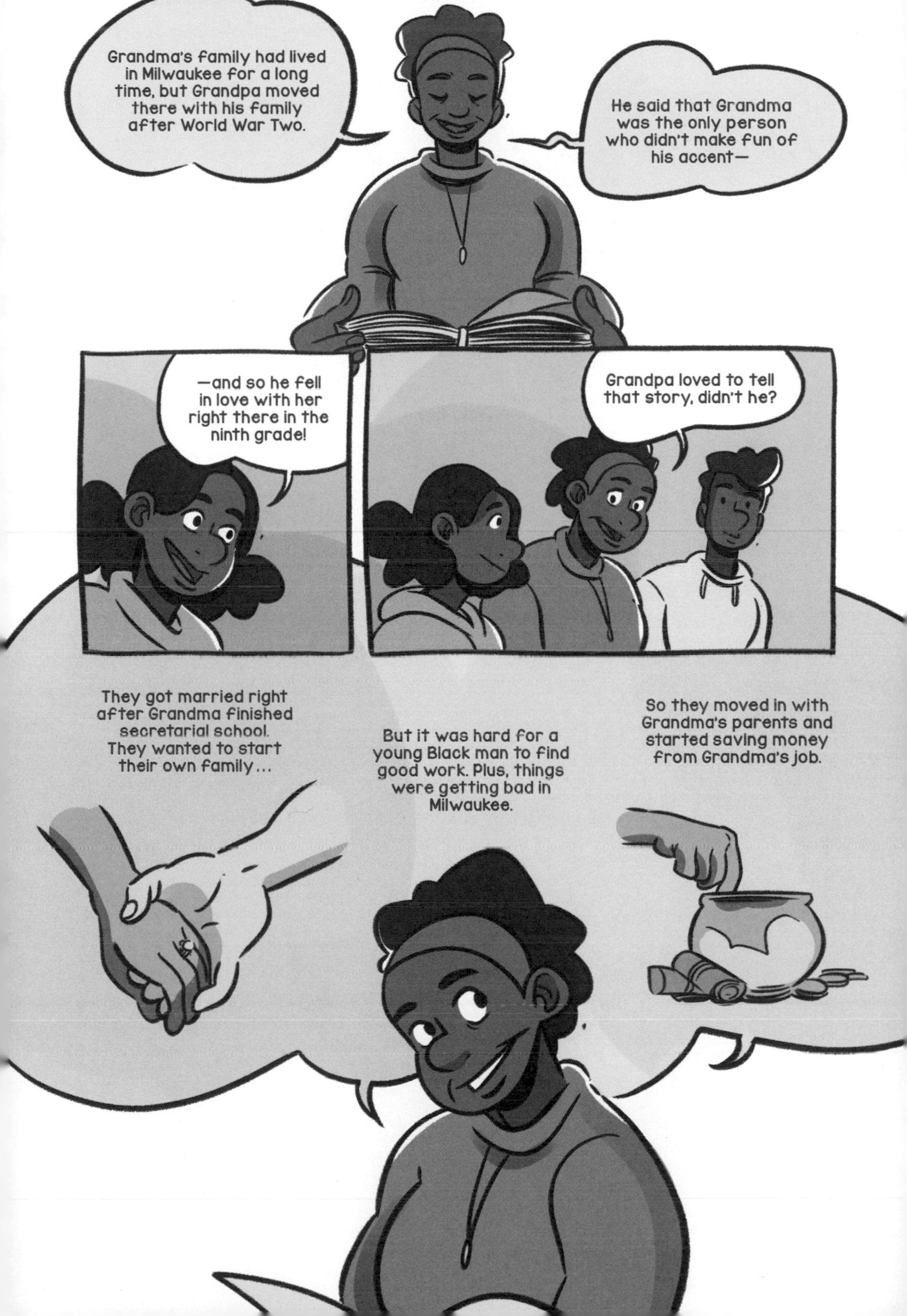

Grandma's family had lived in Milwaukee for a long time, but Grandpa moved there with his family after World War Two.
He said that Grandma was the only person who didn't make fun of his accent—
—and so he fell in love with her right there in the ninth grade!
Grandpa loved to tell that story, didn't he?
They got married right after Grandma finished secretarial school. They wanted to start their own family...
But it was hard for a young Black man to find good work. Plus, things were getting bad in Milwaukee.
So they moved in with Grandma's parents and started saving money from Grandma's job.

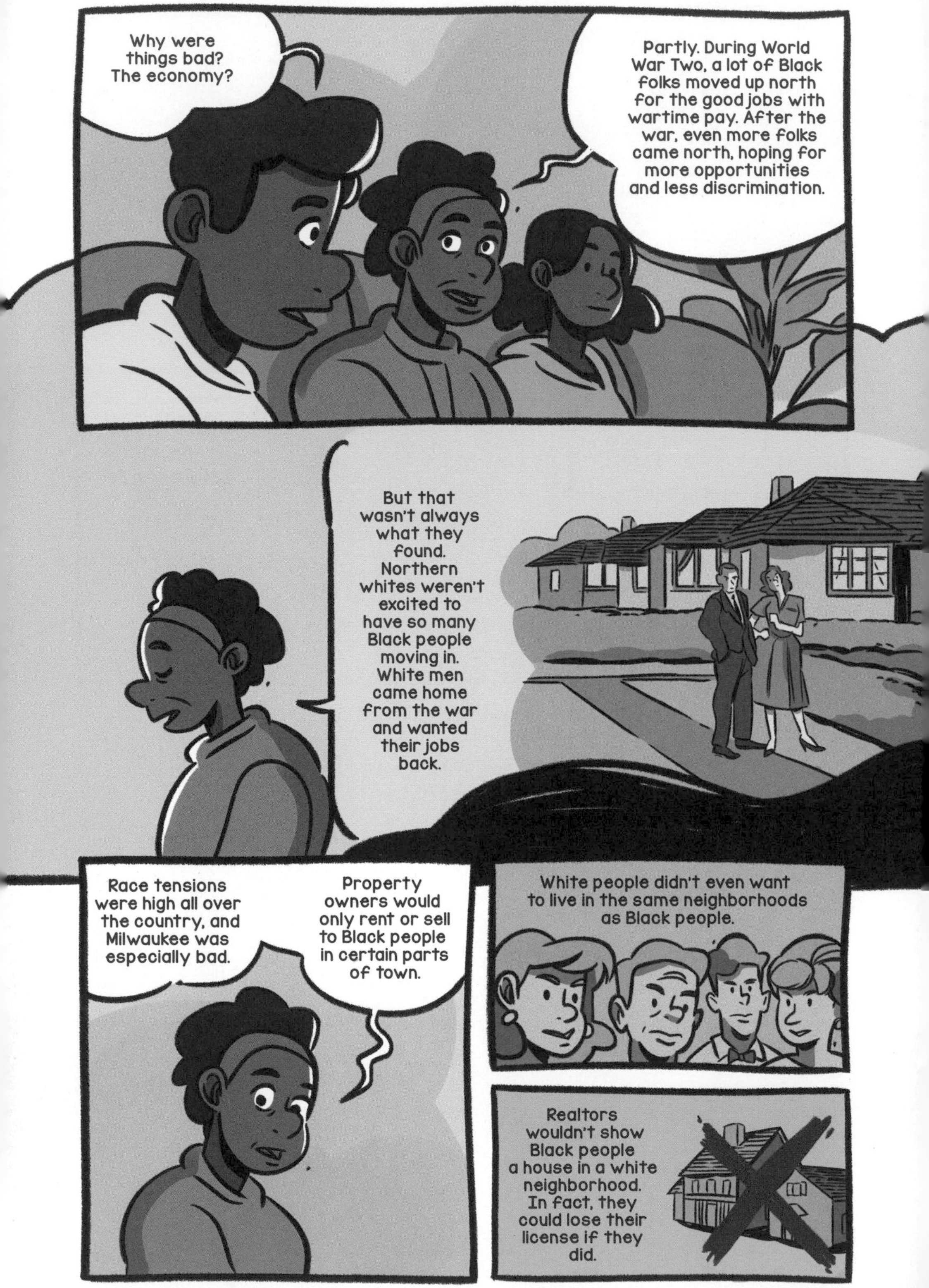
Why were things bad? The economy?
Partly. During World War Two, a lot of Black folks moved up north for the good jobs with wartime pay. After the war, even more folks came north, hoping for more opportunities and less discrimination.
But that wasn't always what they found. Northern whites weren't excited to have so many Black people moving in. White men came home from the war and wanted their jobs back.
Race tensions were high all over the country, and Milwaukee was especially bad.
Property owners would only rent or sell to Black people in certain parts of town.
White people didn't even want to live in the same neighborhoods as Black people.
Realtors wouldn't show Black people a house in a white neighborhood. In fact, they could lose their license if they did.

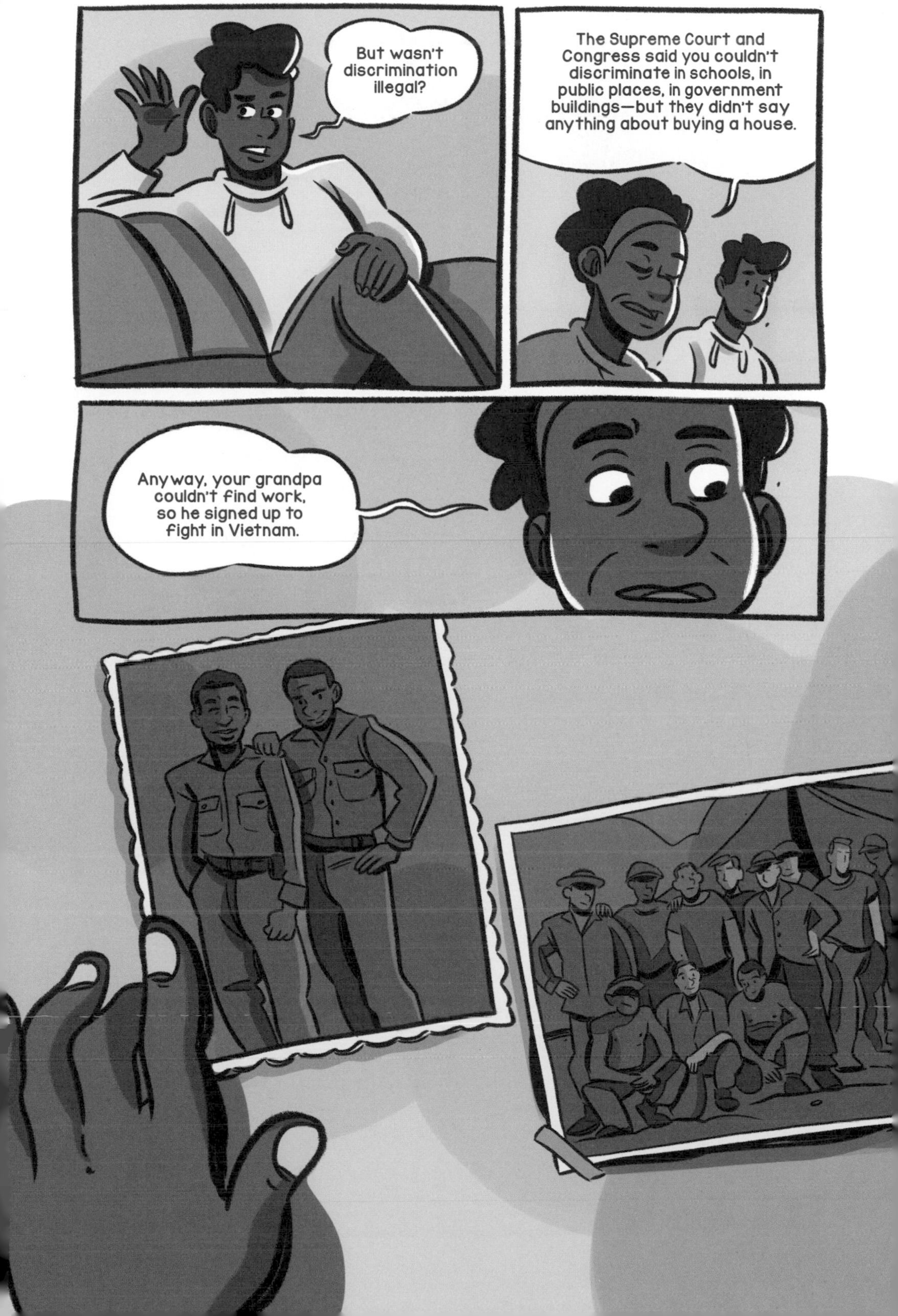
But wasn't discrimination illegal?
The Supreme Court and Congress said you couldn't discriminate in schools, in public places, in government buildings—but they didn't say anything about buying a house.
Anyway, your grandpa couldn't find work, so he signed up to fight in Vietnam.

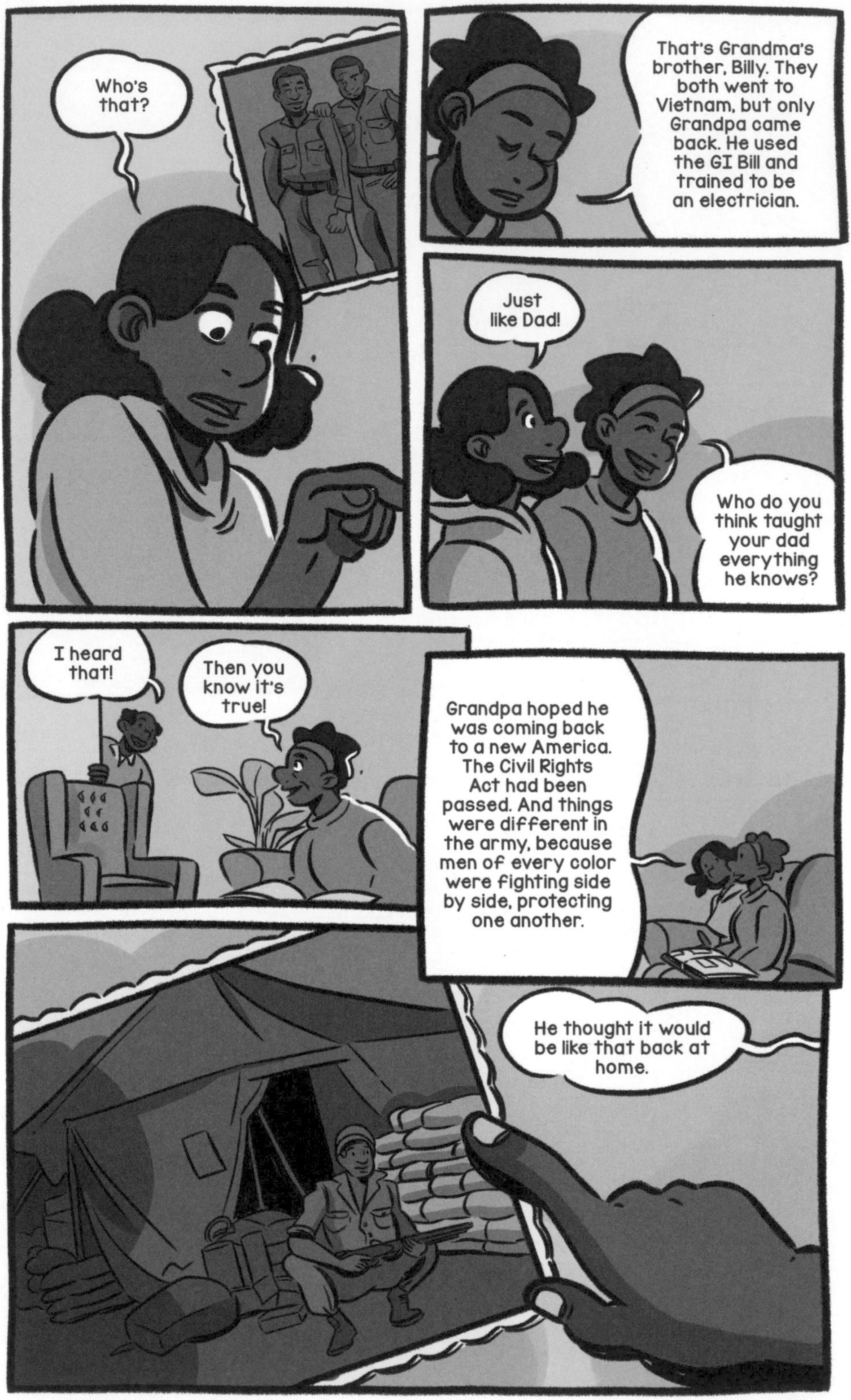

Who's that?
That's Grandma's brother, Billy. They both went to Vietnam, but only Grandpa came back. He used the GI Bill and trained to be an electrician.
Just like Dad!
Who do you think taught your dad everything he knows?
I heard that!
Then you know it's true!
Grandpa hoped he was coming back to a new America. The Civil Rights Act had been passed. And things were different in the army, because men of every color were fighting side by side, protecting one another.
He thought it would be like that back at home.

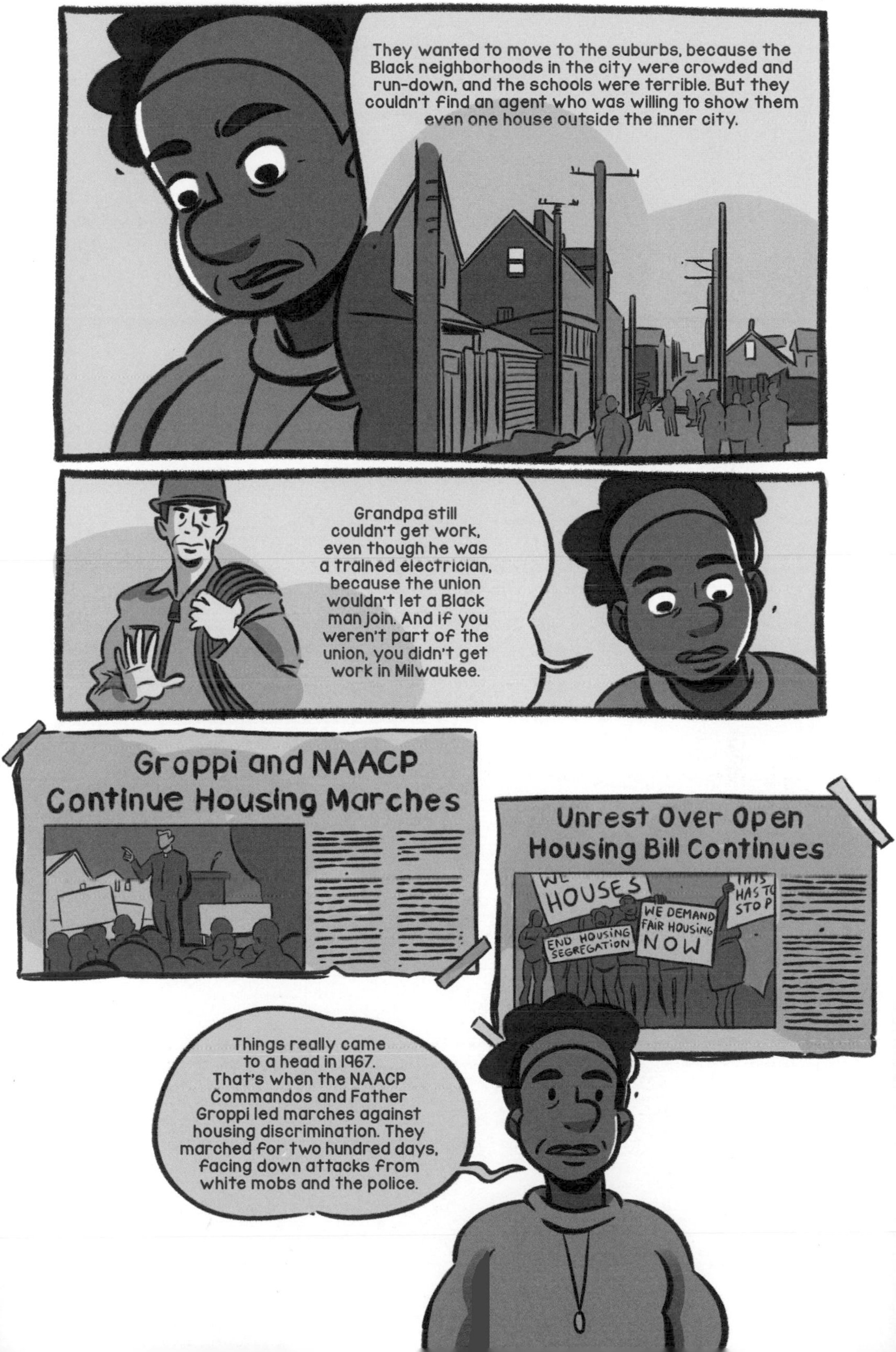
They wanted to move to the suburbs, because the Black neighborhoods in the city were crowded and run-down, and the schools were terrible. But they couldn't find an agent who was willing to show them even one house outside the inner city.
Grandpa still couldn't get work, even though he was a trained electrician, because the union wouldn't let a Black man join. And if you weren't part of the union, you didn't get work in Milwaukee.
Groppi and NAACP Continue Housing Marches
Unrest Over Open Housing Bill Continues
HOUSES
WE DEMAND FAIR HOUSING NOW
END HOUSING SEGREGATION
THIS HAS TO STOP
Things really came to a head in 1967. That's when the NAACP Commandos and Father Groppi led marches against housing discrimination. They marched for two hundred days, facing down attacks from white mobs and the police.

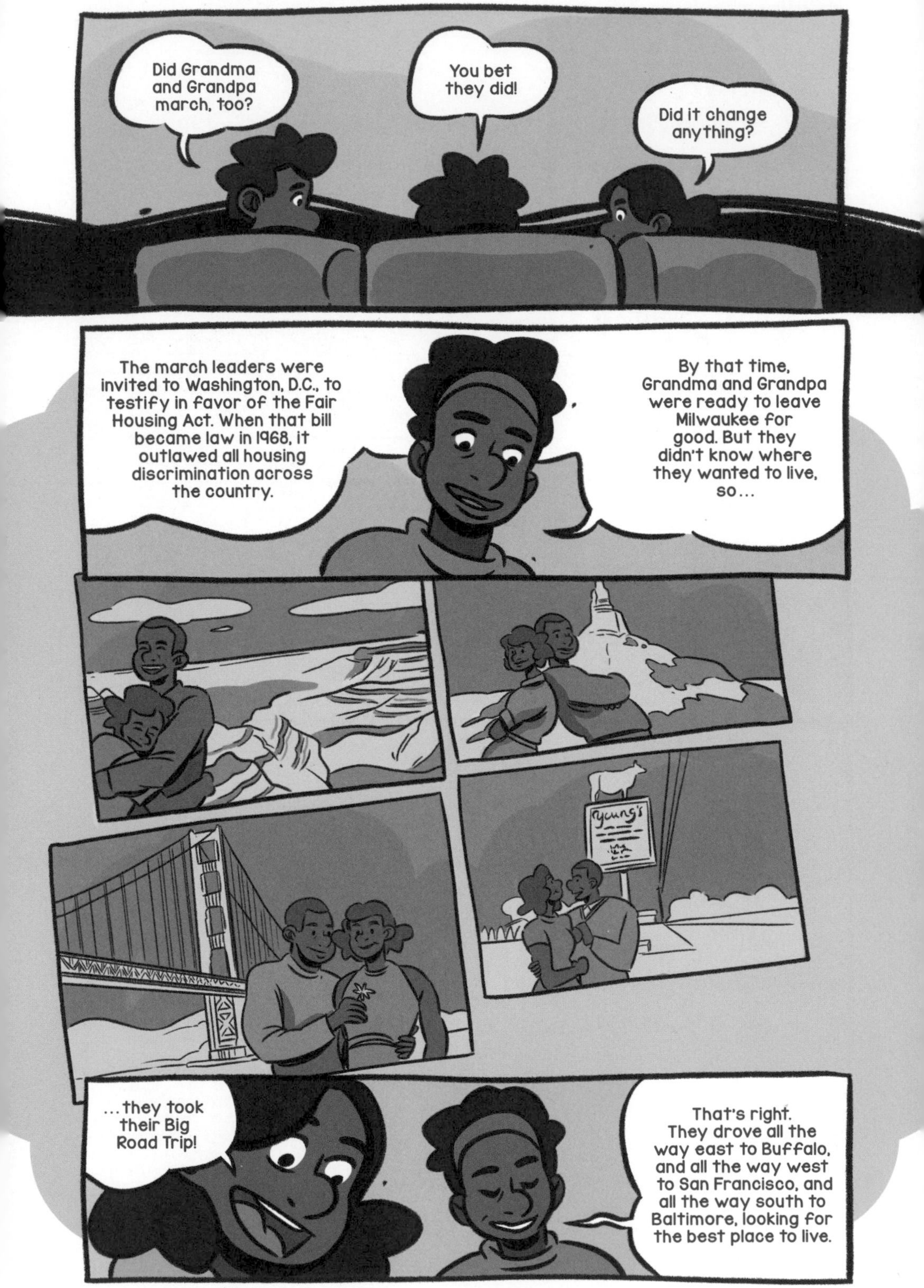

Did Grandma and Grandpa march, too?
You bet they did!
Did it change anything?
The march leaders were invited to Washington, D.C., to testify in favor of the Fair Housing Act. When that bill became law in 1968, it outlawed all housing discrimination across the country.
By that time, Grandma and Grandpa were ready to leave Milwaukee for good. But they didn't know where they wanted to live, so...
Young's
...they took their Big Road Trip!
That's right. They drove all the way east to Buffalo, and all the way west to San Francisco, and all the way south to Baltimore, looking for the best place to live.

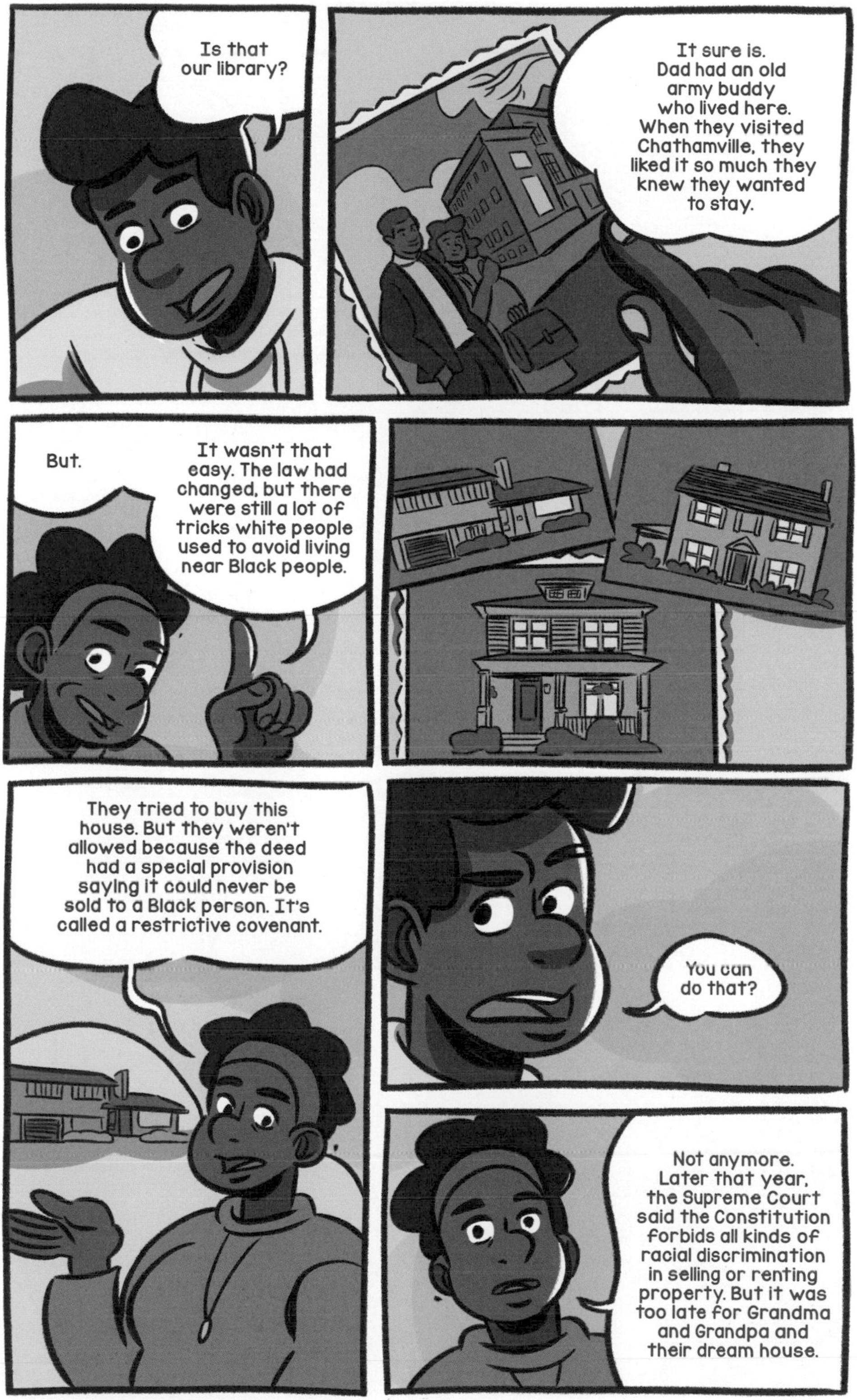

Is that our library?
It sure is. Dad had an old army buddy who lived here. When they visited Chathamville, they liked it so much they knew they wanted to stay.
But.
It wasn't that easy. The law had changed, but there were still a lot of tricks white people used to avoid living near Black people.
They tried to buy this house. But they weren't allowed because the deed had a special provision saying it could never be sold to a Black person. It's called a restrictive covenant.
You can do that?
Not anymore. Later that year, the Supreme Court said the Constitution forbids all kinds of racial discrimination in selling or renting property. But it was too late for Grandma and Grandpa and their dream house.

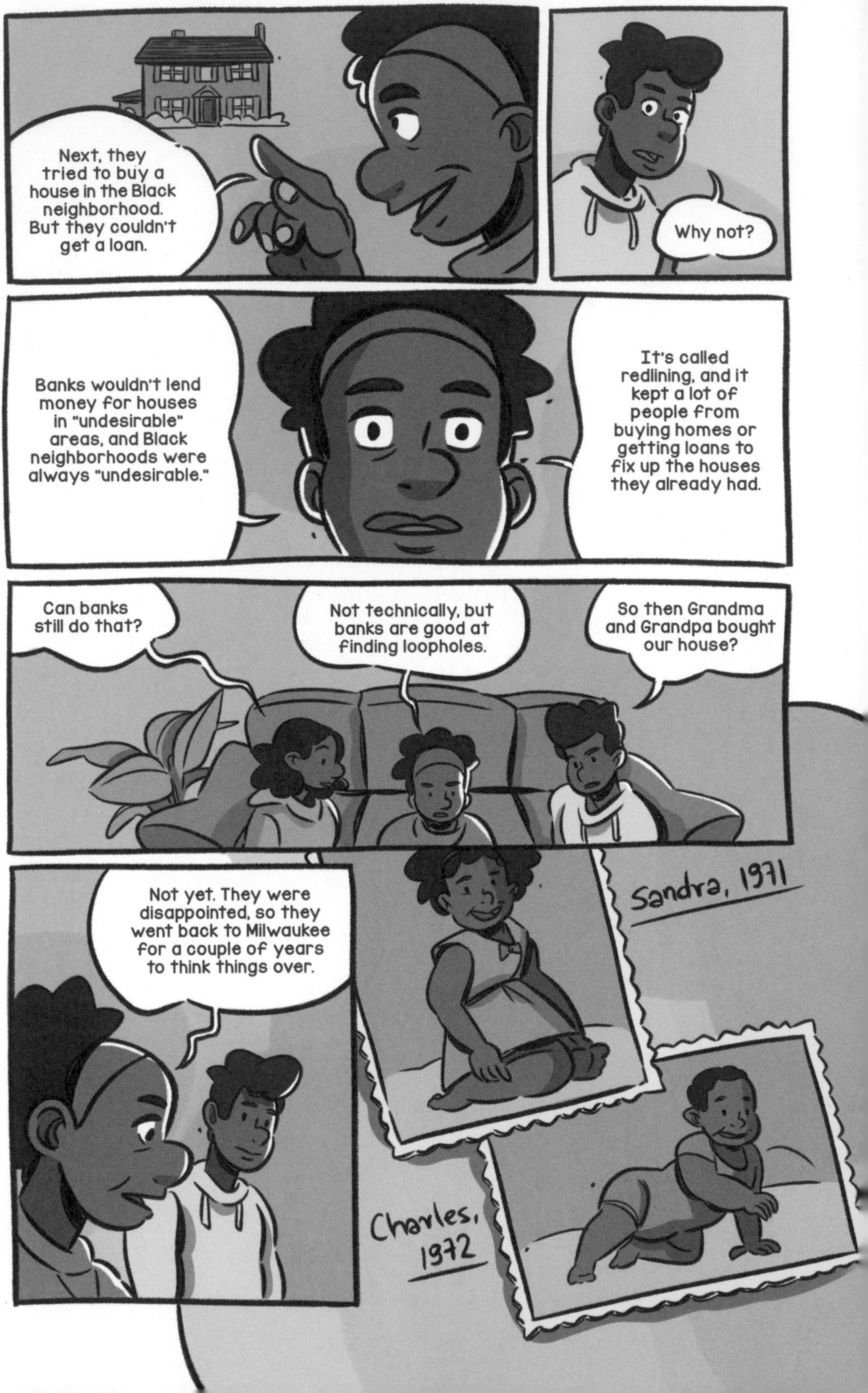
Next, they tried to buy a house in the Black neighborhood. But they couldn't get a loan.
Why not?
Banks wouldn't lend money for houses in "undesirable" areas, and Black neighborhoods were always "undesirable."
It's called redlining, and it kept a lot of people from buying homes or getting loans to fix up the houses they already had.
Can banks still do that?
Not technically, but banks are good at finding loopholes.
So then Grandma and Grandpa bought our house?
Not yet. They were disappointed, so they went back to Milwaukee for a couple of years to think things over.
Sandra, 1971
Charles, 1972

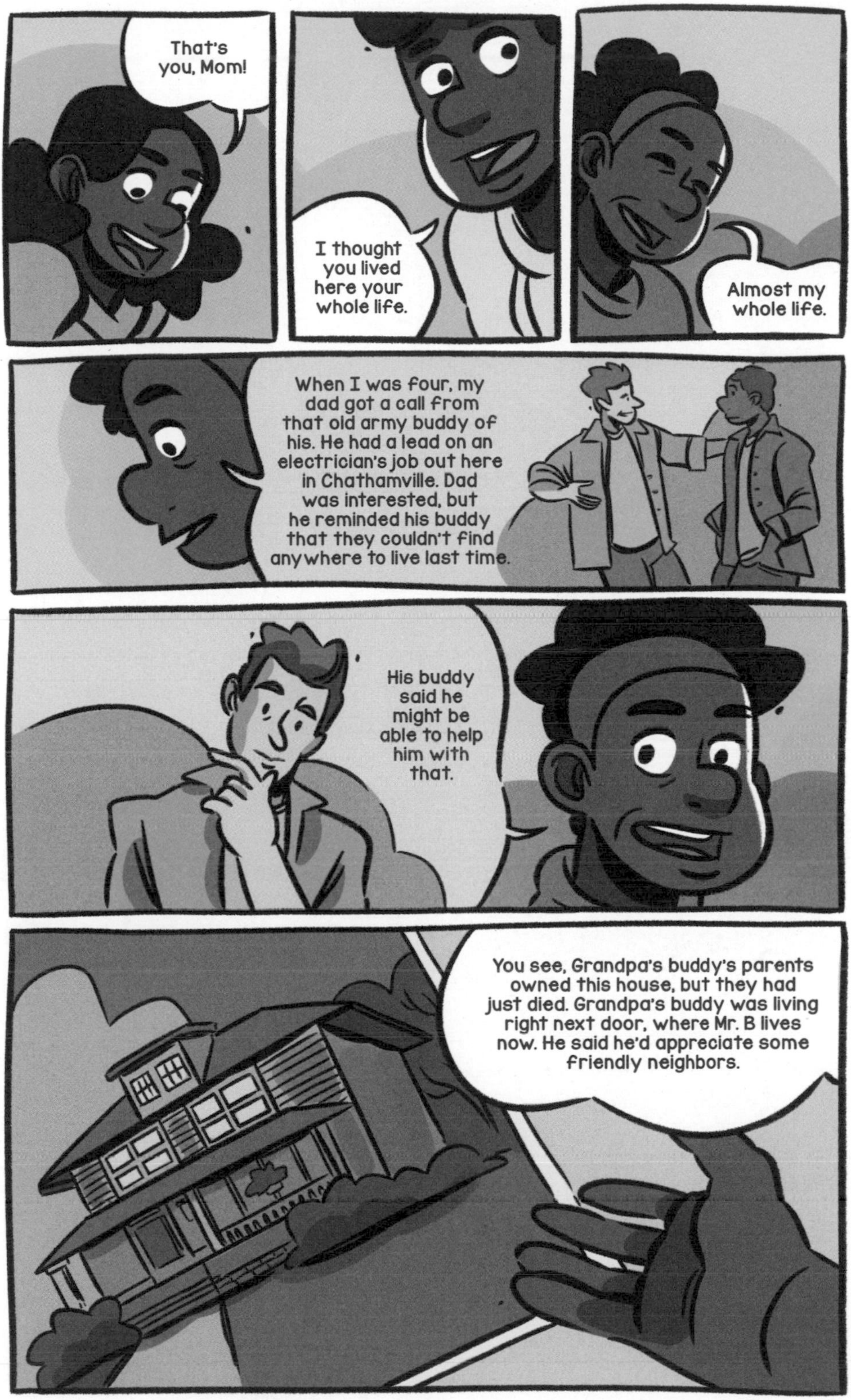
That's you, Mom!
I thought you lived here your whole life.
Almost my whole life.
When I was four, my dad got a call from that old army buddy of his. He had a lead on an electrician's job out here in Chathamville. Dad was interested, but he reminded his buddy that they couldn't find anywhere to live last time.
His buddy said he might be able to help him with that.
You see, Grandpa's buddy's parents owned this house, but they had just died. Grandpa's buddy was living right next door, where Mr. B lives now. He said he'd appreciate some friendly neighbors.

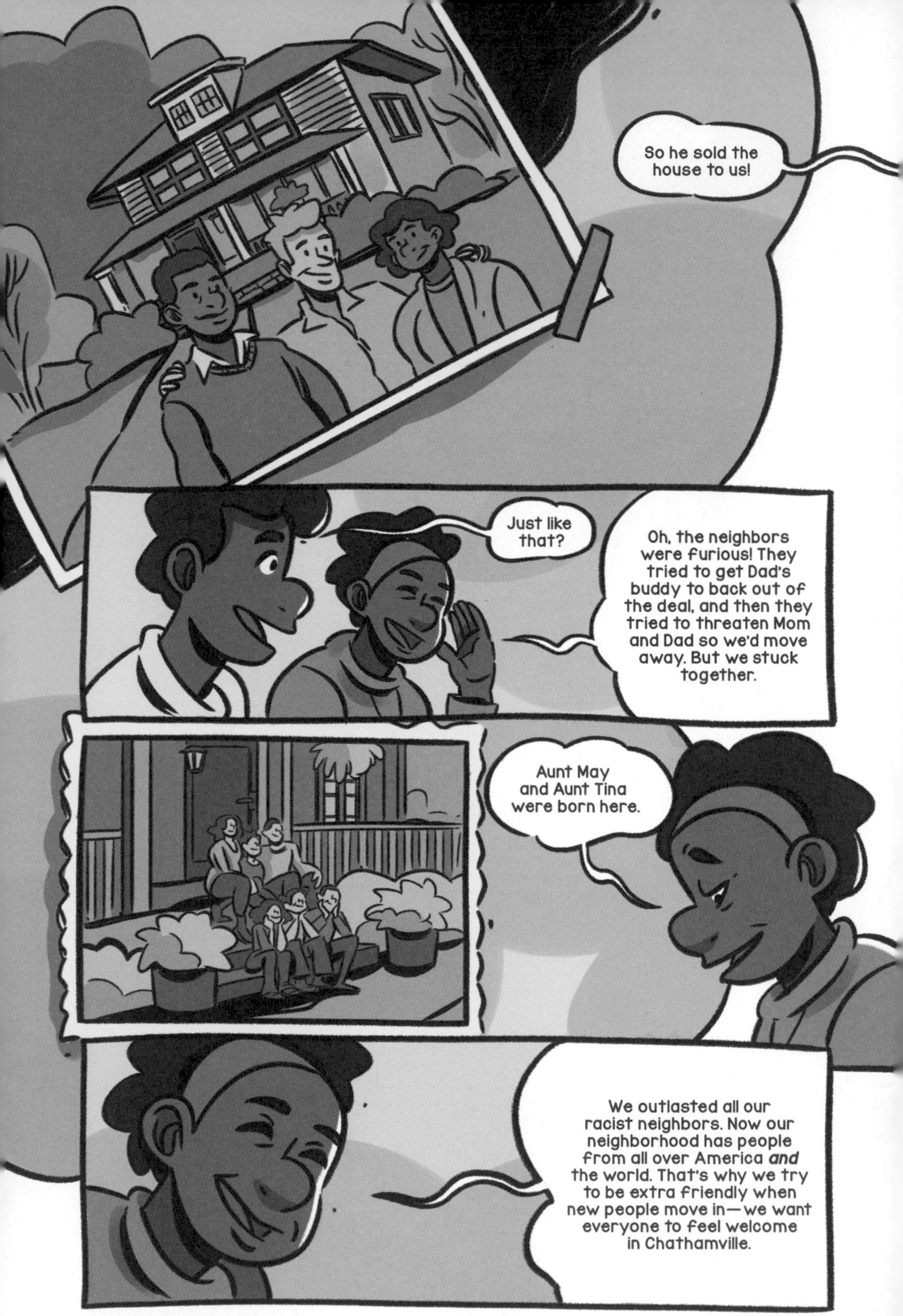
So he sold the house to us!
Just like that?
Oh, the neighbors were furious! They tried to get Dad's buddy to back out of the deal, and then they tried to threaten Mom and Dad so we'd move away. But we stuck together.
Aunt May and Aunt Tina were born here.
We outlasted all our racist neighbors. Now our neighborhood has people from all over America *and* the world. That's why we try to be extra friendly when new people move in—we want everyone to feel welcome in Chathamville.

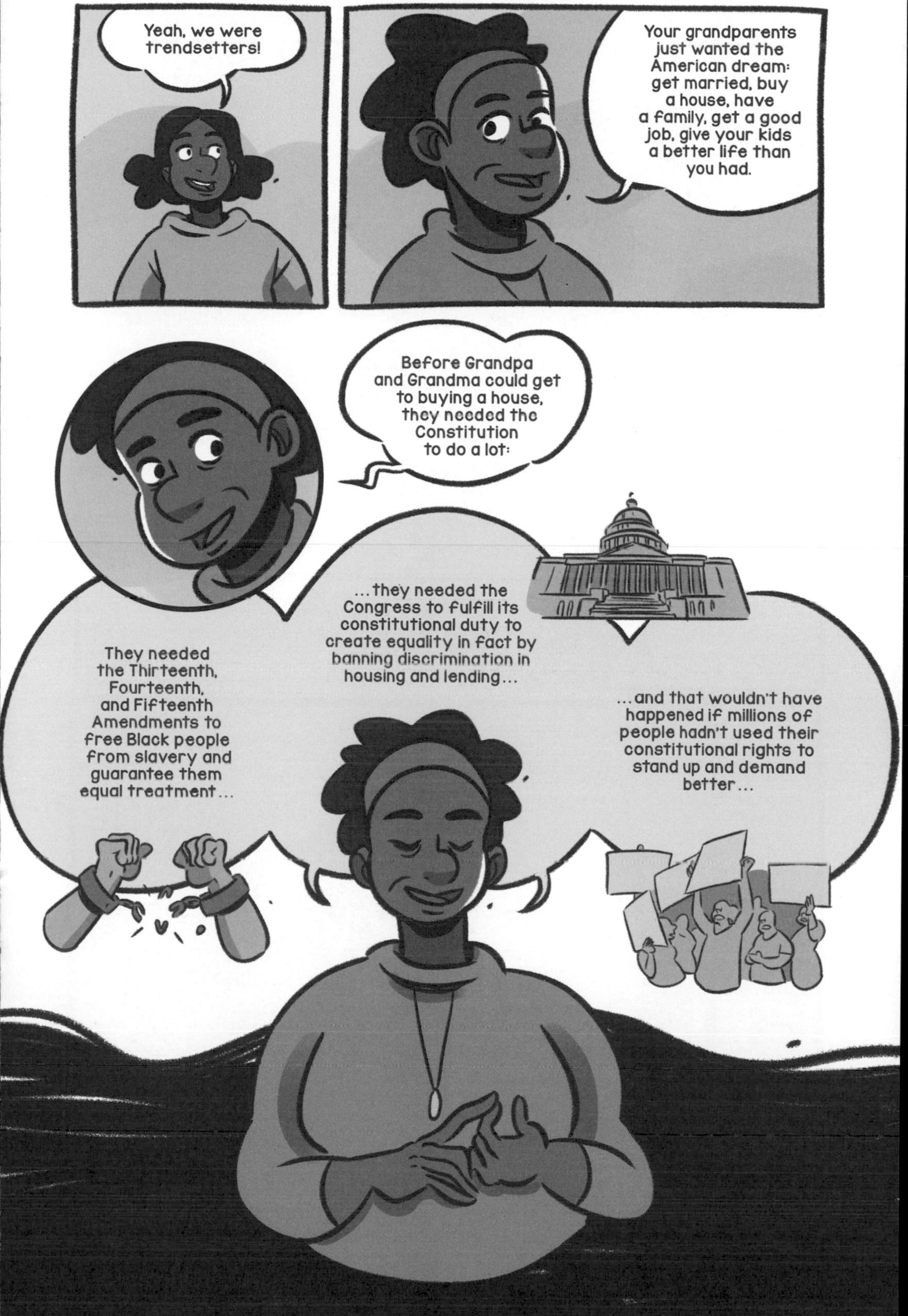
Yeah, we were trendsetters!
Your grandparents just wanted the American dream: get married, buy a house, have a family, get a good job, give your kids a better life than you had.
Before Grandpa and Grandma could get to buying a house, they needed the Constitution to do a lot:
They needed the Thirteenth, Fourteenth, and Fifteenth Amendments to free Black people from slavery and guarantee them equal treatment...
...they needed the Congress to fulfill its constitutional duty to create equality in fact by banning discrimination in housing and lending...
...and that wouldn't have happened if millions of people hadn't used their constitutional rights to stand up and demand better...

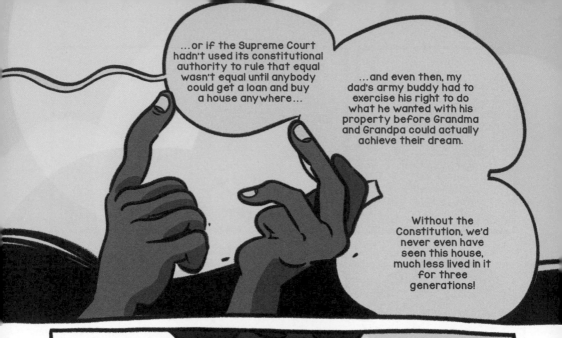

...or if the Supreme Court hadn't used its constitutional authority to rule that equal wasn't equal until anybody could get a loan and buy a house anywhere...

...and even then, my dad's army buddy had to exercise his right to do what he wanted with his property before Grandma and Grandpa could actually achieve their dream.

Without the Constitution, we'd never even have seen this house, much less lived in it for three generations!

Wow, Mom. That's—that's actually kind of cool.

I didn't realize you needed so many parts of the Constitution just to buy a house.

The Constitution doesn't guarantee anybody a house. But it helped your grandparents achieve their version of the American dream. And the American dream is another way of saying what we expect to get out of being citizens of this country.

Does that help you with your project?

Yeah. Yeah, I think that helps a lot.

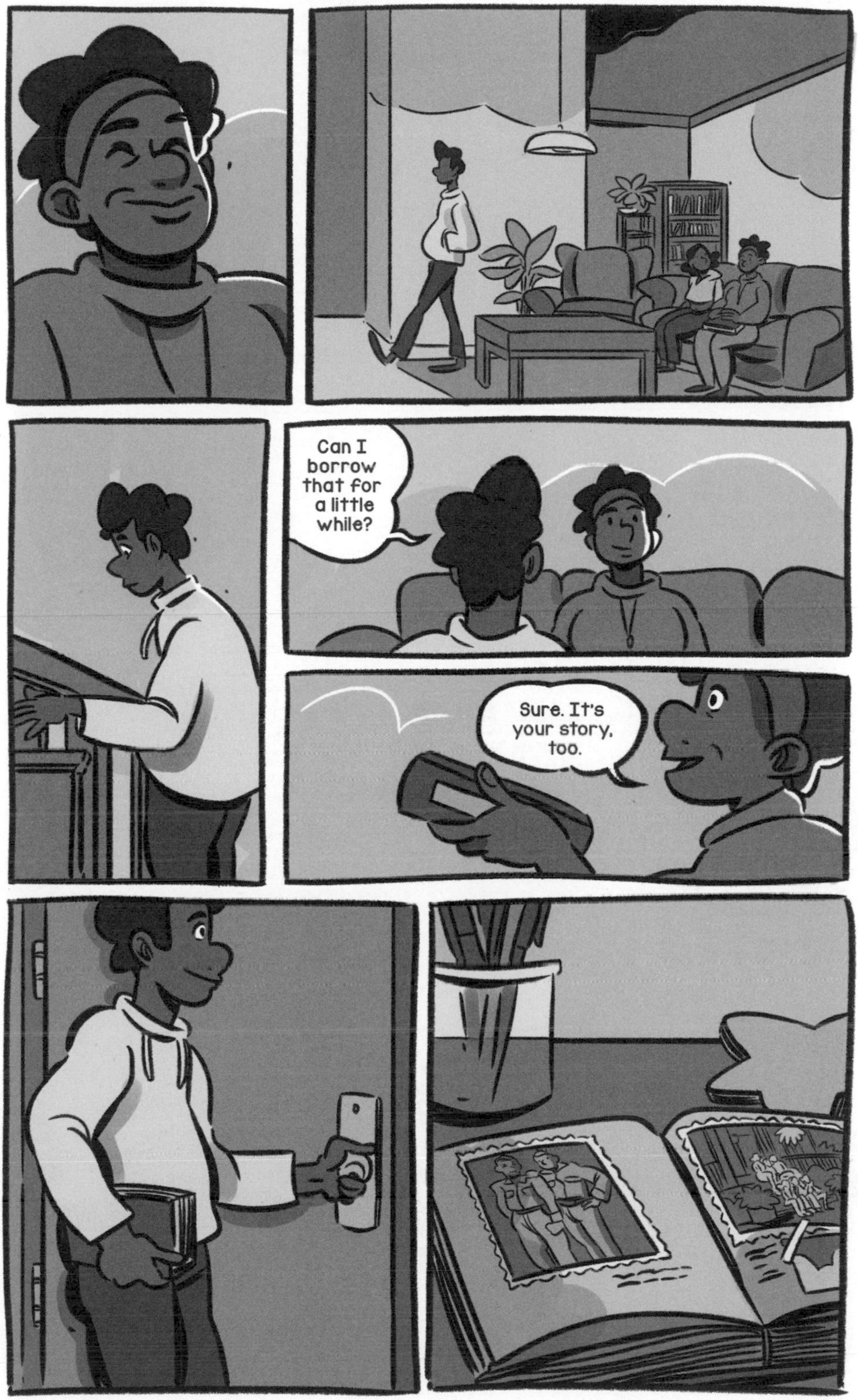
Can I borrow that for a little while?
Sure. It's your story, too.

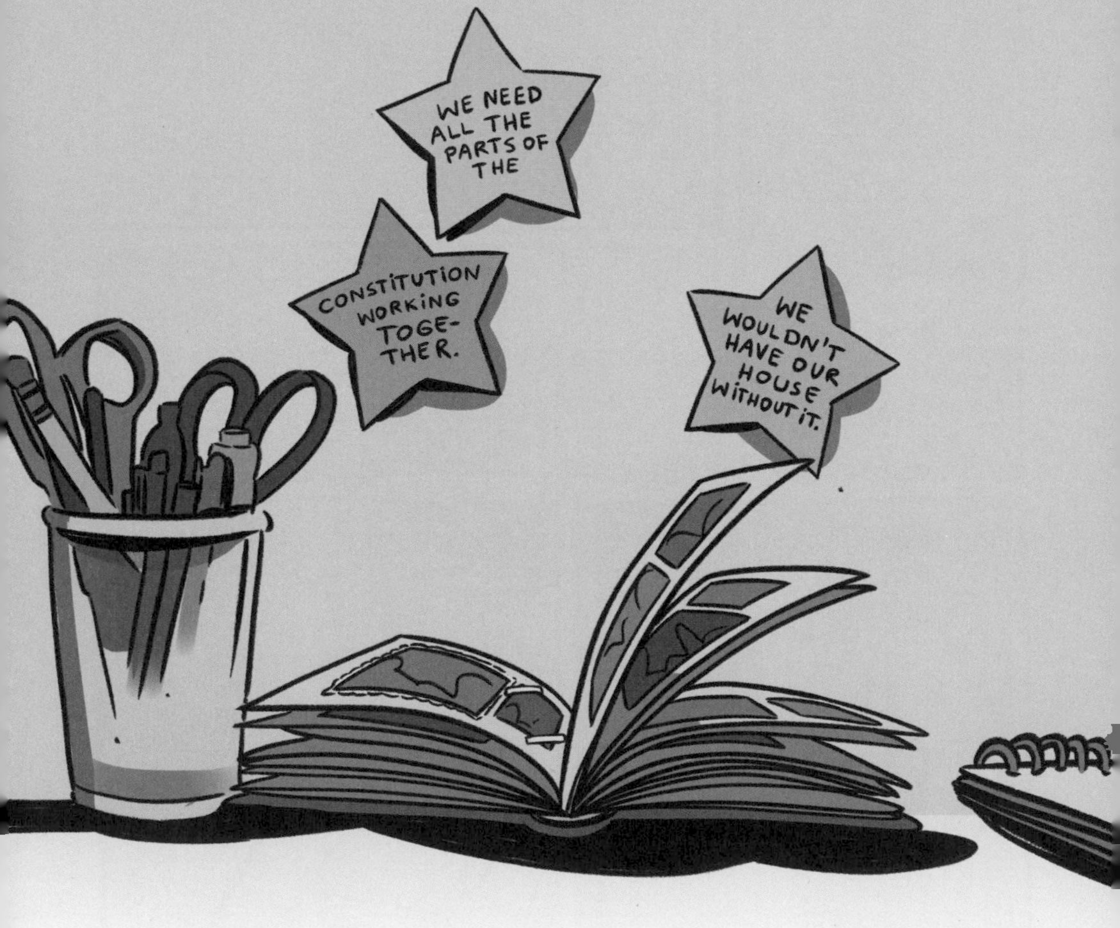
WE NEED ALL THE PARTS OF THE
CONSTITUTION WORKING TOGE-THER.
WE WOULDN'T HAVE OUR HOUSE WITHOUT IT.

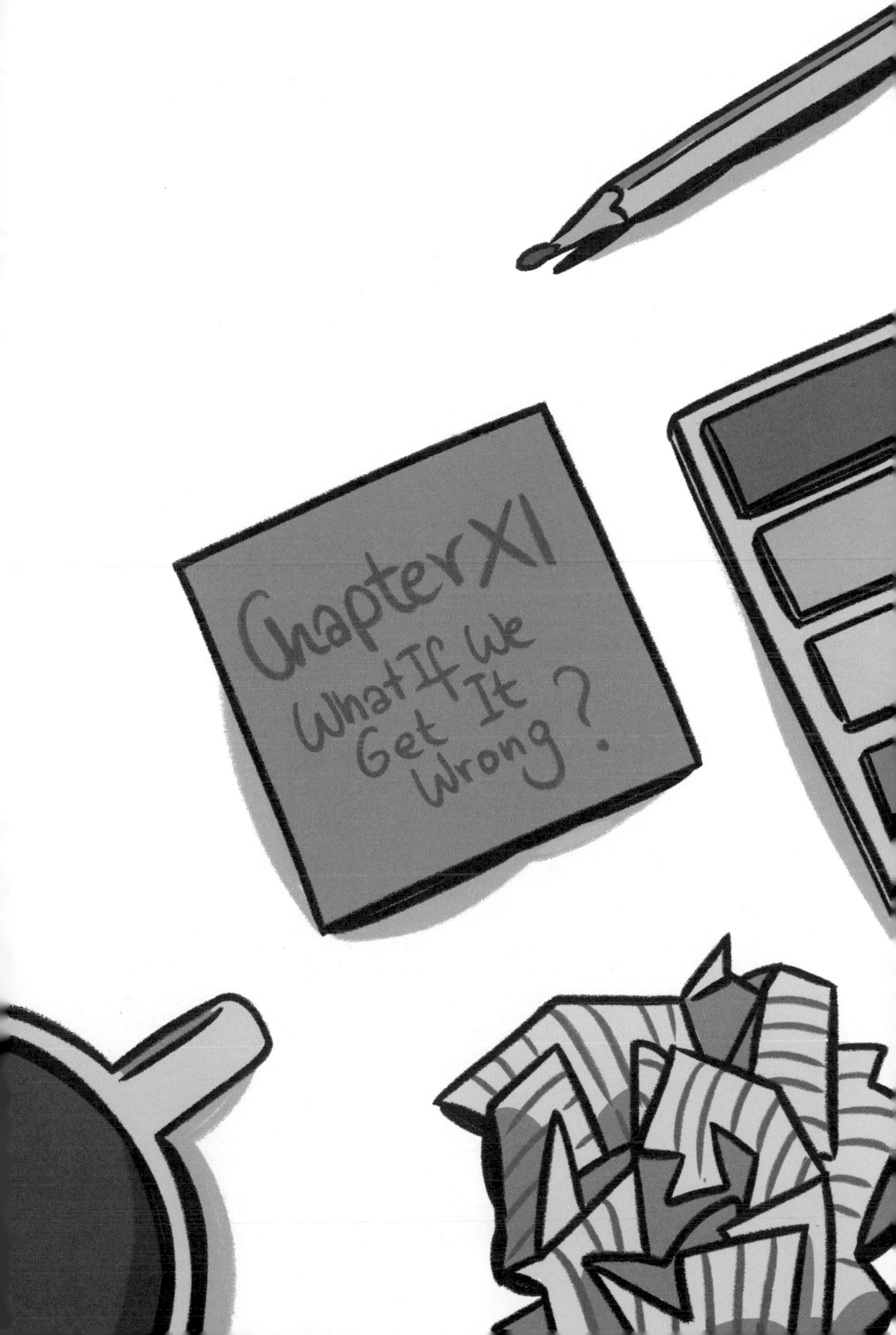
Chapter XI
What If We Get It Wrong?

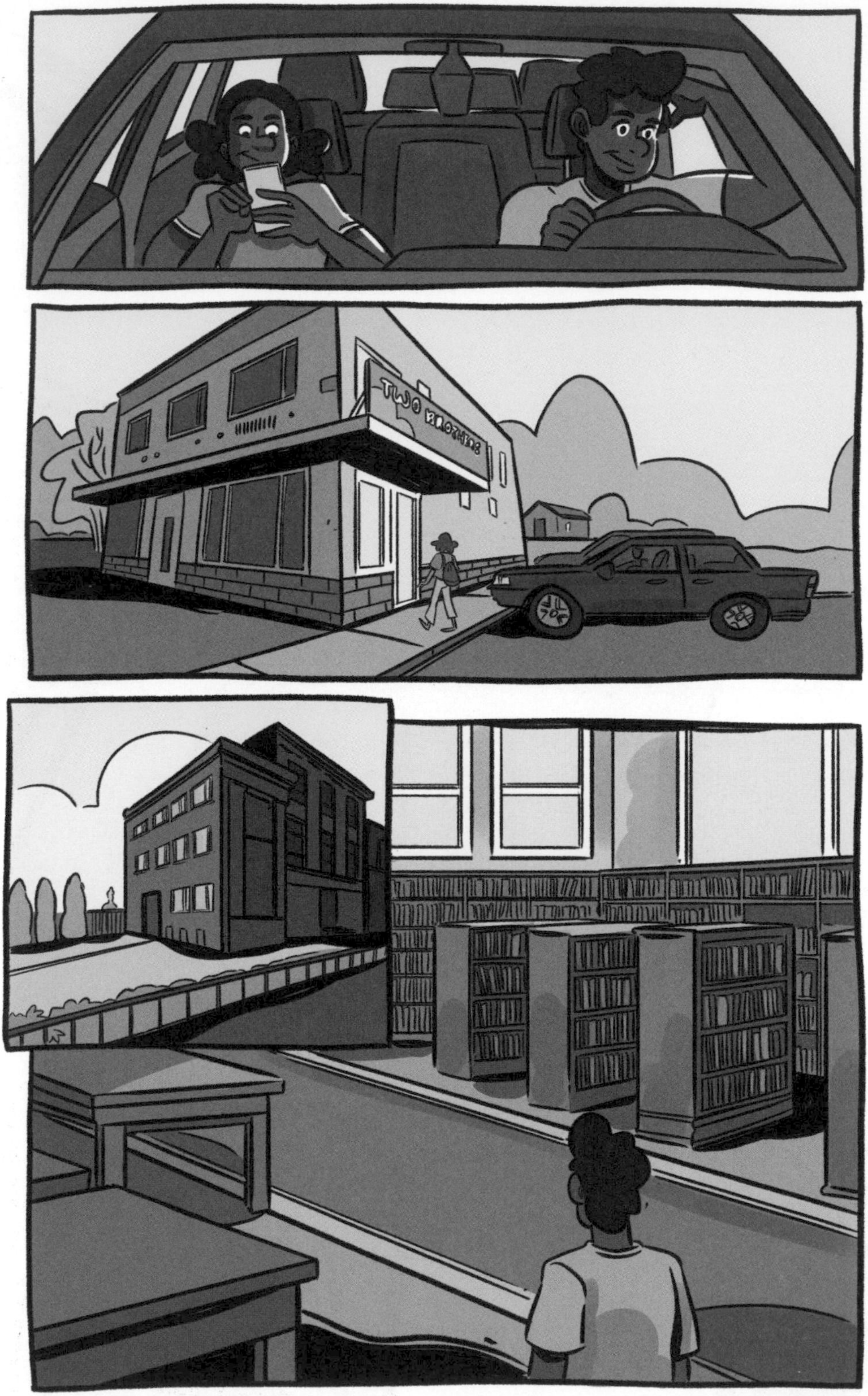
TWO BROTHERS

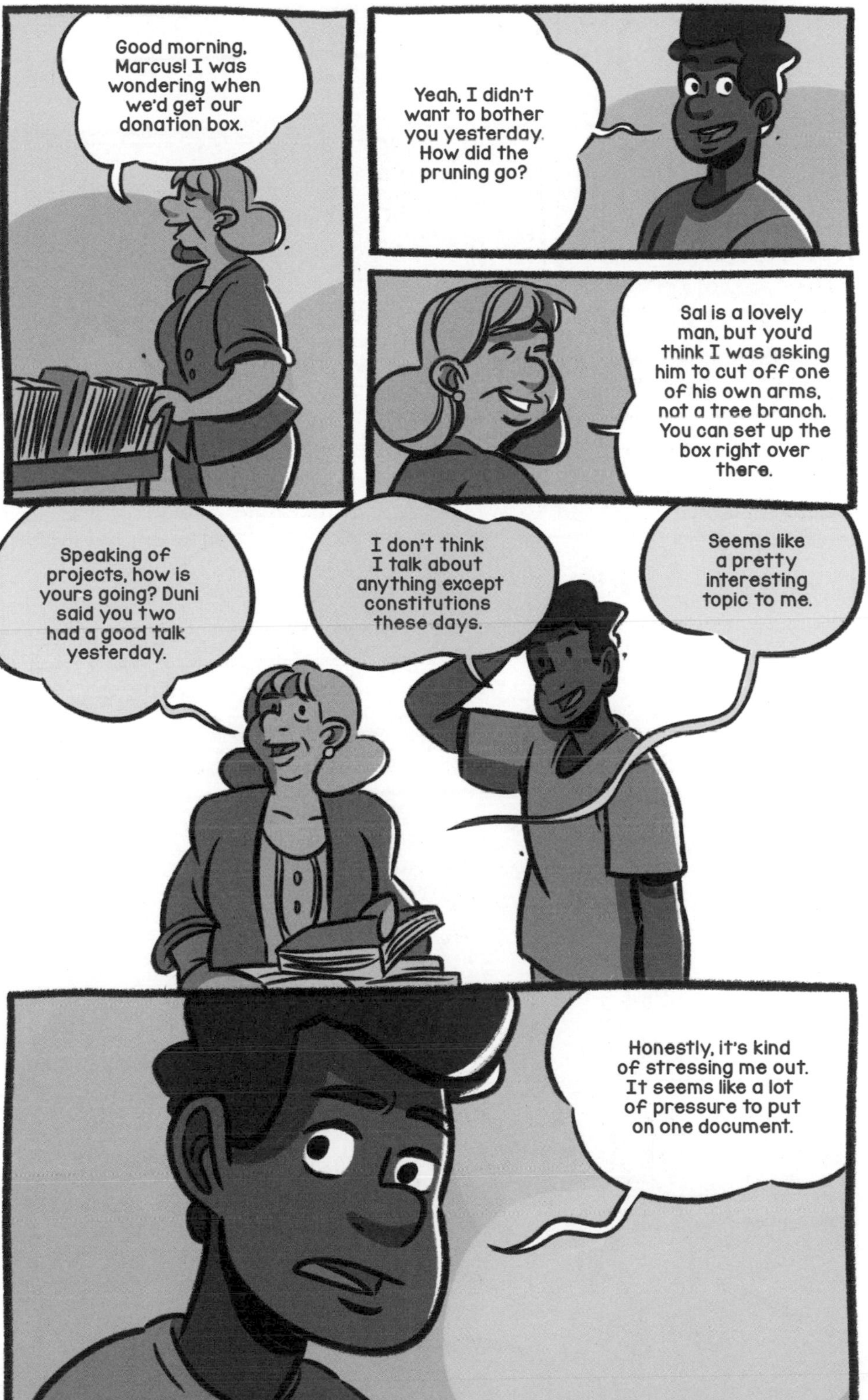
Good morning, Marcus! I was wondering when we'd get our donation box.
Yeah, I didn't want to bother you yesterday. How did the pruning go?
Sal is a lovely man, but you'd think I was asking him to cut off one of his own arms, not a tree branch. You can set up the box right over there.
Speaking of projects, how is yours going? Duni said you two had a good talk yesterday.
I don't think I talk about anything except constitutions these days.
Seems like a pretty interesting topic to me.
Honestly, it's kind of stressing me out. It seems like a lot of pressure to put on one document.

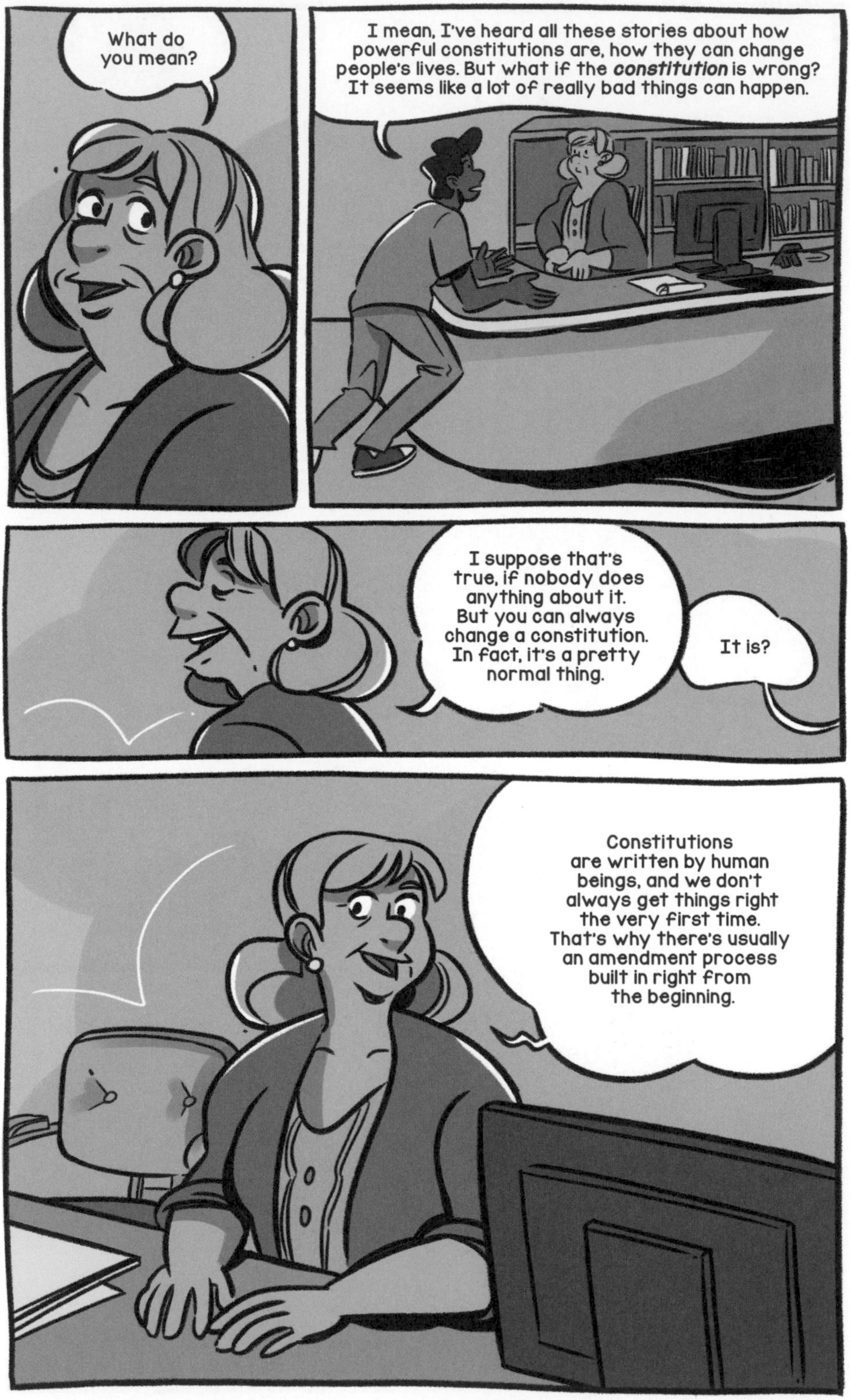
What do you mean?
I mean, I've heard all these stories about how powerful constitutions are, how they can change people's lives. But what if the *constitution* is wrong? It seems like a lot of really bad things can happen.
I suppose that's true, if nobody does anything about it. But you can always change a constitution. In fact, it's a pretty normal thing.
It is?
Constitutions are written by human beings, and we don't always get things right the very first time. That's why there's usually an amendment process built in right from the beginning.

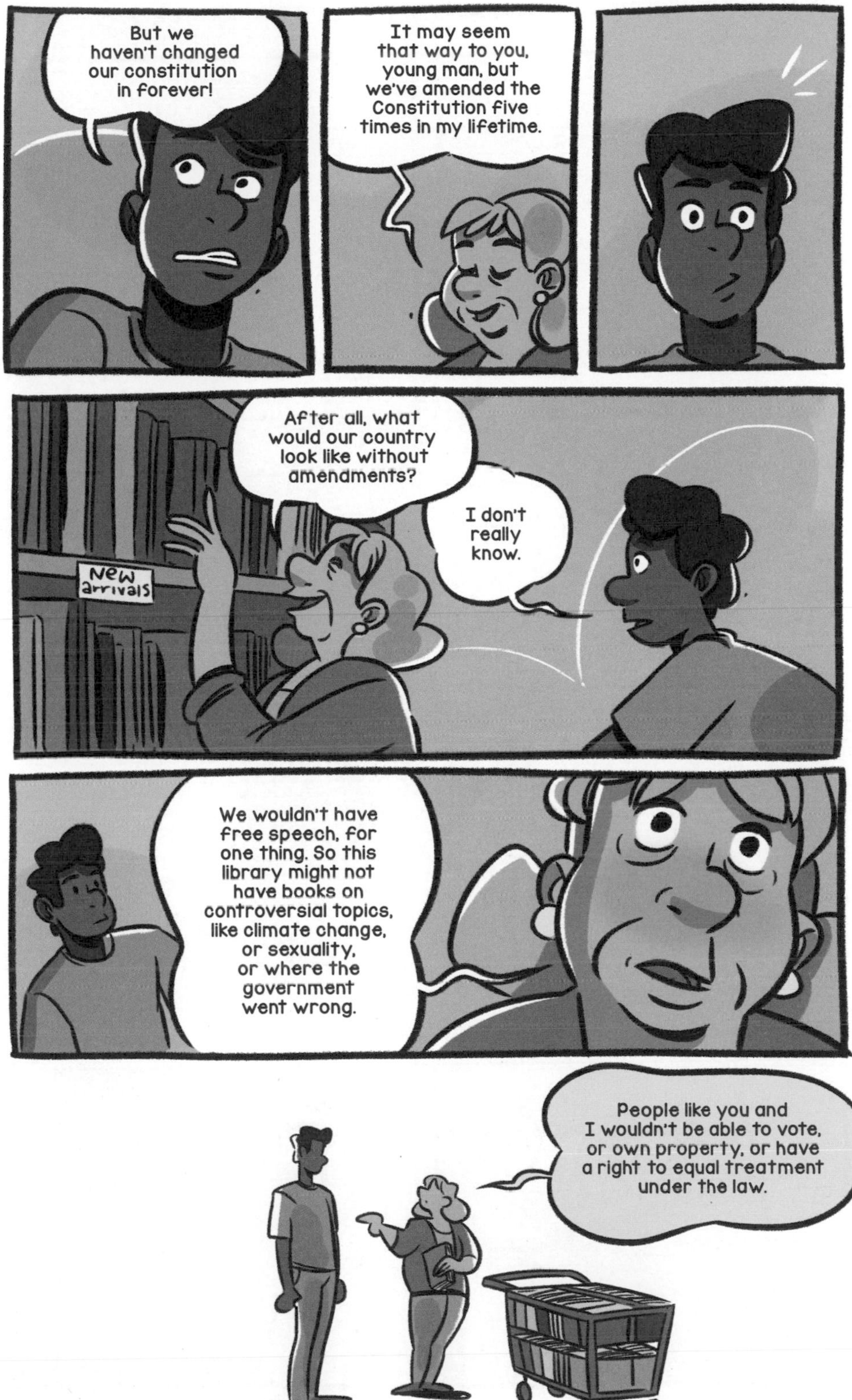
But we haven't changed our constitution in forever!
It may seem that way to you, young man, but we've amended the Constitution five times in my lifetime.
After all, what would our country look like without amendments?
New arrivals
I don't really know.
We wouldn't have free speech, for one thing. So this library might not have books on controversial topics, like climate change, or sexuality, or where the government went wrong.
People like you and I wouldn't be able to vote, or own property, or have a right to equal treatment under the law.

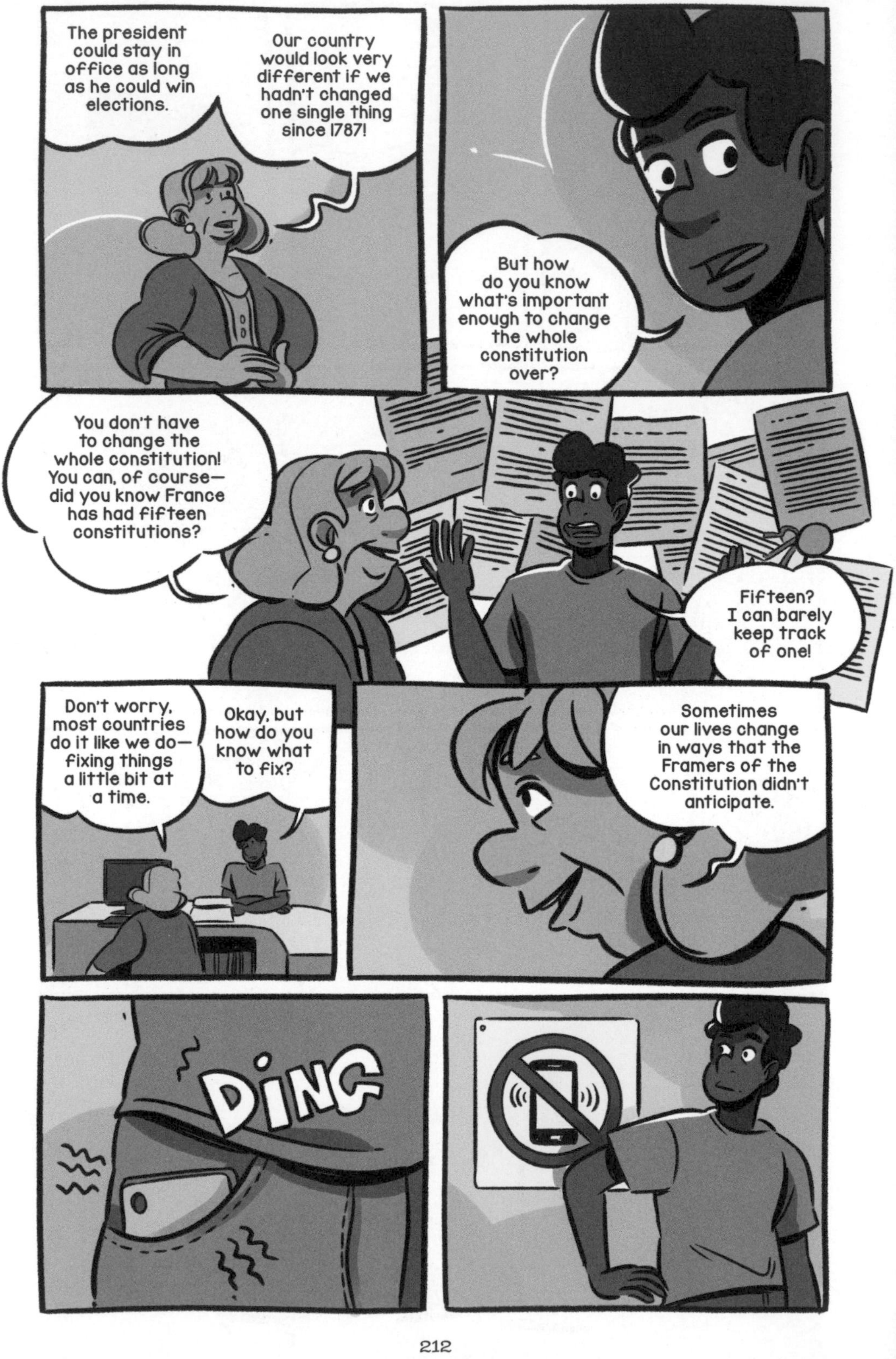

The president could stay in office as long as he could win elections.
Our country would look very different if we hadn't changed one single thing since 1787!
But how do you know what's important enough to change the whole constitution over?
You don't have to change the whole constitution! You can, of course—did you know France has had fifteen constitutions?
Fifteen? I can barely keep track of one!
Don't worry, most countries do it like we do—fixing things a little bit at a time.
Okay, but how do you know what to fix?
Sometimes our lives change in ways that the Framers of the Constitution didn't anticipate.
DING

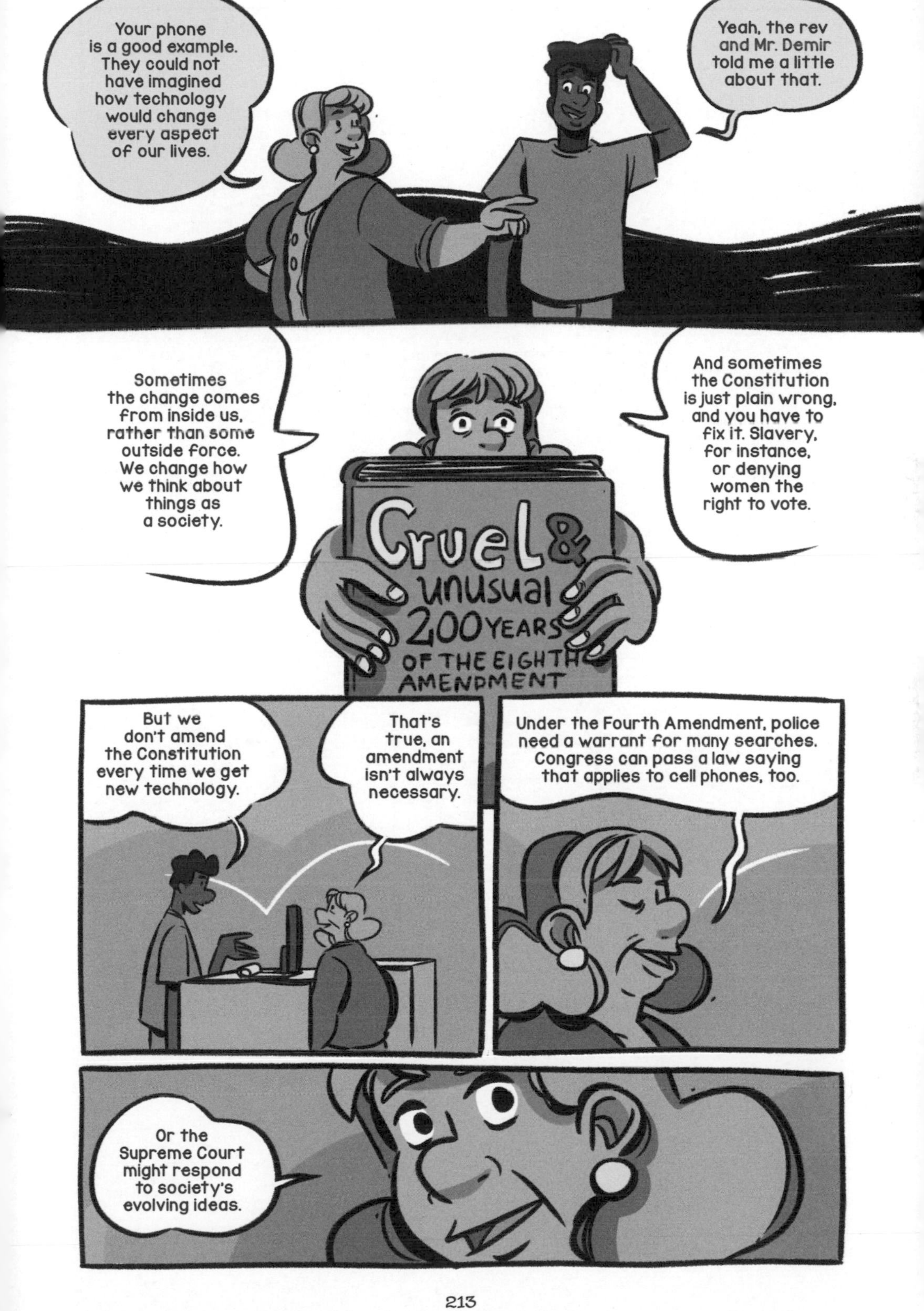
Your phone is a good example. They could not have imagined how technology would change every aspect of our lives.
Yeah, the rev and Mr. Demir told me a little about that.
Sometimes the change comes from inside us, rather than some outside force. We change how we think about things as a society.
Cruel & unusual 200 YEARS OF THE EIGHTH AMENDMENT
And sometimes the Constitution is just plain wrong, and you have to fix it. Slavery, for instance, or denying women the right to vote.
But we don't amend the Constitution every time we get new technology.
That's true, an amendment isn't always necessary.
Under the Fourth Amendment, police need a warrant for many searches. Congress can pass a law saying that applies to cell phones, too.
Or the Supreme Court might respond to society's evolving ideas.

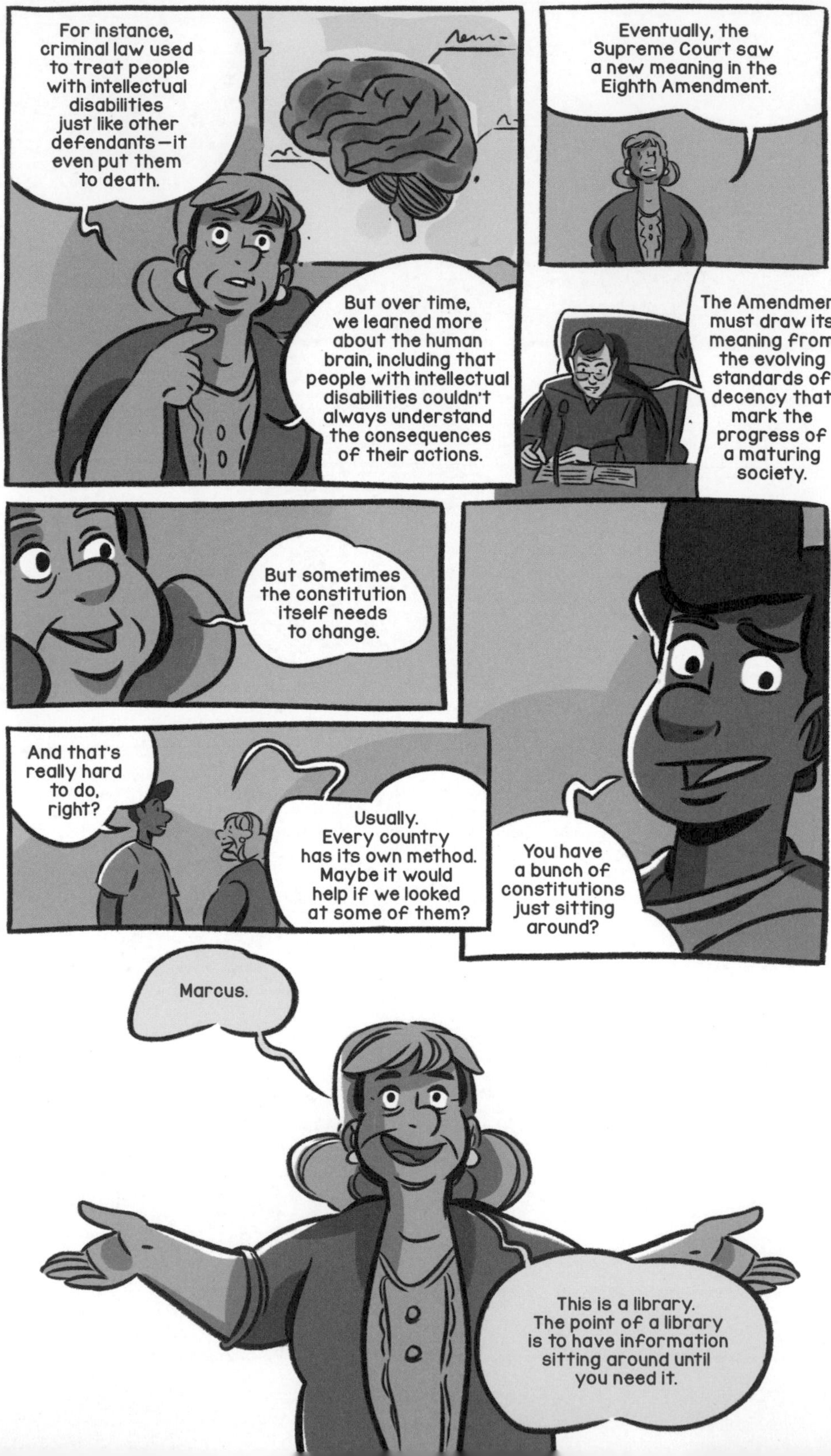
For instance, criminal law used to treat people with intellectual disabilities just like other defendants—it even put them to death.
But over time, we learned more about the human brain, including that people with intellectual disabilities couldn't always understand the consequences of their actions.
Eventually, the Supreme Court saw a new meaning in the Eighth Amendment.
The Amendment must draw its meaning from the evolving standards of decency that mark the progress of a maturing society.
But sometimes the constitution itself needs to change.
And that's really hard to do, right?
Usually. Every country has its own method. Maybe it would help if we looked at some of them?
You have a bunch of constitutions just sitting around?
Marcus.
This is a library. The point of a library is to have information sitting around until you need it.

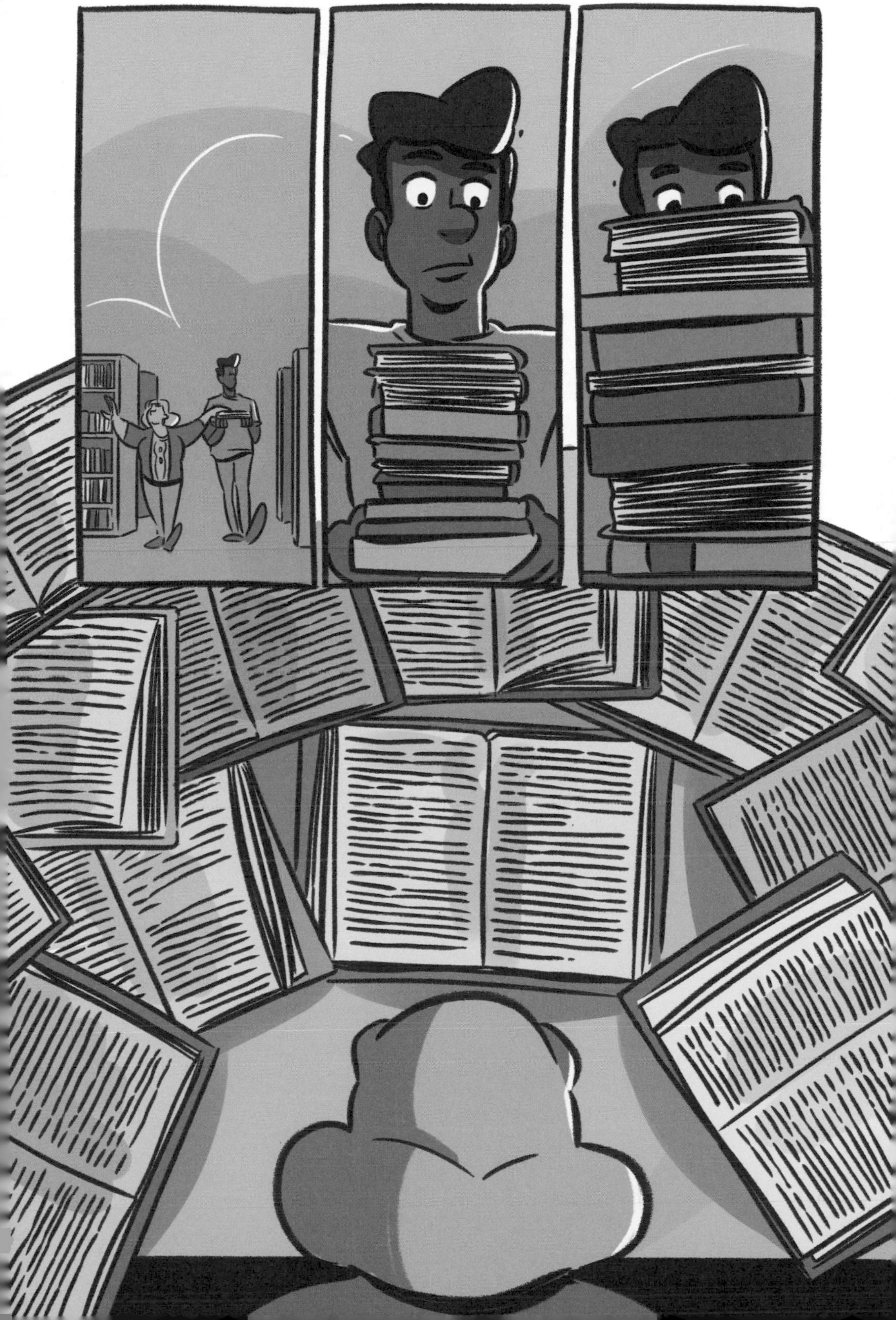

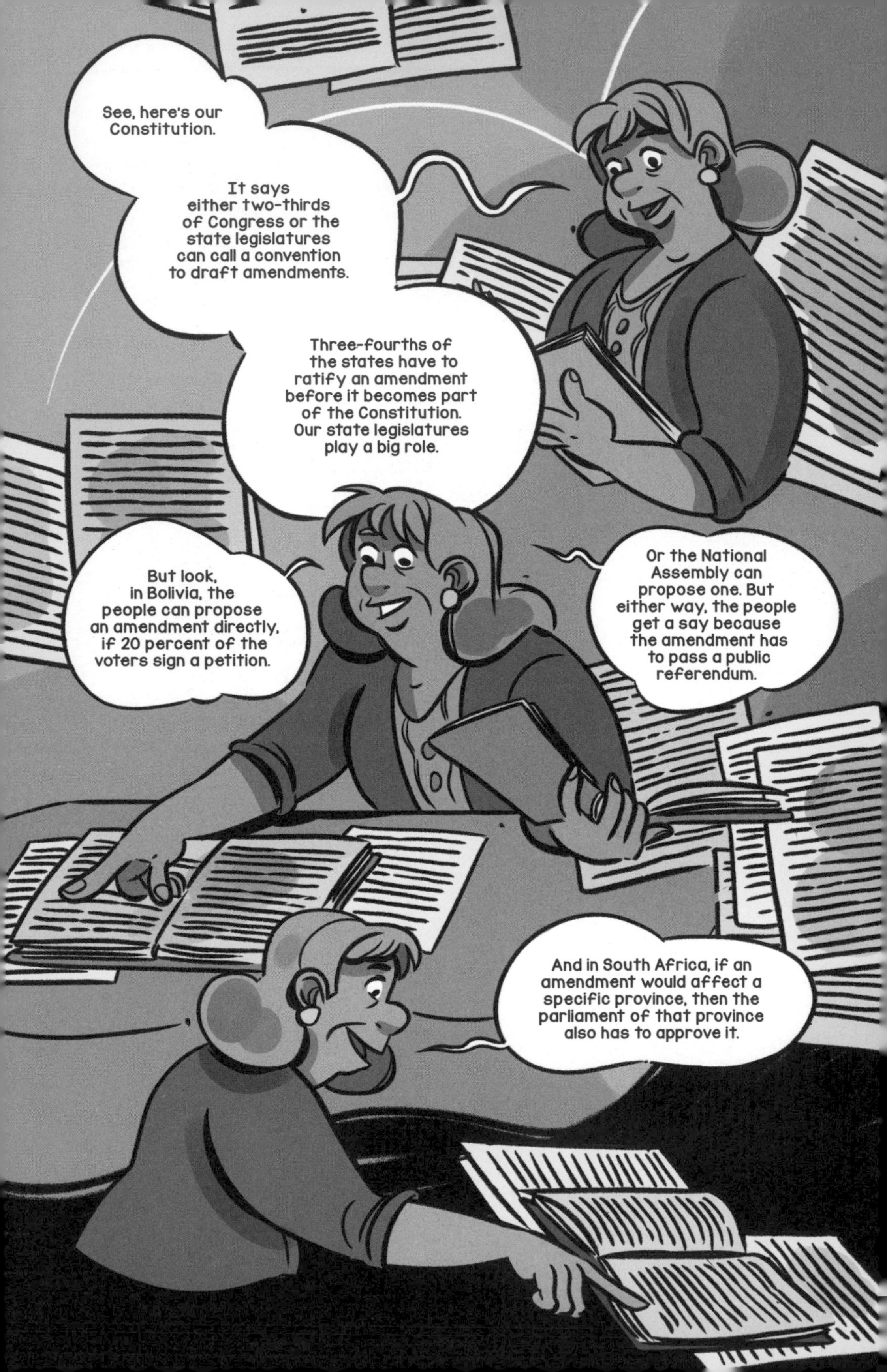
See, here's our Constitution.
It says either two-thirds of Congress or the state legislatures can call a convention to draft amendments.
Three-fourths of the states have to ratify an amendment before it becomes part of the Constitution. Our state legislatures play a big role.
But look, in Bolivia, the people can propose an amendment directly, if 20 percent of the voters sign a petition.
Or the National Assembly can propose one. But either way, the people get a say because the amendment has to pass a public referendum.
And in South Africa, if an amendment would affect a specific province, then the parliament of that province also has to approve it.

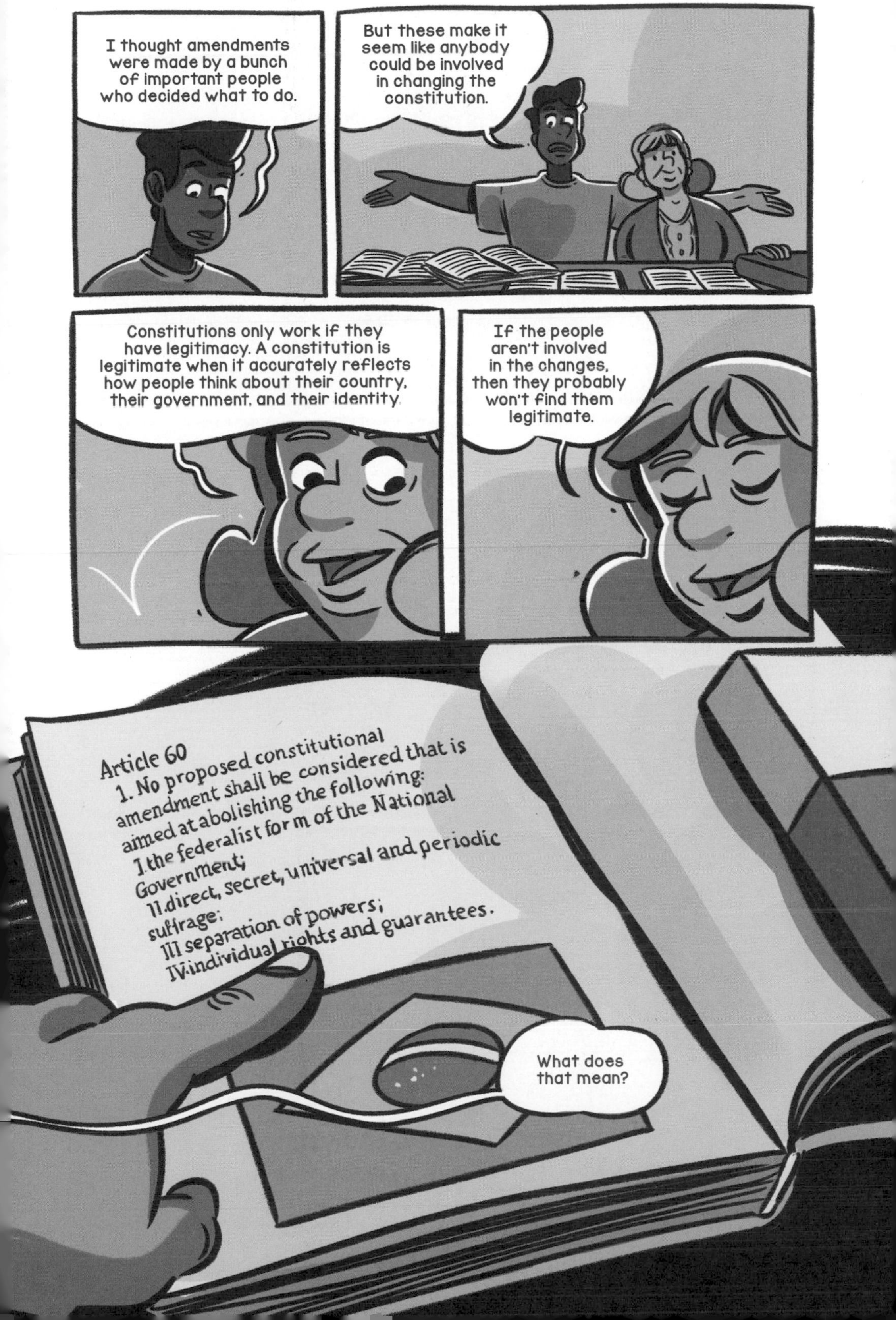
I thought amendments were made by a bunch of important people who decided what to do.
But these make it seem like anybody could be involved in changing the constitution.
Constitutions only work if they have legitimacy. A constitution is legitimate when it accurately reflects how people think about their country, their government, and their identity.
If the people aren't involved in the changes, then they probably won't find them legitimate.
Article 60
1. No proposed constitutional amendment shall be considered that is aimed at abolishing the following:
I the federalist form of the National Government;
II. direct, secret, universal and periodic suffrage;
III separation of powers;
IV. individual rights and guarantees.
What does that mean?

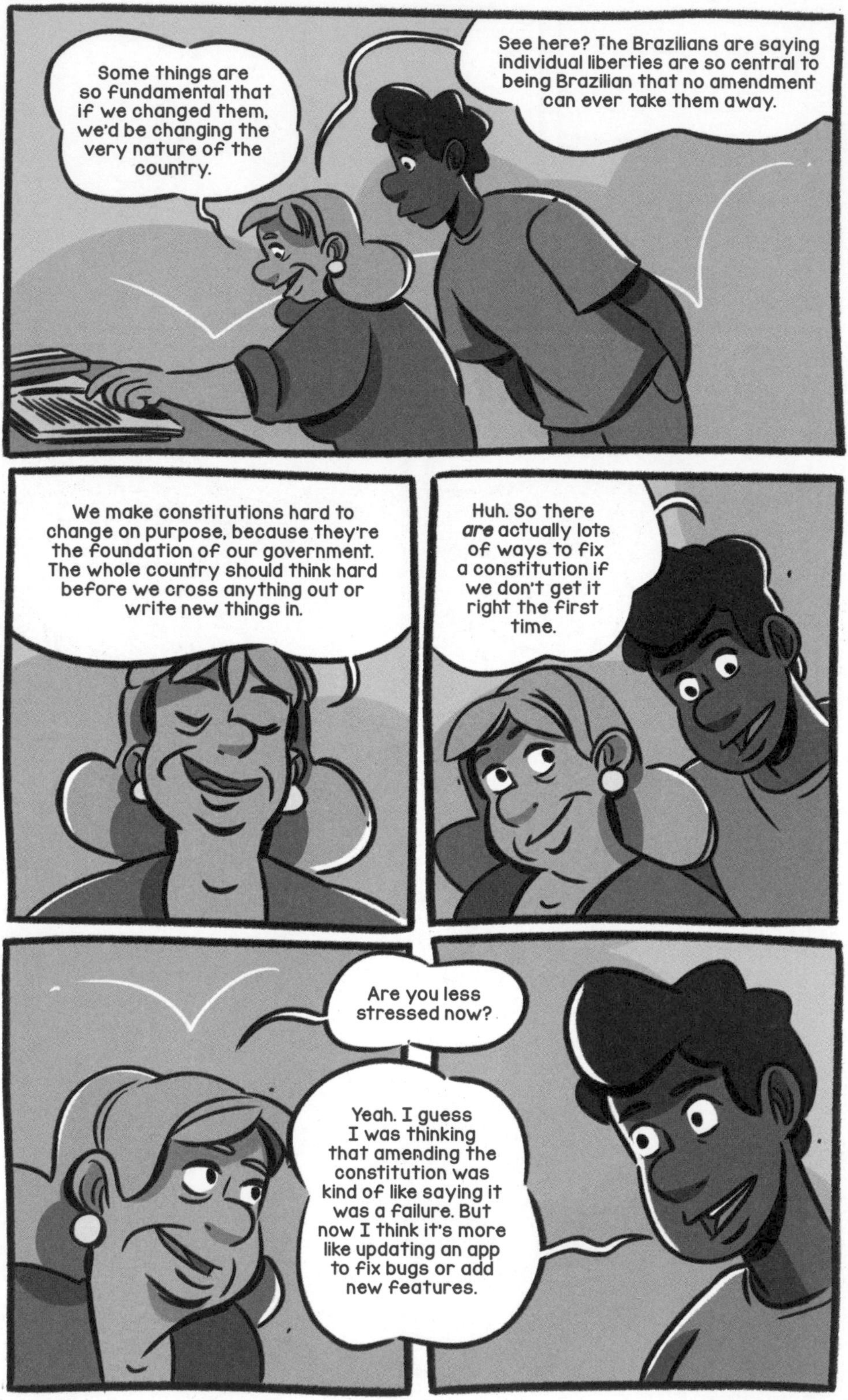
Some things are so fundamental that if we changed them, we'd be changing the very nature of the country.
See here? The Brazilians are saying individual liberties are so central to being Brazilian that no amendment can ever take them away.
We make constitutions hard to change on purpose, because they're the foundation of our government. The whole country should think hard before we cross anything out or write new things in.
Huh. So there *are* actually lots of ways to fix a constitution if we don't get it right the first time.
Are you less stressed now?
Yeah. I guess I was thinking that amending the constitution was kind of like saying it was a failure. But now I think it's more like updating an app to fix bugs or add new features.

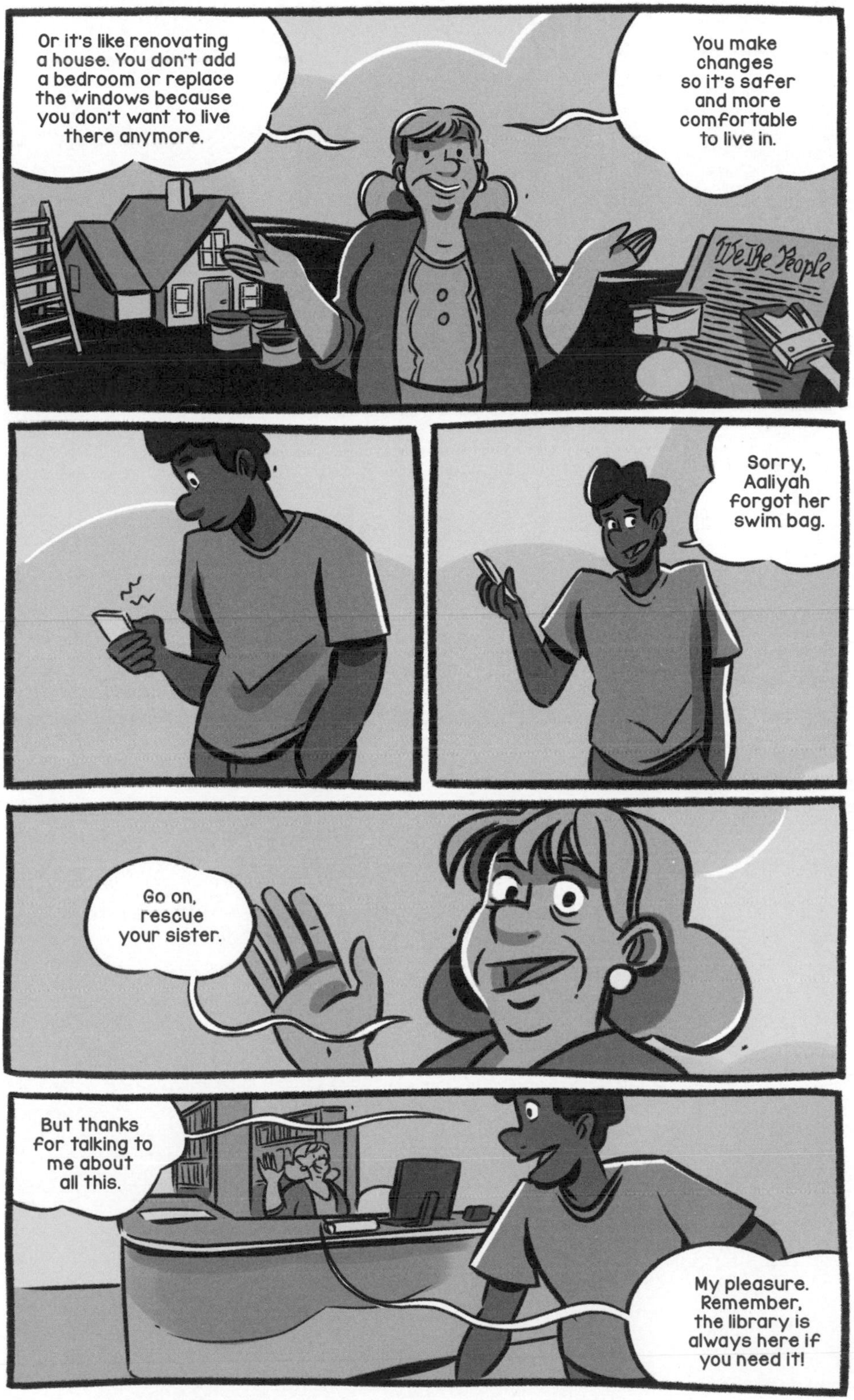
Or it's like renovating a house. You don't add a bedroom or replace the windows because you don't want to live there anymore.
You make changes so it's safer and more comfortable to live in.
We The People
Sorry, Aaliyah forgot her swim bag.
Go on, rescue your sister.
But thanks for talking to me about all this.
My pleasure. Remember, the library is always here if you need it!

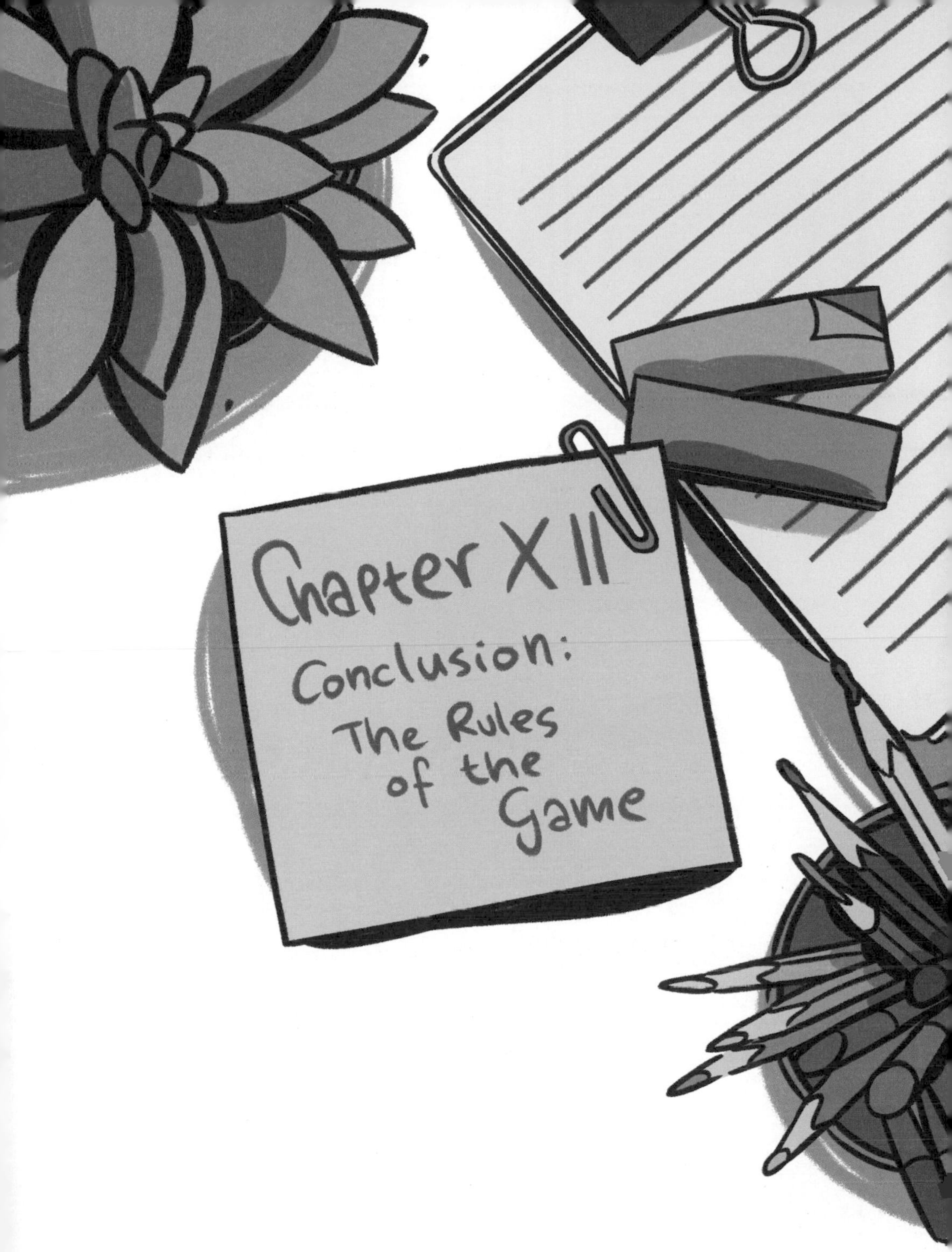
Chapter XII
Conclusion:
The Rules
of the
Game

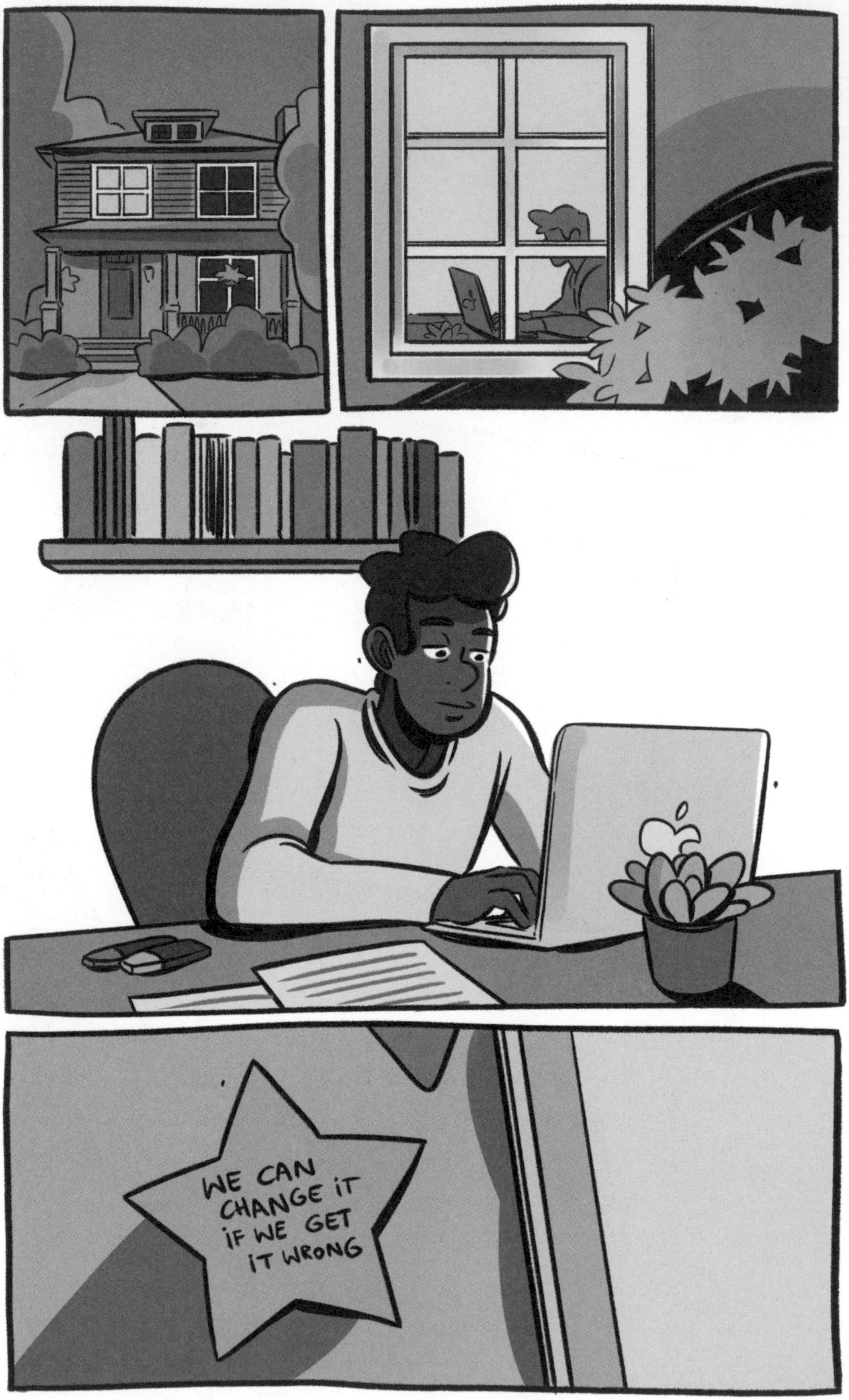
WE CAN CHANGE IT IF WE GET IT WRONG

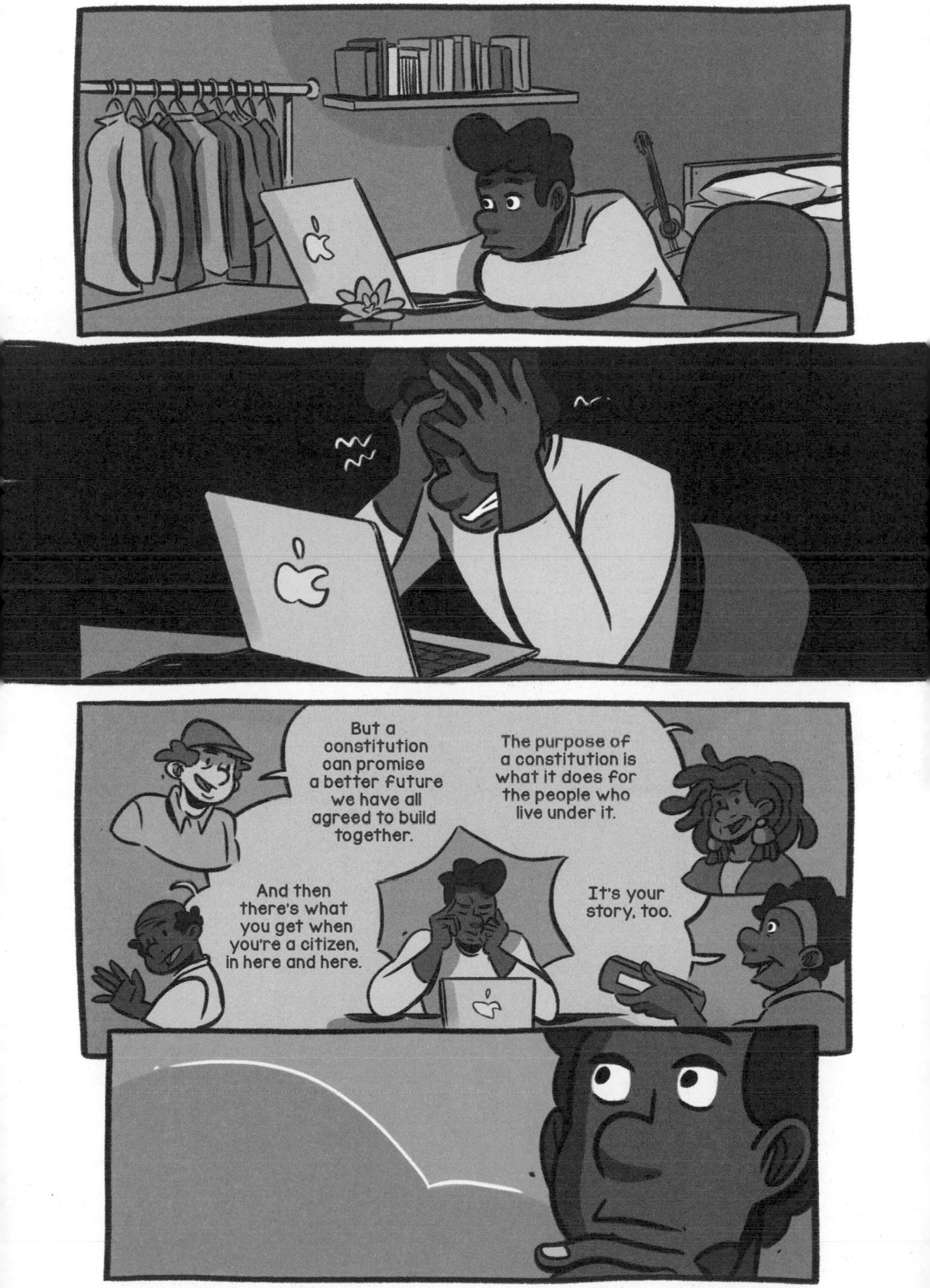
But a constitution can promise a better future we have all agreed to build together.
The purpose of a constitution is what it does for the people who live under it.
And then there's what you get when you're a citizen, in here and here.
It's your story, too.

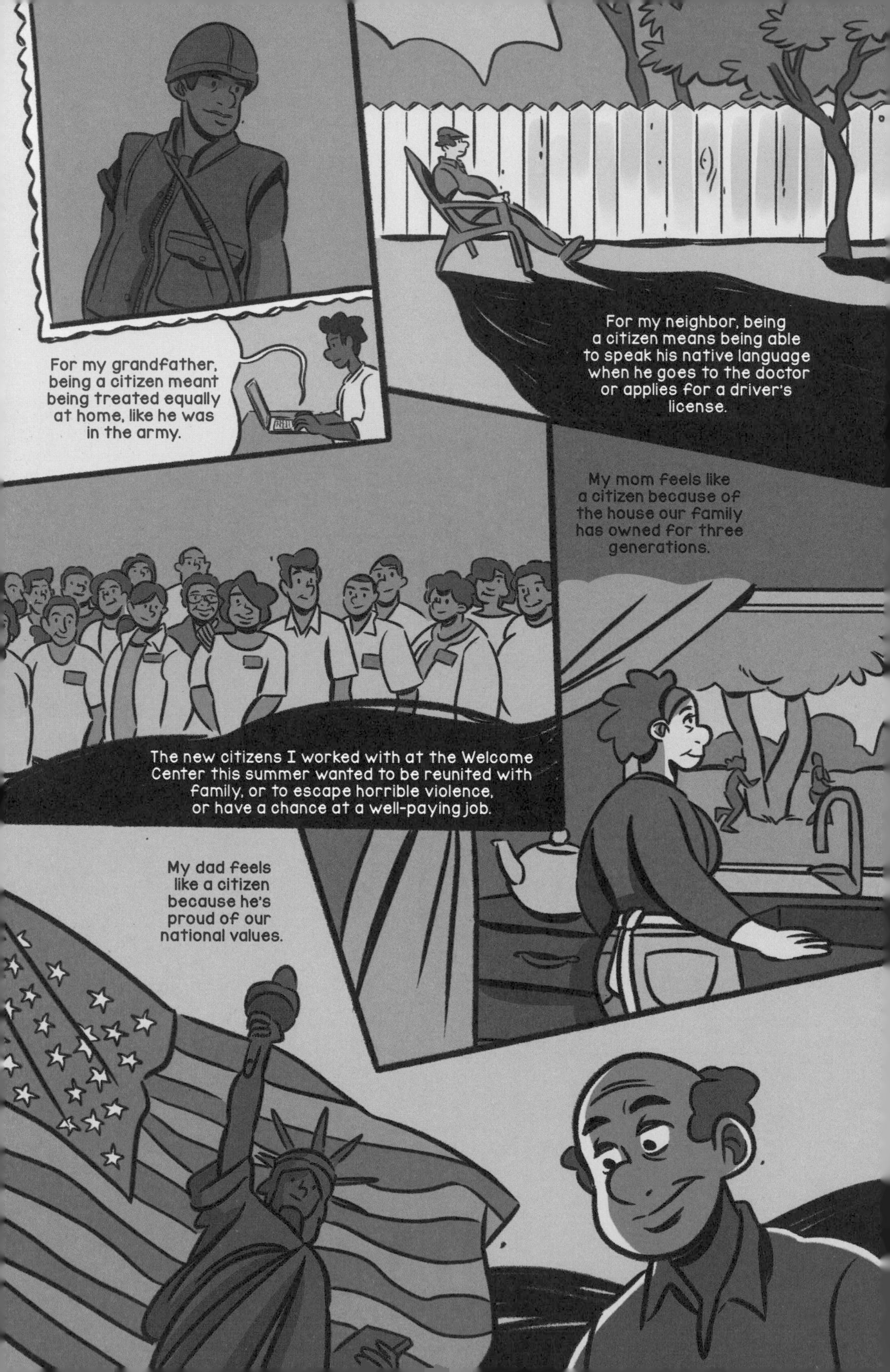
For my grandfather, being a citizen meant being treated equally at home, like he was in the army.
For my neighbor, being a citizen means being able to speak his native language when he goes to the doctor or applies for a driver's license.
My mom feels like a citizen because of the house our family has owned for three generations.
The new citizens I worked with at the Welcome Center this summer wanted to be reunited with family, or to escape horrible violence, or have a chance at a well-paying job.
My dad feels like a citizen because he's proud of our national values.

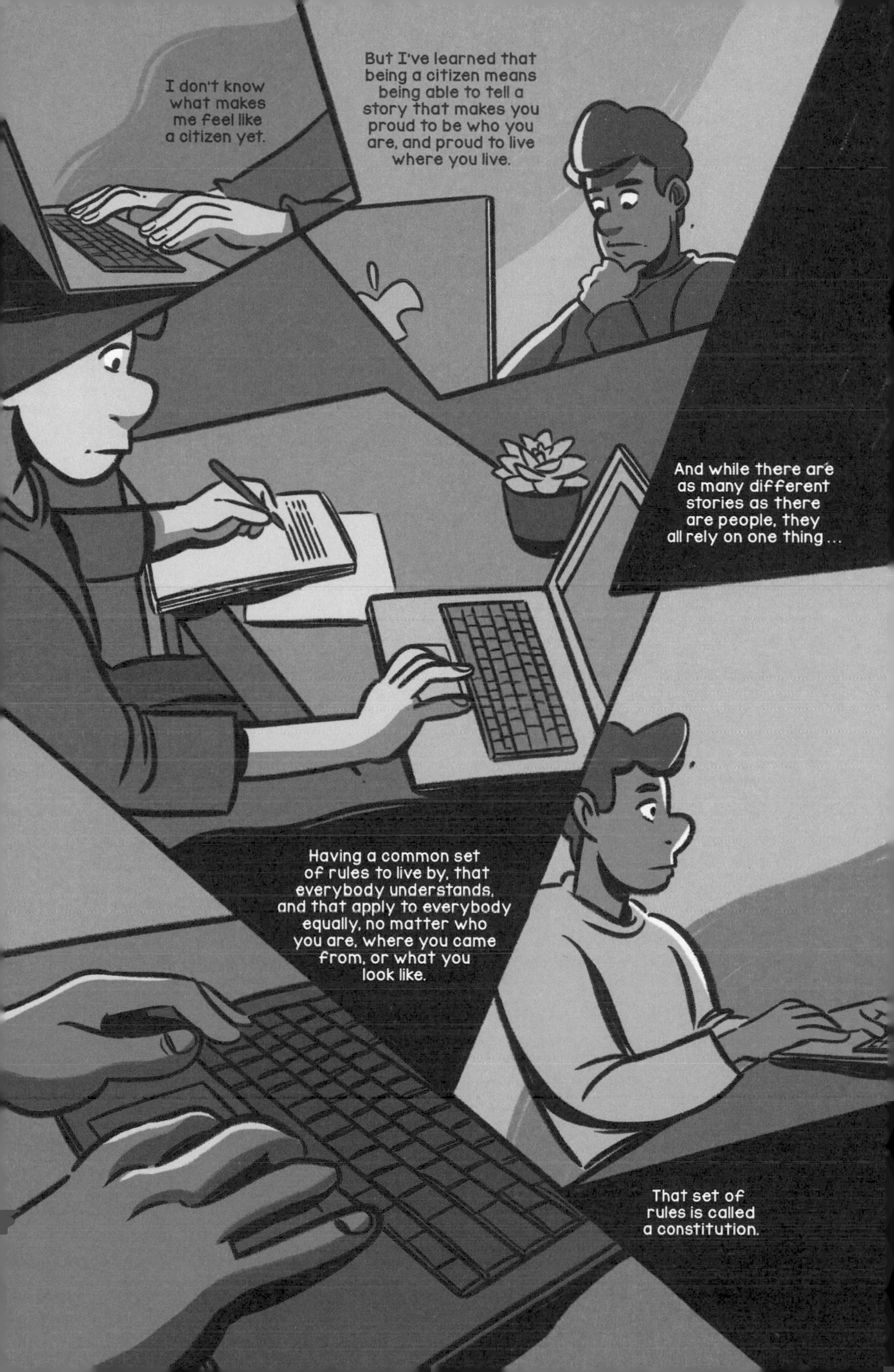
I don't know what makes me feel like a citizen yet.
But I've learned that being a citizen means being able to tell a story that makes you proud to be who you are, and proud to live where you live.
And while there are as many different stories as there are people, they all rely on one thing . . .
Having a common set of rules to live by, that everybody understands, and that apply to everybody equally, no matter who you are, where you came from, or what you look like.
That set of rules is called a constitution.

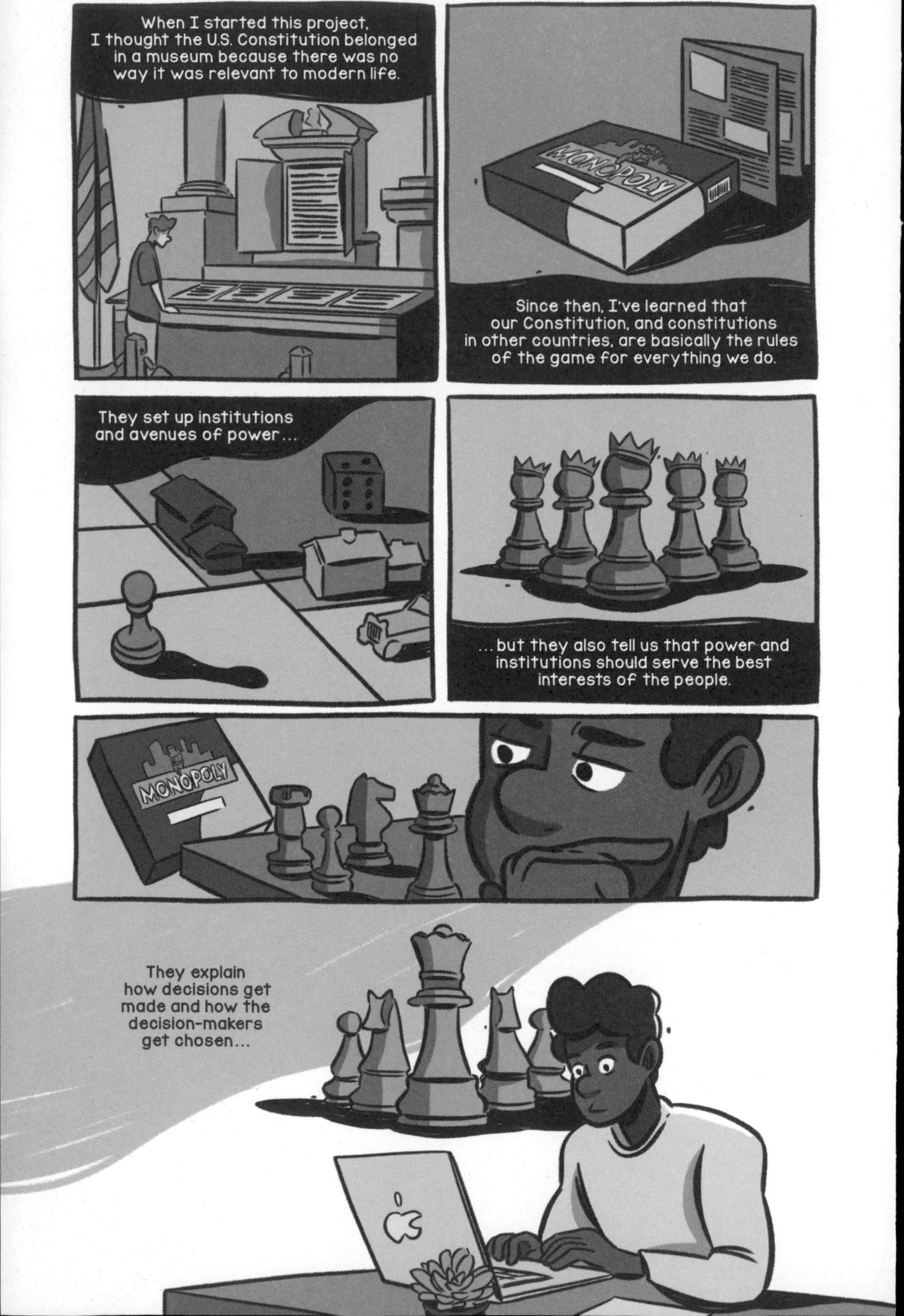
When I started this project, I thought the U.S. Constitution belonged in a museum because there was no way it was relevant to modern life.
MONOPOLY
Since then, I've learned that our Constitution, and constitutions in other countries, are basically the rules of the game for everything we do.
They set up institutions and avenues of power...
...but they also tell us that power and institutions should serve the best interests of the people.
MONOPOLY
They explain how decisions get made and how the decision-makers get chosen...

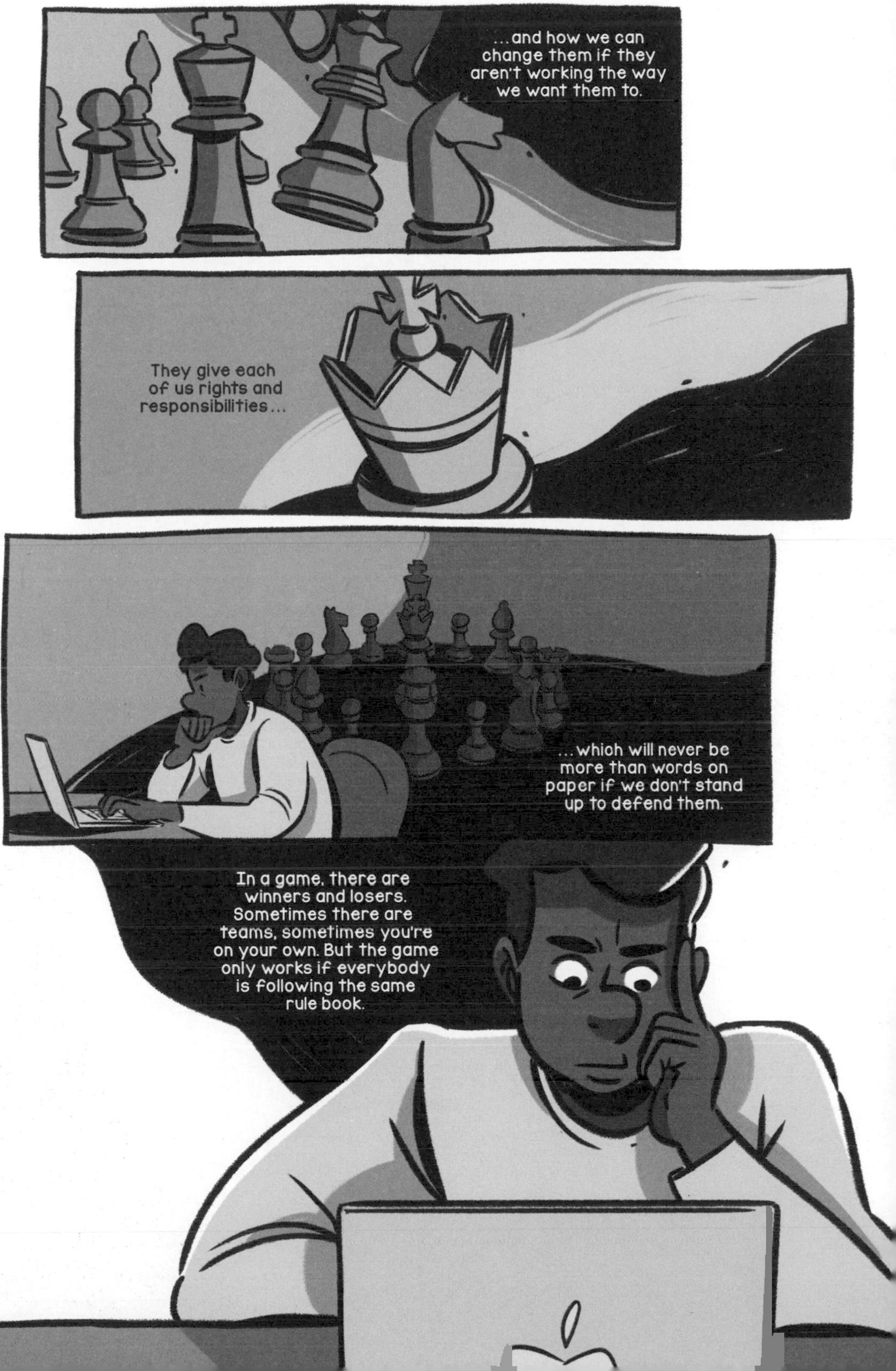
...and how we can change them if they aren't working the way we want them to.
They give each of us rights and responsibilities...
...which will never be more than words on paper if we don't stand up to defend them.
In a game, there are winners and losers. Sometimes there are teams, sometimes you're on your own. But the game only works if everybody is following the same rule book.

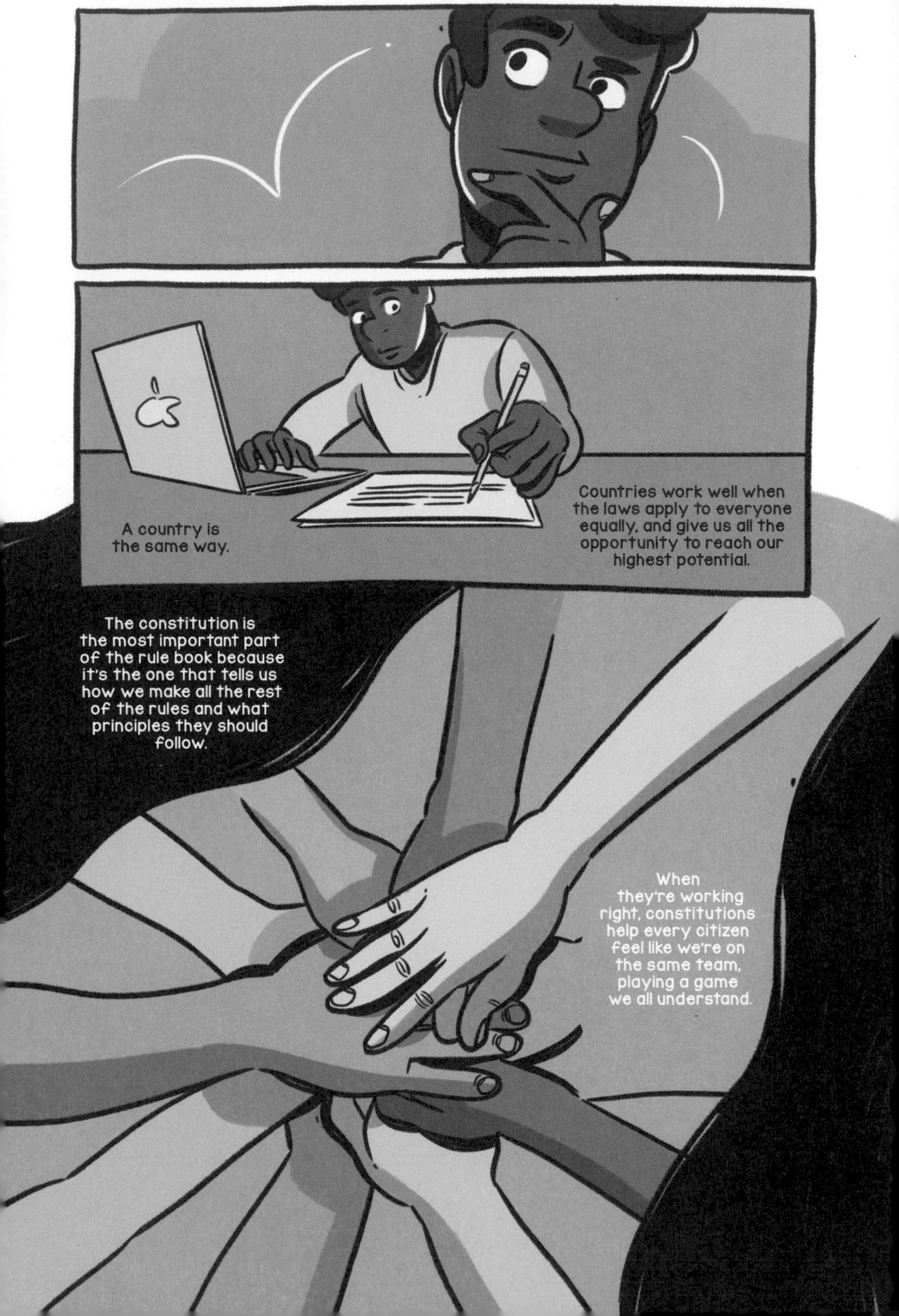
A country is the same way.
Countries work well when the laws apply to everyone equally, and give us all the opportunity to reach our highest potential.
The constitution is the most important part of the rule book because it's the one that tells us how we make all the rest of the rules and what principles they should follow.
When they're working right, constitutions help every citizen feel like we're on the same team, playing a game we all understand.

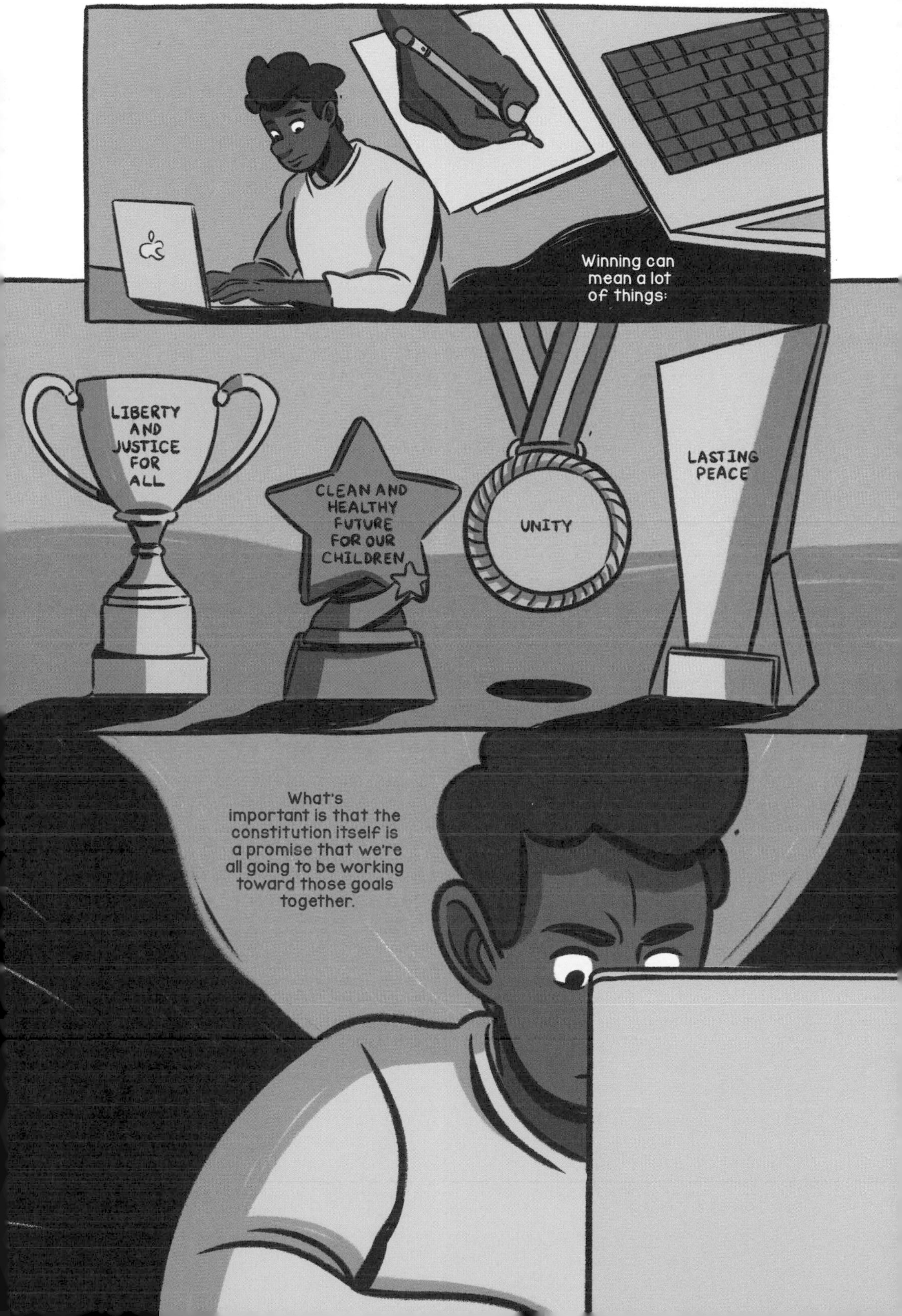
Winning can mean a lot of things:
LIBERTY AND JUSTICE FOR ALL
CLEAN AND HEALTHY FUTURE FOR OUR CHILDREN
UNITY
LASTING PEACE
What's important is that the constitution itself is a promise that we're all going to be working toward those goals together.

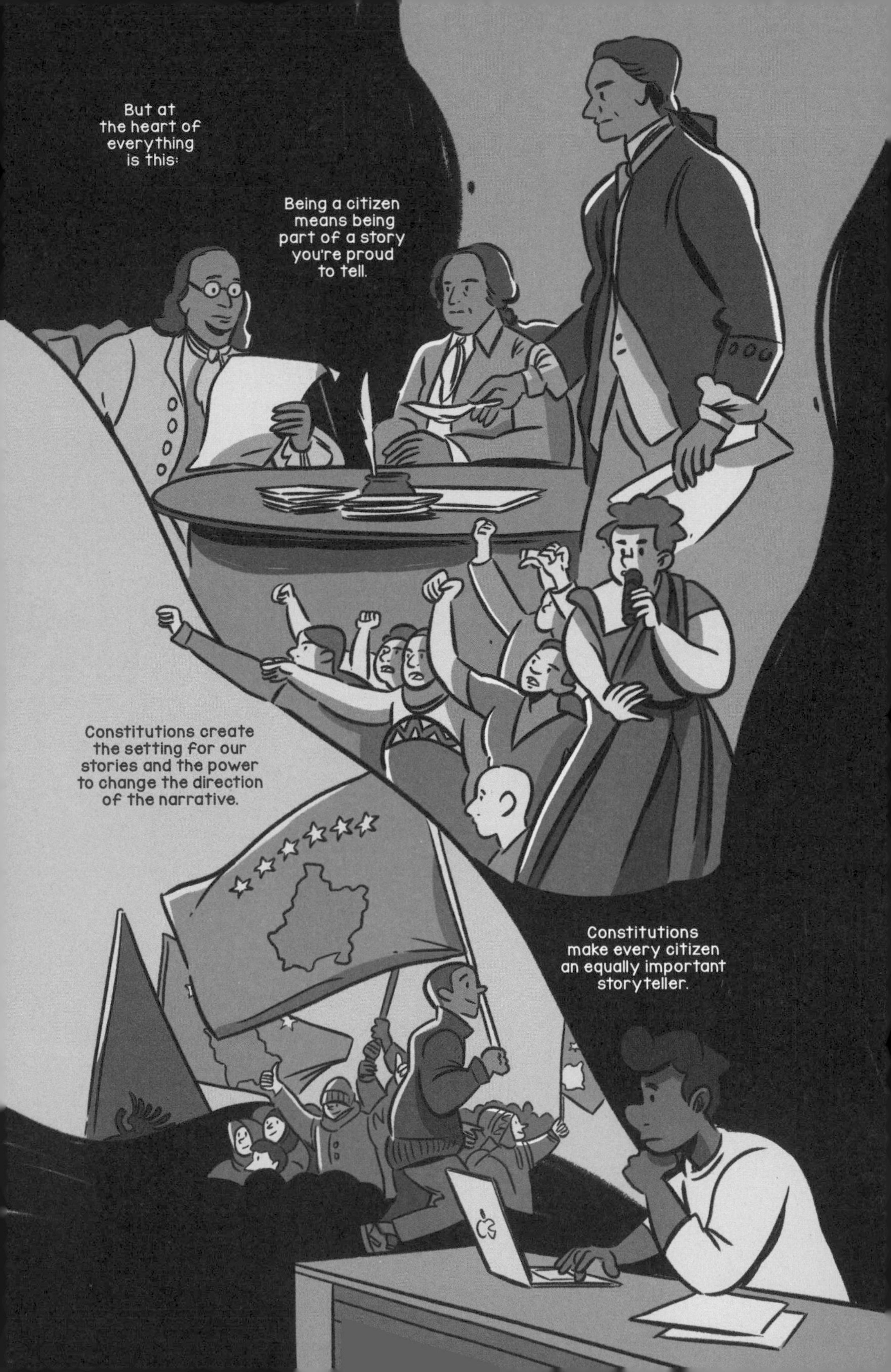
But at the heart of everything is this:
Being a citizen means being part of a story you're proud to tell.
Constitutions create the setting for our stories and the power to change the direction of the narrative.
Constitutions make every citizen an equally important storyteller.

A country is the same way. Countries work we
laws apply to everyone equally, and give us all t
to reach our highest potential. Countries don't
the laws only apply to some, or they mean diff
based on a person's race, gender, sexual orient
place of birth, or how much money they have.

The constitution is the most important part of
because it's the one that tells us how we make

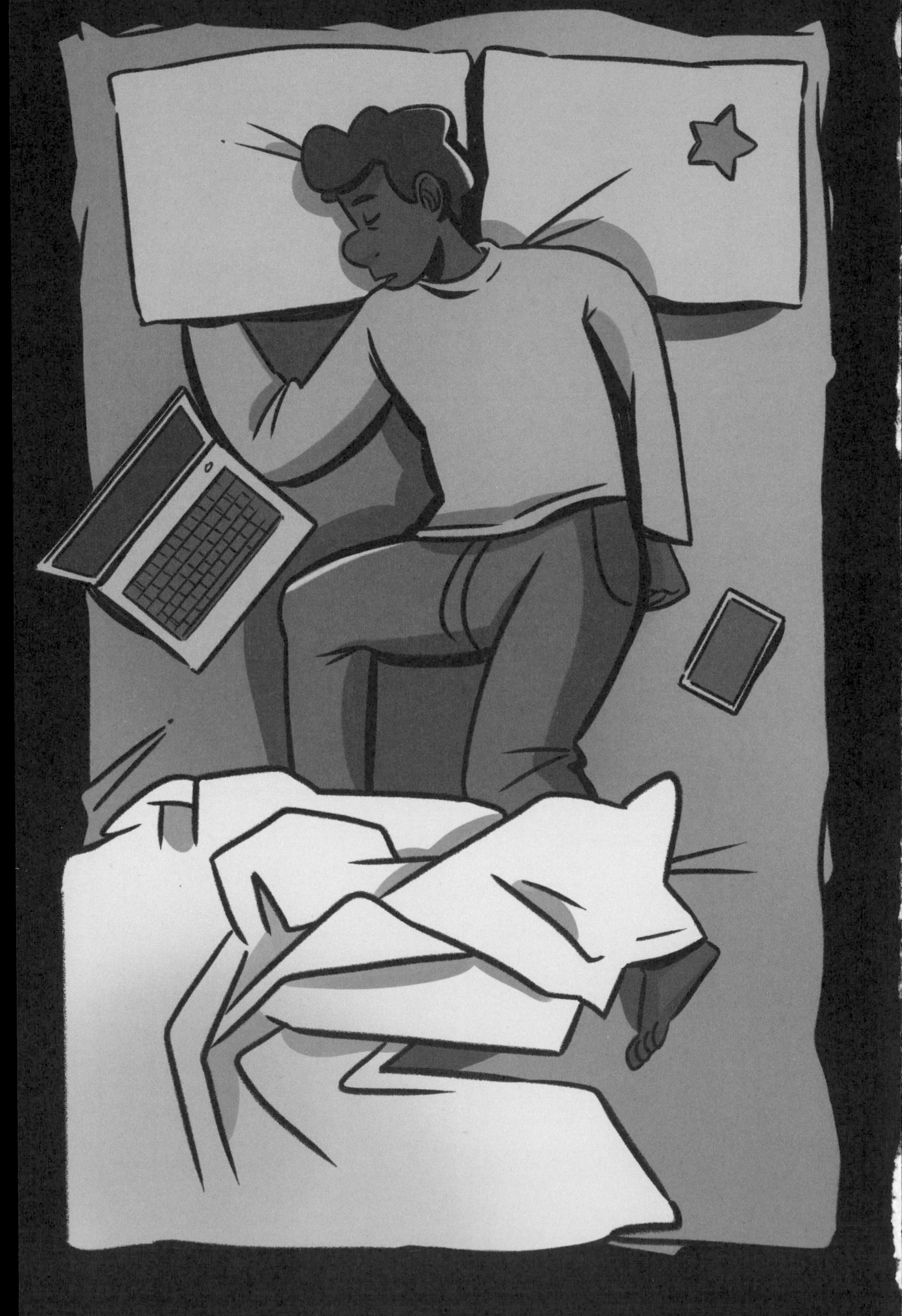

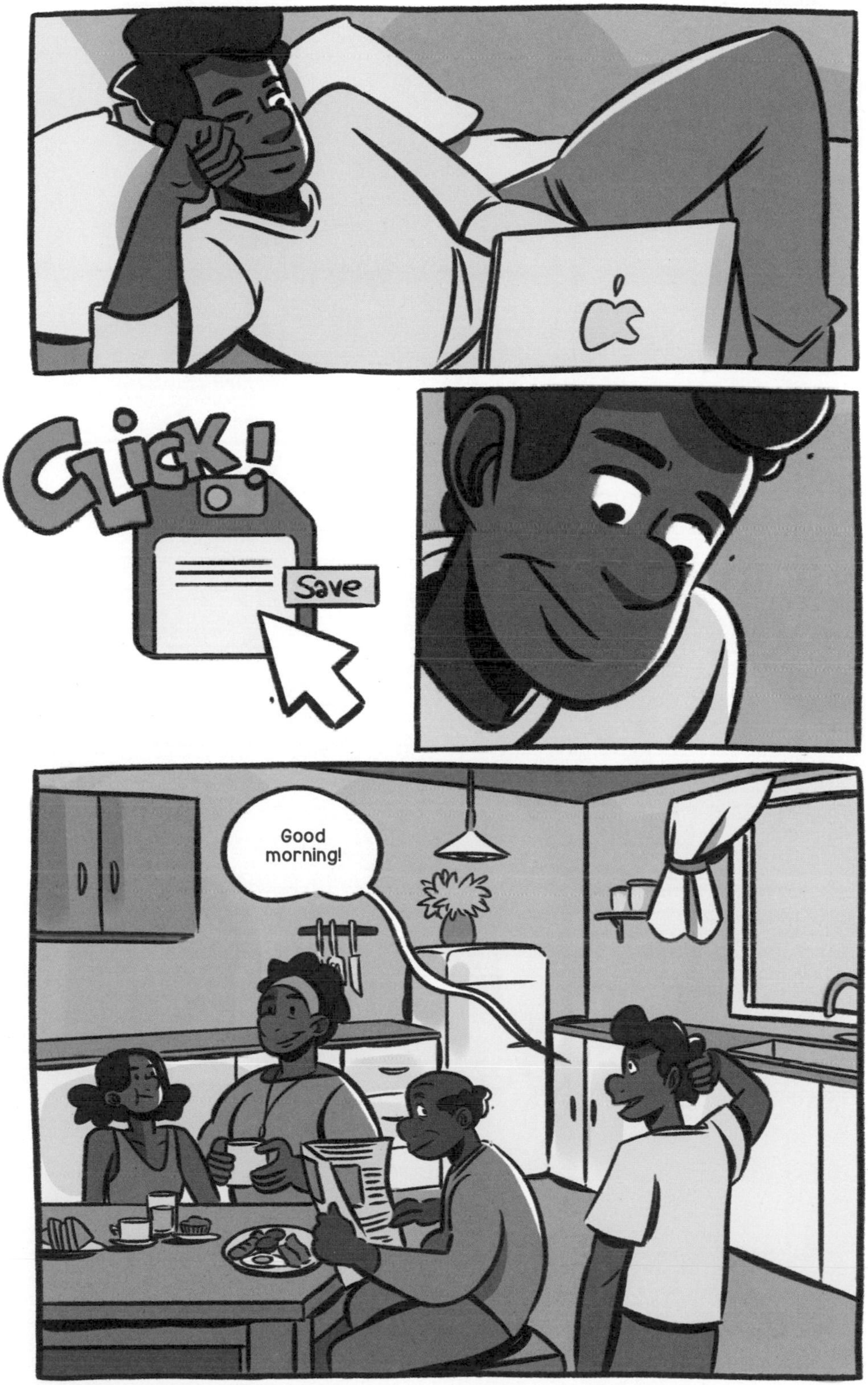
CLICK!
Save
Good morning!

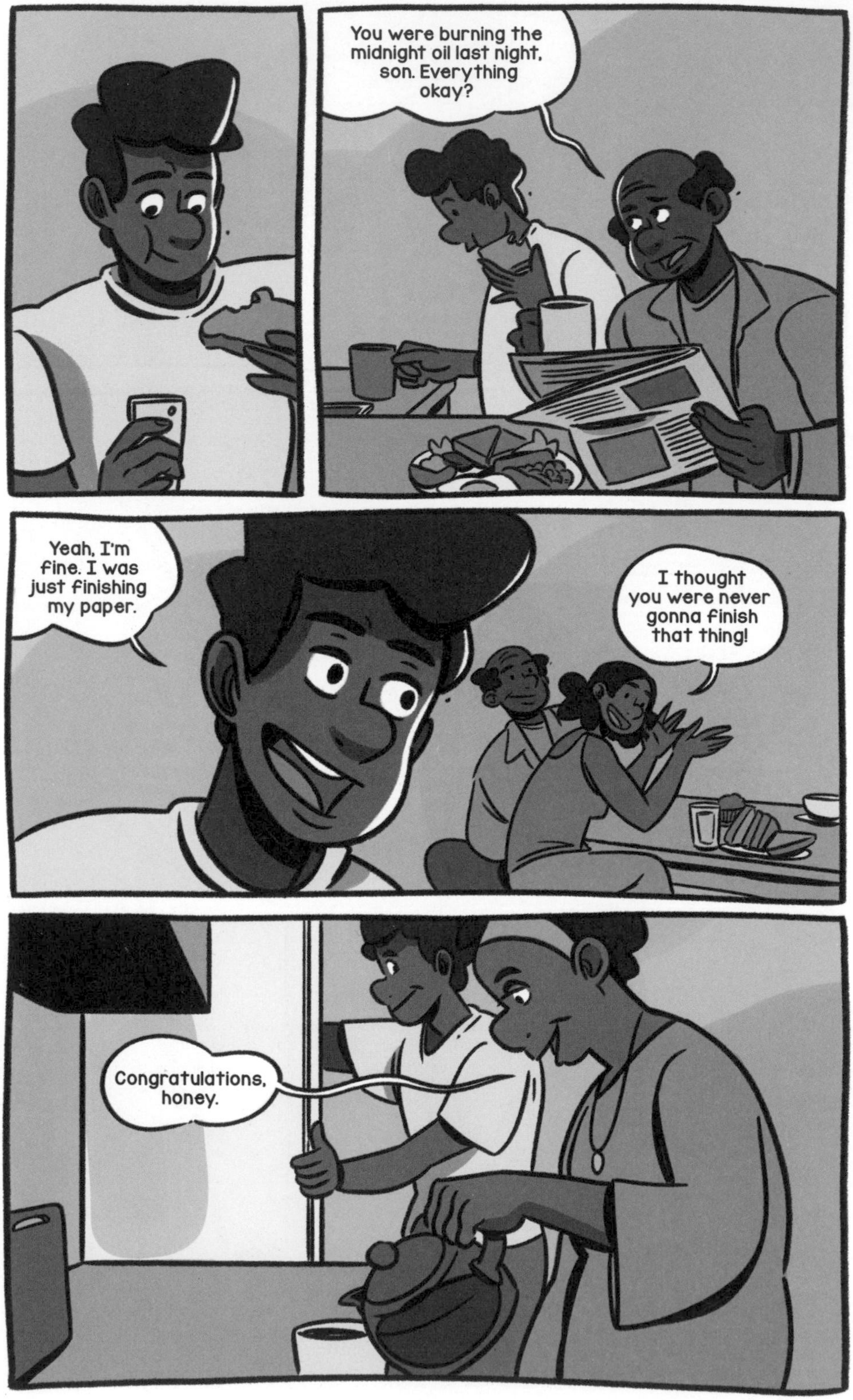
You were burning the midnight oil last night, son. Everything okay?
Yeah, I'm fine. I was just finishing my paper.
I thought you were never gonna finish that thing!
Congratulations, honey.

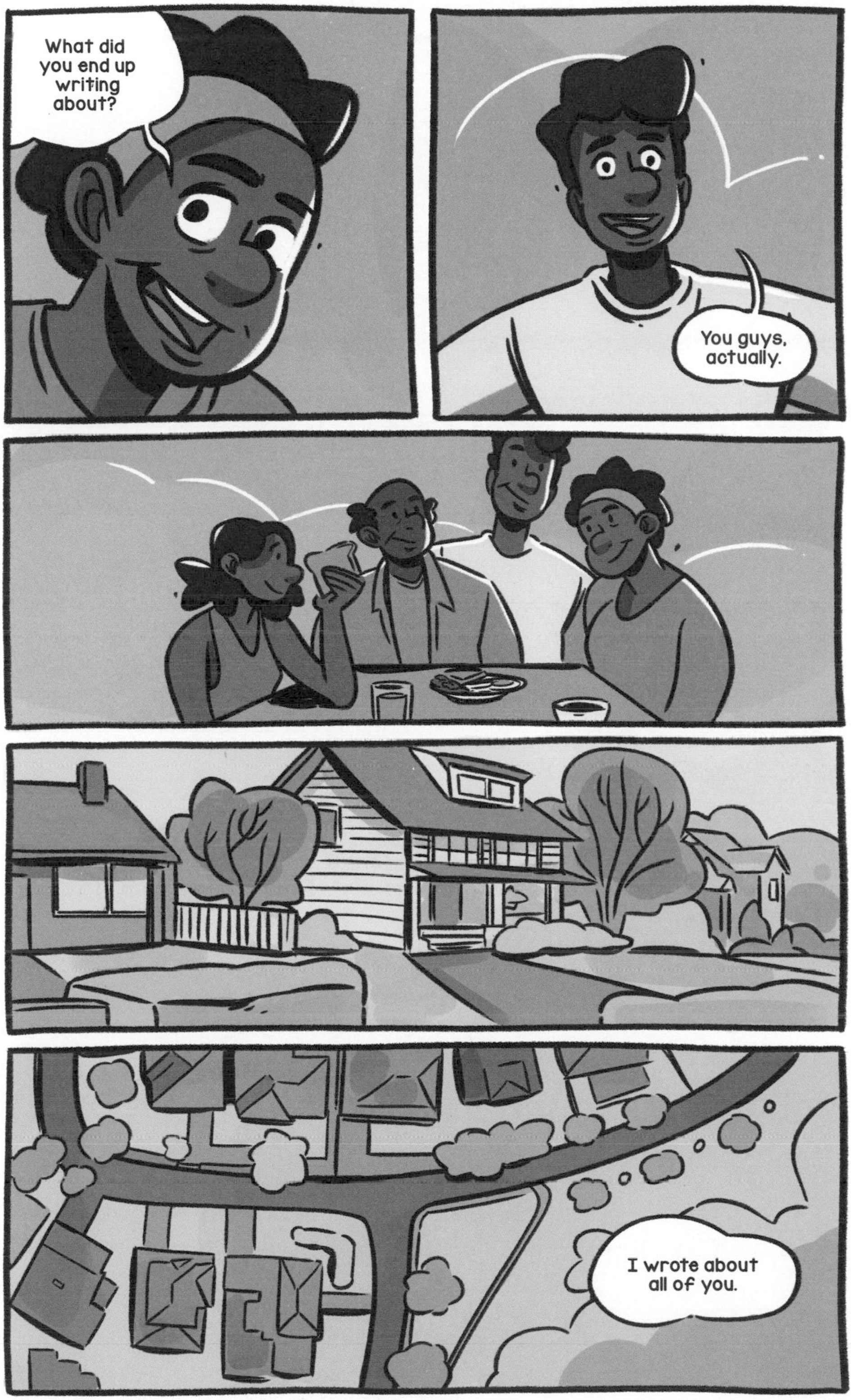
What did you end up writing about?
You guys, actually.
I wrote about all of you.

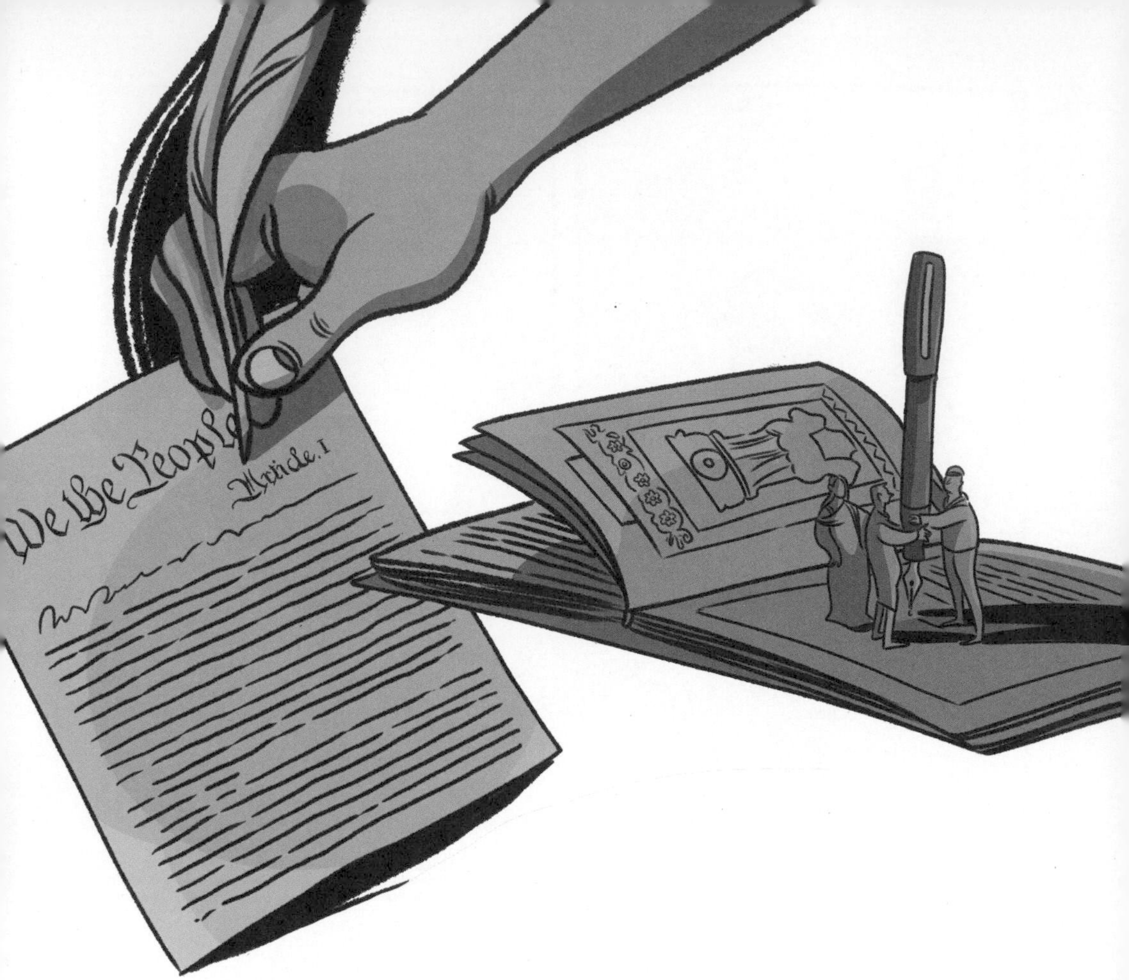
We the People
Article. I

aaliyah's guide to drafting your own constitution

Constitutions are like people: shaped by circumstances, history, and who we know, but sharing some recognizable common elements. Constitutional framers learn from the successes—and the mistakes—of earlier constitutions. They adapt to changing technology, new ideas about whose voice matters, shifting national identity, and specific historical events. They also evolve in response to threats: violent conflict, environmental or economic crises, political scandals, etc.

A constitution builds a government around the principles that are most important to its drafters. It will have legitimacy if those are also principles its citizens share. Of course, constitutions don't stop evolving once they're written down. Citizens change how they use their constitution, what aspects they consider most important and controversial, and whom they expect to benefit from constitutional guarantees. Citizens become constitutional framers, constitutional judges, and constitutional storytellers every time they ask their constitution to go to work for them.

If *you* were designing a constitution, what would it look like? What basic principles would be the foundation of your government? What kind of institutions would be necessary to put your principles into practice? This guide outlines the basic anatomy of most constitutions around the world, so that you can better understand the constitution you live with...or make your own.

PURPOSE

The purpose of a constitution is often, although not always, found in the preamble, which typically describes why a constitution is necessary and the principles it is expected to uphold.

- What is your constitution trying to do? Form a more perfect union, provide for the general welfare, break from a dark past, align government with a religion, ensure justice and peace, defend the nation, affirm national independence?
- What are the foundational principles of your constitution? Individual liberty? Equality under the law? Dignity, development, human rights, and justice for all? National unity? Tolerance and protection of diversity?

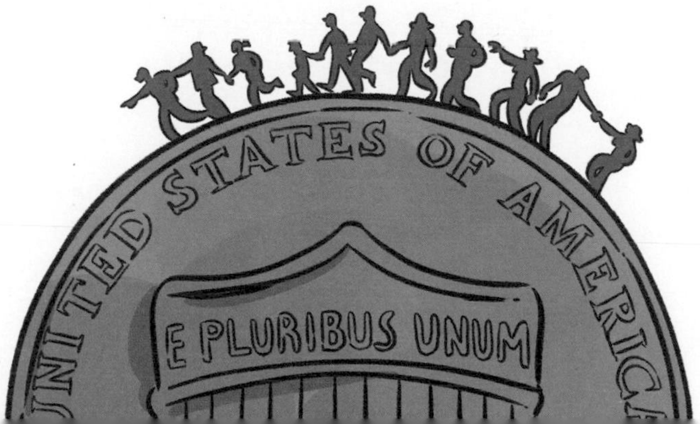
UNITED STATES OF AMERICA
E PLURIBUS UNUM

STRUCTURE OF THE GOVERNMENT

As the supreme law of the land, constitutions define the form of government and lay out some broad rules about how it will be structured.

- Who will hold ultimate governing authority under your constitution? The people? Their representatives? A monarch? God?

- Will your government be unitary, meaning the central government holds all law and decision-making power? Or will it be federal, meaning provincial and local governments can adopt rules and decide how money is spent in their jurisdictions?

- How many levels of government will your constitution establish: national, provincial, municipal, more?

NATIONAL SYMBOLS

Just like Mr. B said, constitutions adopt symbols to help all citizens feel recognized and included.

- What national symbols will your constitution recognize? A flag, a capital city, specific colors, an anthem, a language?

- Maybe you are drafting a constitution for a diverse country. How will your national symbols ensure that everyone feels they belong?

FUNDAMENTAL RIGHTS

Almost every constitution guarantees its citizens at least some fundamental rights. This means the government cannot make laws or policies that violate those rights, and it must try to protect citizens when their rights are violated by others.

- What civil and political rights will your constitution guarantee? The right to free thought and opinion, the right to information, the right to assemble and form organizations, the right to hear the charges against you? What about the right to freedom of movement, the right to free exercise of religion, the right to privacy, or the right to life?

- What economic and social rights will your constitution guarantee? The right to form a family and have children? The right to clean water, to shelter, to health care, to education, to a safe and healthy environment? The right to own property, to establish a business, to choose where you work?

- Will any citizens have special rights? What about children, people accused of a crime, or historically marginalized or oppressed groups?

- Will your constitution prohibit anything to protect these rights? What about the death penalty, or torture, or stripping an individual of their citizenship?

LEGISLATIVE POWER

The core function of any government is making laws and policies that determine how citizens lead their daily lives, including penalties if they break the rules. Constitutions typically describe who makes the laws, how they are made, and how the lawmakers are selected.

- Who will make laws under your constitution? A monarch? Representatives of the people? A council of elders or clan leaders? All citizens meeting together?

- How are the lawmakers chosen? By lottery? By election? Do they inherit their positions? Are all the lawmakers chosen the same way? Are political parties allowed? Are special seats set aside for women, minorities, or other marginalized groups?

- How do laws get made? Are they drafted by committees, or proposed by a single individual like a monarch or president? Can the public give input on proposed legislation? Are laws passed by a legislature, by popular referendum, or a combination?

- What other powers will the legislative branch possess? Oversight of the executive? The power to subpoena private citizens? Is it responsible for appointing senior government officers? Or determining how money is collected and spent?

EXECUTIVE POWER

Constitutions typically establish a head of state, a head of government, or both, who are responsible for representing the country abroad and enforcing the laws at home.

- Who will hold executive power in your constitution? A president, a prime minister, a monarch, a supreme leader, a council?

- How will that person, or those people, be chosen? Election, hereditary leadership, divine favor? Will all citizens get a say, or only some?

- What powers will the executive hold? The power to sign treaties and trade agreements? To make war or give orders to the military? To veto laws, to set the national budget, to propose legislation, to levy fines and enforce penalties? To appoint their own cabinet, to choose senior government officers? To issue pardons?

- Under what circumstances can the executive be replaced? Do they serve a fixed term or can they stay in office as long as they want? If elected, can they be re-elected? How will they be replaced if the current office-holder dies, becomes incapacitated, or commits a crime?

- What special powers, if any, will the executive have during an emergency? Can they make laws without consulting the legislature? Deploy the military domestically? Seize control of critical infrastructure like communication networks, the electricity grid, hospitals, the internet, transportation hubs? Can they close or open borders? For how long, and who ensures they aren't abusing these powers?

JUDICIAL POWER

The judicial branch resolves disputes and decides how a constitution, and the laws made under it, apply to various situations. Constitutions usually emphasize that the judiciary should be fully independent and that judges should meet rigorous qualifications.

- What will be the structure of your court system? Will there be separate courts for different kinds of disputes? If a party loses their case, may they appeal to a higher court? Which court or courts will get the final say?

- What powers will your constitution give to the judiciary? Will just one court have the authority to interpret the constitution, or may all courts do so? Will courts be required to respect past rulings or rulings by higher courts? Can they overrule decisions by the executive or the legislature?

  - How will judges be chosen? Will your constitution establish minimum ages or education requirements? Will they be confirmed by the legislative branch? Will the executive branch have a role? For how long may a judge serve?

  - Will your constitution guarantee the independence and integrity of the judicial system? Will there be rules about conflicts of interest and reporting income? Protection from interference in cases by the executive and legislative branches? Provisions to ensure the judiciary has an adequate budget?

NATIONAL SECURITY

Many constitutions include national defense or national security in their purpose. This typically means protecting the country from external threats, but sometimes includes domestic security as well.

- Does your constitution create a military? Who will be the supreme commander? Can it operate inside the country, or is it limited to external defense? Can it monitor or detain citizens?

- What kinds of threats can the military respond to? Armed invasions? Environmental or economic crises? Mass population movements? Terrorism? Cyberattacks? Who decides what counts as a national security issue?

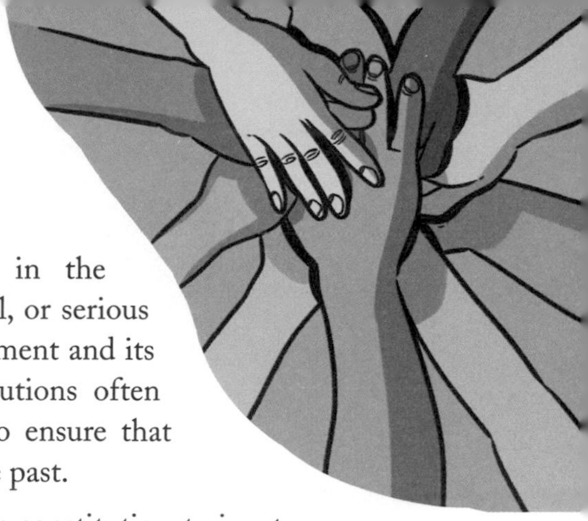

REPAIRING THE PAST

Many constitutions are written in the aftermath of war, political upheaval, or serious breaches of trust between a government and its citizens. Drafters of these constitutions often include institutions or processes to ensure that the future will be different from the past.

- What kind of past is your constitution trying to address? A history of slavery or colonialism? A legacy of conflict, including war crimes, crimes against humanity, or other mass atrocities? Systemic oppression or marginalization of a specific ethnic, religious, or geographic group?
- Will your constitution establish institutions to investigate past abuses or prevent them in the future? A truth and reconciliation commission, a land reform body, an anti-corruption agency, a supreme audit institution?
- Will your constitution require new processes or policies, such as reparations, public education initiatives, memorialization, or public consultations? What about measures to include historically marginalized groups, such as quotas for education, public service, or representation in government?
- Will people who have committed certain crimes, or who have specific political affiliations, be prevented from holding some government posts?

AMENDING THE CONSTITUTION

No constitution gets everything perfect the first time or forever. Constitutions are living documents that need to change in order to remain relevant and legitimate. Amendment provisions usually make it possible, but difficult, to alter the foundational law.

- Who can propose amendments to your constitution? A group of citizens? The legislature or the executive? Provincial governments?

- What is the process by which amendments are adopted? Through a constitutional convention? Ratification by the national or provincial legislatures? A national popular referendum?
- Are there provisions of your constitution that cannot be amended? The form of government? Certain fundamental rights? Provisions related to the separation of powers? The division of territory between provinces?

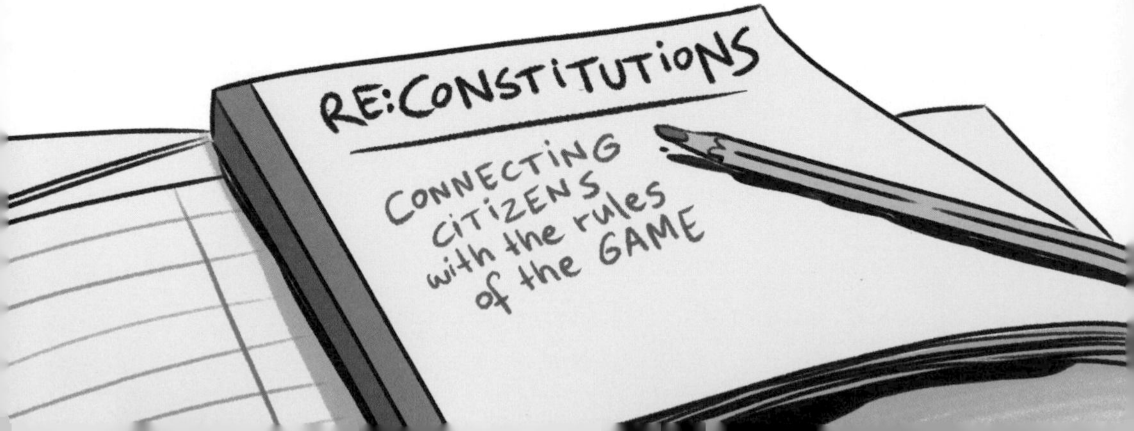
RE:CONSTITUTIONS
CONNECTING CITIZENS with the rules of the GAME

further resources

EXPLORE THE WORLD'S CONSTITUTIONS

Constitute Project: The World's Constitutions to Read, Search, and Compare.
  constituteproject.org/

Rights Around the World, National Constitution Center.
  constitutionalrights.constitutioncenter.org/app/home/world

Bringing the World's Constitutions to the Classroom: Constitute Teaching Guide.
  Comparative Constitutions Project. comparativeconstitutionsproject.org
  /wp-content/uploads/Constitute-Teaching-Guide.pdf

FUNDAMENTALS OF CONSTITUTIONS

What Is a Constitution? Principles and Concepts. International IDEA.
  constitutionnet.org/sites/default/files/what_is_a_constitution_0.pdf

The Fundamentals of a Constitution. International IDEA. idea.int/sites/default/files
  /publications/the-fundamentals-of-a-constitution.pdf

The Constitution-Making Handbook, Interpeace.
  constitutionmakingforpeace.org/the-constitution-making-handbook/

How to Save a Constitutional Democracy, Tom Ginsburg and Aziz Z. Huq (2018).

MORE RESOURCES ON THE U.S. CONSTITUTION

The Annenberg Guide to the United States Constitution. annenbergclassroom.org
  /constitution/

The Citizen's Almanac. US Citizenship and Immigration Services. uscis.gov
  /sites/default/files/USCIS/Office%20of%20Citizenship/Citizenship%20
  Resource%20Center%20Site/Publications/M-76.pdf

The Bill of Rights in Action, quarterly newsletter of the Constitutional Rights
  Foundation. crf-usa.org/r/online-lessons/bill-of-rights-in-action

*FDR and Chief Justice Hughes: The President, the Supreme Court, and the Epic Battle
  Over the New Deal,* James F. Simon (2012).

The Color of Law: A Forgotten History of How Our Government Segregated America,
  Richard Rothstein (2017).

The Constitution Today: Timeless Lessons for the Issues of Our Era, Akhil Reed Amar
  (2016).

acknowledgments

It is impossible to thank everyone who helped bring this book into being. Nevertheless, here is my attempt—where it falls short, please know that you have both my unending gratitude and permanent citizenship in Chathamville. First and foremost, thank you to Kasia Babis, my amazing co-creator. Your art is filled with life and humanity, and I will never understand how you pull images directly from my brain. I am immensely grateful to the entire team at First Second, especially Mark Siegel, Robyn Chapman, Sara Rosenbaum, and Francesca Lynn, who embraced the idea of a book about constitutions, then shepherded it into reality. Speaking of which, I owe a debt of thanks to Gina Gagliano, a friend who opened a door at exactly the right time.

I also want to thank the many people who contributed to the research for this book, both while I was writing and years before the first words were written down. Thank you to Louis Aucoin, Padideh Ala'i, Fernanda Nicola, Hassan Ibrahim, Christina Murray, Zaid al-Ali, and Paul Williams, mentors and guides; to Maria Rosario de la Fuente, Kent Fogg, and others who wish to remain unnamed but let me tap their expertise; and to my friends and family, especially the Thanksgiving crew, who endured numerous "pop quizzes" so I could suss out what constitutions mean to people who aren't writing a book about them. I am fortunate to have a such a generous community. I am also fortunate to have access to the Multnomah County Public Library system, without which most of the research for this book would have been prohibitively difficult and expensive. Support your libraries.

There are a few people whose support was so integral that I could never do it justice in just a few sentences. Whitney, Ryan, Megan, thank you for your love and enthusiasm, which carried me through my most difficult writing days. Most of all, my gratitude and love to my wife, Chelsea, who read every chapter, answered every question, listened to every rambling train of thought, and never let on how she truly felt about becoming an involuntary expert on constitutions.

Finally: the soul of this book would not exist without the brave, determined, hopeful, argumentative, visionary, and pragmatic people of Yemen and South Sudan, who have shown me by example what a constitution can and should mean to its citizens. I believe that you will bring the countries you dream of into being, and I hope with all my heart that it will be soon.

—Beka Feathers

Beka Feathers is a legal adviser on political development in conflict-affected states. She has worked with clients and partners in more than a dozen countries to draft constitutions, design transitional governments, facilitate peace processes, and advocate for improved access to justice. She lives with her talented, pun-loving wife and a suspiciously intelligent dog in Portland, Oregon.

Kasia Babis is a Polish cartoonist, illustrator, and political activist with an online following of more than 100,000 fans. Her viral comics succinctly skewer social issues ranging from racism to street harassment from a distinctly feminist perspective.

First Second

Published by First Second
First Second is an imprint of Roaring Brook Press,
a division of Holtzbrinck Publishing Holdings Limited Partnership
120 Broadway, New York, NY 10271
firstsecondbooks.com

Library of Congress Control Number: 2020919546

Our books may be purchased in bulk for promotional, educational, or business use.
Please contact your local bookseller or the Macmillan Corporate and Premium Sales Department at
(800) 221-7945 ext. 5442 or by email at MacmillanSpecialMarkets@macmillan.com.

First edition, 2021
Edited by Mark Siegel and S. I. Rosenbaum
Cover design by Kirk Benshoff
Interior book design by Sunny Lee
Printed in Singapore

ISBN 978-1-250-23543-5
1 3 5 7 9 10 8 6 4 2

Rough storyboards drawn in Sharpie marker. Final art created digitally in Adobe Photoshop and Procreate.

Don't miss your next favorite book from First Second!
For the latest updates go to firstsecondnewsletter.com and sign up for our enewsletter.